The Global
Findex Database 2025

This book, along with any associated content or subsequent updates,
can be accessed at https://hdl.handle.net/10986/43438.

Reproducible Research Repository

https://reproducibility.worldbank.org

A reproducibility package is available for this book in the Reproducible Research Repository at https://reproducibility.worldbank.org/catalog/299.

Scan to go to this publication online.

The Global Findex Database 2025

Connectivity and Financial Inclusion in the Digital Economy

Leora Klapper
Dorothe Singer
Laura Starita
Alexandra Norris

WORLD BANK GROUP

Contents

Boxes

Figures

Maps

Tables

Acknowledgments

Global Findex 2025 was prepared by the Finance and Private Sector Development team of the Development Research Group in the World Bank's Development Economics Vice Presidency. The team was led by Leora Klapper, Dorothe Singer, Laura Starita, and Alexandra Norris and included Anh Phuong Nguyen, Uzma Sahar Rauf, Ananya Sharma, and Xiaoyu Wang. Fareeza Ibrahim led communications and dissemination efforts. Amani Haque provided administrative support. Strategic guidance was provided by Indermit Gill, senior vice president and chief economist of the World Bank; Deon Filmer, director of the Development Research Group; Somik Lall, senior adviser to the chief economist; and Robert Cull, manager of the Finance and Private Sector Development team.

Special thanks are extended to the senior leadership and managers in the World Bank's Prosperity and Digital Transformation Vice Presidencies for their partnership and guidance in preparing this report. This includes Jean Pesme, global director (Finance, Competitiveness, and Investment [FCI]); Idah Pswarayi-Riddihough, global director (Digital Transformation); Christine Zhenwei Qiang, global director (Digital Transformation); Sophie Sirtaine, CEO, Consultative Group to Assist the Poor; and Harish Natarajan, practice manager (FCI); as well as the FCI and Digital Transformation regional practice managers.

The team is grateful to the Gates Foundation, the Mastercard Foundation, and the World Bank's Development Economics, Digital Transformation, and Prosperity Vice Presidencies for their financial support, which made the collection and dissemination of the data possible.

The team is grateful as well to internal reviewers—Saniya Ansar, Oya Ardic Alper, Claire Casher, Jennifer Chien, Julia Clark, Sheirin Iravantchi, Claudia McKay, Karina Broens Nielsen, Guillermo Alfonso Galicia Rabadan, and Peter Zetterli, as well as other colleagues across the World Bank's Development Economics, Digital Transformation, and Prosperity Vice Presidencies and the International Finance Corporation's Financial Institutions Growth group—who provided important input at different stages of the project. Special thanks also go to Sharada Srinivasan for her contributions to the digital connectivity questionnaire and analysis. The team deeply appreciates the insights of external reviewers Isabelle Carboni and Rebecca Rouse.

We are grateful for helpful discussions with representatives of the Gates Foundation, including Seth Garz, Jason Lamb, Rebecca Mann, Daniel Radcliffe, Michael Wiegand, and Jamie Zimmerman from the Inclusive Financial Systems and Digital Connectivity teams and for communications support from Abigail Faylor and Erin Kelly.

We are also grateful for ongoing consultation with representatives of the Better Than Cash Alliance, the Group of Twenty's Global Partnership for Financial Inclusion, the GSM Association, the Mastercard Center for Inclusive Growth, the Office of the UN Secretary-General's Special Advocate for Inclusive Finance for Development, Visa Social Impact, and Women's World Banking.

Neli Esipova at Multicultural Insights led the update of the Global Findex questionnaire and development of the new module on digital connectivity. Additional thanks go to Saniya Ansar and Seth Garz for supporting pilots of the 2024 questionnaire in Bangladesh, Ghana, Malawi, Malaysia, Pakistan, and Zambia. The team also extends special thanks to the GSM Association for supporting questionnaire development, including contributions from Kalvin Bahia, Nadia Jeffrie, and Rishi Raithatha. The team greatly appreciates the excellent execution of the survey and related support provided by Gallup, Inc., under the direction of Joe Daly and with assistance from Cynthia English and Chris McCarty and the Gallup World Poll survey regional managers.

Ingrid Case of INCase, LLC, provided developmental guidance in drafting the report, and Susanna Roesel of Unleash Creative created the cover and internal infographics, with additional images created by Loaded Pictures. Patricia Anne Janer and Ryan Francis Kemna created the maps, under the guidance of Bruno Bonansea from the World Bank's Map Design unit. The report's reproducibility package was verified by Maria Ruth Jones, Luis Eduardo San Martin, Shreya Suthakar, and Mahin Tariq from the World Bank Reproducible Research Repository team. The databank and Data 360 were set up by Haruna Kashiwase and Hiroko Maeda. An online data visualization tool was originally conceived by Buddy Buruku and created by Rony George and Sreejith KS at ASSYST International. Monica Miller produced the launch event, with editing support from Hannah Long-Higgins. The animation video was designed by Chris Borden at Loaded Pictures. Interview videos were coordinated with support from Mazen Bouri, Patricia da Camara, Laurent Gonnet, Darmy Larroza, Faruk Liriano, and Azrin Rahim. Joseph Rebello developed the communications and engagement strategy, with the support of Kristen Milhollin, Karolina Ordon, and Shane Romig. Giannina Raffo created our social media assets, and Andrew Gilhooly and Kristyn Schrader-King prepared the Global Findex video news release. Roula Yazigi provided web and online services and related guidance.

Special thanks to Stephen Pazdan, who coordinated and oversaw the formal production of the report, as well as to copyeditor Michael Harrup, proofreader Gwenda Larsen, designer Jihane El Khoury Roederer, and print and dissemination coordinator Yaneisy Martinez; to Patricia Katayama, who oversaw the overall publication process; and to the World Bank's Formal Publishing Program.

Finally, the team would like to express its deep gratitude to the more than 750,000 adults around the world who have generously taken the time over the years to participate in the Global Findex survey.

About the Global Findex Database

Financial inclusion is a cornerstone of development, and since 2011, the Global Findex Database has been the definitive source of data on the ways adults around the world use financial services, from payments to saving and borrowing, and manage financial events such as major expenses or losses of income. Results from the first survey were published in 2011 and have been followed by subsequent survey results from 2014, 2017, and 2021.

The 2025 version, based on nationally representative surveys of about 145,000 adults in 141 economies and conducted over the calendar year 2024, includes updated indicators on access to and use of formal and informal financial services to save, borrow, make payments, and manage financial risk, as well as globally comparable data on ownership of mobile phones, internet use, and digital safety. The data also identify gaps in access to and use of digital and financial services by women and poor adults.

The survey results reflect a snapshot in time based on questions that respondents answered about their habits and experiences during the 12 months preceding the survey. Comparing results from the current survey with those from the 2011, 2014, 2017, and 2021 surveys reveals which trends endure, expand, and grow over time.

The Global Findex Database has become a mainstay of global efforts to promote financial inclusion. In addition to being widely cited by policy makers, researchers, and development practitioners, Global Findex data are used to track progress toward the United Nations Sustainable Development Goals.

The database, the full text of the accompanying report, and the economy-level data underlying all figures, along with the questionnaire, the survey methodology, and other relevant materials, are available on the Global Findex website at http://globalfindex.worldbank.org.

The reference citation for the *Global Findex 2025* report is as follows:

Klapper, Leora, Dorothe Singer, Laura Starita, and Alexandra Norris. 2025. *The Global Findex Database 2025: Connectivity and Financial Inclusion in the Digital Economy.* Washington, DC: World Bank. https://doi.org/10.1596/978-1-4648-2204-9.

The database should be cited as follows:

World Bank. 2025. "The Global Findex Database 2025: Data Download and Documentation." http://globalfindex.worldbank.org.

Executive summary

Mobile phones and the internet are revolutionizing financial inclusion, enabling more people to access and use digital financial services to manage their financial lives. From mobile money accounts accessible on basic phones to bank-account-linked wallets used on smartphones, digital services are fulfilling their promise of being more accessible and affordable than alternatives that are not digitally accessible, bringing benefits such as the ability to make daily savings deposits using local agents, to manage loan disbursements and repayments using an app, and to purchase pay-as-you-go renewable electricity directly from a phone, to name just a few.

These increases in access to and use of financial accounts enabled by mobile technology are among the top findings from this fifth edition of the Global Findex, including new data on ownership of mobile phones and internet use from the inaugural Global Findex Digital Connectivity Tracker. The data show high levels of phone ownership and internet use and increased ownership and usage of mobile-enabled accounts in every region of the world. Mobile platforms in particular have given millions of people, including those who were previously too difficult or too expensive to reach, access to financial services, dramatically boosting not just account ownership but also formal saving and digital payments, while in addition enabling a range of nonfinancial digital activities.

The report's main findings are captured in the following sections.

Worldwide, 79 percent of adults have an account at a bank or similar financial institution, with a mobile money provider, or both, up from 74 percent in 2021

Ownership of financial accounts increased globally by 5 percentage points between 2021 and 2024 and by 6 percentage points in low- and middle-income economies, in which 75 percent of adults now have an account.

Account owners increasingly use their mobile phones or debit or credit cards connected to their accounts to make transactions. More than half of all accounts in low- and middle-income economies are digitally enabled in this way,[1] including both

---

A reproducibility package is available for this book in the Reproducible Research Repository at https://reproducibility.worldbank.org/catalog/299.

mobile money accounts[2] and accounts at banks or similar financial institutions such as credit unions, cooperatives, microfinance institutions, or post offices.[3]

Mobile money accounts are driving the increase in account ownership. The growth over the past 10 years in the share of adults who own any kind of account is equivalent to the increase in the share of people owning either only a mobile money account or a mobile money account along with an account at a bank or similar financial institution (refer to figure ES.1).

Telecommunications companies in Sub-Saharan Africa catalyzed the mobile money revolution by offering simple transactional accounts via mobile phones. These companies often operate independently of traditional banks. Though they emerged in East Africa, they have since spread across the continent and are the dominant financial providers in some of the region's economies, supporting a range of financial activities, including making and receiving payments, saving, and borrowing.

Even as mobile money continues as a Sub-Saharan African success story, other regions are reaping the benefits, too. In Latin America and the Caribbean, adoption of mobile money, typically used in combination with or to digitally enable accounts at banks and similar financial institutions, is approaching levels seen in Sub-Saharan Africa. Some economies across Europe and Central Asia are also

Figure ES.1 **Mobile money contributed to the increase overall in account ownership in low- and middle-income economies between 2014 and 2024**

Adults with an account (%), 2014–24

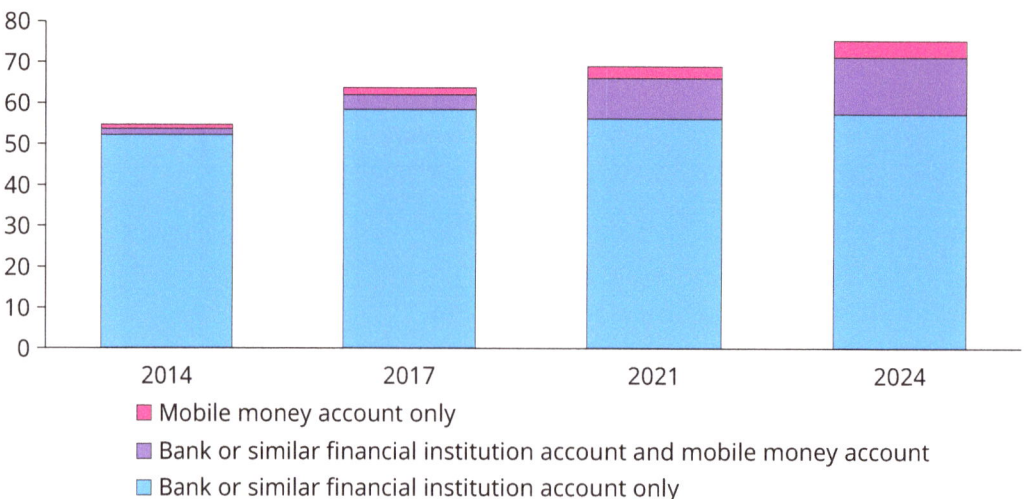

■ Mobile money account only
■ Bank or similar financial institution account and mobile money account
■ Bank or similar financial institution account only

Source: Global Findex Database 2025.

narrowing gaps in financial inclusion by embracing mobile money or other digitally enabled accounts.

To quantify this growth: 40 percent of adults in Sub-Saharan Africa had a mobile money account as of 2024, up from 27 percent in 2021. In Latin America and the Caribbean, 37 percent of adults had a mobile money account as of 2024, up from 22 percent in 2021.

Worldwide, 86 percent of adults own a mobile phone

Most adults with a mobile phone own a smartphone, though basic phones, which do not enable internet access, still play an important role providing more affordable connectivity in the Middle East and North Africa, South Asia, and Sub-Saharan Africa (refer to figure ES.2).

Expanding the prevalence of smartphones is nonetheless important for increasing access to economic opportunities and more robust financial services, as these devices are the primary means by which people in low- and middle-income economies access the internet. Nearly all adults who use the internet, about 70 percent of the global population, use a smartphone to get online.

Figure ES.2 Worldwide, 86 percent of adults own mobile phones, though smartphones are less common in some regions than others

Adults with a phone (%), 2024

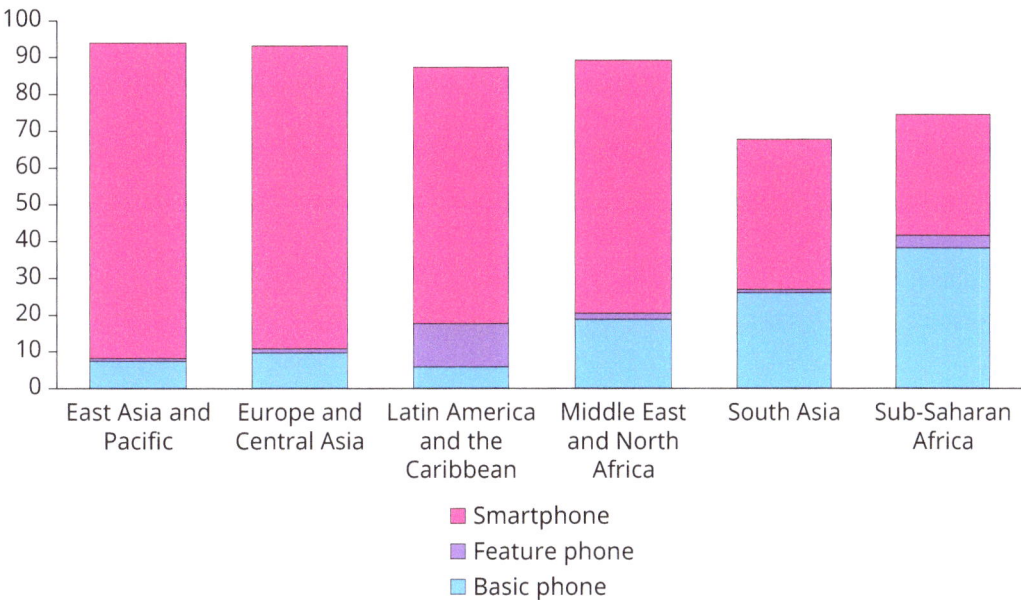

Source: Global Findex Database 2025.

Note: Basic phone, feature phone, and smartphone are defined in chapter 1.1.

Given that, expanding smartphone ownership could likewise make digital activities more accessible to a larger share of adults. Social media is the most popular digital activity: 45 percent of all adults and about 80 percent of internet users engage in it. The popularity of social media is important not just for allowing people to communicate and stay connected but also because digital marketplaces are offering merchants in low- and middle-income economies opportunities to reach new customers through their social media accounts. These merchants may include the 6 percent of adults who use the internet to make money, including the more than 10 percent of adults who do so in all economies in East Asia and Pacific, the region with the highest smartphone penetration, second-highest rate of internet usage, and highest rate of adoption of digital merchant payments.

Gender gaps in account ownership have narrowed, and gender gaps in mobile phone ownership are small

As overall account ownership has increased, a larger share of women are gaining access to their own financial accounts. As of 2024, 73 percent of women in low- and middle-income economies had accounts, up from just 50 percent in 2014 and 66 percent in 2021. East Asia and Pacific continues to stand out, with no statistically significant difference between the share of women in that region who have an account and the share of men who do. Similarly, women and men in India are equally likely to have accounts.

Though meaningful gender gaps in account ownership persist in 65 low- and middle-income economies, these gaps are narrowing in almost all of them. The gender gap is now 4 percentage points globally and 5 percentage points in low- and middle-income economies.

Mobile phone ownership among women likely contributes to the narrowing gender gaps in account ownership. Although women are 9 percentage points less likely than men to own a mobile phone in low- and middle-income economies, this difference is largely driven by the ownership rates in a handful of high-population economies in South Asia and Sub-Saharan Africa with significant gender gaps in smartphone ownership. Basic phone ownership, on the other hand, is more equitable. Overall, being from a poor household has a greater impact on both financial account ownership and mobile phone ownership than does being a woman (refer to figure ES.3).

Figure ES.3 Women and poorer adults are less likely than men and wealthier adults to own a phone, yet income is a bigger driver of phone ownership—and particularly smartphone ownership—than gender

Adults with a mobile phone (%), 2024

a. Differences in mobile phone ownership, by household income and type of phone

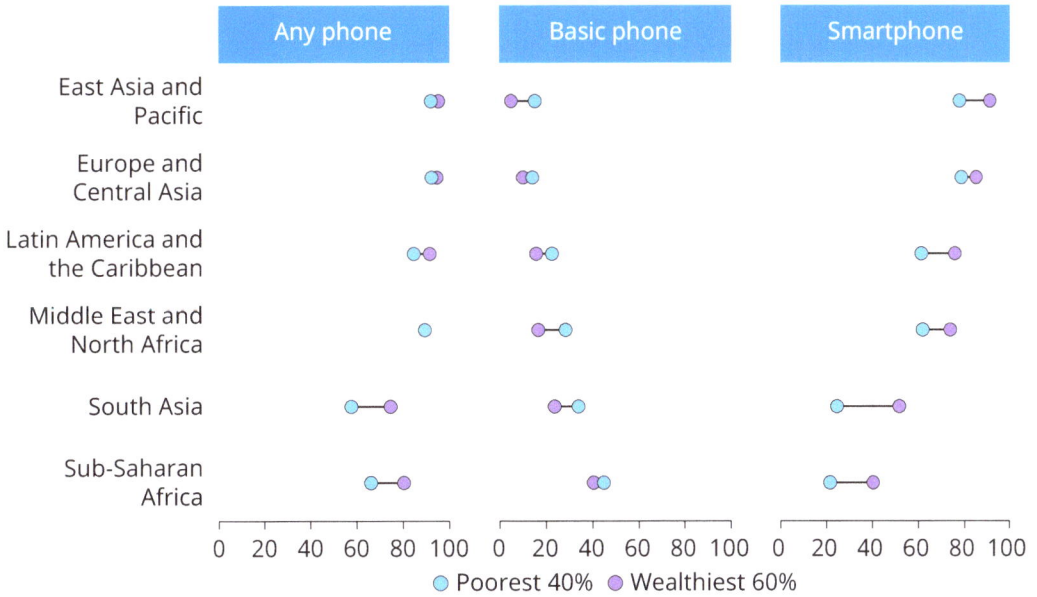

○ Poorest 40% ● Wealthiest 60%

b. Differences in mobile phone ownership, by gender and type of phone

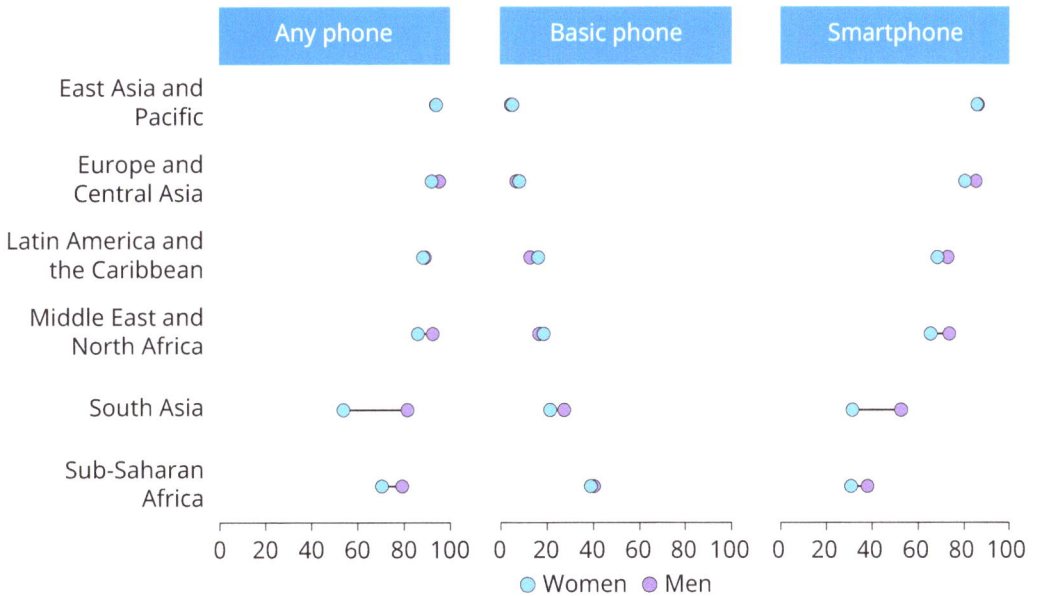

○ Women ● Men

Source: Global Findex Database 2025.

Formal saving has surged globally, enabled by mobile accounts and breaking a long-term trend of slow growth

Formal saving is on the rise, with the increase partly driven in some regions by the convenience, accessibility, and affordability of mobile financial services, which are allowing people to make frequent, small-value savings deposits.

As of 2024, 40 percent of adults in low- and middle-income economies saved formally using an account, a 16 percentage point increase from 2021. Mobile money and other digitally enabled accounts are driving this increase in formal saving. In both Latin America and the Caribbean and Sub-Saharan Africa, the share of adults saving using mobile money increased by more than 10 percentage points, reaching 19 and 23 percent of adults, respectively (refer to figure ES.4). Whereas

Figure ES.4 Mobile money accounts are an important mode of saving in Latin America and the Caribbean and Sub-Saharan Africa

Adults saving any money in the past year (%), 2021–24

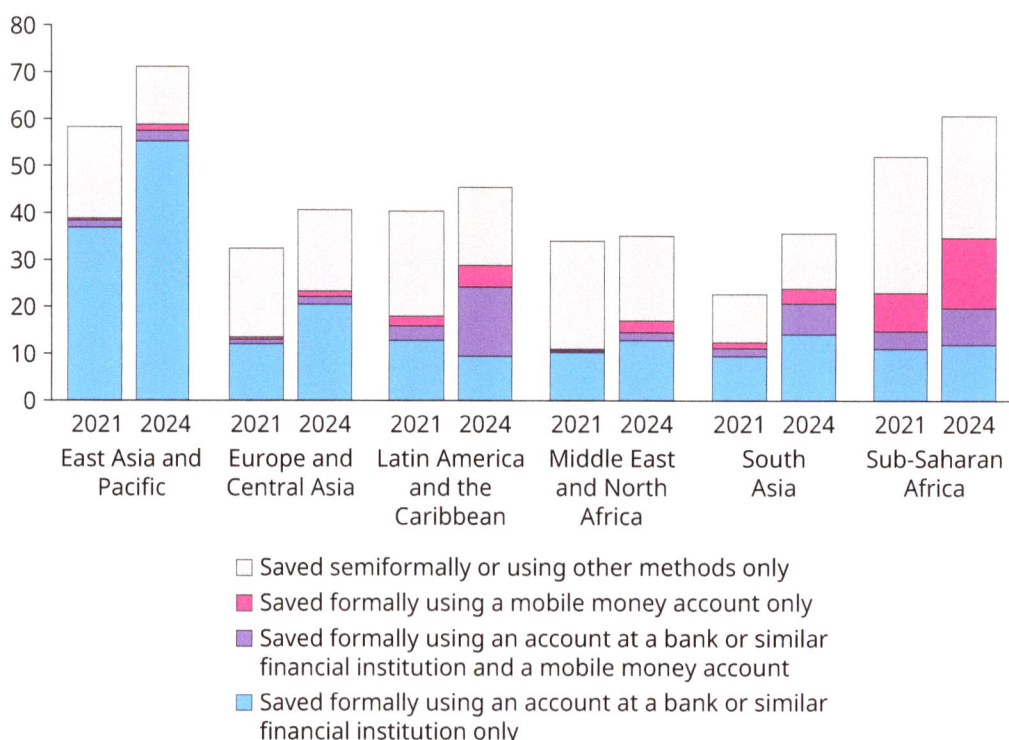

☐ Saved semiformally or using other methods only
▮ Saved formally using a mobile money account only
▮ Saved formally using an account at a bank or similar financial institution and a mobile money account
▮ Saved formally using an account at a bank or similar financial institution only

Source: Global Findex Database 2025.

Note: People may save in multiple ways, but categories in the figure are constructed to be mutually exclusive. *Saved formally* includes all adults who saved any money formally. For comparability over time, regional averages for Europe and Central Asia exclude the Russian Federation across all years.

the largest share of adults in Sub-Saharan Africa who save formally do so using mobile money accounts, in Latin America and the Caribbean, most adults who save formally use both mobile money accounts and accounts at banks or similar financial institutions. The difference between the two regions possibly reflects stronger integration and linkages between mobile platforms and the formal banking system in the latter.

If those who save in either a mobile money account or an account at a bank or similar financial institution are included, 35 percent of adults saved formally in Sub-Saharan Africa in 2024, the second-highest regional rate after that in East Asia and Pacific. Senegal exemplifies this progress, with 67 percent of adults there saving formally in 2024, up from 46 percent in 2021.

East Asia and Pacific continues to have the highest formal saving rate and registered the largest rise in formal saving between 2021 and 2024, at 20 percentage points, with the change driven by an increase of 22 percentage points in China alone.

Despite this growth, women are still less likely to save than men. Although the share of women formally saving nearly doubled between 2021 and 2024, reaching 36 percent, men are still 7 percentage points more likely to save formally.

To build and capitalize on the benefits of formal savings, more could be done to ensure savers get the most out of their balances. For example, in 2024, just over half of adults who saved formally earned interest on their savings balances, highlighting a critical opportunity both to help savers earn more money and to increase capital flows within economies.

More adults are making digital merchant payments

Across low- and middle-income economies, 61 percent of adults, or 82 percent of account owners, made or received a digital payment in 2024, a 27 percentage point increase from 2014. Digital payments are the most popular formal financial service, used by twice as many adults as saved formally and by three times as many as borrowed formally.

Use of digital merchant payments—payments made by retail customers to businesses in stores or online—grew to 42 percent of all adults in 2024, up from 35 percent in 2021, with variations by region (refer to figure ES.5). The share of adults making such payments more than doubled in some economies, including Cameroon, the Kyrgyz Republic, Paraguay, and Viet Nam, and showed widespread adoption in Kazakhstan, Kenya, and Mongolia.

Figure ES.5 Adoption of digital merchant payments has grown since 2021

Adults who made a digital merchant payment (%), 2021–24

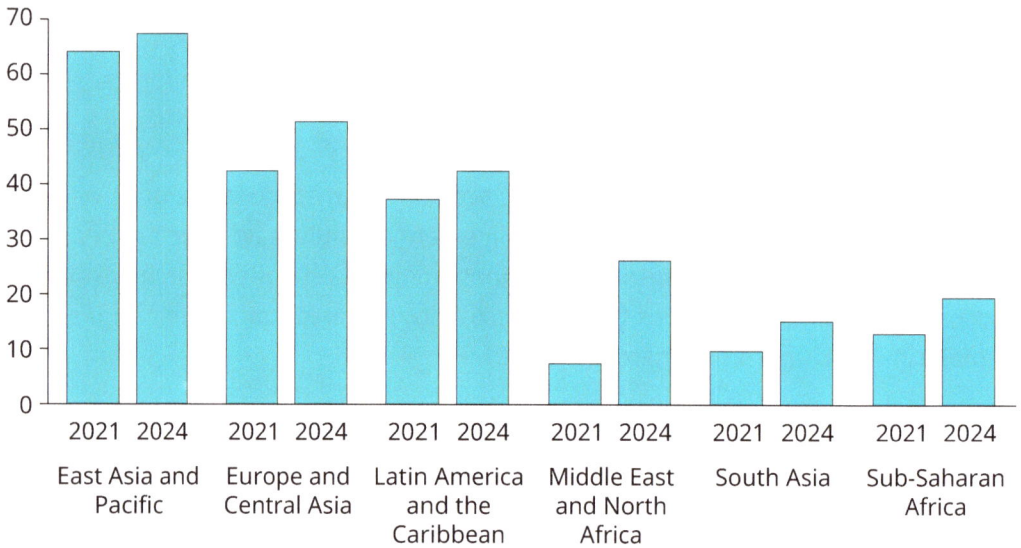

Source: Global Findex Database 2025.

Note: For comparability over time, regional averages for Europe and Central Asia exclude the Russian Federation across all years.

This shift to digital merchant payments benefits both buyers and sellers. Digital payments are safer than cash payments and can help small-scale merchants access credit by giving them real-time records of cash flows they can use to support loan applications aimed at funding working capital or job creation. Digitalizing these payments, however, requires interoperable fast payment systems and national-scale infrastructure for processing payments from any provider to any other.[4]

This is especially important because business-related financial stress is widespread, particularly among the self-employed, 13 percent of whom cite business expenses as their top concern. Access to credit could help, yet in low- and middle-income economies, only about a quarter of adults used formal credit in the past year. An additional 35 percent relied on informal sources such as family or friends. Business borrowing is also mostly informal: Of the 15 percent of self-employed adults who borrowed for business purposes, most of them borrowed only informally. This highlights the need for better access to responsible, formal credit options and the potential of cash flow–based lending models that draw on digital payment histories to assess creditworthiness.

Government and wage payments likewise continued their trend toward digitalization. About 75 percent of recipients of government payments in low- and middle-income economies[5] received their government wage, pension, or social transfer payments directly in accounts. Half of private-sector wage recipients did likewise.

Digital payments also offer opportunities for increased income generation when combined with active internet use. For example, with digital channels enabled by mechanisms for payment, small business owners can more easily reach customers and get paid, thereby growing their businesses and expanding economic opportunities. In low- and middle-income economies, 37 percent of adults paid their bills online, a testament to how digital channels make it easier for people to pay for goods and services. Furthermore, 36 percent of adults purchased goods online, pointing to greater convenience and choice for consumers and increased income-generating opportunities for sellers.

Despite advances, many remain without mobile phones or financial accounts and require focused programs

Not everyone has benefited equally from increased access to and use of financial accounts and digital channels. As mentioned, women are disproportionately less likely than men to have accounts, and being poor remains the biggest barrier to financial access, as adults living in poorer households make up a disproportionate share of people without accounts.

When asked why they do not have accounts, the most common reason people without accounts give is that they do not have enough money to need or use one. But adults without accounts also report that they cannot afford to own an account. These barriers might be addressed with more accessible and affordable accounts that leverage networks of local agents and offer lower pricing. Mobile money and other digitally enabled accounts are often more likely to have these characteristics.

Adults without an account who also do not own any type of mobile phone represent a particularly challenging segment to reach, given that they do not have the means to leverage one of the most accessibility-driving channels for financial services. That share is 31 percent in low- and middle-income economies and about 50 percent in South Asia and Sub-Saharan Africa (refer to figure ES.6).

Adults who lack mobile phones of any kind say that the cost of the device is the biggest barrier they face to owning one. Making digital devices less expensive, whether through product design, innovative pricing models, or both, will be key to equitably increasing digital, and by extension financial, access. Free devices may not be the solution, however, according to research showing that many recipients of free mobile phones lose access to the devices.[6]

Figure ES.6 Thirty-one percent of adults without financial accounts in low- and middle-income economies, including half in South Asia and Sub-Saharan Africa, also do not own mobile phones

Adults without an account (%), 2024

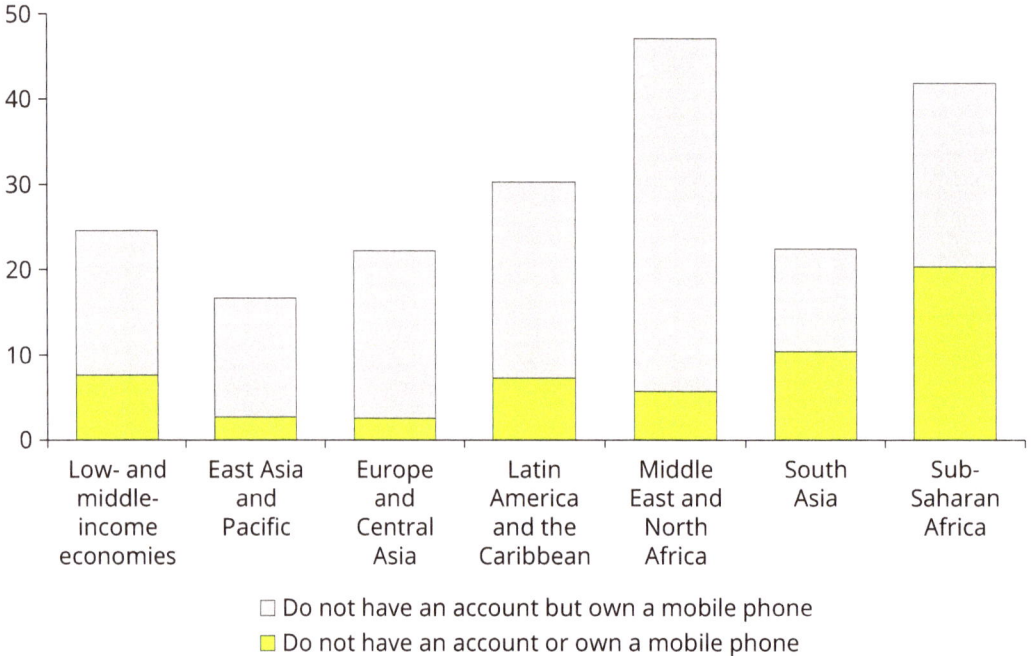

☐ Do not have an account but own a mobile phone
☐ Do not have an account or own a mobile phone

Source: Global Findex Database 2025.

Increased digitalization and mobile financial adoption come with risks, and not everyone is adequately protected

Of the 900 million adults in low- and middle-income economies who use mobile money accounts, only three-quarters use passwords to protect their phones. This could pose a risk of theft when they access their accounts, even though many accounts require additional verification such as a personal identification number (refer to figure ES.7). In Sub-Saharan Africa, only about half of the region's 300 million mobile money account owners protect their phones with passwords. Around the world, women are less likely than men to have passwords.

Financial crime is also a concern. Nearly one in five phone owners in low- and middle-income economies received a text or SMS message from someone they did not know asking for money. Only a small percentage say they sent money in response, but scam prevalence nonetheless poses a risk to adults with digitally enabled accounts.

Figure ES.7 Most owners of mobile money accounts have passwords on their phones, though only about half do in Sub-Saharan Africa

Adults with a mobile money account (%), 2024

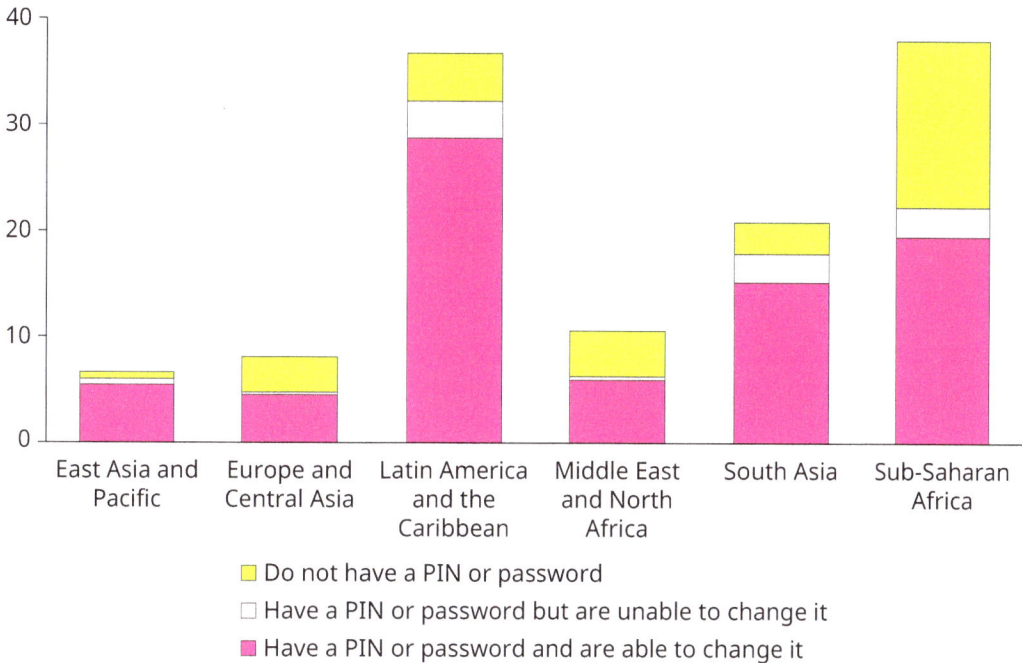

Legend:
- ☐ (yellow) Do not have a PIN or password
- ☐ (white) Have a PIN or password but are unable to change it
- ☐ (pink) Have a PIN or password and are able to change it

Source: Global Findex Database 2025.

Furthermore, as efforts to grow digital financial inclusion continue, governments must set and enforce rules for telecommunications and financial industries. A relatively large share of adults still pay fees they did not expect for receiving wage or government payments in an account. Whether these fees reflect additional charges by an agent or misunderstanding about the fee schedule on the part of the recipient, they nonetheless suggest a lack of financial capability. Setting and enforcing rules for how industry actors market and sell their products, onboard customers, clarify costs and fee schedules, protect deposits, and communicate about safe use and avoiding scams can help equip new users to get the most, safely, from mobile phone and account ownership.

Opportunities remain to better equip people to leverage financial services to reach their goals and increase resilience

Greater account ownership and usage and increased access to digital opportunities have not yet increased overall financial health, defined as the ability to pursue financial goals, manage financial emergencies, and feel confident about one's finances. For example, just 56 percent of adults could easily access extra money to deal with an unexpected event such as a loss of income or an accident (refer to figure ES.8). That percentage is unchanged since 2021. Furthermore, only about half of adults in low- and middle-income economies could cover their expenses for two months or longer if they lost their primary source of income, and the other half could cover no more than a month.

Yet there are opportunities to better link existing services to people's financial needs and goals. An account can be a vital resource for anyone who needs to receive government support payments or financial support from family or friends. Saving, borrowing, and insurance products geared for a specific purpose—such as medical costs, which about a quarter of all adults in low- and middle-income economies say they worry about—could help people mitigate financial stress.

Better tools to enhance people's ability to access extra money during an emergency are particularly important in the context of natural disasters. A quarter of adults in low- and middle-income economies experienced a natural disaster in the three years preceding the survey, and two-thirds of them either lost income or experienced damage to their homes, livestock, or other assets.

Figure ES.8 **The share of financially resilient adults in low- and middle-income economies has held steady since 2021**

Adults identifying the source of, and assessing how difficult it would be to access, emergency money in 30 days or less (%), 2024

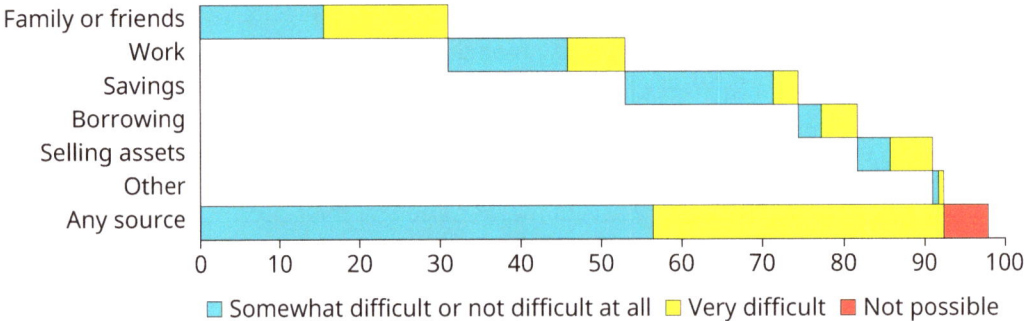

Source: Global Findex Database 2025.

Financial services providers have an opportunity to strengthen household financial health through effective product design. Innovative products could help people pursue their financial aspirations—such as building a business, educating children, or planning for retirement—while also strengthening their ability to manage unexpected financial events. Insurance, affordable loans, well-designed savings accounts, and automatic deposits, transfers, and installment payments can help people achieve their financial goals.

Many of the world's 1.3 billion people without financial accounts already have the tools they would need to get financial services

Despite high mobile phone ownership and growth in account ownership, 1.3 billion people still lack financial accounts. Many of these people have the foundations they would need to get a digitally enabled account, however: They own mobile phones, they have personal ID,[7] and they have SIM cards registered in their names. In an environment with robust consumer protection in which they have access to appropriately designed, affordable, and convenient financial products, this group could be the next beneficiaries of efforts toward financial inclusion, so long as providers take a holistic approach to helping less financially experienced owners of new accounts build their financial skills.

In Sub-Saharan Africa, where mobile money is prevalent, a quarter of adults without accounts, or about 80 million people, have all three digital prerequisites for account ownership (refer to figure ES.9). These digitally connected adults may be able to open and use accounts more easily than their unconnected peers and represent a key opportunity for expanding financial access and use.

One group that could particularly benefit from focused efforts to increase access to and use of formal financial services is the 90 million adults in Sub-Saharan Africa without accounts who receive agricultural payments in cash. Farmers might especially benefit from having a relationship with a formal financial institution, given that such a relationship could provide them with potential access to saving, insurance, and credit products to help them smooth irregular earnings due to seasonal income fluctuations and invest in agricultural inputs at the beginning of the growing season, when cash flows tend to be tight.

Payment digitalization can also help motivate account ownership. Five percent of adults without an account also receive a government payment in cash.[8] Efforts to make these payments directly into accounts can benefit both governments and recipients.[9] An additional 16 percent of adults without accounts receive private wage payments in cash, although digitalizing these payments might face challenges related to firm formalization and compliance with government obligations.

Figure ES.9 Digital enablers are necessary for expanding mobile money account ownership in Sub-Saharan Africa

Adults without an account (%), 2024

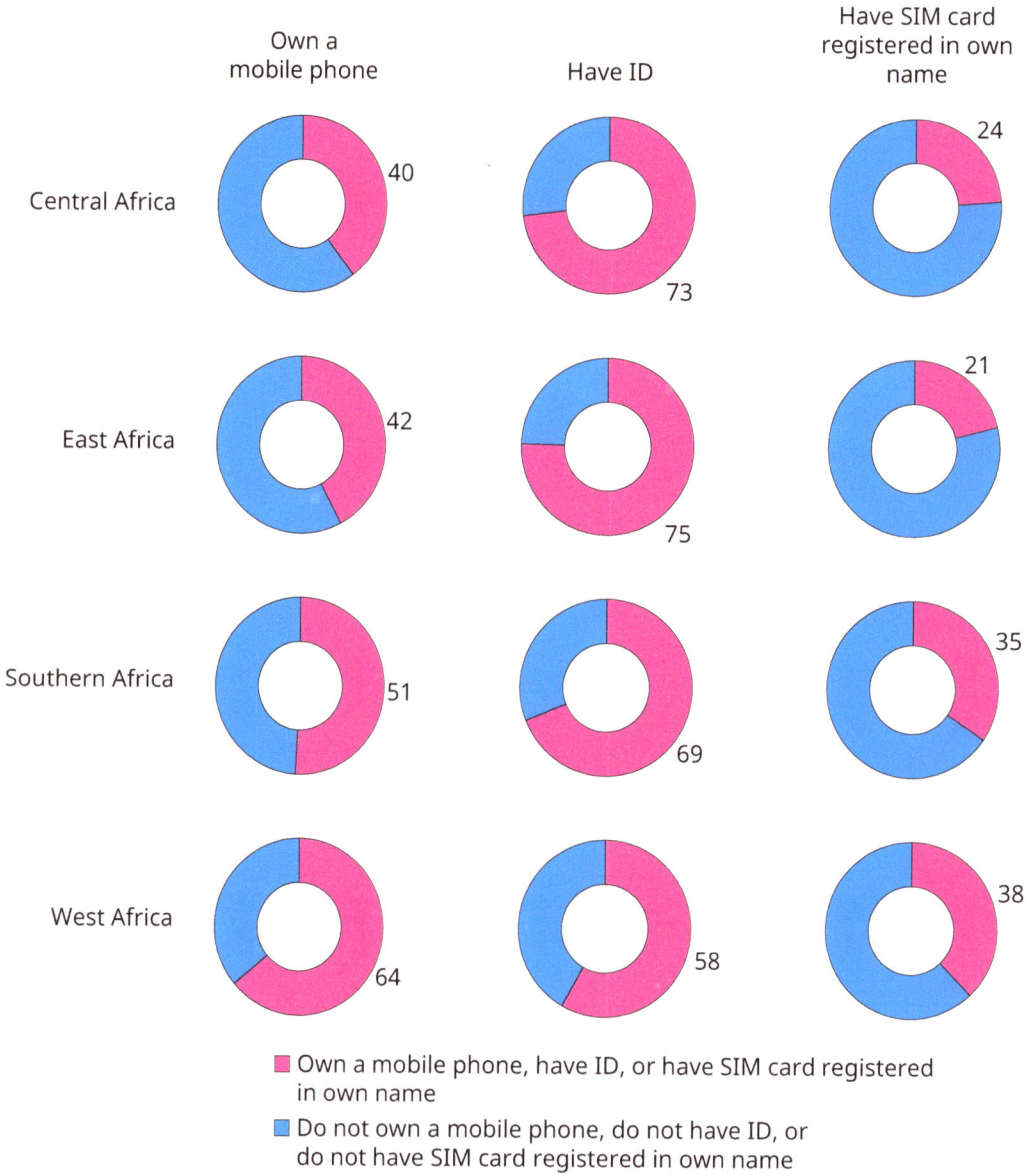

	Own a mobile phone	Have ID	Have SIM card registered in own name
Central Africa	40	73	24
East Africa	42	75	21
Southern Africa	51	69	35
West Africa	64	58	38

■ Own a mobile phone, have ID, or have SIM card registered in own name

■ Do not own a mobile phone, do not have ID, or do not have SIM card registered in own name

Sources: Global Findex Database 2025 and Identification for Development (ID4D)–Global Findex Database 2025.

Conclusion

The high levels of mobile phone ownership and internet use and the increases in financial account ownership and use represent significant development successes. Dedicated financial inclusion efforts are still critical, however, to address two key challenges. The first is reaching the remaining adults without accounts, primarily women and poor adults, through focused, context-appropriate initiatives. The second is developing programs, policies, and products that help everyone improve their financial health so that they can more effectively mitigate sources of financial worry, increase their financial resilience, and more effectively pursue their goals.

Any effort to further expand digital and financial inclusion should take into account the broader context to ensure that the necessary infrastructure and consumer protections are in place. Governments and providers of financial services have a responsibility to establish strong rules ensuring consumer protection and implement them throughout the product design, sales, onboarding, and user experience processes. In this way, they can play a role in designing the next wave of efforts toward financial inclusion for people who remain underserved.

Notes

1. Information on this topic was not collected in high-income economies or the Russian Federation.
2. *Adults with a mobile money account* refers to adults who have personally used a mobile phone in the preceding 12 months to make payments, purchase goods or services, or send or receive money using a mobile money provider included in the GSMA Mobile Money Deployment Tracker, which includes telecom- and fintech-led platforms that offer financial services via mobile phones and typically operate independently of traditional banks. This group generally excludes adults using digital wallets that function primarily as app-based payment tools. Some mobile money account providers listed in the GSMA's tracker, however, could be legally licensed as a bank or supported by a bank partner, or some of their services could be linked to bank accounts. All mobile money accounts are by definition digitally enabled and are primarily accessed through mobile phones.
3. *Adults with an account at a bank or similar financial institution* refers to adults with an account at a regulated institution such as a bank, credit union, microfinance institution, or post office that allows them to store money and make and receive payments. These institutions have historically maintained physical footprints in the form of branch locations. This category also includes adults who say they have a debit card linked to an account, even if they say they do not have an account at a bank or similar financial institution.
4. Refer to the web page for the World Bank's Project FASTT: Frictionless Affordable Safe Timely Transactions: https://fastpayments.worldbank.org/.

5. Data on government and wage payments were not collected in Algeria, China, the Islamic Republic of Iran, Libya, Mauritius, the Russian Federation, or Ukraine.

6. Refer to the web page for the Brookings Institution's *Foresight Africa 2025–2030* report: https://www.brookings.edu/collection/foresight-africa-2025-2030/.

7. The Identification for Development (ID4D)–Global Findex Database 2025 includes data on ID ownership globally. Refer to the web page for the World Bank's ID4D Initiative: https://id4d.worldbank.org/.

8. Data for how adults receive government, private wage, and agricultural payments exclude China.

9. Refer to the web page for the World Bank's G2Px initiative, which aims to contribute to the broader agenda of improving government-to-person payments through digitalization: https://www.worldbank.org/en/programs/g2px/knowledge.

Introduction

Many of today's common financial behaviors barely existed in 2011, when the Global Findex launched its first edition. Since then, digital connectivity, ownership of mobile phones, and internet use, as well as the resulting availability of mobile money and other digitally enabled financial services, have transformed financial sectors in many economies. One of the most visible consequences of this change, as this report shows, is rapid increases in financial account access and usage. In 2011, 51 percent of the world's adults had financial accounts; as of 2024, that share had risen to 79 percent, with half of those accounts being digitally enabled, meaning their owners could use them with a phone or payment card, such as a credit or debit card.

That is a success story for development, given how essential financial services are for equipping people to lift themselves out of poverty or preventing a slide into it. Though there is still important work to be done to include the 1.3 billion adults worldwide who still do not have accounts and to narrow persistent gaps in access and use among poorer adults and women, the trend line is positive—and has been powerfully driven by mobile technology. The impact that mobile phones and the internet are having extends not only to account ownership, but also to potentially productive uses, including saving formally, which 40 percent of adults in low- and middle-income economies now do, and making or receiving digital payments, which more than 60 percent of adults in low- and middle-income economies also do.

The foundational role that digital connectivity plays in financial inclusion and economic opportunities is the central theme of this fifth edition of the *Global Findex*. Consistent with that theme, the report begins with a section on digital connectivity that includes data from the Global Findex 2025 Digital Connectivity Tracker, a new module of the Global Findex focused on digital access and usage. It is followed by sections on the state of financial access, financial use, and financial health.

About the report and the data

As did previous editions, *The Global Findex 2025* describes the data and provides a thorough overview of the survey's coverage and its findings. The data capture respondents' perceptions about their financial habits and access to and use of financial accounts. Those perceptions may differ—sometimes significantly—from supply-side data on account ownership reported by financial institutions to central banks. The latter may show higher account ownership rates because it includes inactive accounts and double counting. The report does not, however, attempt to explain why changes may have occurred, nor does it speculate on the conditions that may help one economy replicate the success of another.

The report summarizes Global Findex survey data from 141 economies collected in the second half of 2024. About 1,000 respondents responded to the survey in each participating economy, and the results are weighted by population. As such, they provide an accurate, nationally representative reflection of behavior across each surveyed economy. Given the timing of the survey, all data in this edition and the corresponding data bank are labeled 2024. In contrast to previous editions, the report and the database—available on the Global Findex website[1]—are dated with the year 2025, based on the publication date of the report rather than the date of data collection.

Unlike what was the case in previous editions, data collection for *The Global Findex 2025* gave priority to low- and middle-income economies. Data on mobile phone ownership, internet use, and account ownership were collected in all economies, but questions on financial use and financial health were asked only in low- and middle-income economies. In addition, in Algeria, China, the Islamic Republic of Iran, Libya, Mauritius, the Russian Federation, and Ukraine, an abridged form of the questionnaire was administered by phone because of economy-specific restrictions. For comparability across time, averages for earlier years exclude data for Russia and may therefore differ from previously published numbers.

Most figures and text in the report provide low- and middle-income economy averages and averages for the six World Bank regions (excluding any high-income economies in them): East Asia and Pacific, Europe and Central Asia, Latin America and the Caribbean, the Middle East and North Africa, South Asia, and Sub-Saharan Africa. Chapters also may include information on specific economies or compare data trends by economy income group classification, specifically, in low-income, lower-middle-income, and upper-middle-income economies. Unless specifically noted, all data are reported as shares of all adults to make economy-to-economy comparisons possible, and all survey questions were asked about recent behavior, usually over the 12 months preceding the survey. Growth levels and comparisons are statistically significant at about 4 percentage points or greater; readers are asked not to overemphasize increases, decreases, or differences of smaller magnitude.

---

1   The website is available at http://globalfindex.worldbank.org.

Given the long history of the Global Findex, readers may encounter occasional inconsistencies between time series data discussed in this report and the same data published in previous years. These inconsistencies usually come about for one of two reasons:

- *Changes in income classification:* The Global Findex uses the World Bank's income designations from fiscal year 2024 for the Global Findex Database 2025. When an economy grows to the point that it "graduates" to a higher income designation or experiences setbacks that place it in a lower income designation, the Global Findex Database reflects that change. This can result in shifts of one or two percentage points in the calculated average for a given indicator for an affected income group; it can also change low- and middle-income averages if economies have graduated to high-income status.

- *COVID-19 data updates:* As a result of COVID-19 mobility restrictions, 22 economies could not be surveyed in time for the release of *The Global Findex 2021*. Those economies were subsequently surveyed in 2022, and the data collected were added to the database. This resulted in small adjustments to the 2021 regional, low- and middle-income, and global averages for several headline indicators.

In addition to these time series inconsistencies, the difference between two reported data points—such as when gender or income gaps are calculated—is occasionally 1 percentage point greater than the value of those points would suggest. This can happen when the difference between the two, rounded to the nearest whole percentage point (as the data in the report are), is less than the difference between the comparable unrounded data (which is what appears in the database). In all such cases, the discrepancies are noted and the circumstances explained in a footnote.

The report progresses as follows:

Section 1, Digital connectivity, reports data from the Global Findex 2025 Digital Connectivity Tracker, including detailed data from 75 low- and middle-income economies on ownership of mobile phones, internet use, and digital safety and the barriers people face across all three.

Section 2, Financial access, provides updated data on the share of adults who have financial accounts and explores opportunities to expand access for those who do not, with analysis of the relationship between financial and digital access.

Section 3, Financial use, explores trends in saving, borrowing, and use of digital payments, as well as how digitally enabled accounts, including mobile money, are encouraging more people to save formally and use digital payments.

Section 4, Financial health, highlights the challenges that adults continue to face— even those with accounts—when managing their financial needs and mitigating the risks associated with unexpected expenses or loss of income, as well as navigating the financial sector itself.

Each section opens with a visual summary of its main findings. In addition, the report includes three spotlights, placed after sections 1, 3, and 4, respectively. Spotlight 1.1 presents select data from the Identification for Development (ID4D)– Global Findex Database 2025, which are collected jointly with the World Bank's ID4D Initiative. This spotlight summarizes ID ownership globally and explores the barriers to digital and financial inclusion that people face when they lack ID. Spotlight 3.1 examines data on account usage frequency and account inactivity. Spotlight 4.1 presents new data on natural disasters and the financial impact they have on those who experience them.

All data included in the report are available on the Global Findex website, on which readers can access the report and subsequent analysis and download the full data bank. The website also includes a tool for reproducing images in the report and customizing them to include particular economies of interest. Finally, readers can visit the World Bank's "Inclusive Digital Financial Services" web page to explore Global Findex data visualized for every world economy. An example from this web page for low- and middle-income economies is included between sections 2 and 3 of the report.[2] Readers are invited to explore and use the data to inform efforts to measure and promote financial inclusion and for research, starting with this report and its core findings.

---

2   The web page is available at http://globalfindex.worldbank.org/visualizations.

Digital connectivity

A reproducibility package is available for this book in the Reproducible Research Repository at https://reproducibility.worldbank.org/catalog/299.

Digital Connectivity

IN LOW- AND MIDDLE-INCOME ECONOMIES

84% of adults own a mobile phone—mostly smartphones, except in Sub-Saharan Africa.

Poorer adults are **8 percentage points and women are 9 percentage points less likely** to own a phone than wealthier adults and men.

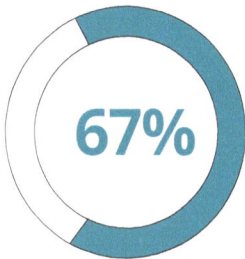

67% of adults use the internet—**primarily through a smartphone.**

Phone ownership **income gaps** exist everywhere—particularly related to smartphones.

Gender gaps are more concentrated. Over **300 MILLION WOMEN** live without phones just in South Asia.

Affordability is by far the **most common reason** people give for not having a mobile phone.

RESPONSIBLE DIGITAL USE

40%
of mobile phone owners do not have a password on their device.

19%
of phone owners have been exposed to online scams. Few say they lost money.

Both **phone owners and internet users** are most likely to use their devices and the web daily.

ONLINE ACTIVITY

Texting and social media are the **most popular digital activities.**

45%
OF ALL ADULTS USE SOCIAL MEDIA.

26%
LEARN ONLINE.

18%
ACCESS GOVERNMENT INFORMATION OR SERVICES.

6%
EARN MONEY.

1.1 Mobile phone ownership

A reproducibility package is available for this book in the Reproducible Research Repository at https://reproducibility.worldbank.org/catalog/299.

1.1 Mobile phone ownership

Mobile phones and the internet have become widespread and essential to daily life in every economy around the world. As of 2024, individual ownership of mobile phones reached 86 percent of adults worldwide (refer to map 1.1.1). For many people, barely an hour goes by without their using a mobile device to make a call, text a friend, read the news, access business information, post a meme on social media, pay for something, play a game, engage with a colleague or a customer, or search for information. As access to and use of digitally connected technologies increase, people, businesses, and governments place an increasingly high priority on online interactions.

Digitally connected technologies have clear, well-documented benefits.[1] Access to mobile phones and the internet is associated with reduced poverty, increased consumption, and more employment for individuals in low- and middle-income economies.[2] Women also experience these benefits, as internet access enables access to flexible jobs[3] and has been shown to increase female labor force participation.[4] Mobile phones also facilitate information sharing. For instance,

Map 1.1.1 Worldwide, 86 percent of adults own a mobile phone

Adults with a mobile phone (%), 2024

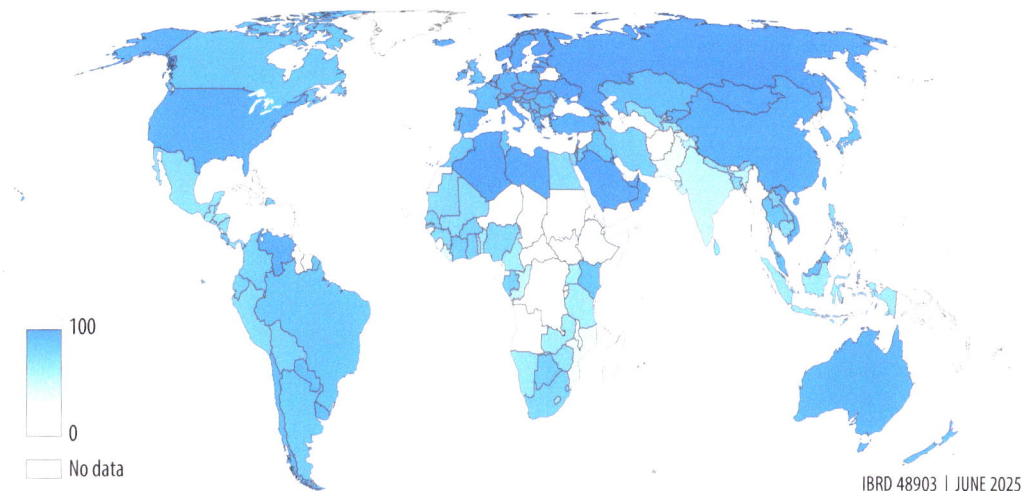

100

0

No data

IBRD 48903 | JUNE 2025

Source: Global Findex Database 2025.

---

1   For an overview of the benefits, especially for women, refer to BIGD (2024).
2   Bahia et al. (2023); Bahia et al. (2024); Blumenstock et al. (2020); Hjort and Poulsen (2019); Simione and Li (2021).
3   Ho, Jalota, and Karandikar (2024).
4   Chiplunkar and Goldberg (2022); Klonner and Nolen (2010); Viollaz and Winkler (2021).

in agricultural contexts, farmers' access to real-time prices and buyer demand data can inform their decisions on where to sell, enhancing market efficiency and reducing the distances they would otherwise travel to get the best return for their product and time.[5] Internet access also helps create jobs[6] and aids individuals and countries in exporting goods and services.[7]

Owning a mobile phone furthermore enables financial access through mobile money and other mobile financial services. These financial accounts and services, typically offered by mobile network operators or fintech firms and accessed via networks of local agents, are associated with lower rates of poverty,[8] increased consumption[9] and savings,[10] and greater resilience to economic shocks.[11]

Given those benefits, and the relationship between mobile phone ownership and adoption of digital financial services, Global Findex 2025 set out to conduct the first global demand-side survey on mobile phone ownership and internet use and the risks people face with both (refer to box 1.1.1).

> ## Box 1.1.1 Measuring digital connectivity: The Global Findex approach
>
> For efficiency, this report uses the term *digital connectivity* to refer to access to and use of the internet or dedicated apps by means of a device—such as a network-connected computer, tablet, or mobile phone—to interact and transact with individuals, businesses, financial institutions, or governments. The goal of digital connectivity is to make these devices and related applications easy, safe, and affordable and enable users to create economic and social value.
>
> The Global Findex survey included a new dedicated module of questions, the Global Findex 2025 Digital Connectivity Tracker. It collected data on personal mobile phone ownership and use, internet use related to a range of digital activities, and responsible digital practices such as password adoption and safe navigation of online scams and harassment.

(Box continued next page)

---

5   Abraham (2007); Aker (2008, 2010); Jensen (2007); Muto and Yamano (2009).
6   Klonner and Nolen (2010).
7   Hjort and Poulsen (2019); Jensen (2007); Schulzrinne and Montpetit (2022).
8   Jack and Suri (2014); Suri and Jack (2016).
9   Blumenstock, Callen, and Ghani (2018); Breza, Kanz, and Klapper (2020).
10   Lee et al. (2021); Munyegera and Matsumoto (2016).
11   Riley (2018).

The tracker employs the following criteria in recording data related to digital connectivity:

Adults *own a mobile phone* if they have any kind of mobile phone for personal use to make and receive calls.

- Adults who own mobile phones can have either *basic phones* or *smartphones*, depending on their response to a survey question on this point. The survey additionally asked adults who have basic phones whether they could use WhatsApp on their phone if they wanted to; those who responded *yes* have *feature phones*.

- *Internet use* is calculated based on adults who said they had used the internet in the past three months. Measuring it in this way aims to capture current and active use, and the definition is aligned with that used by the International Telecommunication Union to measure progress against the Sustainable Development Goals (Indicator 17.8.1).

- Only respondents who said they used the internet or owned a smartphone answered survey questions about digital activities such as social media use or online learning.

The Global Findex 2025 Digital Connectivity Tracker was fielded in person in 75 economies during the second half of 2024. Respondents in all high-income economies and in an additional seven low- and middle-income economies—specifically, Algeria, China, the Islamic Republic of Iran, Libya, Mauritius, the Russian Federation, and Ukraine—were surveyed by phone and therefore were asked only a limited subset of the tracker questions. Data used in calculating regional averages and those for low- and middle-income countries exclude results for several of these economies—China and Russia among them. The "Methodology" tab of the Global Findex website (http://globalfindex.worldbank.org) provides details on the information collected in each surveyed economy.

Mobile phone ownership is widespread nearly everywhere

According to data from the Global Findex 2025 Digital Connectivity Tracker, 86 percent of adults worldwide, and 84 percent of adults in low- and middle-income economies, own personal mobile phones (refer to figure 1.1.1).

Figure 1.1.1 Mobile phone ownership is widespread around the world, though women are less likely than men to own a mobile phone in some economies

Adults with a mobile phone (%), 2024

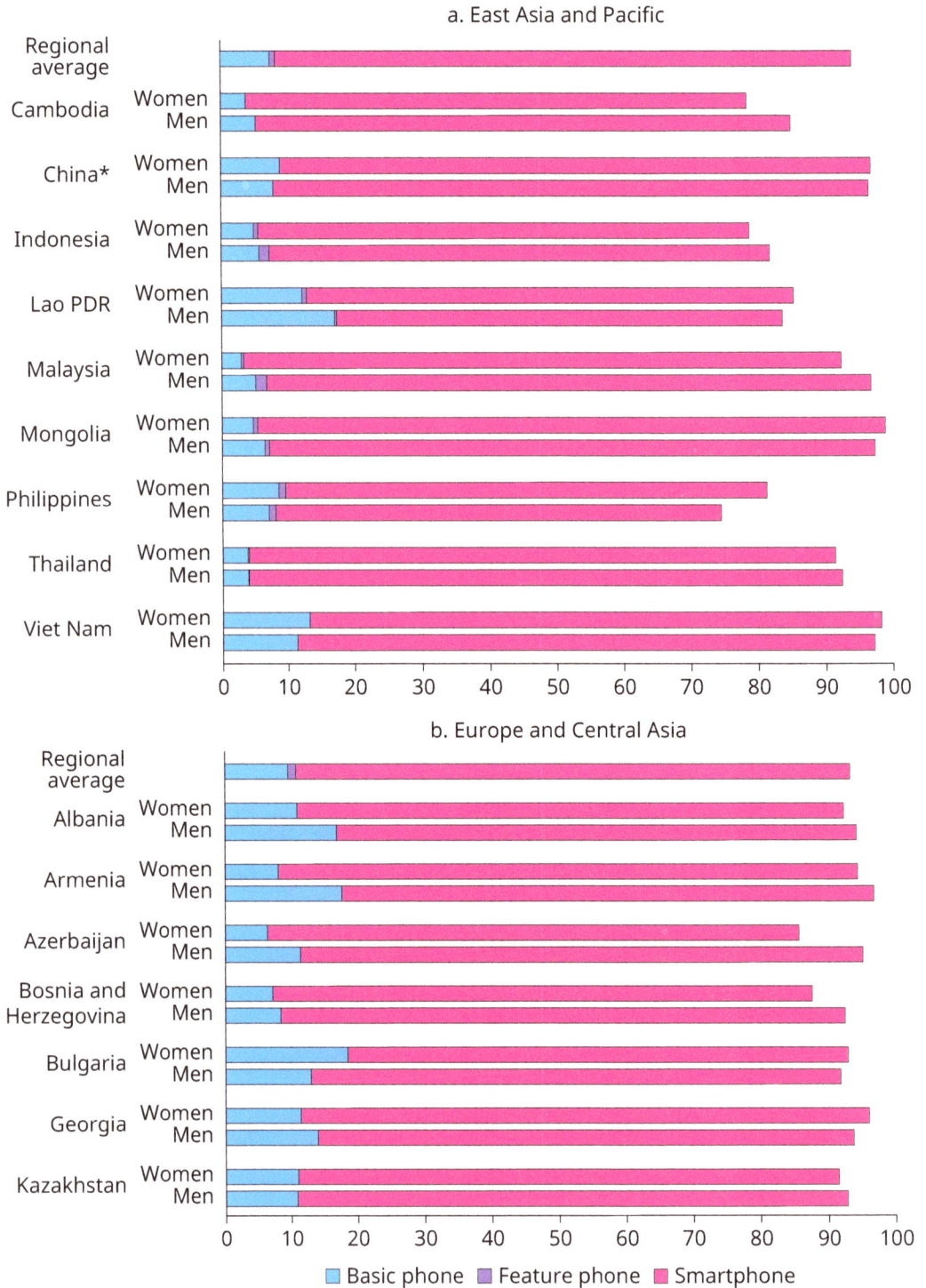

a. East Asia and Pacific

b. Europe and Central Asia

Basic phone   Feature phone   Smartphone

(Figure continued next page)

Figure 1.1.1 Mobile phone ownership is widespread around the world, though women are less likely than men to own a mobile phone in some economies *(continued)*

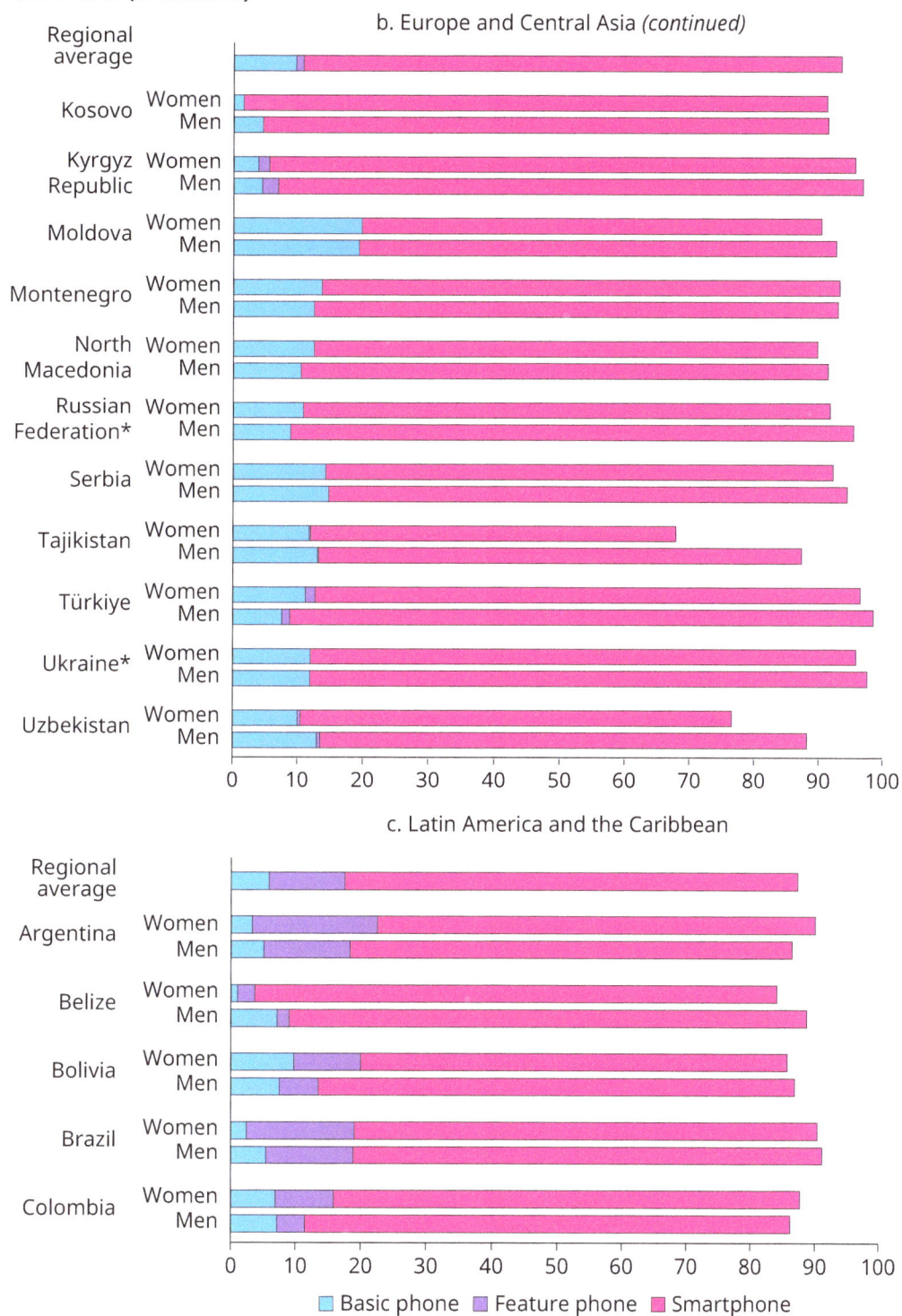

b. Europe and Central Asia *(continued)*

c. Latin America and the Caribbean

Legend: ☐ Basic phone ☐ Feature phone ☐ Smartphone

(Figure continued next page)

Figure 1.1.1 Mobile phone ownership is widespread around the world, though women are less likely than men to own a mobile phone in some economies *(continued)*

c. Latin America and the Caribbean *(continued)*

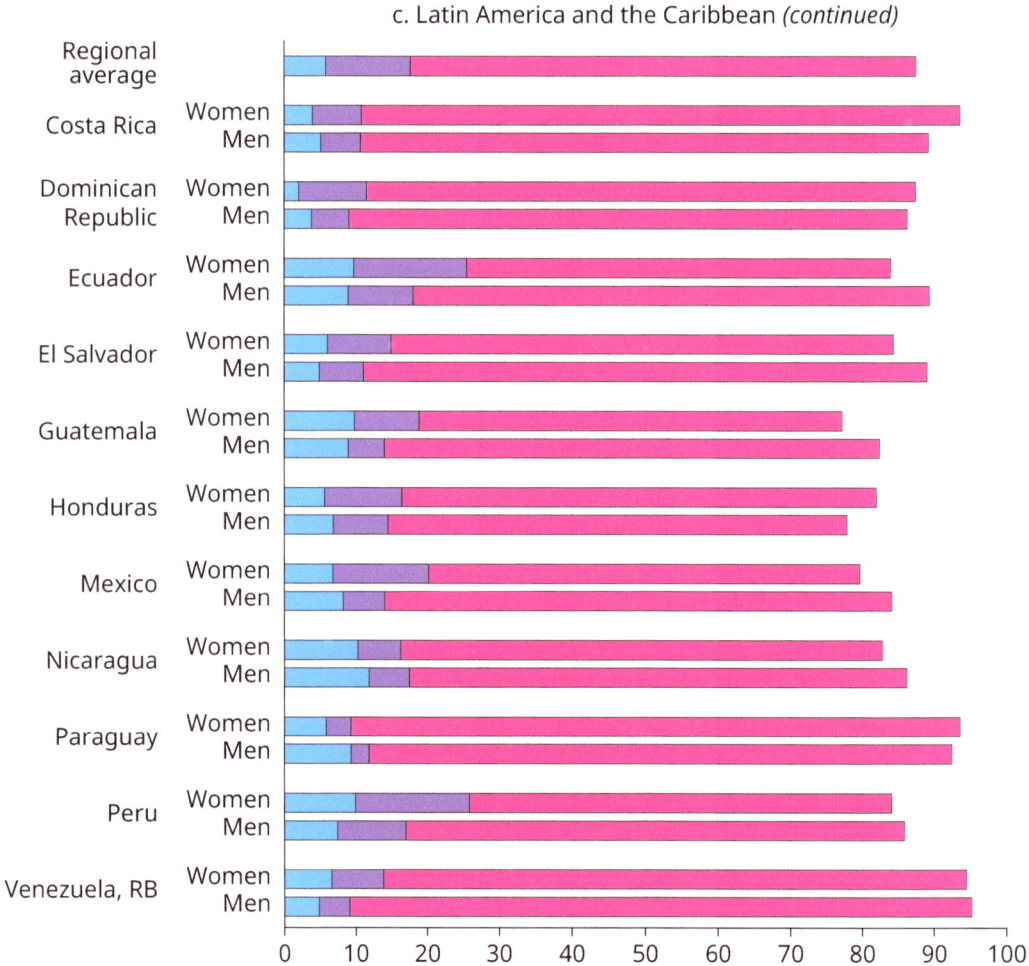

d. Middle East and North Africa

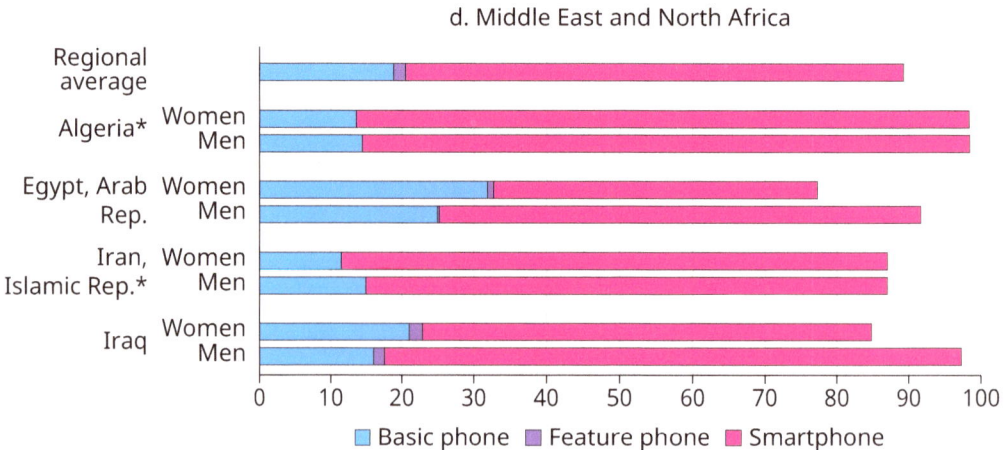

Legend: ☐ Basic phone ☐ Feature phone ☐ Smartphone

(Figure continued next page)

Figure 1.1.1 Mobile phone ownership is widespread around the world, though women are less likely than men to own a mobile phone in some economies *(continued)*

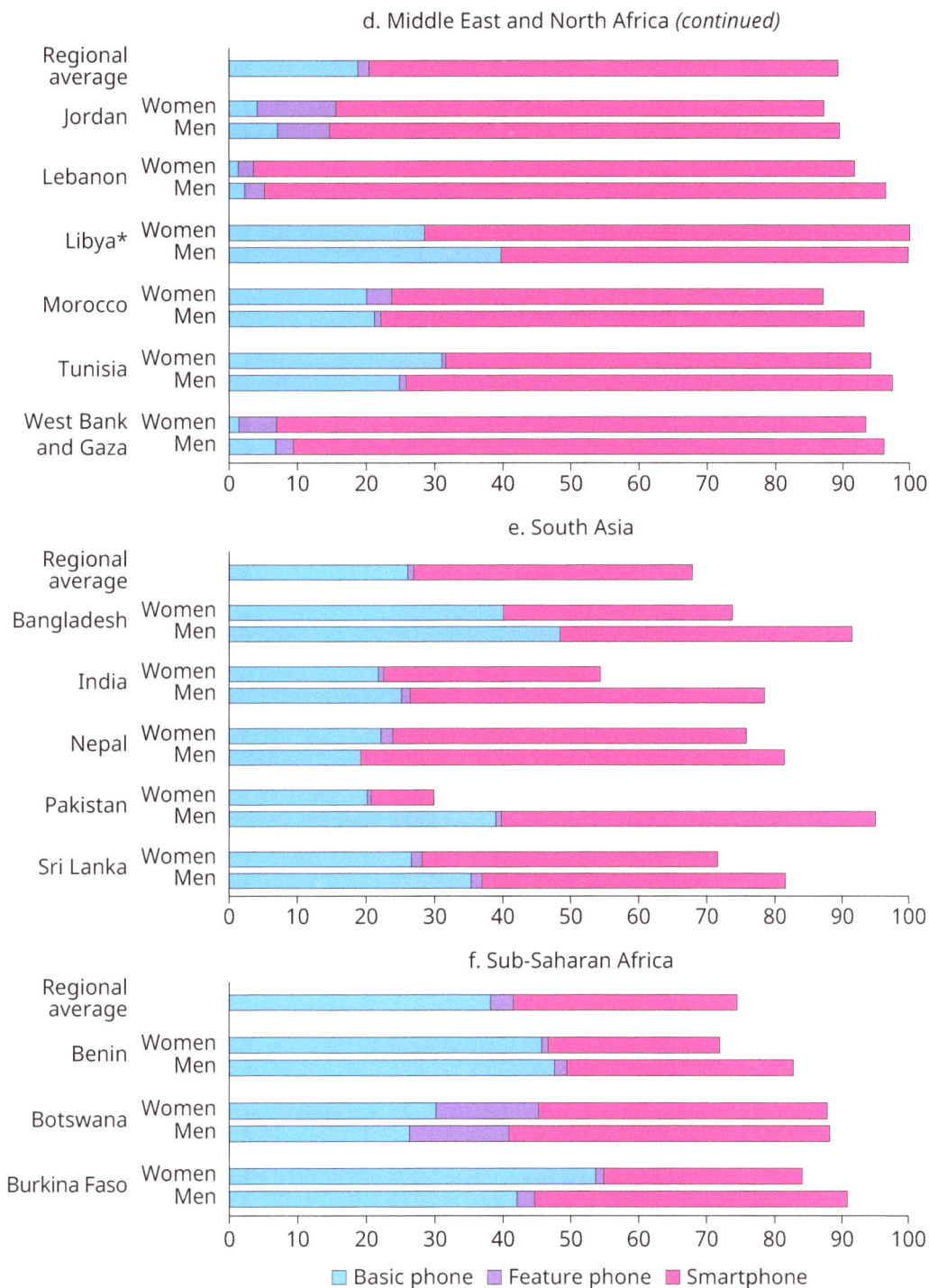

d. Middle East and North Africa *(continued)*

e. South Asia

f. Sub-Saharan Africa

Legend: ☐ Basic phone ☐ Feature phone ☐ Smartphone

(Figure continued next page)

Figure 1.1.1 Mobile phone ownership is widespread around the world, though women are less likely than men to own a mobile phone in some economies *(continued)*

f. Sub-Saharan Africa *(continued)*

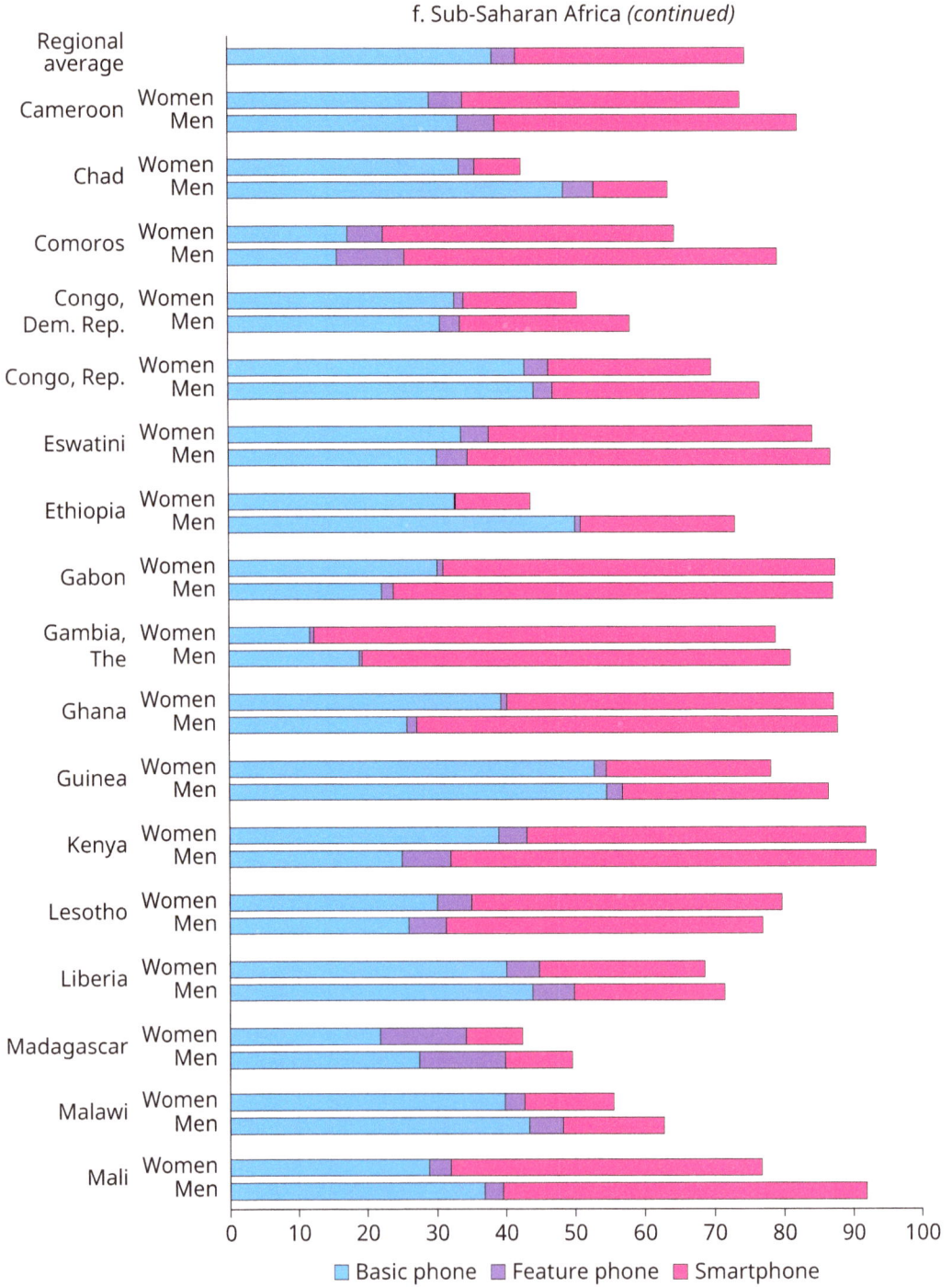

Basic phone ■ Feature phone ■ Smartphone

(Figure continued next page)

Figure 1.1.1 Mobile phone ownership is widespread around the world, though women are less likely than men to own a mobile phone in some economies *(continued)*

f. Sub-Saharan Africa *(continued)*

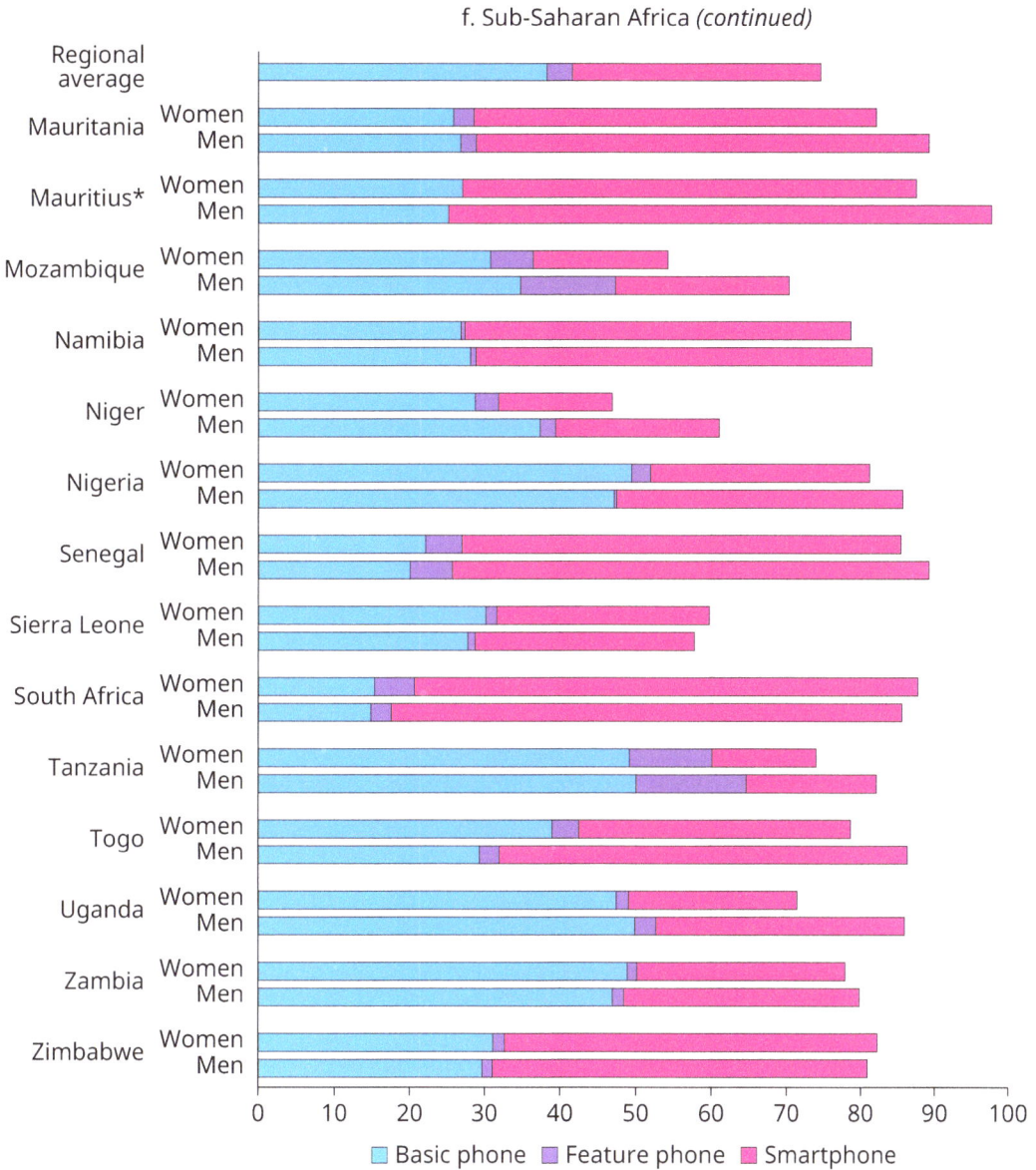

Legend: ☐ Basic phone ☐ Feature phone ☐ Smartphone

Source: Global Findex Database 2025.

Note: See the text for definitions of *basic phones, feature phones,* and *smartphones.* The asterisk next to Algeria, China, the Islamic Republic of Iran, Libya, Mauritius, the Russian Federation, and Ukraine indicates that respondents in these economies were surveyed by phone rather than in person.

These handheld devices have become so popular and ubiquitous that only nine low- and lower-middle-income economies have average mobile phone ownership rates below 65 percent.[12] An additional share of adults do not have their own phone (and therefore are not included among phone owners) and instead use someone else's: depending on the region, between 31 percent and 54 percent of adults without their own phones use someone else's.

Mobile phone ownership varies by type across regions and economies; the survey differentiates between owners of smartphones and owners of basic phones. It defines *smartphones* as having the ability to run applications and having full-function web browsers. Smartphones represent most of the mobile phone stock in all but 18 of the economies surveyed.

Basic phones let users make phone calls, send text messages, and use streamlined services such as mobile money, with payment transactions executed via the Unstructured Supplementary Service Data protocol. Of the 18 economies in which basic phones dominate, 17 are in Sub-Saharan Africa (Bangladesh is the remaining economy). India, Pakistan, and Sri Lanka in South Asia also have relatively large shares of basic phone owners.

A type of basic phone referred to here as a *feature phone* may include preloaded versions of WhatsApp or other basic tools; some feature phones also let owners view text-only HTML web pages. Feature phones represent a very small share of all mobile phones and are more commonly found in the economies of Latin America and the Caribbean relative to those in other regions.

Basic and feature phones' limited functionality and lower levels of data consumption make them more affordable than smartphones, which is particularly important for people with low incomes. Batteries in basic phones also hold their charges for longer, which benefits phone owners in economies in which electricity is intermittent. Their limited functionality may affect owners' access to a range of digital resources, however, including the internet.

Poorer adults and women are less likely to own mobile phones, particularly smartphones

Despite widespread mobile phone ownership, certain adults—particularly those living in the poorest 40 percent of households and those who are out of the

---

12 Most of the economies with mobile phone ownership rates below 65 percent are in Sub-Saharan Africa; these include Chad, the Democratic Republic of Congo, Ethiopia, Madagascar, Malawi, Mozambique, Niger, and Sierra Leone. The only economy outside of Sub-Saharan Africa with a mobile phone ownership rate less than 65 percent is Pakistan.

workforce, as well as people living in rural environments and (in some economies) women—are less likely than those living in higher-income households, those in the workforce, urban dwellers, and men to own their own mobile phones. Income level often influences mobile phone ownership among members of all these groups, likely driving the greater equity seen in basic phone ownership and wider inequity in smartphone ownership, since smartphones are more expensive to buy and to own than basic phones are. The following subsections explore these differences in more detail.

Income gaps in mobile phone ownership exist in nearly every region and economy, though with nuances

In low- and middle-income economies, the overall gap in mobile phone ownership between people living in households in the poorest 40 percent (by income) and those living in the wealthiest 60 percent is 8 percentage points (refer to figure 1.1.2, panel a). Nearly every economy in this group has an income gap in mobile phone ownership.

There are also gaps based on education, employment, and rural residency, each of them strongly associated with income. Specifically, among adults with a primary education or less, 75 percent own a mobile phone, compared with 93 percent of adults with a secondary education or more, an 18 percentage point difference. In addition to often earning less than more-educated peers, people with a primary education or less generally have lower literacy rates and are more likely to live in rural areas. These dynamics are particularly evident in Sub-Saharan Africa. Approaches to digital inclusion for adults with low levels of education must therefore take education into account, because it may affect how people use digital platforms and may make them more vulnerable to digital exploitation.

In regard to employment, 86 percent of wage-employed adults in low- and middle-income economies have a mobile phone compared with 81 percent of self-employed adults and just 68 percent of those who are out of the workforce (refer to figure 1.1.2, panel c).

Making digital connectivity for wage-employed adults a priority can help them leverage financial apps to manage their incomes. The self-employed also have high potential for gaining economic benefit from connectivity, because owning a personal mobile phone can help them communicate with customers and buyers more effectively and make it easier for them to get paid directly in a mobile money account, a topic explored in more detail in chapter 3.3.

Figure 1.1.2 Certain groups are less likely to own any kind of mobile phone, though basic phone ownership is more equitable in every region than smartphone ownership is

Adults with a mobile phone (%), 2024

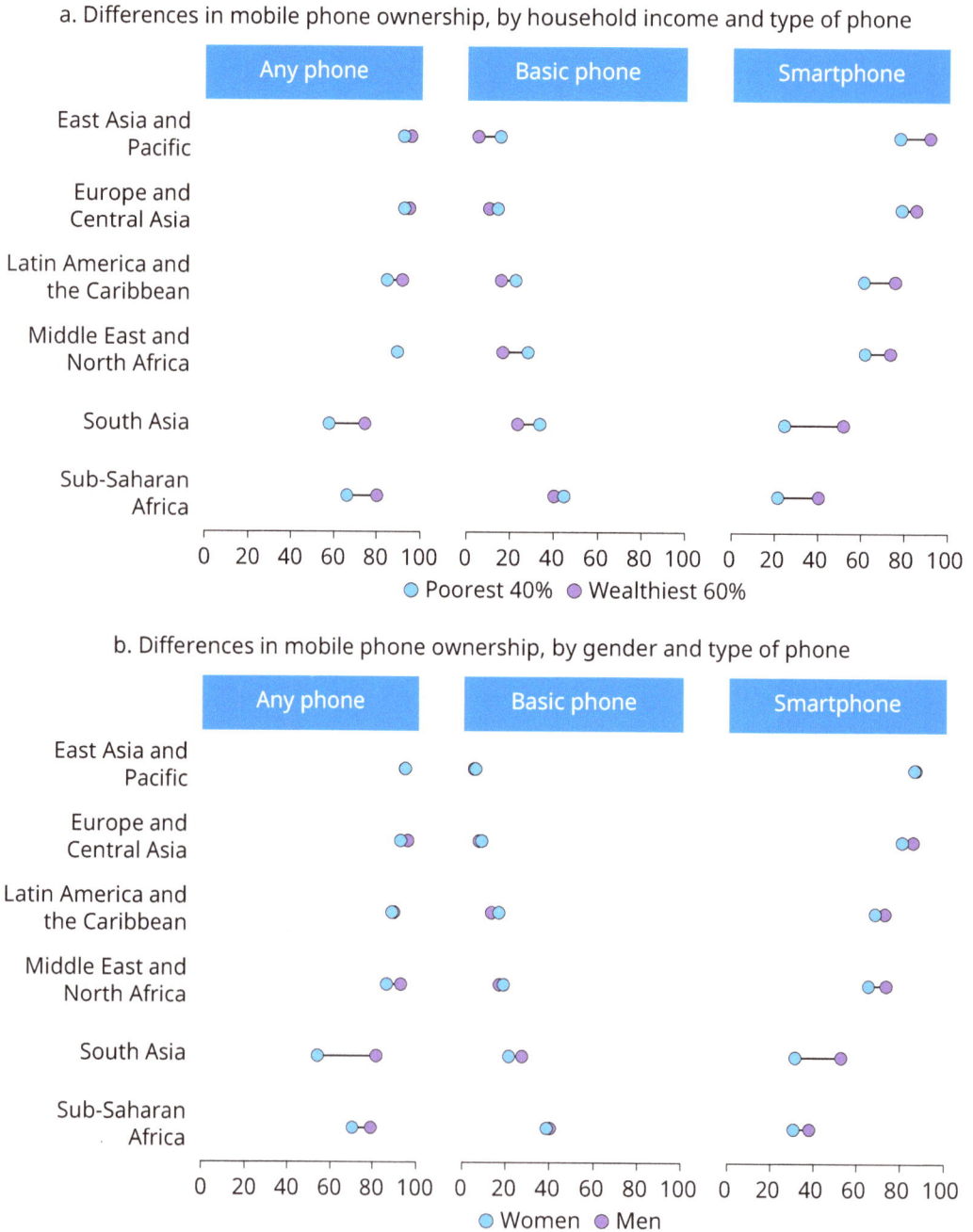

a. Differences in mobile phone ownership, by household income and type of phone

○ Poorest 40% ● Wealthiest 60%

b. Differences in mobile phone ownership, by gender and type of phone

○ Women ● Men

(Figure continued next page)

Figure 1.1.2 Certain groups are less likely to own any kind of mobile phone, though basic phone ownership is more equitable in every region than smartphone ownership is *(continued)*

c. Differences in mobile phone ownership, by employment status and type of phone

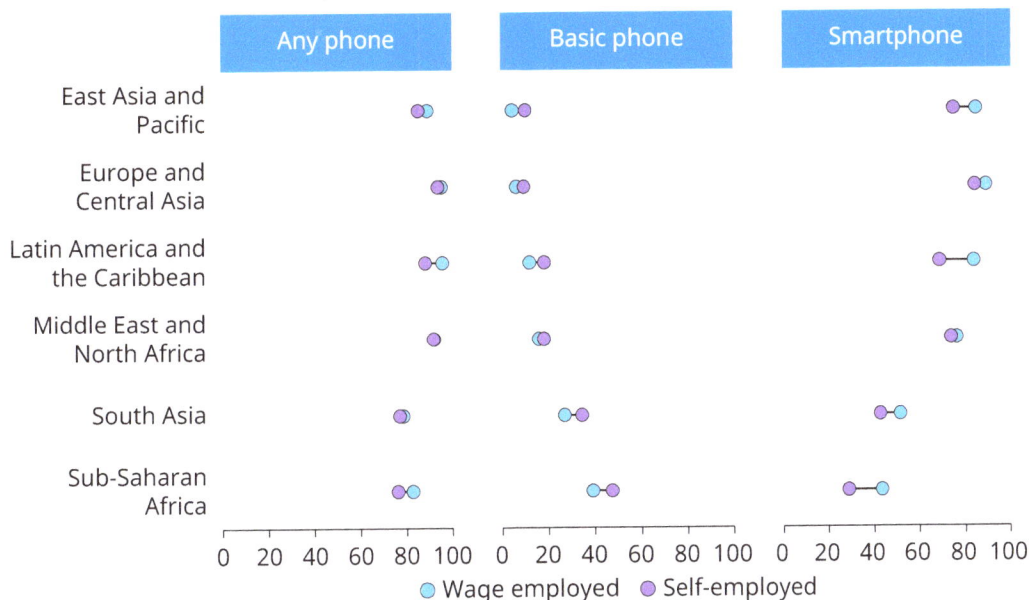

Wage employed   Self-employed

d. Differences in mobile phone ownership, by urban-rural and type of phone

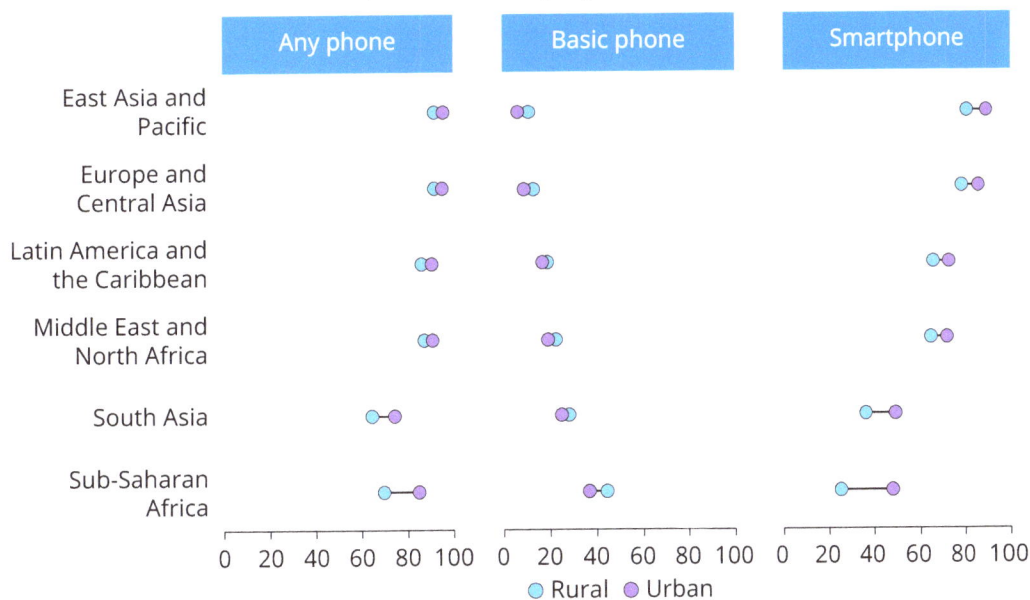

Rural   Urban

(Figure continued next page)

Figure 1.1.2 Certain groups are less likely to own any kind of mobile phone, though basic phone ownership is more equitable in every region than smartphone ownership is *(continued)*

e. Differences in mobile phone ownership, by age and type of phone

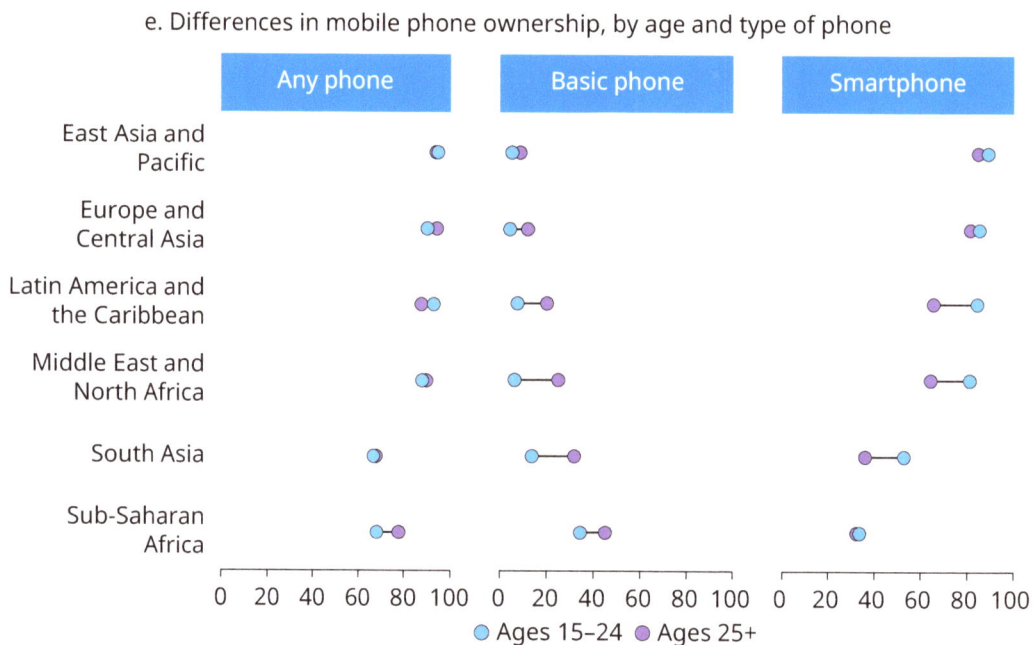

	Any phone	Basic phone	Smartphone

○ Ages 15–24 ● Ages 25+

Source: Global Findex Database 2025.

Note: The data used for regional averages exclude data for several large economies in which respondents were surveyed by phone rather than in person, including China and the Russian Federation. The "Methodology" tab of the Global Findex website (http://globalfindex.worldbank.org) provides details on the information collected in each surveyed economy.

Rural residency is also associated with lower rates of mobile phone ownership: 77 percent of rural residents own a phone compared with 90 percent of urban dwellers, a 12 percentage point difference (refer to figure 1.1.2, panel d).[13] Though there are income and cost factors involved—discussed later in the context of barriers to phone ownership—the connectivity gap between rural and urban residents is also driven by supply-side factors related to limited coverage of cell towers and broadband infrastructure. These barriers will be important to overcome as part of holistic strategies to increase connectivity rates.

---

13   The Global Findex reports data as whole percentage points, although it calculates that whole based on rounding up or down from the tenths place. As such, any discrepancies between the reported size of a gap and the difference between its end points is due to rounding.

Not all groups with low incomes are less likely to own a mobile phone, however. For example, there are generally no statistically significant differences in mobile phone ownership related to age: young adults ages 15 to 24 are as likely to own a mobile phone as adults older than 25 everywhere except Sub-Saharan Africa (refer to figure 1.1.2, panel e).

Though women on average are less likely than men to own mobile phones, the differences are small to nonexistent in most economies

On average, women around the globe are 8 percentage points less likely than men to own a mobile phone. In low- and middle-income economies, women are 9 percentage points less likely (refer to figure 1.1.2, panel b).

Yet unlike differences in mobile phone ownership based on income, which are present at some level in most economies, the gender differences in low- and middle-income economies are driven by larger-than-average differences (between 14 and 25 percentage points) in a small number of high-population economies, specifically, Bangladesh, the Arab Republic of Egypt, Ethiopia, and India. A fifth economy, Pakistan, has an ownership difference of 65 percentage points between women and men. In total, more than 300 million women without phones live in these five economies. On the other hand, 96 economies, including 55 low- and middle-income economies, do not have statistically significant gender gaps in mobile phone ownership.

In every demographic group, the differences by gender in mobile phone ownership are larger when smartphones as opposed to basic phones are considered. Gender differences in basic phone ownership specifically are statistically nonsignificant in every region except for South Asia, where the data for Pakistan drive a larger gap. In contrast, smartphone ownership is equitable only in East Asia and Pacific. Certain economies, including Chad, Ethiopia, and Pakistan, counter that trend, with gender disparities in both basic phone ownership and smartphone ownership; they are the exception, however.

Income and gender also interact to affect how likely women are to own mobile phones, particularly smartphones, with the influence of these two factors varying by region. In the Middle East and North Africa, South Asia, and Sub-Saharan Africa, both poorer women and higher-income women are less likely to own a smartphone than are men in the same income brackets. Smaller differences exist between women and men with similar incomes in Latin America and the Caribbean. In East Asia and Pacific and Europe and Central Asia, women own smartphones as often as men in the same income groups.

SIM card ownership adds another layer of complexity to the income and gender gaps

A SIM card is necessary for using a mobile phone to do almost anything. SIM cards identify a mobile phone to a mobile network and often store information about the phone's owner. In many economies, purchasers need some form of identification to buy a SIM card from a mobile network operator, and certain digital services typically require that the SIM card in the phone of the person using the service be registered in that user's name. In the case of financial services such as mobile money, this is because many of these services use SIMs in the onboarding process for mobile banking or mobile money or to register customers to use a payment platform. They may use customers' SIM card numbers as network IDs to verify the identity of account owners when they make instant payments or apply for credit.

Across low- and middle-income economies, 23 percent of mobile phone owners have SIM cards in their phones that are registered in someone else's name, not their own. In African economies such as the Comoros, the Republic of Congo, Morocco, and Tanzania, as well as in Jordan and Nepal, the share of mobile phone owners whose phones do not have a SIM card registered in their own name exceeds 40 percent (refer to figure 1.1.3).

Women who own mobile phones are as likely as men who own mobile phones to have SIM cards in their own names in East Asia and Pacific and Latin America and the Caribbean. All other regions show fewer women than men owning mobile phones with SIM cards in their own names. The difference is smallest in Sub-Saharan Africa, at 5 percentage points. In Europe and Central Asia, the Middle East and North Africa, and South Asia, the difference is at least 20 percentage points (refer to figure 1.1.4).

There are probably several reasons why people's mobile phones have SIM cards registered to someone else. In some cases, people may use phones they purchased secondhand or phones handed down to them from family members or friends whose SIM cards they never replaced with one of their own. In other cases, one family or community member may travel to a nearby city to buy multiple SIM cards on behalf of others and then distribute them. Finally, in some economies in Sub-Saharan Africa, adults report a lack of identification as a barrier to purchasing a SIM card of a mobile phone (refer to spotlight 1.1). These issues point to secondary disparities in income and by gender.

A small share of adults around the world experience the opposite dynamic: they have SIM cards in their names but do not own a mobile phone. This lets them use a household mobile phone or borrow another person's mobile phone and swap in their own SIM card. This is not a widespread practice, however. In South Asia and Sub-Saharan Africa, the regions where this is most common, only 2 percent of adults have SIM cards in their names but no phone of their own.

Figure 1.1.3 A subset of mobile phone owners do not have a SIM card registered in their name; the share is particularly high in certain economies in Sub-Saharan Africa

Adults with a mobile phone (%), 2024

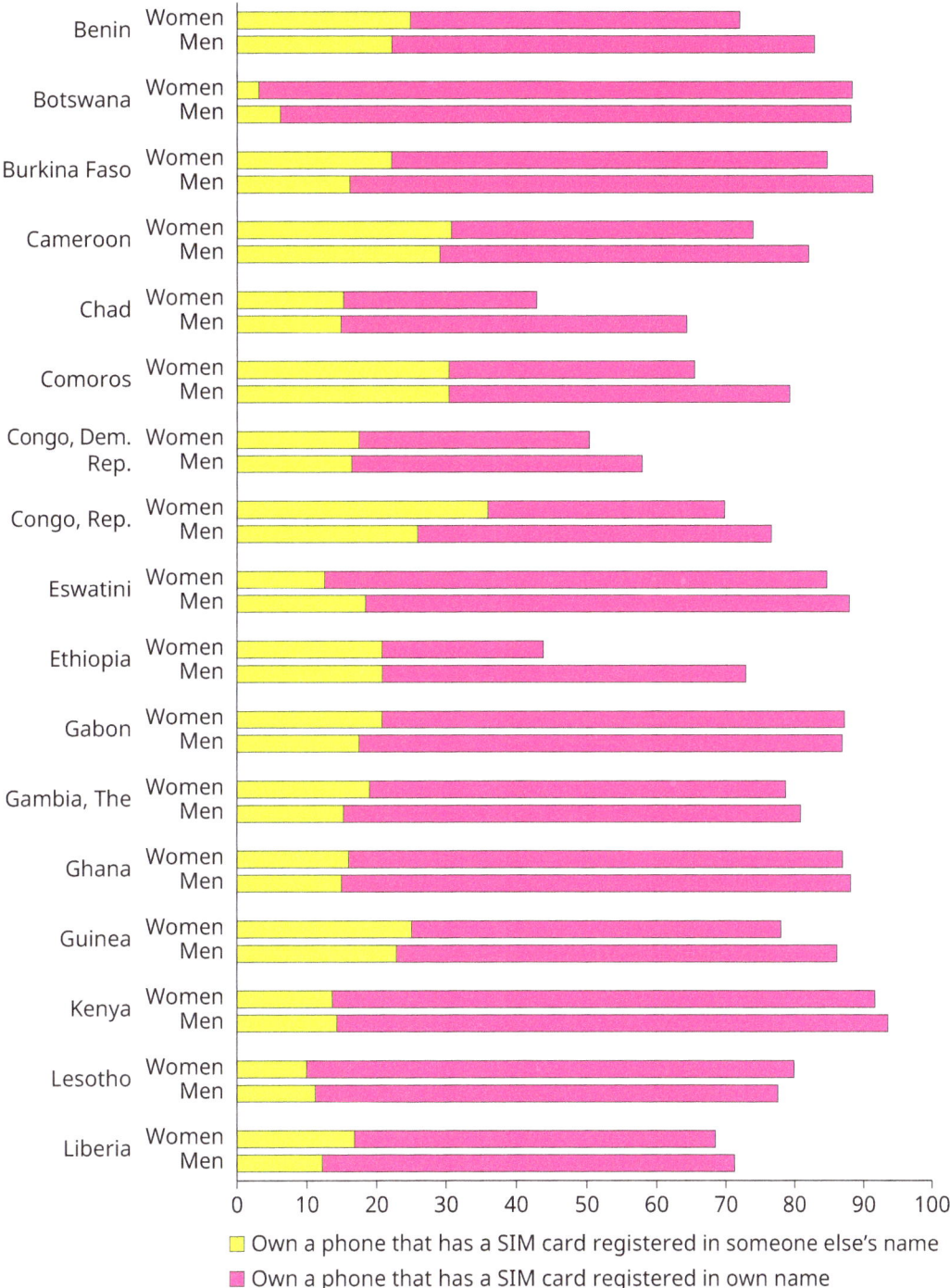

☐ Own a phone that has a SIM card registered in someone else's name
■ Own a phone that has a SIM card registered in own name

(Figure continued next page)

Figure 1.1.3 A subset of mobile phone owners do not have a SIM card registered in their name; the share is particularly high in certain economies in Sub-Saharan Africa *(continued)*

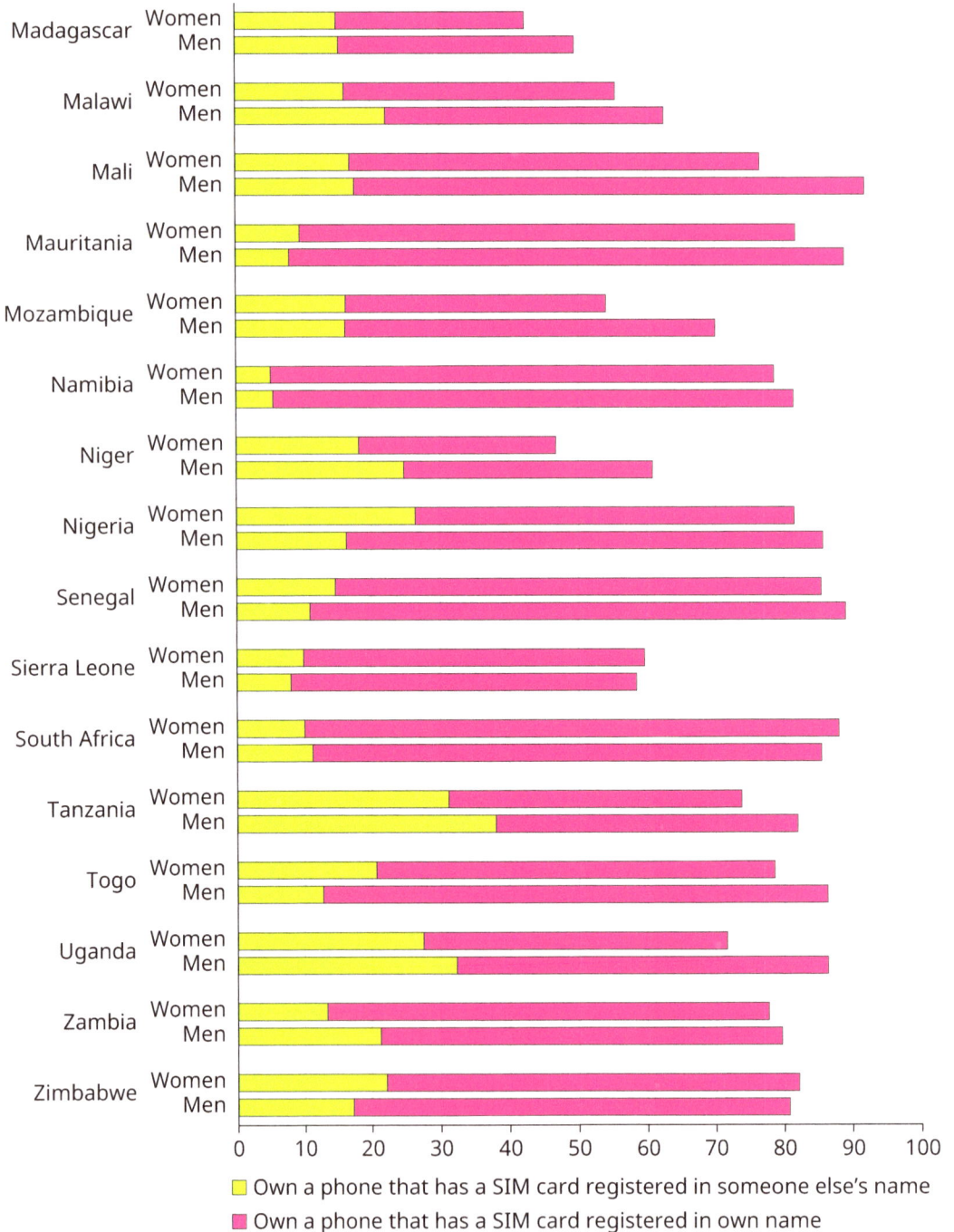

Own a phone that has a SIM card registered in someone else's name

Own a phone that has a SIM card registered in own name

Source: Global Findex Database 2025.

Figure 1.1.4 **Women are often less likely than men to have a SIM card in their own name**

Adults with a mobile phone (%), 2024

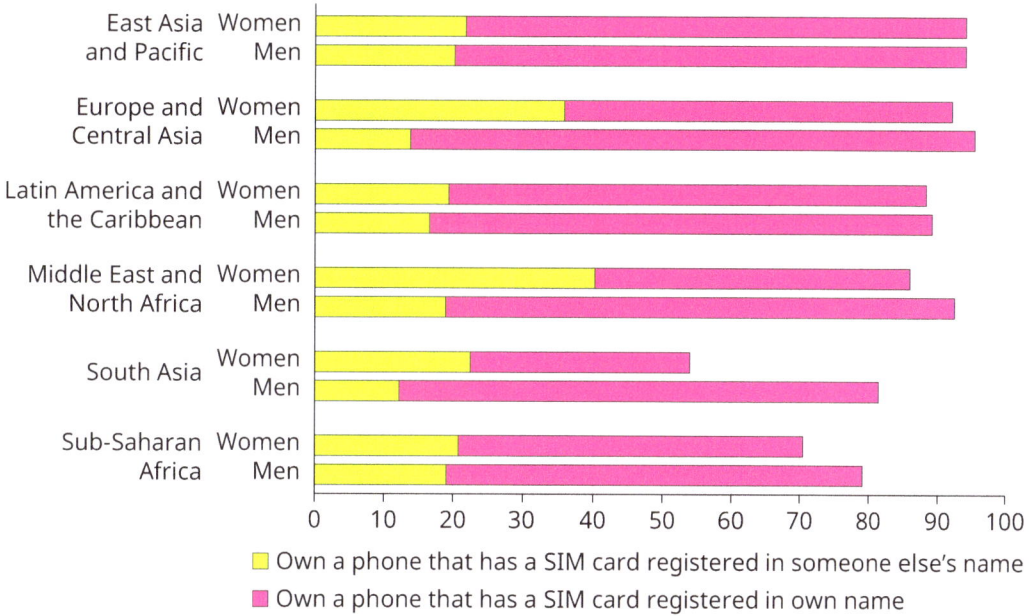

Legend:
- ☐ Own a phone that has a SIM card registered in someone else's name
- ■ Own a phone that has a SIM card registered in own name

Source: Global Findex Database 2025.

Everyone who owns a mobile phone uses it, often for a variety of purposes

People who own mobile phones use them. Across low- and middle-income economies, 91 percent of mobile phone owners—nearly 70 percent of adults in those places—use their phones daily, and an additional 6 percent use them at least weekly. Even in Sub-Saharan Africa, where data rates are among the most expensive in the world, a large majority of mobile phone owners use their phones daily (refer to figure 1.1.5). Daily use rates among mobile phone owners dip below 80 percent in just seven economies, five of them in Sub-Saharan Africa: Chad, the Comoros, Guatemala, Lesotho, Mali, Morocco, and Togo.

Figure 1.1.5 **Mobile phone owners use their devices daily in Sub-Saharan Africa**

Adults with a mobile phone (%), 2024

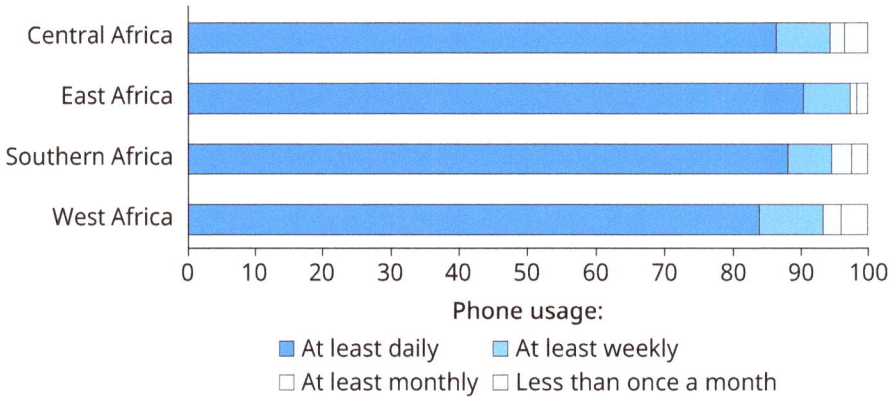

Source: Global Findex Database 2025.

The primary barrier to mobile phone ownership is the cost of the device

Any discussion of digital connectivity would be incomplete if it did not take a close look at adults who do not have their own mobile phones, to understand the barriers to ownership they face.

As mentioned, these adults tend to have low incomes and are more likely to be women than men. Though there are some people without mobile phones in every economy in the world, a disproportionate share live in South Asia and Sub-Saharan Africa (the only regions with mobile phone account ownership rates less than 85 percent), and particularly in large-population economies with lower-than-average connectivity rates, such as Bangladesh, Egypt, Ethiopia, India, and Pakistan.

The Global Findex survey asked respondents without phones to identify all the barriers they faced to owning a mobile phone, then asked them to choose the main barrier.[14] In South Asia and Sub-Saharan Africa, the barrier people overwhelmingly cited most often as among those preventing them from having a mobile phone is that they cannot afford to buy the device: 69 percent and 77 percent, respectively, of adults without a mobile phone in these two regions said this (refer to figure 1.1.6, panels a and b). When they name the main barrier precluding mobile phone ownership, money remains primary. Across both regions, among all adults as well as among women, people in lower-income households, and both people living in rural environments and those living in urban ones, not having enough money for a device is cited as the main barrier to mobile phone ownership.

---

14   Questions regarding barriers to phone ownership are adapted from the questionnaire used in the GSMA Mobile Money Tracker (GSMA 2025).

Figure 1.1.6 A lack of money represents a significant barrier to owning a phone

Adults who do not own a mobile phone citing a given barrier as a reason for having no mobile phone (%), 2024

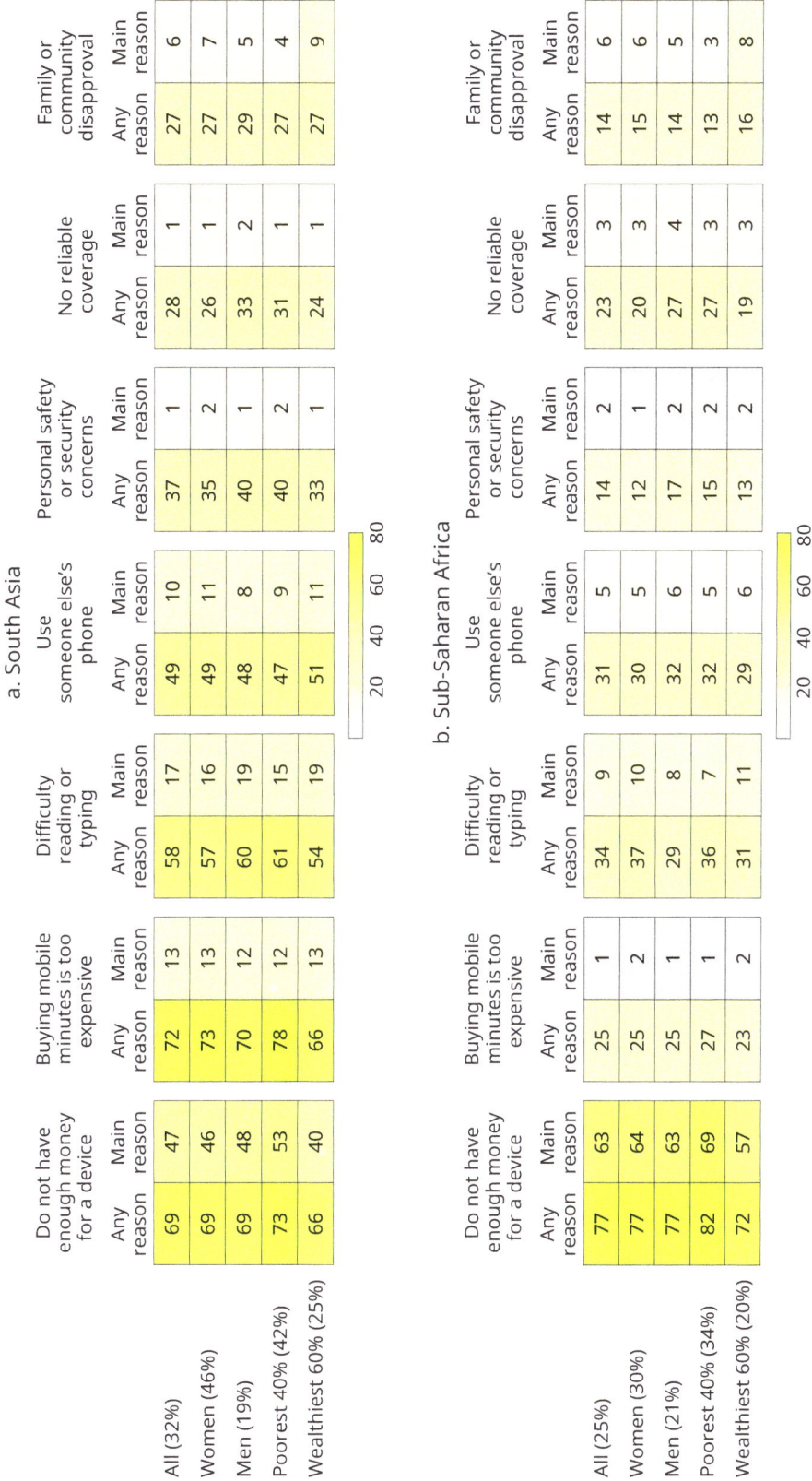

a. South Asia

	Do not have enough money for a device		Buying mobile minutes is too expensive		Difficulty reading or typing		Use someone else's phone		Personal safety or security concerns		No reliable coverage		Family or community disapproval	
	Any reason	Main reason	Any reason	Main reason	Any reason	Main reason	Any reason	Main reason	Any reason	Main reason	Any reason	Main reason	Any reason	Main reason
All (32%)	69	47	72	13	58	17	49	10	37	1	28	1	27	6
Women (46%)	69	46	73	13	57	16	49	11	35	2	26	1	27	7
Men (19%)	69	48	70	12	60	19	48	8	40	1	33	2	29	5
Poorest 40% (42%)	73	53	78	12	61	15	47	9	40	2	31	1	27	4
Wealthiest 60% (25%)	66	40	66	13	54	19	51	11	33	1	24	1	27	9

20 40 60 80

b. Sub-Saharan Africa

	Do not have enough money for a device		Buying mobile minutes is too expensive		Difficulty reading or typing		Use someone else's phone		Personal safety or security concerns		No reliable coverage		Family or community disapproval	
	Any reason	Main reason	Any reason	Main reason	Any reason	Main reason	Any reason	Main reason	Any reason	Main reason	Any reason	Main reason	Any reason	Main reason
All (25%)	77	63	25	1	34	9	31	5	14	2	23	3	14	6
Women (30%)	77	64	25	2	37	10	30	5	12	1	20	3	15	6
Men (21%)	77	63	25	1	29	8	32	6	17	2	27	4	14	5
Poorest 40% (34%)	82	69	27	1	36	7	32	5	15	2	27	3	13	3
Wealthiest 60% (20%)	72	57	23	2	31	11	29	6	13	2	19	3	16	8

20 40 60 80

Source: Global Findex Database 2025.

Note: Respondents could choose more than one reason. Percentages in parentheses represent the share of adults in each group who do not own a mobile phone.

Among those naming any barrier to phone ownership, data costs also come up as a barrier in these two regions, especially South Asia. Low levels of literacy and high rates of illiteracy similarly discourage mobile phone ownership, with difficulty reading or typing cited as a common barrier in both regions.

Costs come up again as a barrier in the context that many people use someone else's phone rather than owning their own. In South Asia, 49 percent of adults who do not own a mobile phone use someone else's, and in Sub-Saharan Africa 31 percent do. Non-owning phone users present an opportunity to increase connectivity, since this group already shows demand for and some skill with digital devices.

Family or community disapproval is a less common, though still statistically significant, barrier to phone ownership. It is the second- or third-most-common reason for people not having phones in the Republic of Congo and Uganda, where it is also cited more commonly by women than by men. Also in Pakistan, 40 percent of women without a phone name family disapproval as a reason for not having one, whereas no men say the same.[15] It is important to note as well that counter to expectations about gender norms, family or community disapproval is among the least commonly cited barriers, and naming it as a barrier is not generally more prevalent among women than among men.

A lack of reliable mobile network coverage also affects mobile phone ownership in some economies. In Chad, for instance, 54 percent of adults who do not own mobile phones name lack of coverage as prohibitive; in India, 29 percent do. One caveat to this observation, however, is that people without mobile phones may not have an accurate sense of mobile network coverage.

Finally, some people say they do not own a mobile phone for reasons of personal safety. This might include fear of phone theft, as well as worries about receiving unwanted, threatening, or harassing calls and messages. South Asia has the highest share of adults without a phone giving this reason, at 37 percent, including about 40 percent of women and men without phones in India.

Expanding mobile phone ownership to those who do not yet own a phone of any kind means overcoming these barriers, with cost being the most salient. However, providing free phones may not be the solution, as the evidence suggests that doing so may lead to limited long-run and often gender-inequitable outcomes.[16]

---

15   Only 5 percent of men in Pakistan do not have a phone.
16   Barboni et al. (2024); Roessler et al. (2021); Roessler et al. (2023).

For example, a study in rural Tanzania for which women were given free smartphones found that the households in which they lived increased their annual consumption of food and basic needs per capita by 20 percent relative to households that received a basic phone or cash. By the end of the intervention, however, only a third of women given smartphones still had them.[17] Another study in rural Malawi similarly assigned smartphones to some women participants, but in this case invited the husbands of half of the women to take part in a training program designed to increase acceptance of women's smartphone use. There were no differences in mobile phone retention and use between those who participated in the couples-based training and those who did not.[18] Finally, in a government program in India to distribute phones and roll out mobile towers in rural communities, nearly 40 percent of women had lost control over their devices within a month after distribution (98 percent of women said they had received the phones). Five years later, researchers found no persistent effects in ownership, gender norms, and economic outcomes in areas eligible to receive free phones compared with other areas.[19] This research suggests that any interventions to overcome barriers to mobile phone ownership must account for intrahousehold dynamics and entrenched gender norms.

In contrast to distribution of free smartphones, pay-as-you-go (PAYGo) financing, which enables users to pay for smartphone purchases in installments over time, attempts to make smartphones more affordable while keeping cost salient. Such an approach in theory could attract people who want a smartphone and will use it (because they have to pay for it) while filtering out, for example, those who view the phone itself as an asset they can sell. PAYGo financing programs include lockout technology, so that lenders can remotely disable phones if borrowers miss a payment. PAYGo-financed smartphones are prevalent in some low- and middle-income economies as part of bundled offerings with solar home systems. Research suggests that PAYGo programs can generate significant welfare gains for users, equivalent to an increase of more than 3 percent in income over a two-year period and as much as 5 percent for lower-risk consumers.[20] Providing incentives to offer these schemes to women—who may otherwise struggle to afford a phone—may hold promise for policies targeting device affordability.

Expanding equity in mobile phone ownership will require solutions that make devices more affordable for everyone. Doing so will be essential for enabling not just phone ownership but the use of the internet and online apps for a range of purposes discussed in the next chapter.

---

17   Roessler et al. (2021).
18   Roessler et al. (2023).
19   Barboni et al. (2024).
20   Gertler et al. (2025).

1.2 Internet use

A reproducibility package is available for this book in the Reproducible Research Repository at https://reproducibility.worldbank.org/catalog/299.

1.2 Internet use

In addition to asking about mobile phone ownership, the Global Findex 2025 Digital Connectivity Tracker asked respondents about their use of the internet and whether they use a mobile phone to get online. To understand the nature of respondents' current and active internet use, the survey asked respondents whether they had engaged in any of a variety of digital activities in the past three months. The survey questions distinguish between activities that require only a basic phone and those that depend on the internet and therefore require a smartphone or other internet-enabled device.

The digital activities discussed in this chapter fall into three categories: communication-focused activities, such as texting, posting on social media, and sending voice messages or photos; information-focused activities, such as keeping up with current events, learning, and accessing government information or services; and income-generating activities, such as looking for jobs and using websites to earn money. The chapter begins with an overview of internet use and then examines each of these types of activity individually.

Most internet users get online with a smartphone

Many people who own mobile phones use them to access the internet, and internet-based uses are often key to the economic and social benefits people derive from these devices. Global Findex 2025 Digital Connectivity Tracker data show that 71 percent of adults worldwide and 67 percent of adults in low- and middle-income economies used the internet in the three months before taking the survey.[1] Most of them used the internet at least weekly.

Internet use differed by region (refer to figure 1.2.1). Whereas 80 percent or more of adults in East Asia and Pacific, Europe and Central Asia, and Latin America and the Caribbean used the internet in the three months preceding the survey, only 45 percent or less of adults in South Asia and Sub-Saharan Africa did so. Trends in internet use in Middle Eastern economies resemble those in Europe and Central Asia, whereas trends in North African economies resemble those in Sub-Saharan Africa.

---

1   The Global Findex 2025 asked adults whether they used the internet in the week preceding the survey interview. If the answer was *no*, respondents were asked a follow-up question about whether they used the internet in the past three months. Adults who answered *yes* to either of these questions were coded as having used the internet in the past three months.

Figure 1.2.1 **Across low- and middle-income economies, 67 percent of adults use the internet, though rates vary widely by region**

Adults who used the internet in the past three months (%), 2024

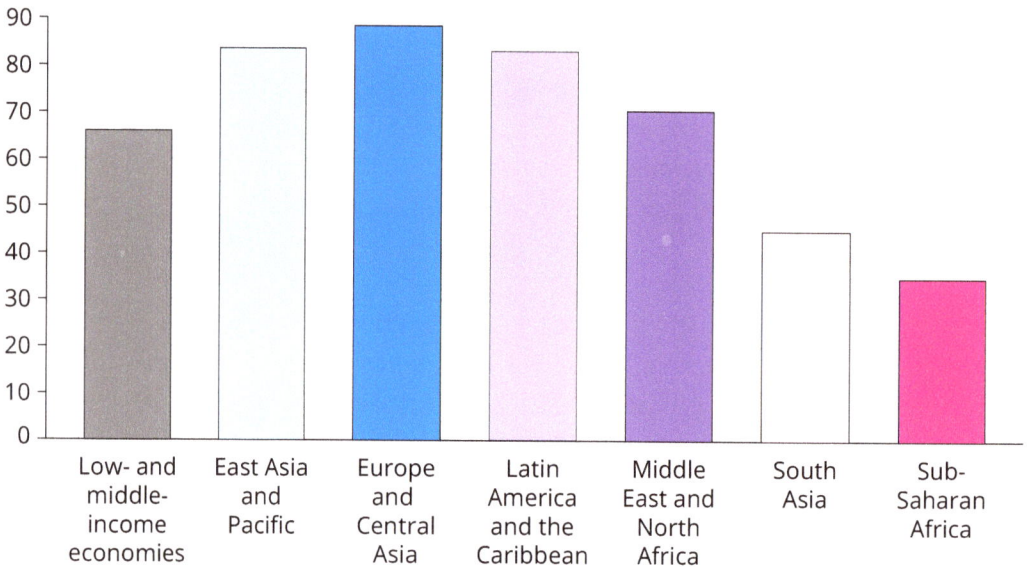

Source: Global Findex Database 2025.

Note: The data used for regional averages and for the average for low- and middle-income economies exclude data for several large economies in which respondents were surveyed by phone rather than in person, including China and the Russian Federation. The "Methodology" tab of the Global Findex website (http://globalfindex.worldbank.org) provides details on the information collected in each surveyed economy.

Adults in the poorest 40 percent of households by income and women are less likely than wealthier adults and men to use the internet. In low- and middle-income economies, the internet use gap by income is 20 percentage points: more than twice the size of the overall mobile phone gap by income. It is analogous to the income gap among smartphone users of 18 percentage points. A detailed look at individual economies shows that almost every economy has an income gap in internet use.

The gender gap in internet use is considerably narrower than the income gap and less consistent across different regions. In low- and middle-income economies, women are 6 percentage points less likely than men to use the internet (a difference that is not exclusively a function of access, as it holds as well among people who own smartphones). Only the Middle East and North Africa, South Asia, and Sub-Saharan Africa have statistically significant gender gaps in internet use, at 9 percentage points, 21 percentage points, and 12 percentage points, respectively (refer to figure 1.2.2). Only one in three individual economies shows a gender gap in internet use.

Figure 1.2.2 Internet use is widespread, though there are gaps according to gender and income

Adults who used the internet in the past three months (%), 2024

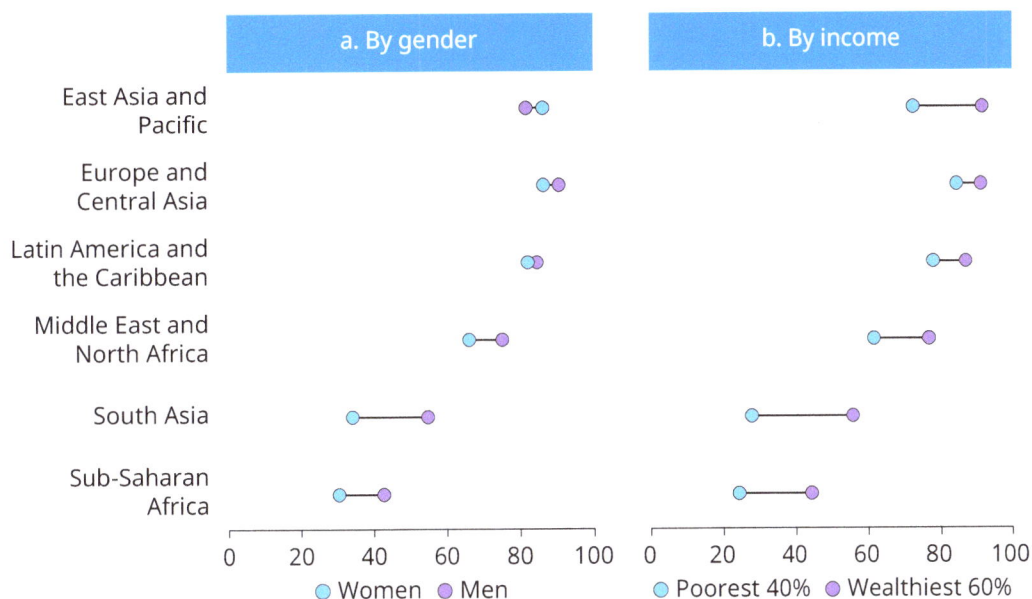

Source: Global Findex Database 2025.

Note: The data used for regional averages exclude data for several large economies in which respondents were surveyed by phone rather than in person, including China and the Russian Federation. The "Methodology" tab of the Global Findex website (http://globalfindex.worldbank.org) provides details on the information collected in each surveyed economy.

Smartphones are the primary channel for internet access. In low- and middle-income economies, 92 percent of smartphone owners used the internet in the three months preceding the 2024 survey (refer to figure 1.2.3). The inverse is also true: 89 percent of internet users in low- and middle-income economies own a smartphone. This finding corroborates earlier data on the relationship between smartphone ownership and internet access.[2] In contrast, just 20 percent of adults with a basic phone use the internet. The correlation between smartphone ownership and internet use is so strong that the income and gender gaps in smartphone ownership are both within 4 percentage points of the income and gender gaps in internet usage.

---

2   ITU (2023a).

Figure 1.2.3 **Among smartphone owners, 92 percent use the internet**

Adults who used the internet in the past three months (%), 2024

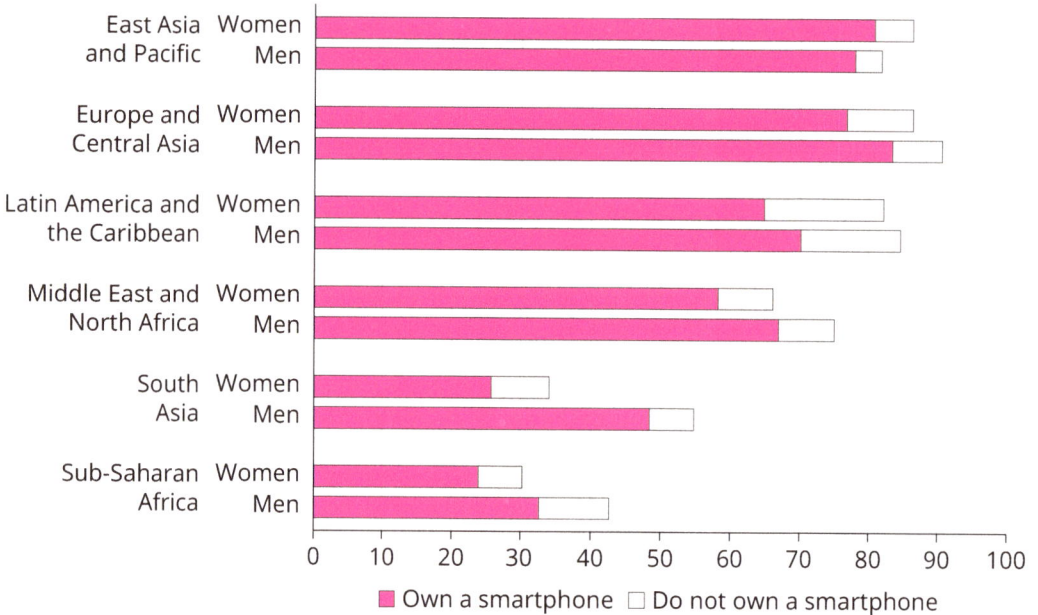

■ Own a smartphone   □ Do not own a smartphone

Source: Global Findex Database 2025.

Note: The data used for regional averages exclude data for several large economies in which respondents were surveyed by phone rather than in person, including China and the Russian Federation. The "Methodology" tab of the Global Findex website (http://globalfindex.worldbank.org) provides details on the information collected in each surveyed economy.

Latin America and the Caribbean—in part because feature phones are prevalent there—has the largest share of adults using the internet without owning a smartphone. People who use someone else's device account for a small part of that share.

Another 11 percent of adults in the region use free wifi or internet connections available in cafes, libraries, schools, or other public spaces, the largest share anywhere in the world. Overall, just 5 percent of adults in all low- and middle-income economies access the internet exclusively using free resources.

This tight association between smartphone ownership and internet use also means that specific digital activities are largely contingent on owning a smartphone, regardless of income status or gender.

With this perspective on use of the internet and how people are accessing it, the next subsection considers how connected adults use their mobile phones and the internet across the three categories of digital activities mentioned earlier: communication-focused, information-focused, and income-generating activities.

Internet users engage in a wide variety of digital activities

Internet usage patterns vary greatly in regard to how people engage in different digital activities over time. To provide a better understanding of patterns of use, Global Findex 2025 examines the data to identify clusters of people using the internet in similar ways. The largest cluster of adults, representing about 9 percent of internet users, use their mobile phones exclusively for four digital activities: texting, using social media, sending voice messages, and sending photos. These happen to be the four most popular digital activities, in order of popularity. Another 9 percent of internet users learn online using their phones, as well as engaging in the preceding four activities.

The next-largest cluster of internet users, about 7 percent, do not use the internet for any of the specific digital activities asked about in the survey. This group also uses the internet less frequently than the average, suggesting potential pressure resulting from data costs. Frequency of use is discussed later in this subsection.

Such wide variation in usage patterns points to significant diversity of digital experiences, as well as widespread opportunities to increase internet use for a range of activities.

Most mobile phone owners embrace the ability to communicate

The Global Findex asked adults whether in the previous three months they had engaged in four distinct, communication-based activities that require either a basic phone or a smartphone: texting, reading or posting on social media, sending recorded audio messages, and sending photos. The survey asked all respondents about texting, and only those who either said they used the internet or that they had a smartphone about the other three and all subsequent digital activities.

Texting is broadly popular in almost every economy and does not require a smartphone; any type of mobile phone provides a user with the ability to text. Among adults in low- and middle-income economies, 47 percent both receive and send texts, and 56 percent of mobile phone owners do so. Only in a few Sub-Saharan African (refer to figure 1.2.4) and South Asian economies do 50 percent or less of mobile phone owners send and receive texts, potentially because of low degrees of literacy skills.

Figure 1.2.4 **Most mobile phone owners in Sub-Saharan Africa both receive and send text messages**

Adults with a mobile phone (%), 2024

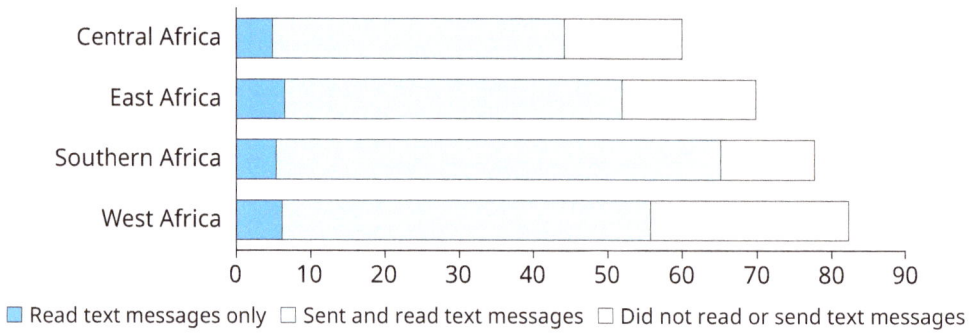

■ Read text messages only ☐ Sent and read text messages ☐ Did not read or send text messages

Source: Global Findex Database 2025.

Literacy in this context is more nuanced than whether someone can read and write. In some economies, people who can read their native alphabet or script but cannot read Latin characters may experience literacy barriers to sending and receiving text messages. This is especially true in places where basic phones are common, as these phones' touchpads may offer only Latin characters. For example, women in South Asia are less likely than men to be able to read Latin characters. They may therefore be unable to read and respond to a text message written using the Latin alphabet, even if the message is in phonetic Hindi or Urdu (refer to figure 1.2.5).

Expanding access to smartphones can help in this regard, as they enable users to employ a range of character-based keyboards, which allow them to type in the script they prefer. For basic phone users, particularly those with low levels of literacy, interactive voice response technologies can also provide an accessible solution. These audio-based technologies allow users to navigate menu options verbally or via keypad inputs, helping them access critical services without requiring text literacy. Governments in low- and middle-income economies often use such technologies for service delivery, with evidence suggesting that doing so can help improve health care and agricultural outcomes and enhance consumer protection.[3]

---

3   Refer to Chikowo, Christensen, and Snapp (2020); Fink (2024); and Ouedraogo et al. (2024).

Figure 1.2.5 In South Asia, women are less likely than men to be able to read text messages written using the Latin alphabet

Adults with a mobile phone (%), 2024

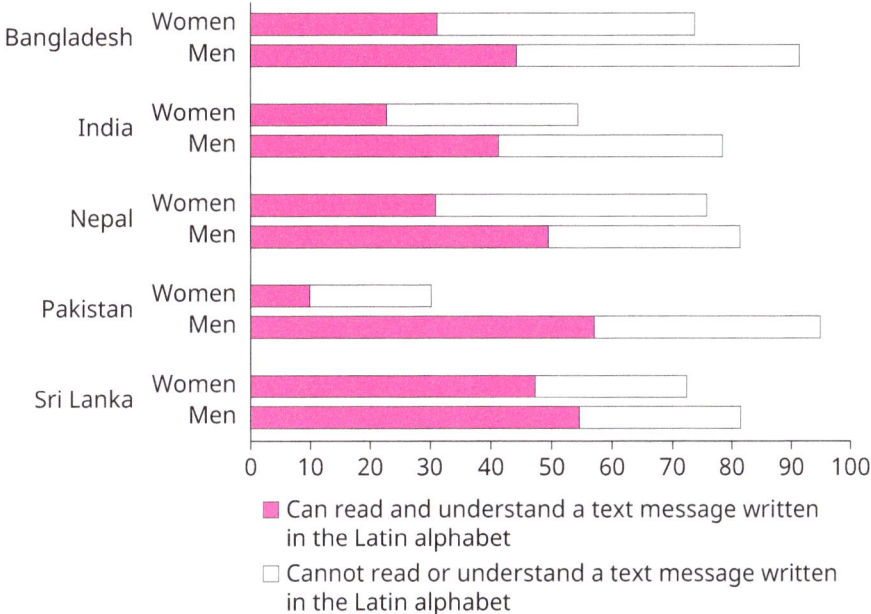

Source: Global Findex Database 2025.

Social media is the next-most-popular digital activity after texting.[4] Across low- and middle-income economies, 45 percent of adults and 80 percent of internet users were active on social media in the three months before taking the survey. East Asia and Pacific had the highest average share of adults who were active on social media. A slightly smaller share of all adults used social media than the share who sent text messages (refer to figure 1.2.6).

Though most people think of social media as a way to keep up with friends and family (hence its position among the communication activities) and sometimes to gather information or simply pass the time, it can also help small and medium enterprises communicate with new customers, which can increase sales. In fact, studies have shown that social media use is positively associated with improved firm performance in Pakistan[5] and Oman.[6] Another study measured the welfare effects of 10 digital services (like Google Search, YouTube, and Facebook) across 13 countries. It estimates that these platforms generate more than US$2.5 trillion in consumer benefits, with a larger share of the gains going to lower-income individuals.[7]

4   Respondents were asked whether they "used social media, like Facebook or TikTok, on a mobile phone."
5   Qalati et al. (2022).
6   Alraja et al. (2020).
7   Brynjolfsson et al. (2023).

Figure 1.2.6 Social media is the most popular digital use after texting

Adults who did the following digital activities in the past three months (%), 2024

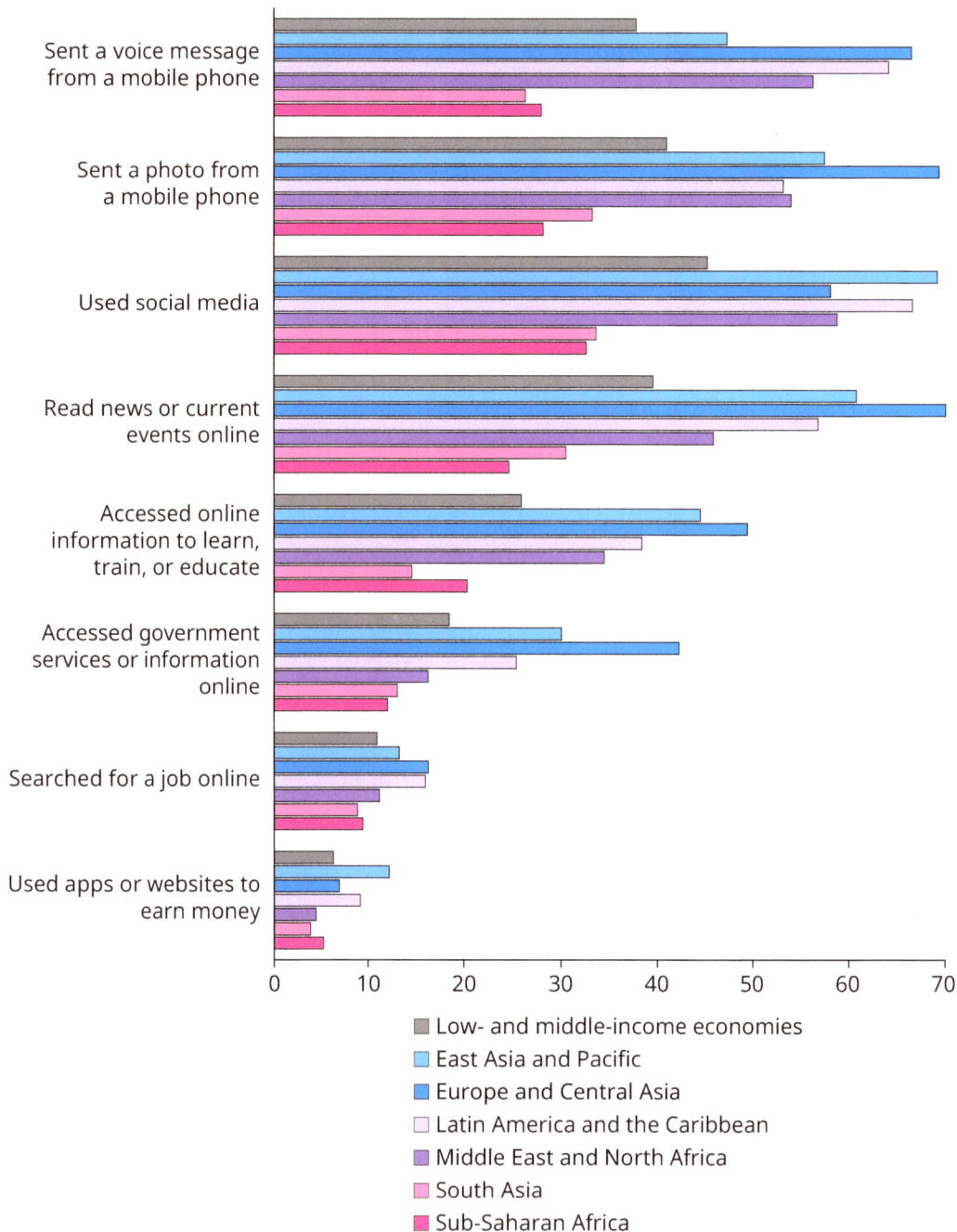

Legend:
- Low- and middle-income economies
- East Asia and Pacific
- Europe and Central Asia
- Latin America and the Caribbean
- Middle East and North Africa
- South Asia
- Sub-Saharan Africa

Source: Global Findex Database 2025.

Note: Respondents could choose more than one digital activity.

Those who use social media to generate income typically must be able to upload product photos and record and post audio messages. In low- and middle-income economies, 41 percent of adults and 74 percent of smartphone owners uploaded or sent a photo in the three months preceding the survey, and 38 percent of adults and 68 percent of smartphone owners sent a recorded audio message. These activities also have value for people who leverage online channels to earn money independent of their personal social media use.

Informational activities such as consuming news and learning are also popular

The Global Findex 2025 Digital Connectivity Tracker includes answers to questions about three common information-focused activities: reading about news; accessing online learning, training, or educational information; and accessing government services or information.

In low- and middle-income economies, 39 percent of adults and 71 percent of internet users read or watch the news online. The benefits of doing this include knowledge of current events locally and across their economies, including political happenings. A study on political knowledge in the United States found that after news outlets introduced paywalls there in the early 2010s, survey respondents were between 2 and 3 percentage points less likely to answer questions about political subjects correctly.[8] This positive relationship between news access and civic knowledge can affect how citizens interact with their governments and even how those governments allocate and disburse public funds. For example, mobile applications have been shown to be useful for holding middle management accountable in health care and agricultural settings, enhancing bureaucratic accountability.[9] Better-informed populations have in some instances received more and larger relief payments in times of crisis,[10] and they demand greater political accountability.[11]

Accessing learning, training, or educational materials is the next-most-popular information activity. An average of 26 percent of adults in low- and middle-income economies and 46 percent of internet users used the web for this purpose. The popularity of online learning is much higher in some economies, some of which had mobility restrictions in 2024 due to extreme weather events or conflict.[12]

8   Streyczek (2025).

9   Callen et al. (2020); Dal Bó et al. (2021).

10   Besley and Burgess (2002); Strömberg (2004).

11   Ferraz and Finan (2008); Snyder and Strömberg (2008).

12   These economies include Malaysia and Thailand in East Asia and Pacific, Belize in Latin America and the Caribbean, Jordan and West Bank and Gaza in the Middle East and North Africa, and Gabon in Sub-Saharan Africa.

Widespread access to online learning could reduce educational inequality, in theory, by enabling learners to access high-quality instruction previously available only to students of elite institutions.[13] Simultaneously, online resources could enhance the effectiveness and skills of local teachers who provide services complementary to the online experience, like personalized guidance, application support, and responsive feedback.[14] Evidence also shows some benefit for teachers in the form of resource and information access from leveraging internet and artificial intelligence search tools.[15] Empirical research testing this theory shows limited effects on labor market outcomes, however, in part because of low retention rates in most online-learning settings.[16] Nonetheless, the internet can be a lifeline during interruptions to schooling. During the COVID-19 pandemic, combined phone and SMS-based educational interventions in Botswana increased learning by 0.121 standard deviation and reduced absolute innumeracy by 31 percent.[17] Researchers are continuing to investigate where and in what circumstances technology-enabled learning can bring the most benefit.[18]

The final category of informational activity included in the Global Findex 2025 Digital Connectivity Tracker is accessing government resources or searching for government information online. In low- and middle-income economies, 18 percent of adults did this, and 33 percent of internet users. These rates depend on whether a government offers online services and information, however, and rates reflect that availability (or lack thereof) as much as they do end-user demand.

Both citizens and governments can benefit when people access government services and information online. When this information is digitally available, citizens with internet access can retrieve any information they need at any time of day. In an extreme example, Estonia provides online access to all its government services. Residents can file taxes in just three minutes, and entrepreneurs can fill out the forms they need to start a business and have them approved in just three hours. Providing online access to government services saves the economy an estimated 2 percent of GDP annually.[19]

Digitalization of government services also has the potential to increase transparency and enable real-time data sharing between agencies, addressing fragmentation

---

13   Bianchi, Lu, and Song (2022).
14   Acemoglu, Laibson, and List (2014); Björkegren et al. (2025); Rodriguez-Segura (2022).
15   Björkegren et al. (2025).
16   Novella, Rosas-Shady, and Freund (2024).
17   Angrist, Bergman, and Matsheng (2022).
18   Rodriguez-Segura (2022).
19   Vassil (2016).

in business-government interactions. In Croatia, for example, using digital tools such as an integrated case management system to record and track the progress of all court cases directly improved judicial efficiency.[20] Evaluations of the system also showed a reduction in firm costs, since tying up resources in prolonged court proceedings can impede firm operations. Other examples show that e-procurement in India and Indonesia substantially improved the quality of goods and services procured by facilitating the engagement of high-quality contractors.[21]

A relatively small share of adults use online channels to earn money or search for a job

Development advocates herald the internet as a potential place for people to earn money. Some research even shows digital work opportunities can boost income for women.[22] Yet only 6 percent of adults in low- and middle-income economies and 11 percent of internet users use apps or websites to earn money. Outside East Asia and Pacific, where 12 percent of all adults earn money on the internet—more than 10 percent of adults in every economy in the region—only a small number of economies breach the 10 percent threshold: Argentina, Eswatini, and Iraq, with 11 percent; Brazil, Mauritania, and South Africa, with 12 percent; Lesotho, with 13 percent; Senegal, with 15 percent; Belize, with 16 percent; and Namibia, with 17 percent. All have mobile phone ownership rates near or above 80 percent.

Notwithstanding those low participation rates, research shows that online selling platforms can help sellers connect with potential buyers more efficiently. A survey of small firms in South Asia without formal registration (that is, informal firms) finds that sellers that joined e-commerce platforms saw their businesses expand.[23]

Searching for or applying for jobs online is more common than earning money online. In low- and middle-income economies, 11 percent of adults and 20 percent of internet users look for or apply for work online. In the Middle East and North Africa, South Asia, and Sub-Saharan Africa, the share totals 10 percent or less, whereas it is between 10 and 16 percent in East Asia and Pacific, Europe and Central Asia, and Latin America and the Caribbean. In a handful of economies across the world, more than 20 percent of adults look for jobs online.

Many people in low- and middle-income economies seek government jobs because they are among the most consistent salaried jobs available to people with lower

---

20   World Bank Independent Evaluation Group (2020).
21   Lewis-Faupel et al. (2016).
22   Ho, Jalota, and Karandikar (2024).
23   Bussolo et al. (2023).

incomes.[24] Furthermore, efforts to train workers to use online job platforms have increased employment opportunities.[25] Job postings give people a big motivator to stay connected in economies in which federal and local governments post open positions on the web. Online job postings are not associated with shorter periods of unemployment[26] but do enable individuals who are already employed to find new job opportunities more easily than through word of mouth or printed job advertisements.[27]

In general, those who use the web to earn money are not the same people who use it to look for jobs. A small share of adults in low- and middle-income economies do both.

Barriers to internet use start with smartphone device costs

Given the important role smartphones play as an internet access channel, the most significant barrier for people who do not use the internet is that they do not own a smartphone. Given that, the Global Findex asked adults with only a basic phone why they did not own a smartphone.

As they were regarding ownership of any kind of mobile phone, survey respondents were asked first about any of the barriers they faced to smartphone ownership and then were asked to choose the main barrier. The discussion here focuses on the regions in which about 20 percent or more of adults do not have smartphones: Latin America and the Caribbean, the Middle East and North Africa, South Asia, and Sub-Saharan Africa.

As is the case in regard to owning any phone, among survey respondents who specified any barriers, the main barrier to owning a smartphone is device cost (refer to figure 1.2.7, panels a–d). As a point of reference, across low- and middle-income economies, an entry-level internet-enabled handset costs 18 percent of the average adult's monthly income, according to a GSMA cost analysis using supply-side data.[28] It is 24 percent of women's average monthly income, compared with 12 percent of men's. In Sub-Saharan Africa specifically, an entry-level device costs 73 percent of the average monthly income for adults in the poorest 40 percent of households.

24   Lorenceau, Rim, and Savitki (2021).
25   Wheeler et al. (2022).
26   Kuhn and Skuterud (2004).
27   Stevenson (2008).
28   GSMA (2024).

Figure 1.2.7 Lack of money to buy a smartphone is the biggest barrier to smartphone ownership and therefore to internet use

Adults without a smartphone citing a given barrier as a reason for having no smartphone (%), 2024

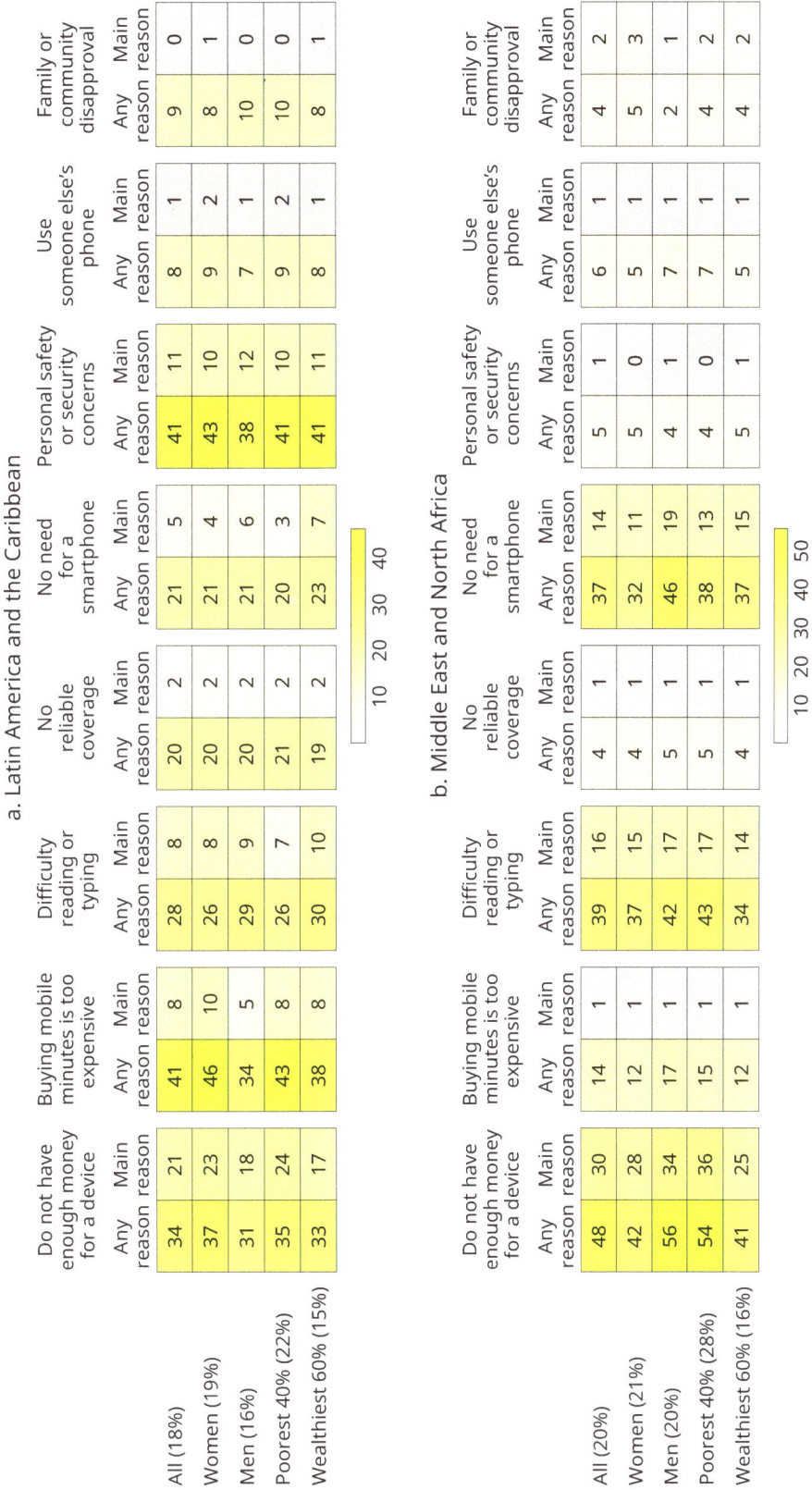

a. Latin America and the Caribbean

	Do not have enough money for a device		Buying mobile minutes is too expensive		Difficulty reading or typing		No reliable coverage		No need for a smartphone		Personal safety or security concerns		Use someone else's phone		Family or community disapproval	
	Any reason	Main reason	Any reason	Main reason	Any reason	Main reason	Any reason	Main reason	Any reason	Main reason	Any reason	Main reason	Any reason	Main reason	Any reason	Main reason
All (18%)	34	21	41	8	28	8	20	2	21	5	41	11	8	1	9	0
Women (19%)	37	23	46	10	26	8	20	2	21	4	43	10	9	2	8	1
Men (16%)	31	18	34	5	29	9	20	2	21	6	38	12	7	1	10	0
Poorest 40% (22%)	35	24	43	8	26	7	21	2	20	3	41	10	9	2	10	0
Wealthiest 60% (15%)	33	17	38	8	30	10	19	2	23	7	41	11	8	1	8	1

10 20 30 40

b. Middle East and North Africa

	Do not have enough money for a device		Buying mobile minutes is too expensive		Difficulty reading or typing		No reliable coverage		No need for a smartphone		Personal safety or security concerns		Use someone else's phone		Family or community disapproval	
	Any reason	Main reason	Any reason	Main reason	Any reason	Main reason	Any reason	Main reason	Any reason	Main reason	Any reason	Main reason	Any reason	Main reason	Any reason	Main reason
All (20%)	48	30	14	1	39	16	4	1	37	14	5	1	6	1	4	2
Women (21%)	42	28	12	1	37	15	4	1	32	11	5	0	5	1	5	3
Men (20%)	56	34	17	1	42	17	5	1	46	19	4	1	7	1	2	1
Poorest 40% (28%)	54	36	15	1	43	17	5	1	38	13	4	0	7	1	4	2
Wealthiest 60% (16%)	41	25	12	1	34	14	4	1	37	15	5	1	5	1	4	2

10 20 30 40 50

(Figure continued next page)

Figure 1.2.7 Lack of money to buy a smartphone is the biggest barrier to smartphone ownership and therefore to internet use (*continued*)

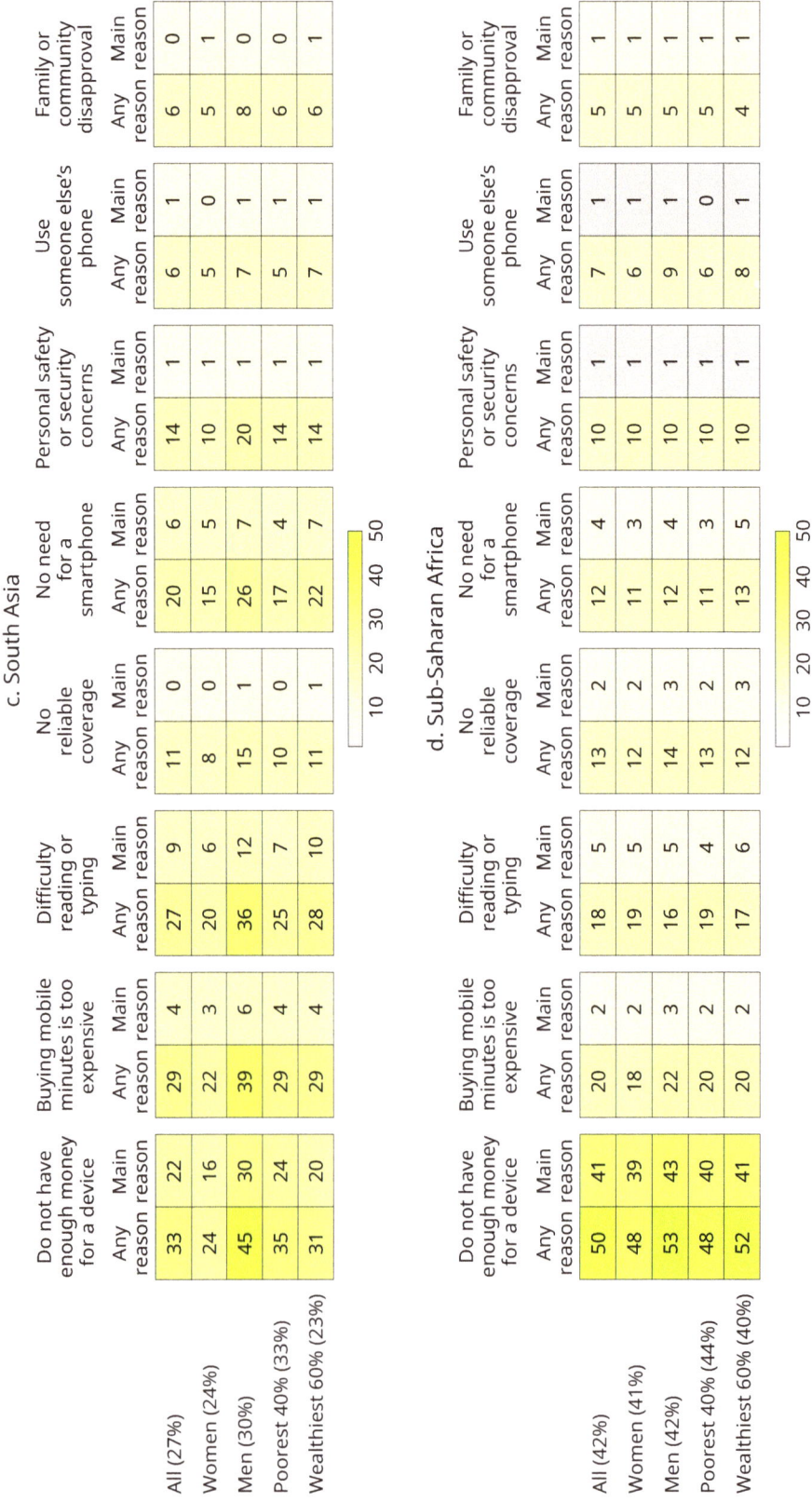

c. South Asia

	Do not have enough money for a device		Buying mobile minutes is too expensive		Difficulty reading or typing		No reliable coverage		No need for a smartphone		Personal safety or security concerns		Use someone else's phone		Family or community disapproval	
	Any reason	Main reason	Any reason	Main reason	Any reason	Main reason	Any reason	Main reason	Any reason	Main reason	Any reason	Main reason	Any reason	Main reason	Any reason	Main reason
All (27%)	33	22	29	4	27	9	11	0	20	6	14	1	6	1	6	0
Women (24%)	24	16	22	3	20	6	8	0	15	5	10	1	5	0	5	1
Men (30%)	45	30	39	6	36	12	15	1	26	7	20	1	7	1	8	0
Poorest 40% (33%)	35	24	29	4	25	7	10	0	17	4	14	1	5	1	6	0
Wealthiest 60% (23%)	31	20	29	4	28	10	11	1	22	7	14	1	7	1	6	1

10 20 30 40 50

d. Sub-Saharan Africa

	Do not have enough money for a device		Buying mobile minutes is too expensive		Difficulty reading or typing		No reliable coverage		No need for a smartphone		Personal safety or security concerns		Use someone else's phone		Family or community disapproval	
	Any reason	Main reason	Any reason	Main reason	Any reason	Main reason	Any reason	Main reason	Any reason	Main reason	Any reason	Main reason	Any reason	Main reason	Any reason	Main reason
All (42%)	50	41	20	2	18	5	13	2	12	4	10	1	7	1	5	1
Women (41%)	48	39	18	2	19	5	12	2	11	3	10	1	6	1	5	1
Men (42%)	53	43	22	3	16	5	14	3	12	4	10	1	9	1	5	1
Poorest 40% (44%)	48	40	20	2	19	4	13	2	11	3	10	1	6	0	5	1
Wealthiest 60% (40%)	52	41	20	2	17	6	12	3	13	5	10	1	8	1	4	1

10 20 30 40 50

Source: Global Findex Database 2025.

Note: Respondents could choose more than one reason. Percentages in parentheses represent the share of adults who do not own a smartphone.

The expense of mobile minutes is the next-most-common barrier mentioned among those naming any reason. It registers as particularly important for people in Latin America and the Caribbean, where more women than men and more poor than wealthier adults cite it as a barrier.

Difficulty reading or typing is also a major hurdle cited in each region. Overcoming this barrier is challenging, given its likely connection to low levels of literacy or illiteracy, but technology advances now becoming more available on smartphones could help. Current generative artificial intelligence (GenAI) tools increasingly embedded in smartphone-based applications can help convert speech to text easily and vice versa, making digital services potentially accessible to those with limited literacy or with physical disabilities. Nonetheless, there are real challenges regarding "low-resource languages," as there is a limited body of digital texts available to train the large language models on which GenAI runs. With time, targeted investments in linguistic data sets for underrepresented languages, coupled with development of specialized AI, may serve users with low levels of literacy much better.[29]

The remaining barriers—unreliable coverage, personal safety concerns, no need for a phone, and disapproval from family or community—all play a role in nonownership of smartphones, but at different levels of relevance depending on the region. Safety concerns are particularly salient for nonowners of smartphones in Latin America and the Caribbean, for example, and are the second-most-prevalent reason people there give.

Data costs are a barrier to more, and more frequent, internet use in low- and middle-income economies

For people with smartphones, additional barriers to internet use potentially arise in the cost of mobile data. As discussed in chapter 1.1, data costs are not a primary barrier to ownership among those without any kind of phone. They do come up as a reason for not owning a smartphone, however, and they influence behavioral patterns among those who use the internet.

Monthly unlimited data plans for mobile phone owners are uncommon outside high-income economies. Instead, people buy a certain amount of data (1 gigabyte, for example), and then top up their data when they run low. This can be prohibitively expensive, especially in Sub-Saharan Africa, which has the highest mobile data costs in the world as a percentage of household income and 6 of the world's 10 most expensive economies for mobile data.[30] According to analysis by GSMA, 1 gigabyte

---

29   Pava et al. (2025).
30   Broadband Genie (n.d.); ITU (2023b).

of data in the region costs an average 2.4 percent of monthly income and 5 percent of the average income of people in the poorest 40 percent.[31]

Data costs track with internet use when how frequently phone owners purchase data is compared with how often they use the internet. In every region but Sub-Saharan Africa, the largest share of adults use the internet daily and buy data monthly. In India, for example, almost three-quarters of internet users purchase data monthly. In Sub-Saharan Africa, however, it is more common to see internet use tightly aligned with data purchases. Daily is still the most common frequency at which internet use occurs, but Sub-Saharan Africa has a much smaller share of daily internet users than any other region. Yet nearly three times as many users make weekly or daily data purchases as make monthly ones (refer to figure 1.2.8). This may suggest that high costs and limited liquidity prevent many adults in Sub-Saharan Africa from affording larger data bundles, even if these bundles offer lower costs per minute and align with their expected usage.

Expanding access to high-quality broadband internet in low- and middle-income economies by, among other things, increasing competition and pursuing policies that support equitable access may help lower data costs in these economies and generally help expand digital connectivity. Failure to do so risks exacerbating the existing digital divide between high-income and low- and middle-income economies.[32] Broadband internet also will become more essential for increasing access to data-heavy applications, such as those that enable digital learning, much of whose content is in video formats.

Other opportunities to expand internet use will depend on the individual and the hoped-for benefit. Since there is no universal definition of "low" internet use, it is hard to know what specific incentives could motivate expanded internet use or whether they are even necessary or helpful.

31   GSMA (2024).
32   World Bank (2024).

Figure 1.2.8 Internet users typically use the web daily and pay for data monthly

Adults who used the internet in the past three months (standardized to 100%), 2024

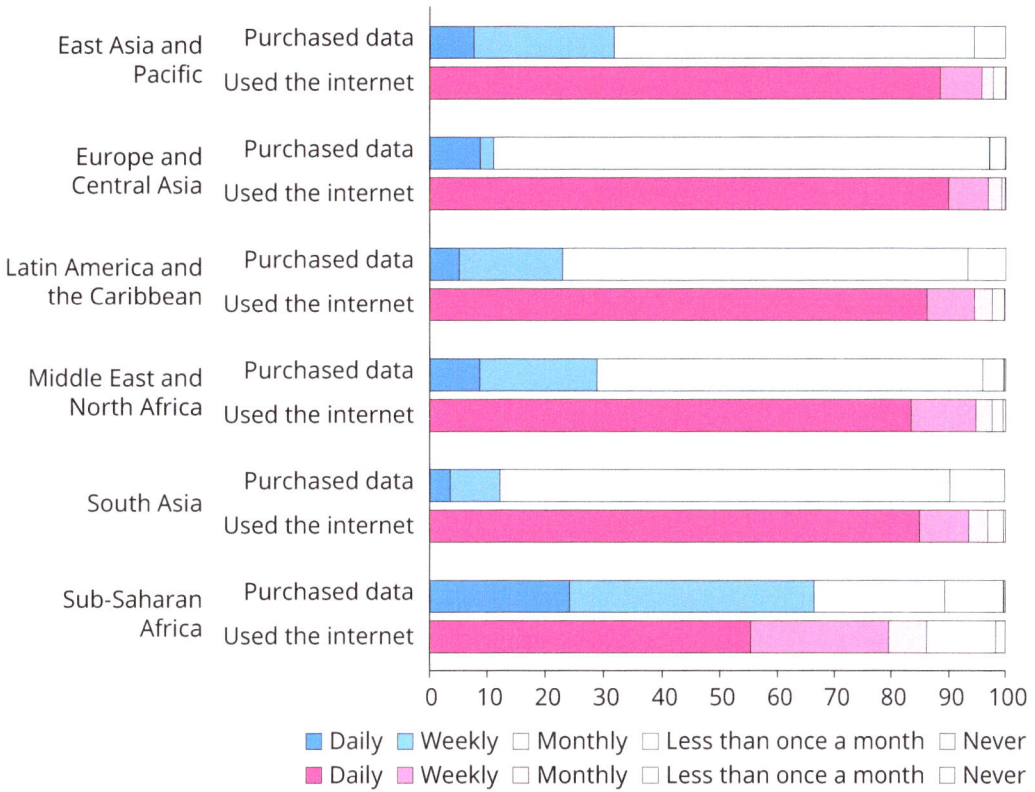

Source: Global Findex Database 2025.

Note: The data used for regional averages exclude data for several large economies in which respondents were surveyed by phone rather than in person, including China and the Russian Federation. The "Methodology" tab of the Global Findex website (http://globalfindex.worldbank.org) provides details on the information collected in each surveyed economy.

There are, however, several design characteristics that digitally enabled products, platforms, devices, and inclusion initiatives can adopt to help people maximize the benefits of connectivity while minimizing its risks. Those characteristics include safety, ease of use, and features that protect people's personal information. The next chapter explores those topics, collectively referred to as *responsible digital use*.

1.3 Digital safety and responsible use

A reproducibility package is available for this book in the Reproducible Research Repository at https://reproducibility.worldbank.org/catalog/299.

1.3 Digital safety and responsible use

Having a mobile phone and using the internet potentially gives connected people worldwide the ability to access information and resources more readily. It also exposes users to certain risks and requires them to develop the digital skills they need to get the most out of digital channels.

To understand more about the digital risks people face and how vulnerable they may be to them, the Global Findex asked respondents about their use of passwords, their exposure to scams or extortion, and whether they had experienced online harassment. It also asked whether others imposed rules on how and when they used their phones. The results show that there are opportunities to encourage people to take steps to protect themselves, even though only a small share of adults currently experience scams and harassment. Awareness could help keep those rates low.

Passwords are not universal

Not all mobile phone owners take advantage of the most basic digital security measure: setting up and using passwords on their personal devices. Only 60 percent of mobile phone owners use this essential first-line defense against exploitation and digital theft in low- and middle-income economies (refer to figure 1.3.1).

Rates of password adoption show some regional patterns. Seventeen of the twenty economies with the lowest rates of password adoption are in Sub-Saharan Africa.[1] In contrast, password adoption reaches two-thirds to three-quarters of mobile phone owners in the economies of East Asia and Pacific, Europe and Central Asia, and Latin America and the Caribbean, consistent with their high phone penetration rates.

Women mobile phone owners in Europe and Central Asia and the Middle East and North Africa, South Asia, and Sub-Saharan Africa are about 10 percentage points less likely than their male counterparts to protect their phones with passwords. In East Asia and Pacific and Latin America and the Caribbean, however, women phone owners are just as likely as men to use passwords with phones.

---

1   The exceptions to the low rate of password adoption in Africa are Botswana, Kenya, Namibia, Senegal, and South Africa, where about two-thirds or more of mobile phone owners use passwords. These economies also show high engagement with the digital activities discussed in the previous chapter.

Figure 1.3.1 In low- and middle-income economies, only 60 percent of mobile phone owners have a password on their mobile phones; more men than women mobile phone owners have passwords on their devices

Adults with a mobile phone (%), 2024

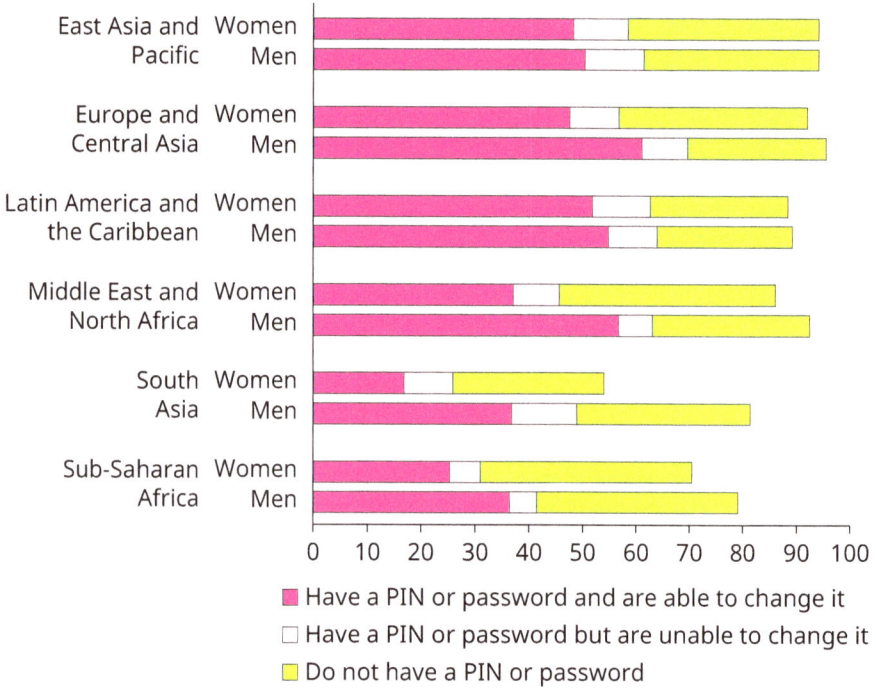

Legend:
- ■ (pink) Have a PIN or password and are able to change it
- □ (white) Have a PIN or password but are unable to change it
- ■ (yellow) Do not have a PIN or password

Source: Global Findex Database 2025.

Note: The data used for regional averages exclude data for several large economies in which respondents were surveyed by phone rather than in person, including China and the Russian Federation. The "Methodology" tab of the Global Findex website (http://globalfindex.worldbank.org) provides details on the information collected in each surveyed economy. PIN = personal identification number.

The Global Findex also asked people who had password-protected mobile phones whether they could change that password themselves. The responses show that in most economies, between 15 percent and 30 percent of phone owners with passwords cannot change them. This could be for benign reasons. For example, a shopkeeper or a more digitally skilled family member may have helped set up a user's phone and its password at purchase, after which the owner forgot the steps for changing it. Phones passed down after a family member upgrades to a more recent model may also have the original owner's password. In other instances, however, someone other than the owner may control a password, creating the potential for exploitation.

The danger of going without a password is greater in the context of digital financial services, particularly mobile money. Across the economies of Sub-Saharan Africa, about half of adults with mobile money accounts do not have passwords on their mobile phones. Thus anyone who has the person's phone—whether it is a family member or a phone thief—could potentially access any balance in the associated mobile account (with the caveat that most mobile money providers require users to input a personal identification number, or PIN, when signing in or transacting, thus mitigating the danger). Given that a lack of trust is often a barrier to mobile money adoption, ensuring that people know about the benefits of passwords and PIN use, and know how to use passwords and PINs, is important. Women mobile money account owners are not more likely to lack a phone password than men with mobile money are in any region.

Almost one in five mobile phone owners has rules set for them

About 15 percent of all adults in low- and middle-income economies, and 19 percent of mobile phone owners, say that someone else sets rules about when and how they use their devices. That share is about 5 percentage points higher in East Asia and Pacific and Latin America and the Caribbean. In the Middle East and North Africa, women phone owners are twice as likely as men with phones to be subject to someone else's rules about their phone use (refer to figure 1.3.2).

Young adults between the ages of 15 and 25 are generally more likely than those in other age groups to say that rules for mobile phone use are imposed on them. In Europe and Central Asia, younger adults with phones are 18 percentage points more likely than older adults to have rules imposed on them regarding phone use. In Latin America and the Caribbean, in contrast, younger and older adults are equally likely to have rules imposed on them.

As with password controls, imposed rules for phone use can be relatively benign, or they can indicate a lack of autonomy. A concerned family member, for example, might worry about a less digitally savvy person's exposure to inappropriate content or to online harassment or about "excessive" digital use, and thus may set rules to protect that person. Alternatively, those rules may be a form of control by an authoritarian relative or intimate partner.

Exposure to digital harassment in the form of offensive messages, photos, or videos is less common than having rules set for phone use: 7 percent of adults (9 percent of mobile phone owners) have experienced this form of harassment in low- and middle-income economies. Women are in general as likely as or less likely than men to experience online harassment (refer to figure 1.3.2). It is worth noting, however, that the question is subjective, and women may perceive harassment differently from men. Only in a handful of economies in Sub-Saharan Africa do digital harassment rates exceed 20 percent of adults with mobile phones, among them Ghana, Kenya, Mauritania, Senegal, Sierra Leone, Uganda, and Zambia.

Figure 1.3.2 Women and men both confront risks associated with digital connectivity

Adults with a mobile phone (%), 2024

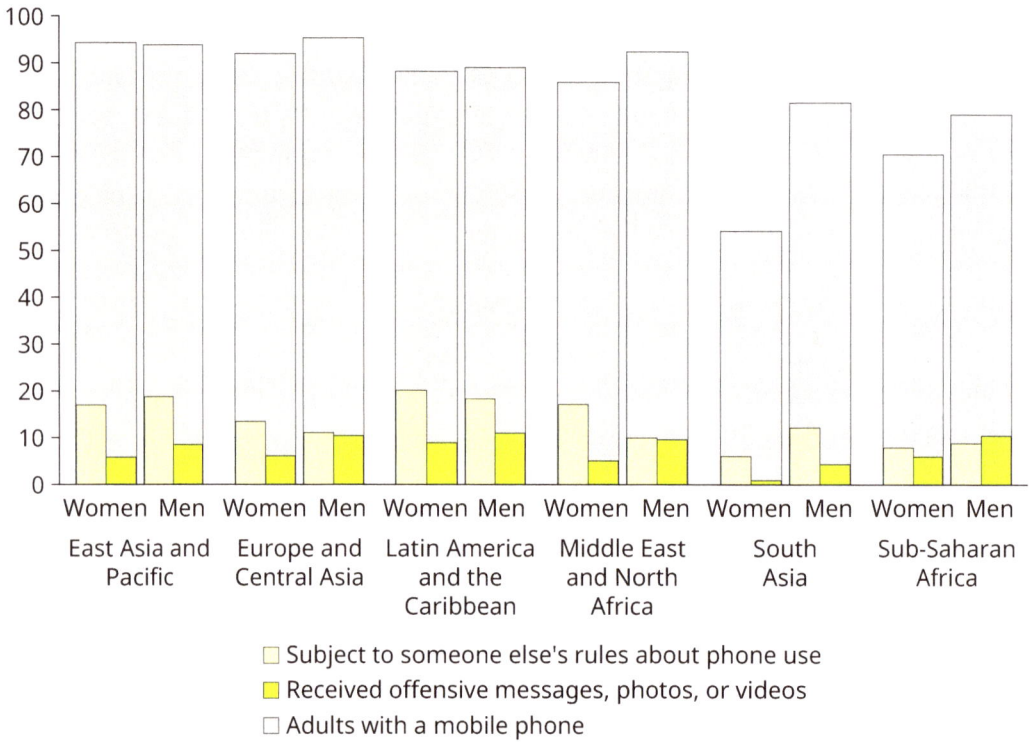

☐ Subject to someone else's rules about phone use
☐ Received offensive messages, photos, or videos
☐ Adults with a mobile phone

Source: Global Findex Database 2025.

Note: The data used for regional averages exclude data for several large economies in which respondents were surveyed by phone rather than in person, including China and the Russian Federation. The "Methodology" tab of the Global Findex website (http://globalfindex.worldbank.org) provides details on the information collected in each surveyed economy.

Exposure to scams or extortion attempts is high among online users, though few lose money to them

Exposure to digital exploitation is more common than online harassment. In low- and middle-income economies, 14 percent of adults, or 19 percent of phone owners, report having received a text or SMS message from someone they don't know asking for money in the context of a scam or online extortion. Latin America and the Caribbean and Sub-Saharan Africa both have regional averages of about 30 percent. In about a dozen different economies worldwide, about a third or more of adults have received messages asking for money.

Figure 1.3.3 A significant share of mobile phone owners in Sub-Saharan Africa are exposed to scams, though only a small minority report falling for them

Adults with a mobile phone (%), 2024

■ Received a scam call or text message and sent money to the scammer
■ Received a scam call or text message but did not send money to the scammer
■ Did not receive a scam call or text message

Source: Global Findex Database 2025.

Adults who are exposed to a digital scam are asked if they sent money to their scammers; only a small share say they did. In a few economies, however, mobile phone owners have both high levels of exposure to scams or extortion and a high tendency to send funds, including Gabon, Ghana, and Senegal (refer to figure 1.3.3). Women are not overall more likely than men to receive scams or extortion attempts or to send money in response.

Opportunities exist to increase responsible digital use

Consumer awareness about scams and the methods of scammers has shown promise for increasing people's ability to avoid them. For example, a study in Uganda that employed interactive games, delivered through interactive voice response, to teach people about fraud decreased the shares of both women and men falling for scams.[2]

---

2   Mazer et al. (2025).

There has also been increased attention to the risks of technology-facilitated violence, which includes online bullying, offensive messages, doxing, and sharing doctored photos. Though the Global Findex 2025 Digital Connectivity Tracker shows that a relatively small share of people experience such harassment, any level is unacceptable. International efforts to address issues surrounding such violence include the UN's Global Digital Compact, which aims to establish principles for an open, free, and secure digital future that respects human rights. Complementary efforts at the national level may span multiple domains. Globally, only 53 out of 190 economies reviewed in one study impose criminal penalties for offenses associated with cyberharassment.[3] Legal frameworks must evolve to recognize online harassment and treat it with the same seriousness as physical harassment. At the same time, tailored training programs in digital literacy for vulnerable populations— particularly women, adolescent girls, and marginalized communities—can help build preventive capacity by teaching users to recognize warning signs and employ privacy-enhancing settings on their mobile phones. Finally, accessible, confidential reporting channels with transparent processes for handling cases can enable victims to seek help without stigma.

Users in all regions are moving from connectivity to inclusion

The view provided by the Global Findex 2025 Digital Connectivity Tracker highlights the ways that people who own a mobile phone and SIM card and use the internet are taking advantage of opportunities to communicate, access information, and earn an income. Digital channels have also become essential for accessing and using financial services to fulfill daily needs, pursue goals, and manage risk. The next section explores these topics, starting with an overview of the current state of financial account ownership.

---

3   Recavarren and Elefante (2023).

References

Abraham, Reuben. 2007. "Mobile Phones and Economic Development." *Information Technologies and International Development* 4 (1): 5–17. https://itidjournal.org/index .php/itid/article/download/241/241-577-2-PB.pdf.

Acemoglu, Daron, David Laibson, and John A. List. 2014. "Equalizing Superstars: The Internet and the Democratization of Education." *American Economic Review* 104 (5): 523–27. https://www.aeaweb.org/articles?id=10.1257/aer.104.5.523.

Aker, Jenny C. 2008. "Does Digital Divide or Provide? The Impact of Cell Phones on Grain Markets in Niger." Center for Global Development Working Paper 154, Center for Global Development, Washington, DC. https://doi.org/10.2139/SSRN.1093374.

Aker, Jenny C. 2010. "Information from Markets Near and Far: Mobile Phones and Agricultural Markets in Niger." *American Economic Journal: Applied Economics* 2 (3): 46–59. https://doi.org/10.1257/app.2.3.46.

Alraja, Mansour Naser, Sarfraz Fayaz Khan, Basel Khashab, and Raghad Aldaas. 2020. "Does Facebook Commerce Enhance SMEs Performance? A Structural Equation Analysis of Omani SMEs." *SAGE Open* 10 (1). https://doi.org/10.1177/2158244019900186.

Angrist, Noam, Peter Bergman, and Moitshepi Matsheng. 2022. "Experimental Evidence on Learning Using Low-Tech When School Is Out." *Nature Human Behaviour* 6 (7): 941–50. https://doi.org/10.1038/s41562-022-01381-z.

Bahia, Kalvin, Pau Castells, Genaro Cruz, Takaaki Masaki, Xavier Pedrós, Tobias Pfutze, Carlos Rodríguez-Castelán, and Hernán Winkler. 2024. "The Welfare Effects of Mobile Broadband Internet: Evidence from Nigeria." *Journal of Development Economics* 170 (September): 103314. https://doi.org/10.1016/J.JDEVECO.2024.103314.

Bahia, Kalvin, Pau Castells, Genaro Cruz, Takaaki Masaki, Carlos Rodríguez-Castelán, and Viviane Sanfelice. 2023. "Mobile Broadband, Poverty, and Labor Outcomes in Tanzania." *World Bank Economic Review* 37 (2): 235–56. https://doi.org/10.1093/WBER /LHAD003.

Barboni, Giorgia, Anwesha Bhattacharya, Erica Field, Rohini Pande, Natalia Rigol, Simone Schaner, Aruj Shukla, and Charity Troyer Moore. 2024. "Hold the Phone: The Short- and Long-Run Impacts of Connecting Indian Women to Digital Technology." EGC Discussion Paper 1109, Economic Growth Center, Yale University, New Haven, CT. https://elischolar.library.yale.edu/egcenter-discussion-paper-series/1109/.

Besley, Timothy, and Robin Burgess. 2002. "The Political Economy of Government Responsiveness: Theory and Evidence from India." *Quarterly Journal of Economics* 117 (4): 1415–51. https://doi.org/10.1162/003355302320935061.

Bianchi, Nicola, Yi Lu, and Hong Song. 2022. "The Effect of Computer-Assisted Learning on Students' Long-Term Development." *Journal of Development Economics* 158 (September): 102919. https://doi.org/10.1016/J.JDEVECO.2022.102919.

BIGD (BRAC Institute of Governance and Development). 2024. "Women's Economic Empowerment and Digital Connectivity: The White Paper; Version 1.0." BIGD, BRAC University, Dhaka, Bangladesh. https://bigd.bracu.ac.bd/wp-content/uploads/2024/02/WEE-Connect-White-Paper_Version-1.0.pdf.

Björkegren, Daniel, Jun Ho Choi, Divya Budihal, Dominic Sobhani, Oliver Garrod, and Paul Atherton. 2025. "Could AI Leapfrog the Web? Evidence from Teachers in Sierra Leone." *arXiv*:2502.12397v2. https://arxiv.org/abs/2502.12397.

Blumenstock, Joshua, Michael Callen, and Tarek Ghani. 2018. "Why Do Defaults Affect Behavior? Experimental Evidence from Afghanistan." *American Economic Review* 108 (10): 2868–901. https://doi.org/10.1257/aer.20171676.

Blumenstock, Joshua, Niall Keleher, Arman Rezaee, and Erin Troland. 2020. "The Impact of Mobile Phones: Experimental Evidence from the Random Assignment of New Cell Towers." Working paper, School of Information, University of California, Berkeley. https://www.jblumenstock.com/publications.

Breza, Emily, Martin Kanz, and Leora F. Klapper. 2020. "Learning to Navigate a New Financial Technology: Evidence from Payroll Accounts." NBER Working Paper 28249, National Bureau of Economic Research, Cambridge, MA. https://doi.org/10.3386/W28249.

Broadband Genie. n.d. "Mobile Data Affordability Index: A Global Comparison." Accessed April 10, 2025. https://www.broadband.co.uk/mobile-data-world-affordability.

Brynjolfsson, Erik, Avinash Collis, Asad Liaqat, Daley Kutzman, Haritz Garro, Daniel Deisenroth, Nils Wernerfelt, and Jae Joon Lee. 2023. "The Digital Welfare of Nations: New Measures of Welfare Gains and Inequality." NBER Working Paper 31670, National Bureau of Economic Research, Cambridge, MA. https://doi.org/10.3386/w31670.

Bussolo, Maurizio, Akshay Dixit, Anne Golla, Ananya Kotia, Jean N. Lee, Prema Narasimhan, and Siddharth Sharma. 2023. "How Selling Online Is Affecting Informal Firms in South Asia." Policy Research Working Paper 10306, World Bank, Washington, DC. https://doi.org/10.1596/1813-9450-10306.

Callen, Michael, Saad Gulzar, Ali Hasanain, Muhammad Yasir Khan, and Arman Rezaee. 2020. "Data and Policy Decisions: Experimental Evidence from Pakistan." *Journal of Development Economics* 146 (September): 102523.

Chikowo, Regis, Kennet Christensen, and Sieglinde S. Snapp. 2020. "Towards Large-Scale Decision Support for Farmers: Site and Season Specific Advice for Maize Agronomy in Malawi." Alliance of Biodiversity CIAT Report. https://cgspace.cgiar.org/items/c9c38bfb-d562-44e6-905e-58c6c9ff4994.

Chiplunkar, Gaurav, and Pinelopi Koujianou Goldberg. 2022. "The Employment Effects of Mobile Internet in Developing Countries." NBER Working Paper 30741, National Bureau of Economic Research, Cambridge, MA. https://doi.org/10.3386/W30741.

Dal Bó, Ernesto, Frederico Finan, Nicholas Y. Li, and Laura Schechter. 2021. "Information Technology and Government Decentralization: Experimental Evidence from Paraguay." *Econometrica* 89: 2677–701. https://onlinelibrary.wiley.com/doi/10.3982/ECTA17497.

Ferraz, Claudio, and Frederico Finan. 2008. "Exposing Corrupt Politicians: The Effects of Brazil's Publicly Released Audits on Electoral Outcomes." *Quarterly Journal of Economics* 123 (2): 703–45. https://doi.org/10.1162/QJEC.2008.123.2.703.

Fink, Günther. 2024. "Encouraging Women to Use Call-In Health Information Services Improves Health Knowledge and Practices in Uganda." Innovations for Poverty Action, New York. https://poverty-action.org/encouraging-women-use-call-health -information-services-improves-health-knowledge-and-practices.

Gertler, Paul, Brett Green, Renping Li, and David Sraer. 2025. "The Welfare Benefits of Pay-as-You-Go Financing." NBER Working Paper 33484, National Bureau of Economic Research, Cambridge, MA. https://www.nber.org/system/files/working_papers /w33484/w33484.pdf.

GSMA. 2024. "The State of Mobile Internet Connectivity: Key Findings 2024." GSMA, London. https://www.gsma.com/r/wp-content/uploads/2024/10/The-State-of-Mobile-Internet -Connectivity-Report-Key-Findings-2024.pdf.

GSMA. 2025. "The Mobile Gender Gap Report 2025." GSMA, London. https://www.gsma .com/r/wp-content/uploads/2025/05/The-Mobile-Gender-Gap-Report-2025.pdf.

Hjort, Jonas, and Jonas Poulsen. 2019. "The Arrival of Fast Internet and Employment in Africa." *American Economic Review* 109 (3): 1032–79. https://doi.org/10.1257 /aer.20161385.

Ho, Lisa, Suhani Jalota, and Anahita Karandikar. 2024. "Bringing Work Home: Flexible Arrangements as Gateway Jobs for Women in West Bengal." STEG Working Paper 080, Structural Transformation and Economic Growth, Centre for Economic Policy Research, Paris. https://steg.cepr.org/publications/bringing-work-home-flexible-arrangements -gateway-jobs-women-west-bengal.

ITU (International Telecommunication Union). 2023a. "Facts and Figures 2023." Accessed April 10, 2025. https://www.itu.int/itu-d/reports/statistics/facts-figures-2023/.

ITU (International Telecommunication Union). 2023b. "Facts and Figures 2023: Affordability of ICT Services." https://www.itu.int/itu-d/reports/statistics/2023/10/10/ff23-affordability -of-ict-services/.

Jack, William, and Tavneet Suri. 2014. "Risk Sharing and Transactions Costs: Evidence from Kenya's Mobile Money Revolution." *American Economic Review* 104 (1): 183–223. https://doi.org/10.1257/aer.104.1.183.

Jensen, Robert. 2007. "The Digital Provide: Information (Technology), Market Performance, and Welfare in the South Indian Fisheries Sector." *Quarterly Journal of Economics* 122 (3): 879–924. https://www.jstor.org/stable/25098864.

Klonner, Stefan, and Patrick J. Nolen. 2010. "Cell Phones and Rural Labor Markets: Evidence from South Africa." In "Proceedings of the German Development Economics Conference, Hannover 2010," no. 56. https://www.econstor.eu/handle/10419/39968.

Kuhn, Peter, and Mikal Skuterud. 2004. "Internet Job Search and Unemployment Durations." *American Economic Review* 94 (1): 218–32. https://doi.org/10.1257/000282804322970779.

Lee, Jean N., Jonathan Morduch, Saravana Ravindran, Abu Shonchoy, and Hassan Zaman. 2021. "Poverty and Migration in the Digital Age: Experimental Evidence on Mobile Banking in Bangladesh." *American Economic Journal: Applied Economics* 13 (1): 38–71. https://doi.org/10.1257/app.20190067.

Lewis-Faupel, Sean, Yusuf Neggers, Benjamin A. Olken, and Rohini Pande. 2016. "Can Electronic Procurement Improve Infrastructure Provision? Evidence from Public Works in India and Indonesia." *American Economic Journal: Economic Policy* 8 (3): 258–83. https://doi.org/10.1257/pol.20140258.

Lorenceau, Adrien, Ji-Yeun Rim, and Toma Savitki. 2021. "Youth Aspirations and the Reality of Jobs in Africa." OECD Development Policy Paper 38, OECD Publishing, Paris. https://doi.org/10.1787/2d089001-en.

Mazer, Rafe, Matthew Bird, Anthony Kamwesigye, and Jessica Massie. 2025. "How Interactive Storytelling Is Protecting Ugandans from Mobile Money Fraud." March 28, 2025. https://poverty-action.org/how-interactive-storytelling-protecting-ugandans -mobile-money-fraud.

Munyegera, Ggombe Kasim, and Tomoya Matsumoto. 2016. "Mobile Money, Remittances, and Household Welfare: Panel Evidence from Rural Uganda." *World Development* 79 (March): 127–37. https://doi.org/10.1016/J.WORLDDEV.2015.11.006.

Muto, Megumi, and Takashi Yamano. 2009. "The Impact of Mobile Phone Coverage Expansion on Market Participation: Panel Data Evidence from Uganda." *World Development* 37 (12): 1887–96. https://doi.org/10.1016/J.WORLDDEV.2009.05.004.

Novella, Rafael, David Rosas-Shady, and Richard Freund. 2024. "Is Online Job Training for All? Experimental Evidence on the Effects of a Coursera Program in Costa Rica." *Journal of Development Economics* 169 (June): 103285. https://www.sciencedirect.com/science /article/pii/S0304387824000348#bib2.

Ouedraogo, Ismaila, Borlli Michel Jonas Some, Kiemute Oyibo, Roland Benedikter, and Gayo Diallo. 2024. "Evaluating a Phone-Based Interactive Voice Response System for Reducing Misinformation and Improving Malaria Literacy." *Information Technology for Development* (October): 1–27. https://doi.org/10.1080/02681102.2024.2414193.

Pava, Juan N., Caroline Meinhardt, Haifa Badi Uz Zaman, Toni Friedman, Sang T. Truong, Daniel Zhang, Elena Cryst, Vukosi Marivate, and Sanmi Koyejo. 2025. "Mind the (Language) Gap: Mapping the Challenges of LLM Development in Low-Resource Language Contexts." Policy White Paper, Stanford University Human-Centered Artificial Intelligence, Stanford, CA. https://hai.stanford.edu/policy/mind-the-language-gap -mapping-the-challenges-of-llm-development-in-low-resource-language-contexts.

Qalati, Sikandar Ali, Dragana Ostic, Mohammad Ali Bait Ali Sulaiman, Aamir Ali Gopang, and Asadullah Khan. 2022. "Social Media and SMEs' Performance in Developing Countries: Effects of Technological-Organizational-Environmental Factors on the Adoption of Social Media." *SAGE Open* 12 (2). https://doi.org/10.1177/21582440221094594.

Recavarren, Isabel Santagostino, and Marina Elefante. 2023. "Protecting Women and Girls from Cyber Harassment: A Global Assessment." *Let's Talk Development* (blog), November 27, 2023. https://blogs.worldbank.org/en/developmenttalk/protecting -women-and-girls-cyber-harassment-global-assessment.

Riley, Emma. 2018. "Mobile Money and Risk Sharing against Village Shocks." *Journal of Development Economics* 135 (November): 43–58. https://doi.org/10.1016/J .JDEVECO.2018.06.015.

Rodriguez-Segura, Daniel. 2022. "EdTech in Developing Countries: A Review of the Evidence." *World Bank Research Observer* 37 (2): 171–203. https://openknowledge .worldbank.org/handle/10986/40100.

Roessler, Philip, Peter Carroll, Flora Myamba, Cornel Jahari, Blandina Kilama, and Daniel Nielson. 2021. "The Economic Impact of Mobile Phone Ownership: Results from a Randomized Controlled Trial in Tanzania." CSAE Working Paper Series 2021-05, Centre for the Study of African Economics, University of Oxford, Oxford, UK. https://ideas .repec.org/p/csa/wpaper/2021-05.html.

Roessler, Philip, Tanu Kumar, Shreya Bhattacharya, Peter Carroll, Boniface Dulani, and Daniel Nielson. 2023. "Smartphone Ownership, Economic Empowerment and Women's Property Rights: Experimental Evidence from Malawi." Working paper, College of William and Mary, Williamsburg, VA. https://bigd.bracu.ac.bd/wp-content /uploads/2024/06/Smartphone-Ownership-Economic-Empowerment-and-Womens -Property-Rights-Experimental-Evidence-from-Malawi_Working-Paper.pdf.

Schulzrinne, Henning, and Marie-José Montpetit. 2022. "NSF Broadband Research 2020 Report." https://ssrn.com/abstract=4048023.

Simione, Felix F., and Yiruo Li. 2021. "The Macroeconomic Impacts of Digitalization in Sub-Saharan Africa: Evidence from Submarine Cables." IMF Working Paper 2021/110, International Monetary Fund, Washington, DC. https://www.imf.org/en/Publications /WP/Issues/2021/04/29/The-Macroeconomic-Impacts-of-Digitalization-in-Sub -Saharan-Africa-Evidence-from-Submarine-50337.

Snyder, James M., Jr., and David Strömberg. 2008. "Press Coverage and Political Accountability." NBER Working Paper 13878, National Bureau of Economic Research, Cambridge, MA. https://www.nber.org/papers/w13878.

Stevenson, Betsey. 2008. "The Internet and Job Search." NBER Working Paper 13886, National Bureau of Economic Research, Cambridge, MA. https://papers.ssrn.com /abstract=1111979.

Streyczek, Julian. 2025. "Political Effects of Newspaper Paywalls." Department of Economics, Bocconi University, Milan. https://doi.org/10.2139/SSRN.5124655.

Strömberg, David. 2004. "Radio's Impact on Public Spending." *Quarterly Journal of Economics* 119 (1): 189–221. https://doi.org/10.1162/003355304772839560.

Suri, Tavneet, and William Jack. 2016. "The Long-Run Poverty and Gender Impacts of Mobile Money." *Science* 354 (6317): 1288–92. https://www.science.org/doi/10.1126/science .aah5309.

Vassil, Kristjan. 2016. "Estonian e-Government Ecosystem: Foundation, Applications, Outcomes." Background paper for *World Development Report 2016.* World Bank, Washington, DC. https://thedocs.worldbank.org/en/doc/165711456838073531 -0050022016/original/WDR16BPEstonianeGovecosystemVassil.pdf.

Viollaz, Mariana, and Hernan Winkler. 2021. "Does the Internet Reduce Gender Gaps? The Case of Jordan." *Journal of Development Studies* 58 (3): 436–53. https://doi.org/10.1080 /00220388.2021.1965127.

Wheeler, Laurel, Robert Garlick, Eric Johnson, Patrick Shaw, and Marissa Gargano. 2022. "LinkedIn(to) Job Opportunities: Experimental Evidence from Job Readiness Training." *American Economic Journal: Applied Economics* 14 (2): 101–25. https://doi.org/10.1257 /app.20200025.

World Bank. 2024. *The Path to 5G in the Developing World: Planning Ahead for a Smooth Transition.* Sustainable Infrastructure Series. Washington, DC: World Bank. http://hdl .handle.net/10986/41689.

World Bank Independent Evaluation Group. 2020. "Project Performance Assessment Report: Croatia." Justice Sector Support Project, Independent Evaluation Group, World Bank, Washington, DC. https://documents1.worldbank.org/curated/en/786741595517900211 /pdf/Croatia-Justice-Sector-Support-Project.pdf.

SPOTLIGHT 1.1

Identification, digital connectivity, and financial inclusion

The World Bank's Identification for Development (ID4D) Initiative partners with the Global Findex team to collect data on worldwide ownership and use of government-issued forms of identification (ID) as part of the Global Findex survey.[1] ID is often a prerequisite for accessing and using digital services and for transacting with governments, financial institutions, medical providers, educational institutions, and other entities that handle personal information.[2]

Across low- and middle-income economies, 95 percent of adults have ID. Ownership of ID is nearly universal across regions except for Sub-Saharan Africa (refer to figure S1.1.1).

Figure S1.1.1 **Ownership of ID is nearly universal across regions except for Sub-Saharan Africa**

Adults with ID (%), 2024

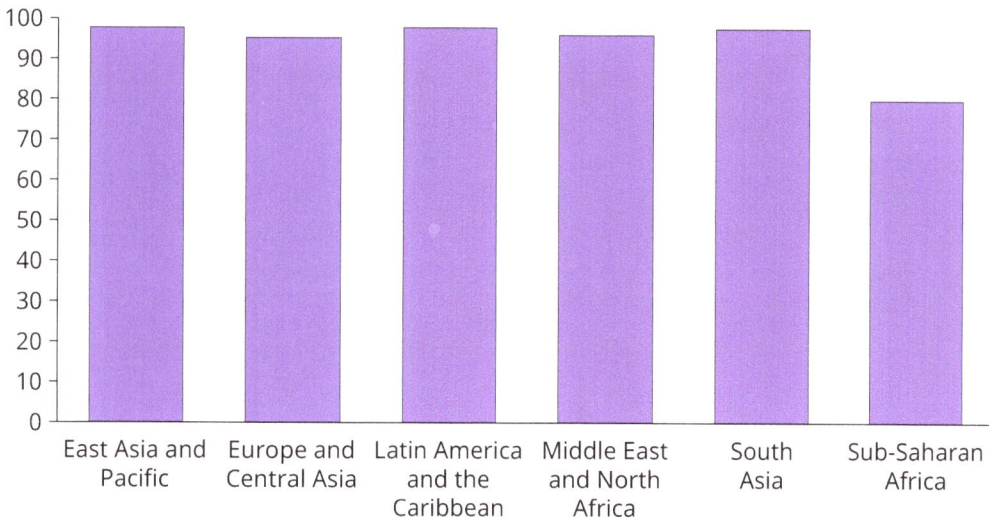

Source: Identification for Development (ID4D)–Global Findex Database 2025.

---

1   To ensure accuracy and local relevance, the survey was administered using locally appropriate terminology for ID in local languages.

2   G20 and UNDP (2023).

Some countries in Sub-Saharan Africa have low rates of ID ownership

Though not universal in the region, ID is pervasive in most Sub-Saharan African economies. In all four subregions of Sub-Saharan Africa, average ID ownership rates exceed 70 percent among all adults, and only the West and East African regions have statistically significant gender gaps in these rates (of 5 percentage points, on average; refer to figure S1.1.2). Eight economies have ID ownership rates below 70 percent, however: the Republic of Congo, Guinea, Mozambique, Niger, Sierra Leone, Tanzania, Togo, and Uganda.[3]

Examination of data from just the eight economies with ID rates below 70 percent reveals that five of them have significant gender gaps in ID ownership (refer to figure S1.1.3). In Guinea, for example, the rates are 42 percent of women versus 52 percent of men, and in Niger, 43 percent of women have ID, compared with 63 percent of men.

Figure S1.1.2 **Even though eight economies in Sub-Saharan Africa have low rates of ID ownership, average rates among both women and men exceed 70 percent in all four subregions**

Adults with ID (%), 2024

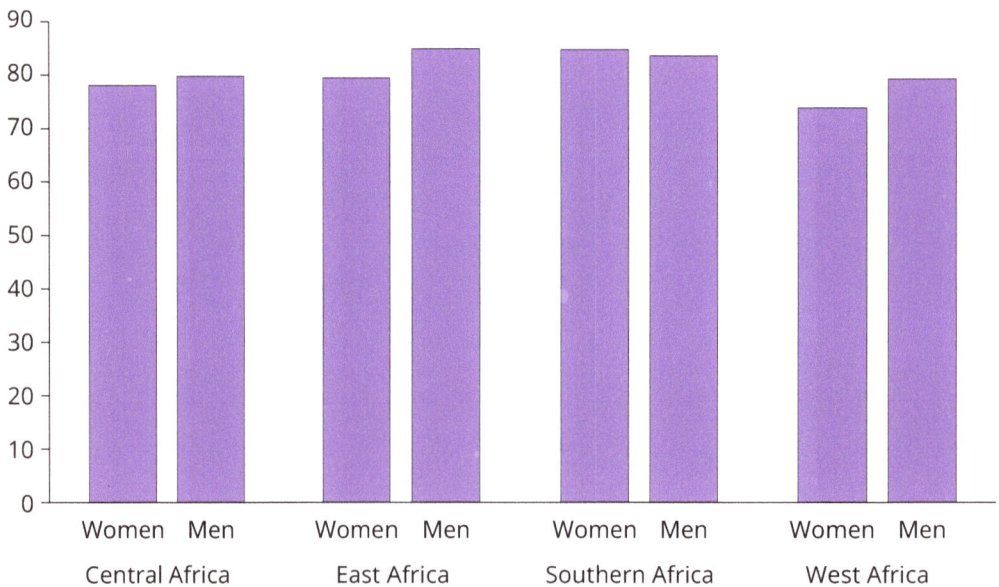

Source: Identification for Development (ID4D)–Global Findex Database 2025.

---

3   Data for Chad and Liberia have been suppressed because of possible misinterpretation of the question as referring to other acceptable forms of ID that could fulfill a similar purpose. This issue is particularly relevant in these two economies, where new ID systems are being introduced while older systems remain in use.

Figure S1.1.3 Five of the economies in Sub-Saharan Africa with low rates of ID ownership also have large gender gaps in those rates

Adults with ID (%), 2024

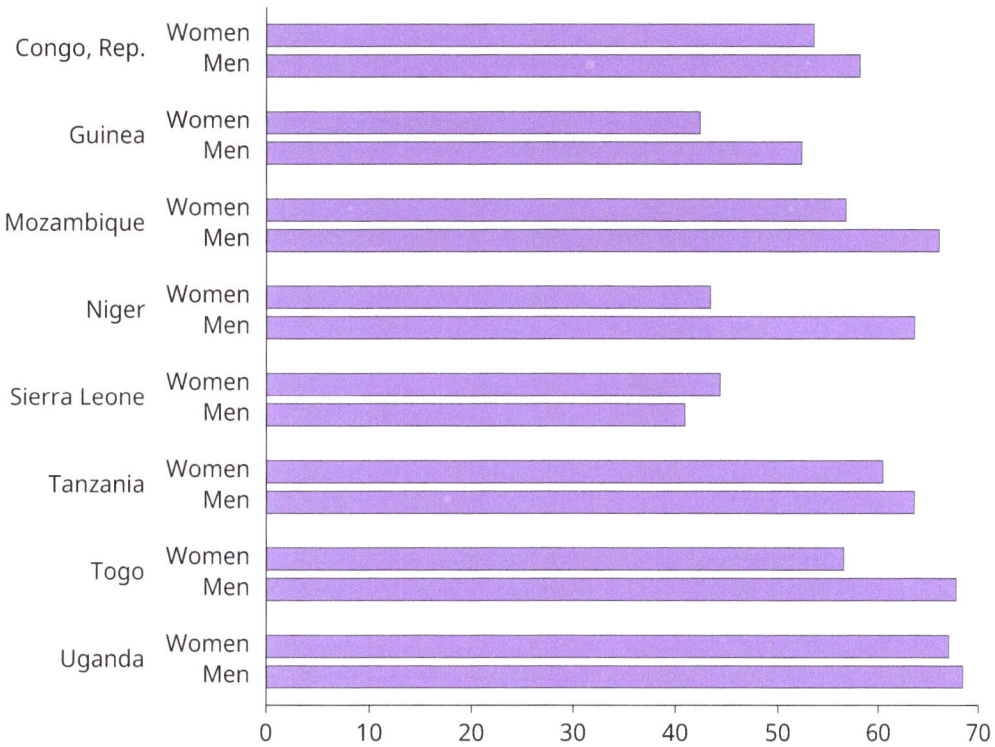

Source: Identification for Development (ID4D)–Global Findex Database 2025.

ID matters for connectivity and accessing financial services, among other benefits

People without ID face challenges participating in important activities. Specifically, people without ID often have difficulty buying SIM cards; participating in elections; accessing financial services, government support, and medical care; and applying for jobs.

In six of the eight Sub-Saharan African economies with low rates of ID ownership, the largest share of adults without ID cited having difficulty buying SIM cards.[4] In the Republic of Congo, 58 percent of adults without ID experienced this challenge; in Guinea, 57 percent did; in Tanzania, 67 percent did; and in Uganda, 79 percent did. Put another way, at least one in four adults in each of these economies was unable to buy and register a SIM card in their own name (refer to figure S1.1.4). This directly affects their ability to own and use a mobile phone and related digital services.

---

4   Respondents were able to choose multiple responses to the survey question.

Figure S1.1.4 People without ID have trouble buying SIM cards; participating in elections; accessing financial services, government support, and medical care; and applying for jobs

Adults without ID citing difficulty doing a given activity (%), 2024

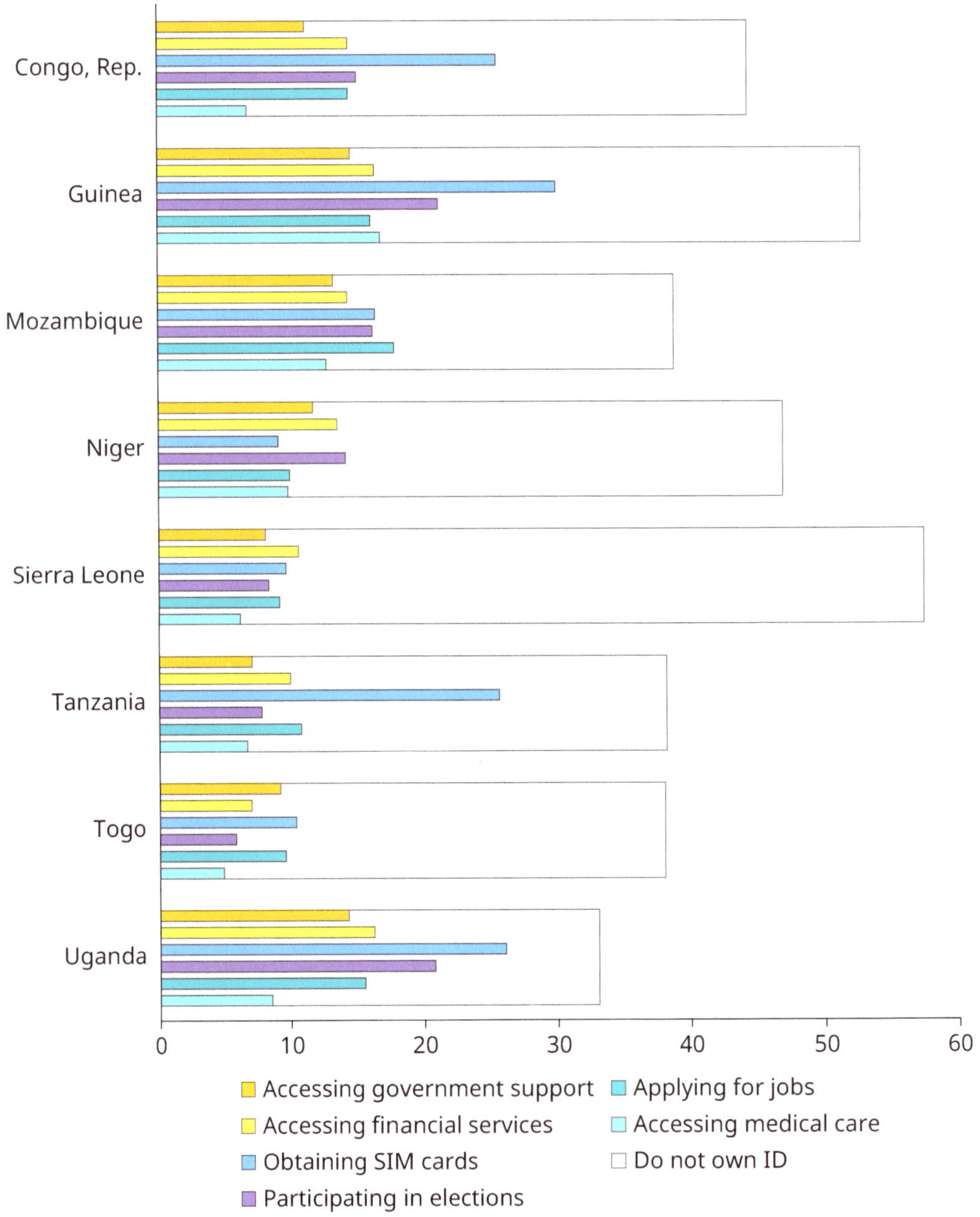

Congo, Rep.
Guinea
Mozambique
Niger
Sierra Leone
Tanzania
Togo
Uganda
0
10
20
30
40
50
60
Accessing government support
Accessing financial services
Obtaining SIM cards
Participating in elections
Applying for jobs
Accessing medical care
Do not own ID

Source: Identification for Development (ID4D)–Global Findex Database 2025.

Note: Respondents could choose more than one activity.

Challenges in buying and registering SIM cards are just the beginning for people who lack ID, however. They also find it difficult to participate in elections. In Guinea and Uganda, one in five adults said they face this problem.

For people in Sub-Saharan Africa without ID, access to financial services is also uncertain. Across the eight low-ID economies, a third of adults without ID report that their lack of ID makes it difficult for them to use financial services. In Uganda, about half of adults without ID report having this difficulty. This aligns with Global Findex 2025 data showing that 15 percent of adults without an account in Sub-Saharan Africa do not have a mobile money account because they lack the documentation they would need to open one.

Finally, some adults without ID say that they have had problems accessing government support, applying for jobs, or accessing medical care. Across all low-ID economies except Sierra Leone and Tanzania, about a quarter or more of adults with no ID had difficulty accessing government services as a result. In the Republic of Congo, Guinea, Mozambique, and Uganda, more than 30 percent of adults without ID—generally between 10 and 15 percent of all adults in these economies—faced difficulties applying for a job. More than 20 percent of adults without ID found it challenging to access medical care in Guinea, Mozambique, Niger, and Uganda.

Why don't people have ID?

The process of applying for government ID requires people to travel to the nearest location where registration services are offered; they must bring documentation supporting their identity, such as a birth certificate, which can be difficult to obtain; they may have to pay a fee for ID and cover travel costs for the trip; and they risk either lost wages as a result of taking time away from work or challenges arising from leaving their domestic duties. Each of these factors creates a barrier to accessing ID.

When the Global Findex asked people without ID why they don't have it, three of these barriers came up most often in the eight economies in Sub-Saharan Africa with low rates of ID ownership: getting ID is too expensive, the distance to travel to obtain ID is too great, or they lack the supporting documentation they would need to get ID. Smaller but statistically significant shares of adults without ID say they use another form of ID instead, such as a voter card or a birth registration certificate, do not need ID, or are uncomfortable with sharing their personal information to get ID.

Different barriers dominate in different economies (refer to figure S1.1.5). At least half of adults without ID in Guinea, Mozambique, and Sierra Leone say getting ID is too expensive. Half or more in Guinea, Mozambique, Niger, and Sierra Leone say it is too far to travel to get ID. More than 60 percent in Guinea and Togo say they lack the necessary documentation.

Figure S1.1.5 The expense of ID and the burden of travel to get it are the most common barriers to ID ownership

Adults without ID citing a given barrier as a reason for having no ID (%), 2024

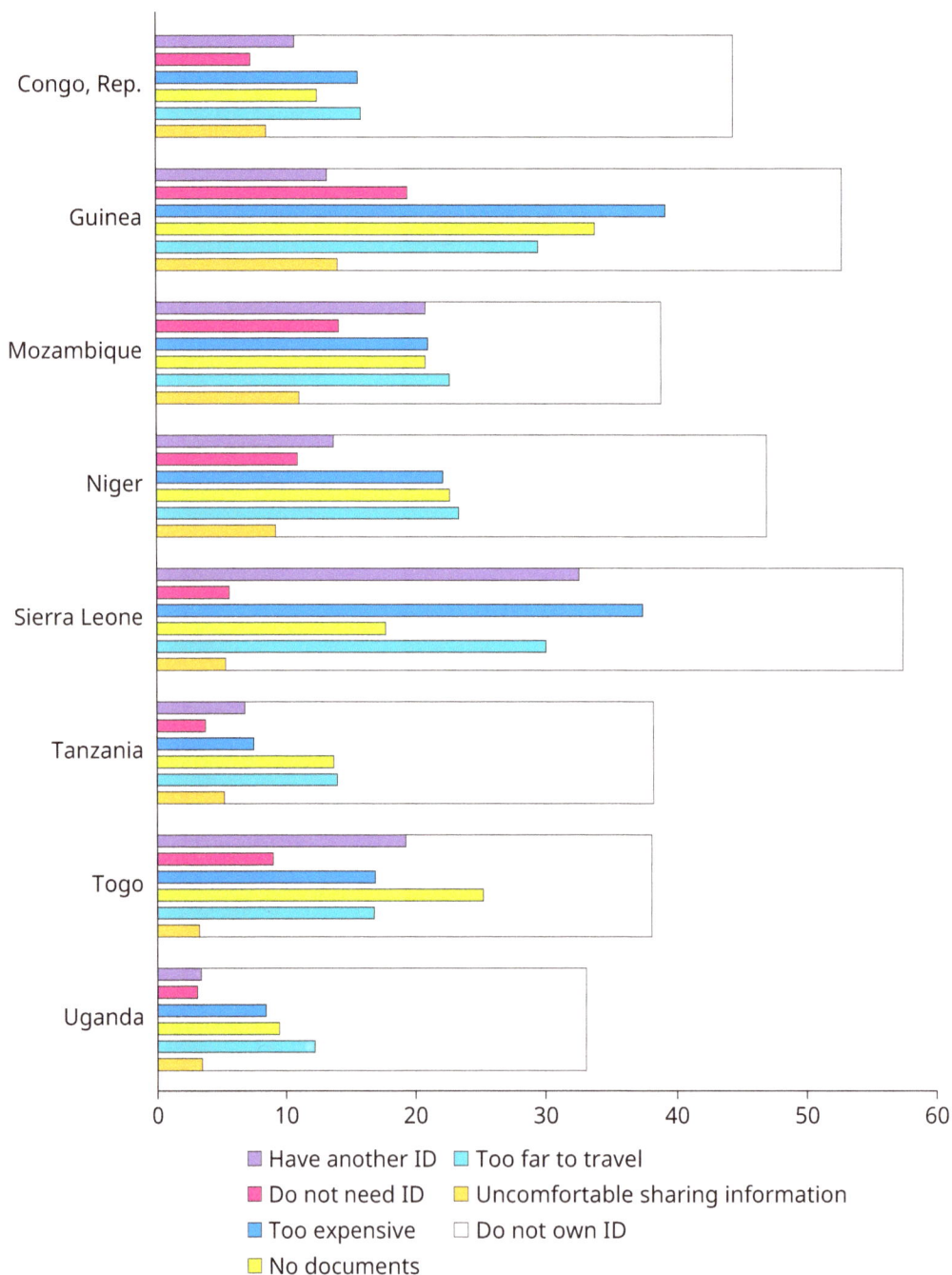

Legend:
- Have another ID
- Do not need ID
- Too expensive
- No documents
- Too far to travel
- Uncomfortable sharing information
- Do not own ID

Source: Identification for Development (ID4D)–Global Findex Database 2025.
Note: Respondents could choose more than one reason.

What approaches can facilitate increased ID access?

Successful approaches to facilitating greater access to ID consider both the services that they want to enable and the barriers people face. For example, reducing travel time to get ID and streamlining the registration process can lower associated costs and particularly benefit the people most likely not to have ID, such as women and rural residents.

Access to ID is essential, but equally important is ensuring that ID systems are trustworthy, effectively managed, and designed to safeguard individuals' rights and data while supporting development goals. Possession of ID does not necessarily mean people have access to high-quality ID systems, indicating that coverage alone should not be the primary focus for those working on ID and civil registration.[5]

For more information on approaches to improving access to and quality of ID systems, visit the World Bank's ID4D web page at http://id4d.worldbank.org.

References

Clark, Julia, Anna Metz, and Claire Casher. 2022. *ID4D Global Dataset*, vol. 1, *Global ID Coverage Estimates*. Washington, DC: World Bank. https://documents1 .worldbank.org/curated/en/099705012232226786/pdf/P176341132c1ef0b21adf11abad 304425ef.pdf.

G20 (Group of Twenty) and UNDP (United Nations Development Programme). 2023. "Accelerating the SDGs through Digital Public Infrastructure: A Compendium of the Potential of Digital Public Infrastructure." G20, New Delhi, and UNDP, New York. https://www.undp.org/sites/g/files/zskgke326/files/2023-08/undp-g20-accelerating -the_sdgs-through-digital-public-infrastructure.pdf.

---

5   Clark, Metz, and Casher (2022).

Financial access

A reproducibility package is available for this book in the Reproducible Research Repository at https://reproducibility.worldbank.org/catalog/299.

Financial Access

GLOBALLY, UNLESS OTHERWISE NOTED

79% OF ADULTS HAVE AN ACCOUNT.

That's an increase of 28 percentage points since 2011.

75% OF ADULTS IN LOW- AND MIDDLE-INCOME ECONOMIES HAVE ACCOUNTS.

77% of women have an account, narrowing the global gender gap to 4 percentage points.

Over half of all adults in low- and middle-income economies now make payments from an account using a mobile phone or card.

MOBILE MONEY ACCOUNTS HAVE SPREAD WORLDWIDE.

15% OF ALL ADULTS NOW HAVE ONE.

IN SUB-SAHARAN AFRICA AND LATIN AMERICA AND THE CARIBBEAN:

Around 40% of adults have mobile money.

Poorer adults are still **11 percentage points less likely** than wealthier adults to have an account.

1.3 billion adults worldwide still lack accounts.

650 MILLION OF THEM LIVE IN JUST EIGHT ECONOMIES.

Adults without accounts who own a mobile phone, basic ID, and a SIM card registered in their name have the **foundations for account ownership.**

THERE ARE 80 MILLION OF THEM IN SUB-SAHARAN AFRICA ALONE.

☑ **WOMEN**

☑ **POOR ADULTS**

☑ **THOSE OUT OF THE WORKFORCE**

are **more likely to lack an account** than men, wealthier adults, and the wage- or self-employed.

Affordability, accessibility, and not having enough money to use accounts are the top three barriers to having one in low- and middle-income economies.

2.1 Account ownership

A reproducibility package is available for this book in the Reproducible Research Repository at https://reproducibility.worldbank.org/catalog/299.

2.1 Account ownership

Accounts are the cornerstone of financial access and the foundation of financial inclusion. They provide people with a safe way to store money and build savings for the future; they also help them make and receive payments or receive loan disbursements. Account ownership is associated with multiple positive development outcomes for both account owners and the broader economy, including increased consumption,[1] reduced poverty,[2] elevated productivity,[3] higher savings levels,[4] and greater ability to share resources.[5]

Worldwide, 79 percent of adults have an account either at a bank or similar financial institution such as a credit union, microfinance institution, or post office or through a mobile money provider (refer to box 2.1.1). Rates of account ownership vary widely across economies, however (refer to map 2.1.1). Among the 139 economies included in Global Findex 2025, account ownership ranges from just 15 percent in Niger, a low-income and fragile and conflict-affected economy, to universal in such high-income economies as Canada, Japan, and the Netherlands.

> ### Box 2.1.1 *Account ownership* defined
>
> Global Findex 2025 defines "account ownership" as having an account at a bank or similar institution such as a credit union, microfinance institution, or post office, or with a mobile money provider that is included in the GSMA's Mobile Money Deployment Tracker.[a] Owners can use these accounts at a minimum to store money and to send and receive payments.
>
> The Global Findex 2025 collected data separately for accounts at these two types of providers and uses the following definitions:
>
> - *Adults with an account at a bank or similar financial institution* refers to adults with an individual or jointly owned account at a regulated institution such as a bank or similar financial institution. Such institutions have historically maintained a physical footprint in the form of branch locations. This category also includes adults who say they have a debit card linked to an account, even if they say they do not have an account at a bank or similar financial institution.
>
> *(Box continued next page)*

---

1   Burgess and Pande (2005); Karlan and Zinman (2012).
2   Beck, Demirgüç-Kunt, and Levine (2004); Suri and Jack (2016).
3   Allen et al. (2016); Bruhn and Love (2014).
4   Gertler et al. (2023); Karlan, Ratan, and Zinman (2014).
5   Jack and Suri (2014); Lee et al. (2021); Munyegera and Matsumoto (2016); Riley (2018).

Box 2.1.1 *Account ownership* defined *(continued)*

A subcategory of "digitally enabled" account at a bank or similar financial institution allows the account owner to make or receive payments using a card or phone.

Each economy identifies the banks and financial institutions that offer transaction accounts and are subject to prudential regulation by a government authority. This category excludes accounts with mobile money providers as well as those with nonbank financial institutions, such as pension funds and retirement accounts, and with other nonbank financial institutions like insurance companies and brokerage firms.

- *Adults with a mobile money account* refers to adults who have personally used a mobile phone in the preceding 12 months to make payments, purchase goods or services, or send or receive money and have also used a mobile money provider included in the GSMA Mobile Money Deployment Tracker. The GSMA's tracker includes telecom- and fintech-led platforms that offer financial services via mobile phones and typically operate independently of traditional banks. This group generally excludes adults using digital wallets that function primarily as app-based payment tools. Some mobile money account providers listed in the GSMA's tracker, however, could be legally licensed as a bank or are typically supported by a bank partner, or some of their services could be linked to bank accounts, although they can also be used without a traditional bank account. All mobile money accounts are by definition digitally enabled, and are primarily accessed through mobile phones.

The *total account ownership rate* includes respondents who said *no* when asked if they had an account or debit card yet also reported that they had received wages, government transfers, public sector pensions, or payments for the sale of agricultural products in an account in the preceding 12 months or that they had paid utility bills directly from an account at a bank or similar financial institution in the preceding 12 months. Among low- and middle-income economies, this adds 2 percent of respondents to the share of adults with an account; each of these respondents is added to the share of adults with the type of account they say they used to receive or make the relevant payment (that is, an account at a bank or similar financial institution or a mobile money account).

For most high-income economies and the Russian Federation, the Global Findex 2025 included only questions on account ownership, not questions that resulted in these additions. In Algeria, China, the Islamic Republic of Iran, Libya, Mauritius, and Ukraine, an abridged form of the questionnaire was administered by phone. As a result, account ownership in these economies may be underestimated, because the questionnaire did not include all relevant questions. The "Methodology" tab of the Global Findex website (http://globalfindex.worldbank.org) provides details on the information collected in each surveyed economy.

a. The complete list of providers included in the GSMA Mobile Money Deployment Tracker is available at https://www.gsma.com/mobile-money-metrics/#deployment-tracker.

Map 2.1.1 Account ownership rates vary around the world

Adults with an account (%), 2024

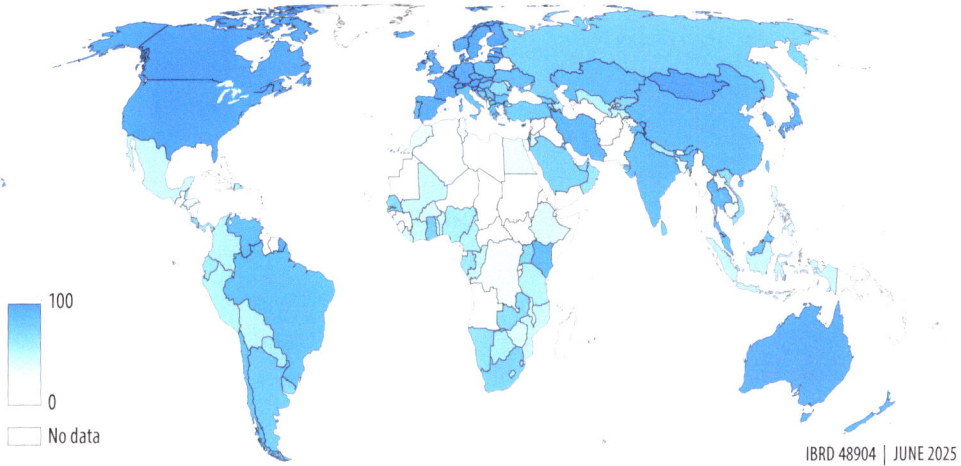

Source: Global Findex Database 2025.

Figure 2.1.1 Account ownership differs significantly even within income groups

Adults with an account (%), 2024

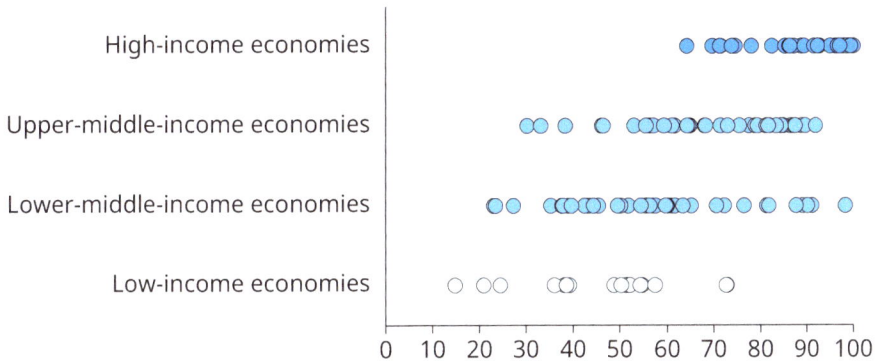

Source: Global Findex Database 2025.

The data show significant differences in account ownership rates across economies in the same income group (refer to figure 2.1.1). For example, among low-income economies, account ownership ranges from 15 percent in Niger to 73 percent in Uganda. Among high-income economies, Panama has the lowest account ownership rate, at 64 percent. Thailand has the highest account ownership rate among upper-middle-income economies, at 92 percent. In lower-middle-income economies, account ownership ranges from 23 percent in Lebanon to 98 percent in Mongolia.[6]

---

6   Mongolia's near-universal Child Money Programme drives the economy's high rate of account ownership.
     The program, introduced in 2005, provides a monthly allowance for every child under the age of 18, which the
     Mongolian government deposits directly into an account.

Account ownership increased by 28 percentage points, or more than 50 percent, worldwide between 2011 and 2024

In 2024, the global account ownership rate stood at 79 percent, a 28 percentage point increase from the worldwide average of 51 percent in 2011, when the first round of Global Findex data was collected (refer to figure 2.1.2). Account ownership increased in both high-income and low- and middle-income economies, but the average growth rate in the latter group of economies was steeper. Account ownership is nearly universal in most high-income economies, yet nevertheless increased for this group by 7 percentage points, from 87 percent in 2011 to 95 percent in 2024.[7] In low- and middle-income economies, account ownership grew by 34 percentage points, from 42 percent in 2011 to 75 percent in 2024, an 80 percent increase.

Despite the large increase overall, account ownership grew at different rates in individual economies between 2011 and 2024 (refer to figure 2.1.3). For instance, it grew by about 70 percentage points in both the Kyrgyz Republic and Senegal over this period. This is twice the average increase for low- and middle-income economies and by far the largest increase among economies in this income group, albeit from 2011 account ownership percentages in the single digits.

Figure 2.1.2 Global account ownership increased from 51 percent to 79 percent between 2011 and 2024

Adults with an account (%), 2011–24

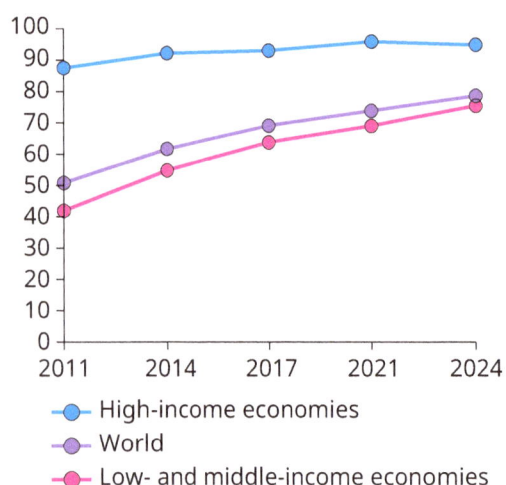

- High-income economies
- World
- Low- and middle-income economies

Account ownership increased by more than 50 percentage points in Armenia, Uganda, and Zambia, from about 20 percent in 2011 to just over 70 percent in 2024. In Ghana and India, account ownership similarly grew by more than 50 percentage points, reaching 81 percent in the former and 89 percent in the latter. Account ownership rates also increased to more than 80 percent in additional economies, including Argentina, Kazakhstan, and Kenya.

Source: Global Findex Database 2025.

---

7   The Global Findex reports data as whole percentage points, although it calculates that whole based on rounding up or down from the tenths place. As such, any discrepancies between the reported size of a gap and the difference between its end points is due to rounding.

Other economies, however, experienced much smaller increases. In 16 economies that were at or below the global average of 51 percent in 2011, account ownership grew by 20 percentage points or less between 2011 and 2024. This includes six economies in which it grew by 10 percentage points or less.

Figure 2.1.3 **Account ownership has increased dramatically over time**

Adults with an account (%), 2011–24

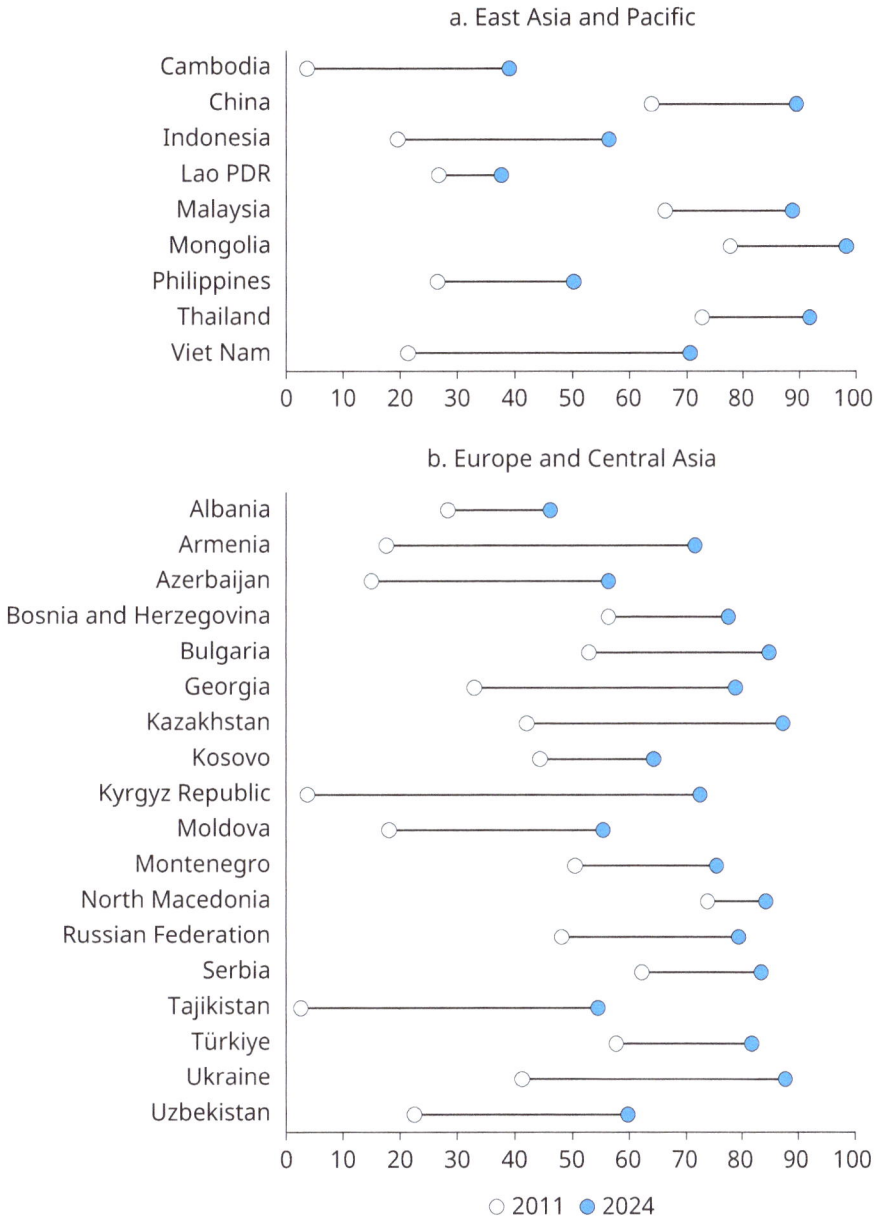

a. East Asia and Pacific

b. Europe and Central Asia

○ 2011   ● 2024

(Figure continued next page)

Figure 2.1.3 Account ownership has increased dramatically over time *(continued)*

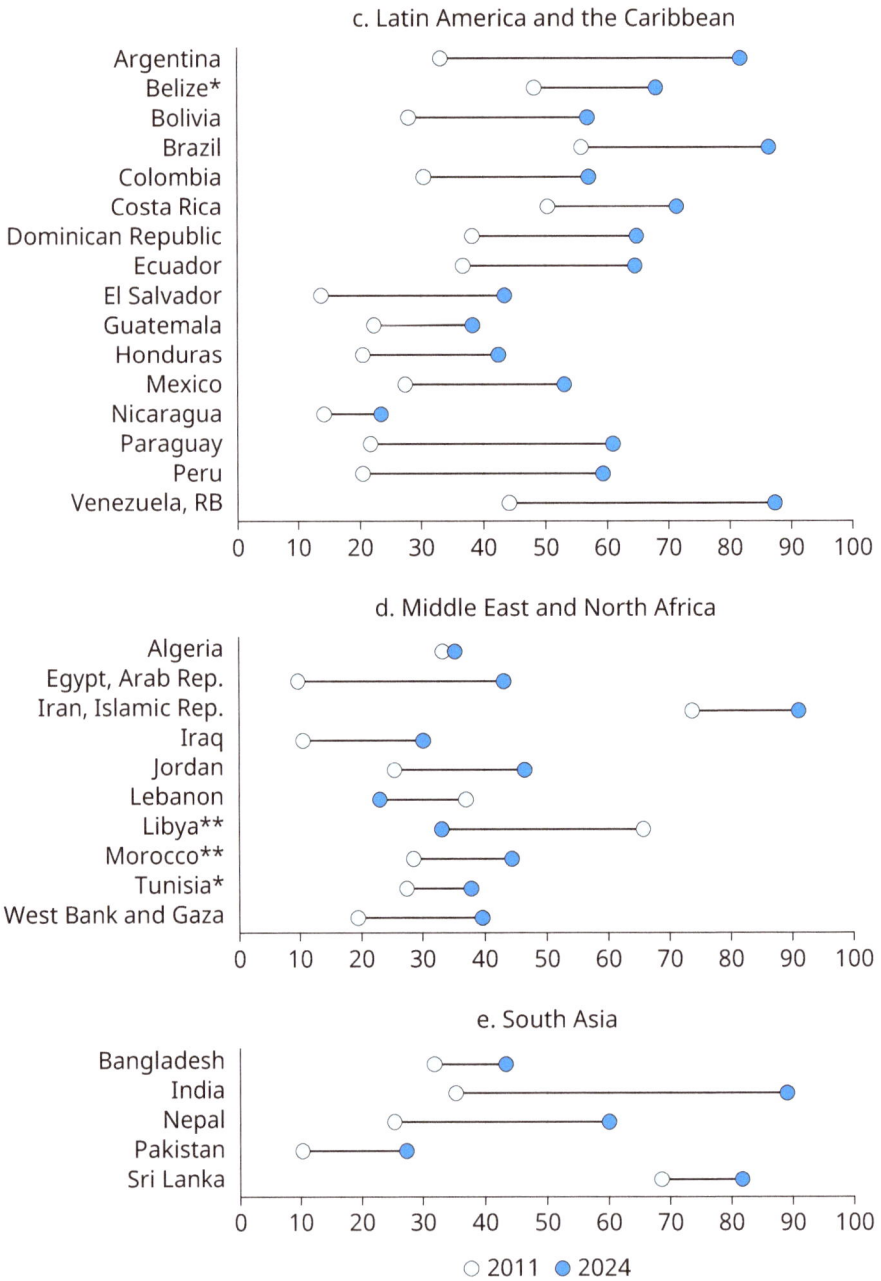

c. Latin America and the Caribbean

Country	2011	2024
Argentina	33	81
Belize*	48	68
Bolivia	28	56
Brazil	56	86
Colombia	30	56
Costa Rica	50	71
Dominican Republic	38	64
Ecuador	37	65
El Salvador	14	43
Guatemala	22	38
Honduras	21	42
Mexico	27	53
Nicaragua	14	24
Paraguay	22	60
Peru	20	60
Venezuela, RB	44	87

d. Middle East and North Africa

e. South Asia

○ 2011　● 2024

(Figure continued next page)

Figure 2.1.3 Account ownership has increased dramatically over time *(continued)*

f. Sub-Saharan Africa

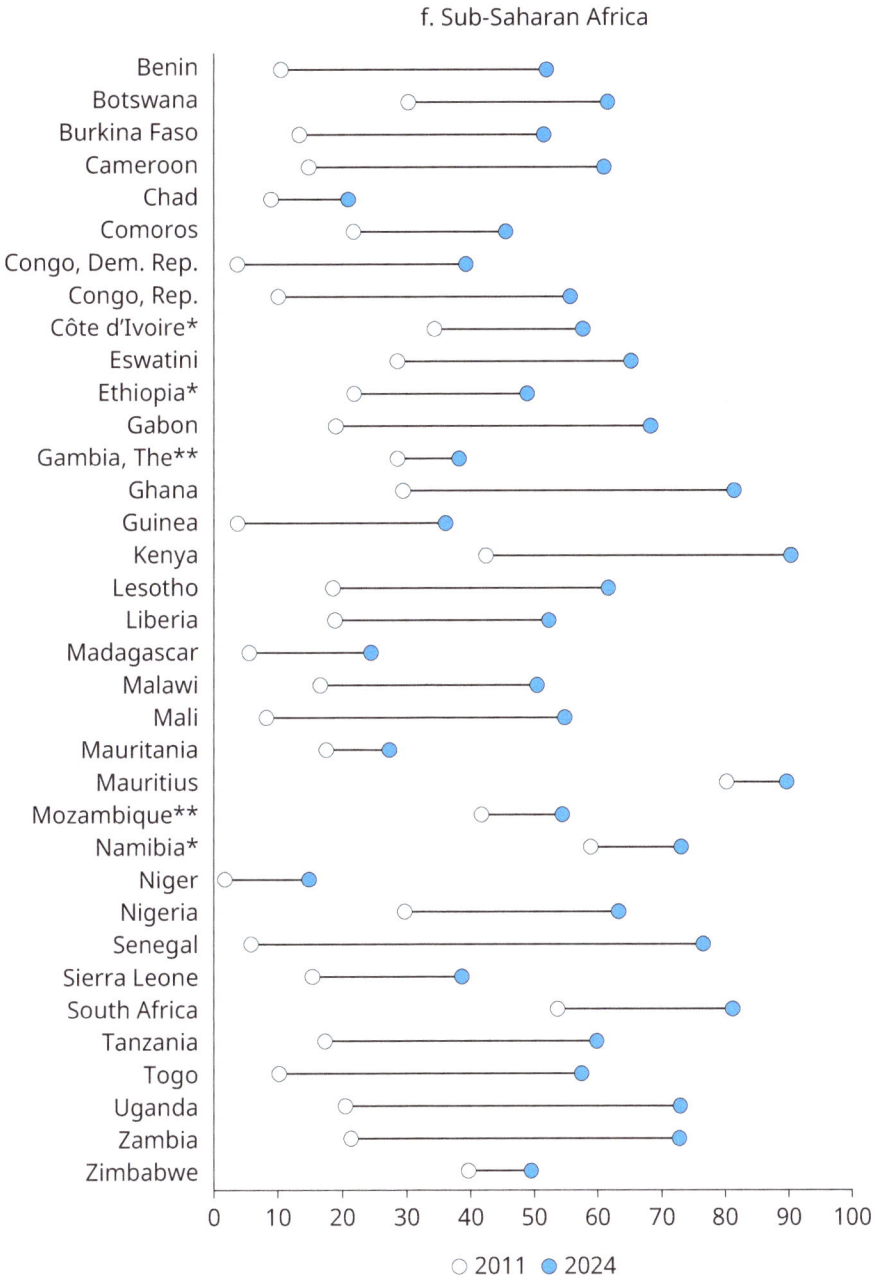

○ 2011 ● 2024

(Figure continued next page)

Figure 2.1.3 **Account ownership has increased dramatically over time** *(continued)*

g. High-income economies

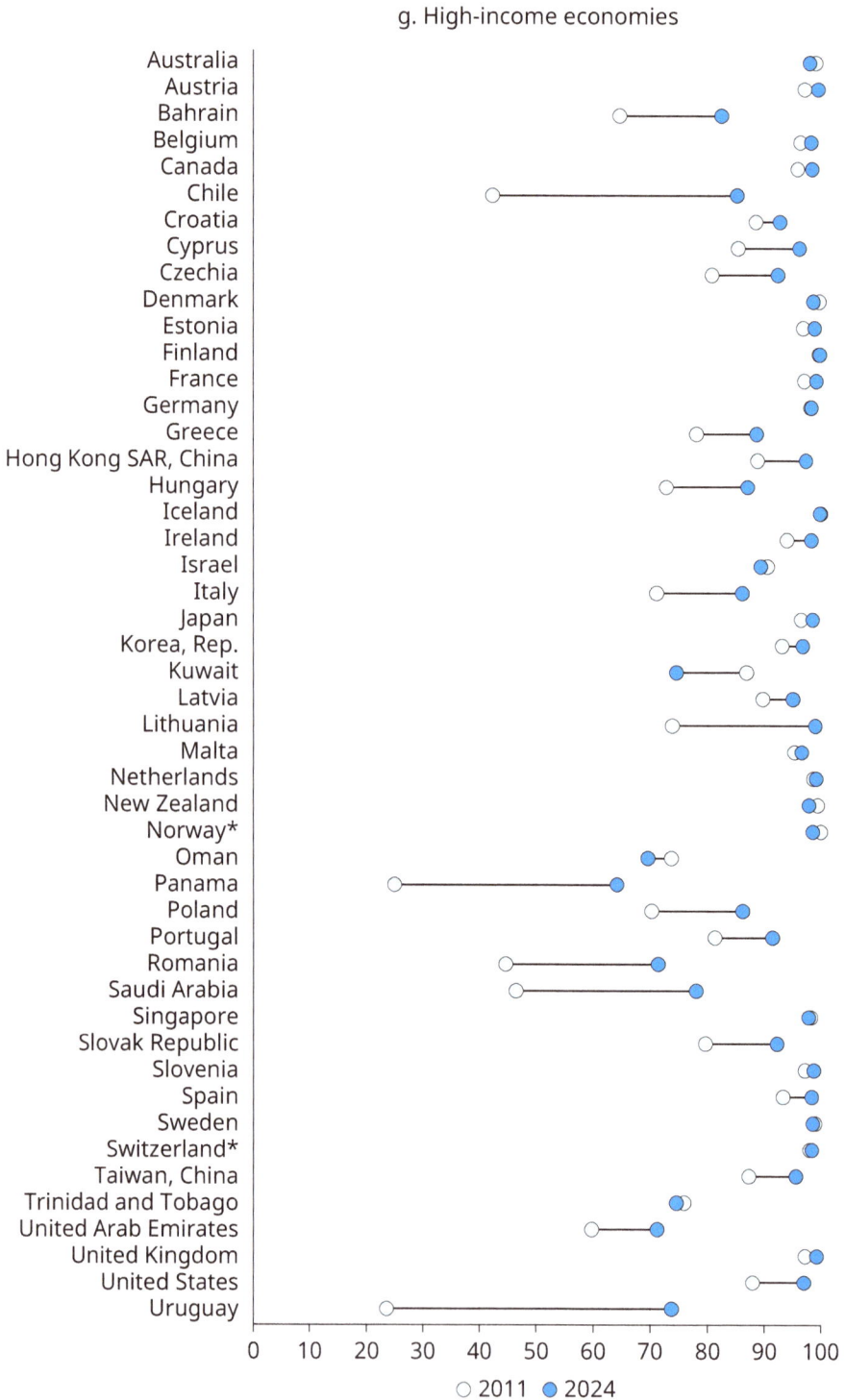

Source: Global Findex Database 2025.

Note: A single asterisk (or double asterisk) next to an economy's name indicates that 2014 (or 2017) is the first year for which account ownership data are available for that economy. For West Bank and Gaza, data collection in 2024 took place in West Bank and East Jerusalem only. SAR = special administrative region.

More recently, between 2021 and 2024, the Kyrgyz Republic, Senegal, and Zambia each experienced account ownership increases of more than 20 percentage points. An additional 18 economies also experienced double-digit increases in account ownership, each gaining between 10 and 20 percentage points during this period: Argentina, Armenia, Azerbaijan, Burkina Faso, the Comoros, the Democratic Republic of Congo, the Dominican Republic, the Arab Republic of Egypt, Ghana, India, Iraq, Kenya, Mali, Nigeria, Panama, Tajikistan, Uzbekistan, and Viet Nam.

Mobile money has spread from Sub-Saharan Africa around the world and increased total account ownership

Motivated by the growing impact of mobile money on financial inclusion, since 2014 the Global Findex survey has asked respondents about their use of mobile money services, in addition to their use of accounts at a bank or similar financial institution (refer to map 2.1.2). In 2014, just 2 percent of adults globally had a mobile money account. As of 2024, that share had increased to 15 percent globally and 18 percent in low- and middle-income economies (refer to figure 2.1.4).[8]

Map 2.1.2 **Mobile money account ownership varies across economies**

Adults with a mobile money account (%), 2024

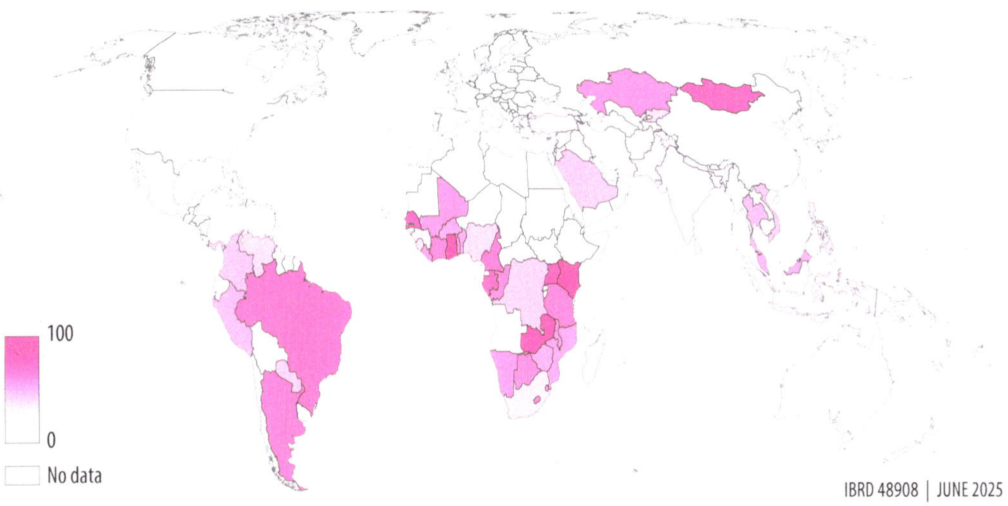

IBRD 48908 | JUNE 2025

Source: Global Findex Database 2025.

---

8   The only high-income economies in which the Global Findex 2025 asked respondents about mobile money accounts were Panama and Saudi Arabia.

Figure 2.1.4 Mobile money contributed to the increase overall in account ownership in low- and middle-income economies between 2014 and 2024

Adults with an account (%), 2014–24

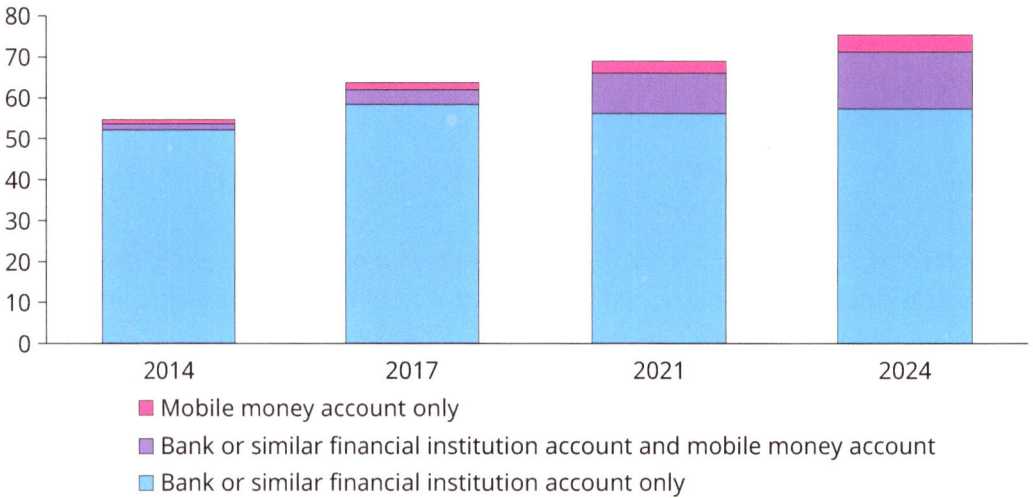

- Mobile money account only
- Bank or similar financial institution account and mobile money account
- Bank or similar financial institution account only

Source: Global Findex Database 2025.

Sub-Saharan Africa continues to have the highest rate of mobile money account ownership of any world region, at 40 percent of adults. Sub-Saharan Africa is no longer the only world region enjoying high rates of mobile money account ownership, however. In Latin America and the Caribbean, 37 percent of adults have a mobile money account (refer to figure 2.1.5). Compared with the rate in 2021, mobile money account ownership had increased by 13 and 15 percentage points in Sub-Saharan Africa and Latin America and the Caribbean, respectively, in 2024. In South Asia, 22 percent of adults have a mobile money account, a 10 percentage point increase since 2021.

Yet Sub-Saharan Africa still stands out for having a large share of adults with only a mobile money account. A third of the region's account owners—20 percent of adults—have no other kind of account. In all other regions, less than 5 percent of all adults and less than 6 percent of account owners have only a mobile money account.

Notwithstanding mobile money's growth, accounts at banks or similar financial institutions remain the most common type of account for adults in low- and middle-income economies. In that group of countries, 57 percent of adults have only an account at a bank or similar financial institution, and 14 percent have both an account at a bank or similar financial institution and a mobile money account.

Figure 2.1.5 Sub-Saharan Africa remains the region with the largest share of adults with only mobile money accounts

Adults with an account (%), 2024

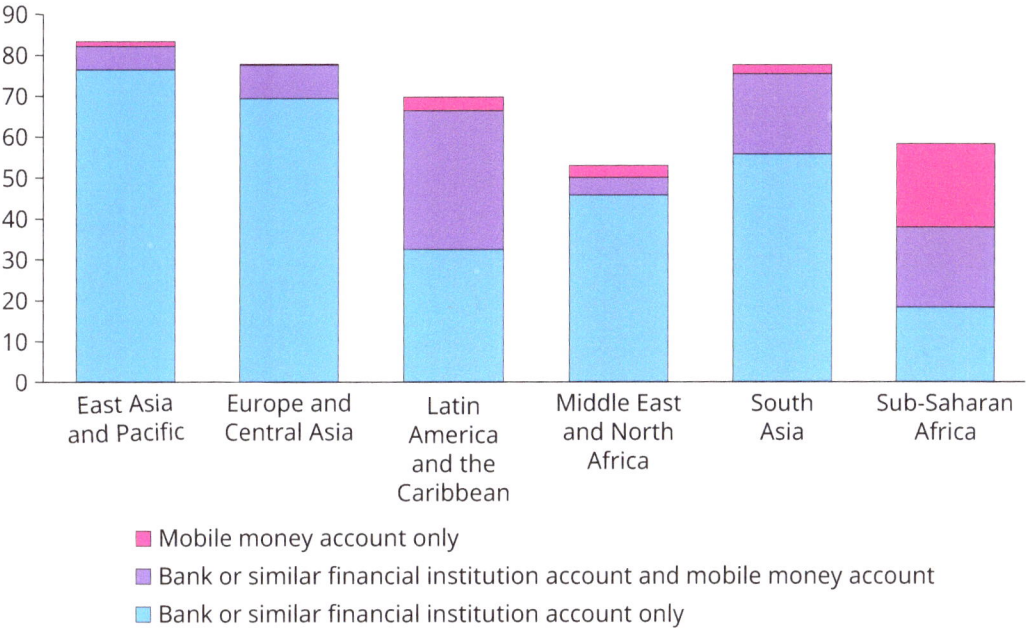

■ Mobile money account only
■ Bank or similar financial institution account and mobile money account
■ Bank or similar financial institution account only

Source: Global Findex Database 2025.

Almost half of adults in low- and middle-income economies have a digitally enabled account

A mobile money account is not the only way to use financial services with a mobile phone. Many adults who have only an account at a bank or similar financial institution, and not a mobile money account, make payments from their account using a card or app on a mobile phone, which means their accounts are digitally enabled. Since mobile money accounts are also by definition digitally enabled, more than half of adults in low- and middle-income economies today have a digitally enabled account.

In Latin America and the Caribbean and Sub-Saharan Africa, most adults have a digitally enabled account as a function of the fact that they have mobile money accounts. In East Asia and Pacific, Europe and Central Asia, and the Middle East and North Africa, however, accessing an account at a bank or similar financial institution using a card or mobile phone is more common than using mobile money (refer to figure 2.1.6). South Asia is the only region where fewer than half of account owners have a digitally enabled account.

Figure 2.1.6 Most account owners in low- and middle-income economies have a digitally enabled account

Adults with an account (%), 2024

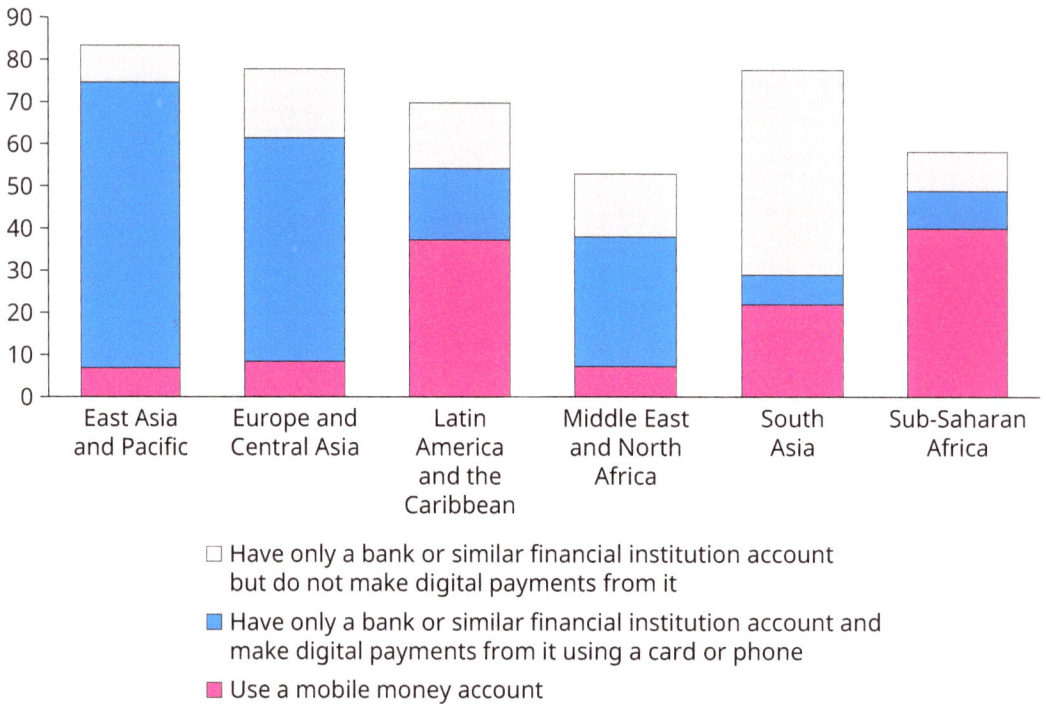

Legend:
- ☐ Have only a bank or similar financial institution account but do not make digital payments from it
- ■ (blue) Have only a bank or similar financial institution account and make digital payments from it using a card or phone
- ■ (pink) Use a mobile money account

Source: Global Findex Database 2025.

The role of mobile money accounts in Sub-Saharan Africa

In Sub-Saharan Africa, mobile money rather than traditional banks or similar financial institutions increasingly drives account ownership. The region is home to all 19 world economies in which more banked adults have only a mobile money account than have an account at a bank or similar financial institution: Benin, Burkina Faso, Cameroon, the Democratic Republic of Congo, the Republic of Congo, Côte d'Ivoire, Gabon, Ghana, Guinea, Liberia, Madagascar, Malawi, Mali, Mozambique, Sierra Leone, Tanzania, Uganda, Zambia, and Zimbabwe. In 2014, mobile money accounts were concentrated in the economies of East Africa. Since then, however, mobile money has spread to economies in West Africa and beyond (refer to map 2.1.3). In 2024, average mobile money account ownership in each of the four subregions of Sub-Saharan Africa—Central, East, Southern, and West—was about 40 percent (refer to figure 2.1.7).[9]

---

9   Subregions here are as defined by the African Union.

Map 2.1.3 Mobile money accounts both grew and spread across Sub-Saharan Africa between 2014 and 2024

Adults with a mobile money account (%)

a. 2014

b. 2024

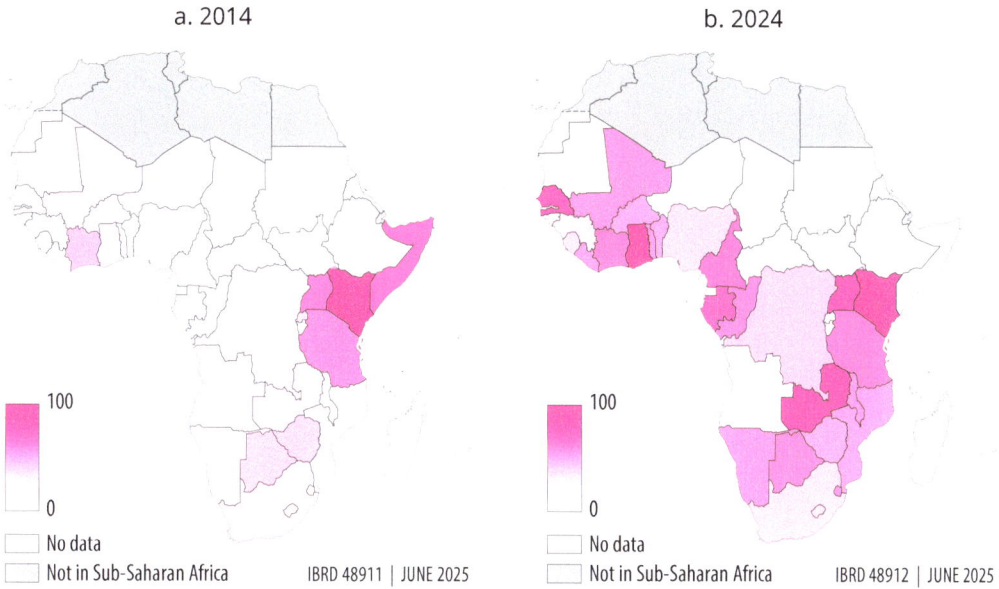

100

0

☐ No data
☐ Not in Sub-Saharan Africa   IBRD 48911 | JUNE 2025

100

0

☐ No data
☐ Not in Sub-Saharan Africa   IBRD 48912 | JUNE 2025

Source: Global Findex Database 2025.

Figure 2.1.7 Across the four subregions of Sub-Saharan Africa, about 40 percent of adults have a mobile money account

Adults with an account (%), 2014–24

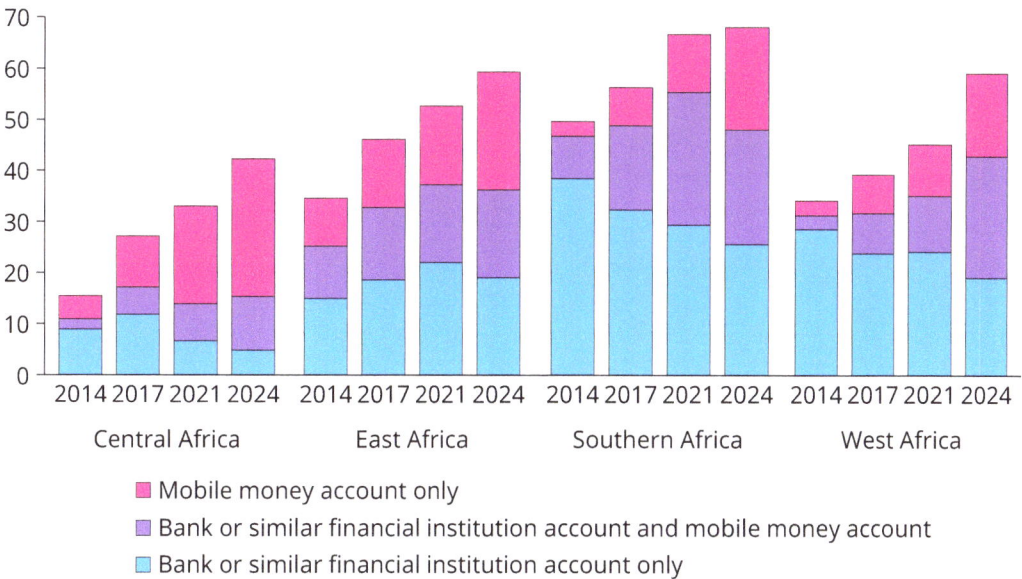

■ Mobile money account only
■ Bank or similar financial institution account and mobile money account
■ Bank or similar financial institution account only

Source: Global Findex Database 2025.

Account ownership gaps are narrowing, but not everywhere and not for everyone

Not all groups have benefited equally from growth in account ownership since 2011. Although progress continues, women, the poor, the young, the less educated, people who are out of the workforce, and people living in rural environments remain less likely than men, the rich, older adults, educated adults, those in the workforce, and urban residents to have an account (refer to figure 2.1.8).[10]

Figure 2.1.8 **Gaps in account ownership among underserved groups remain in nearly every region of the world**

Adults with an account (%), 2024

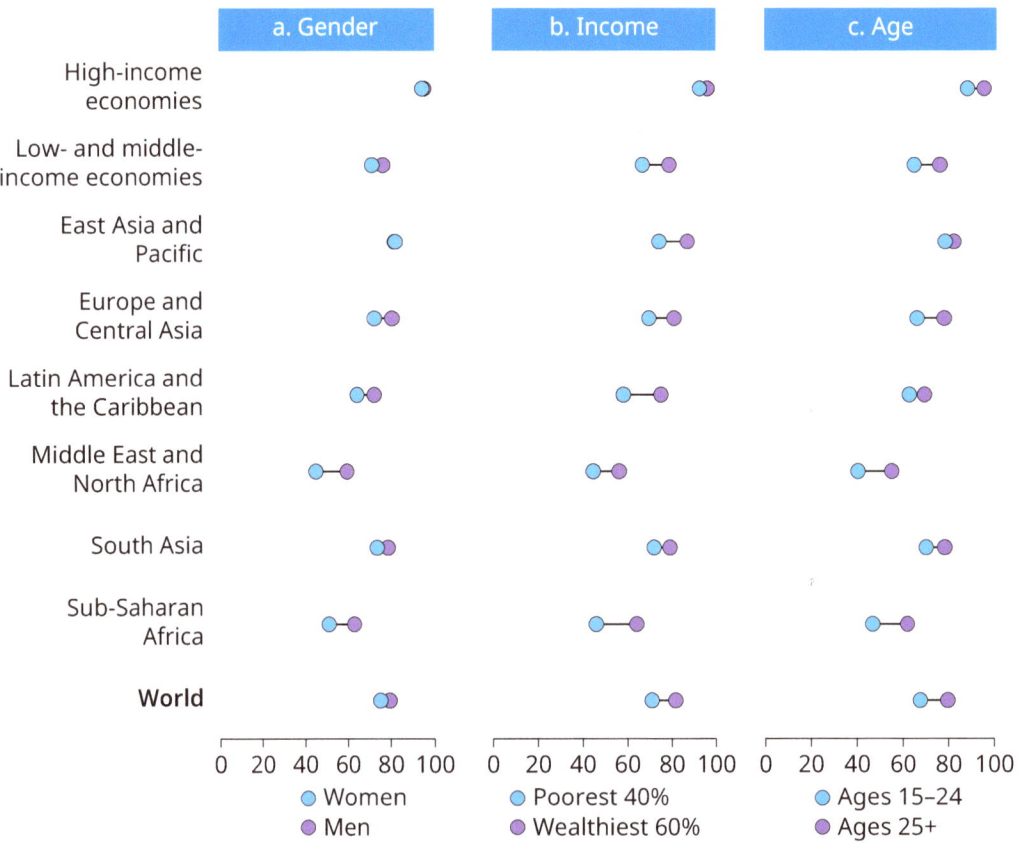

(Figure continued next page)

---

10   Regression results for a pooled sample with country fixed effects confirm this, and the results are statistically significant.

Figure 2.1.8 Gaps in account ownership among underserved groups remain in nearly every region of the world *(continued)*

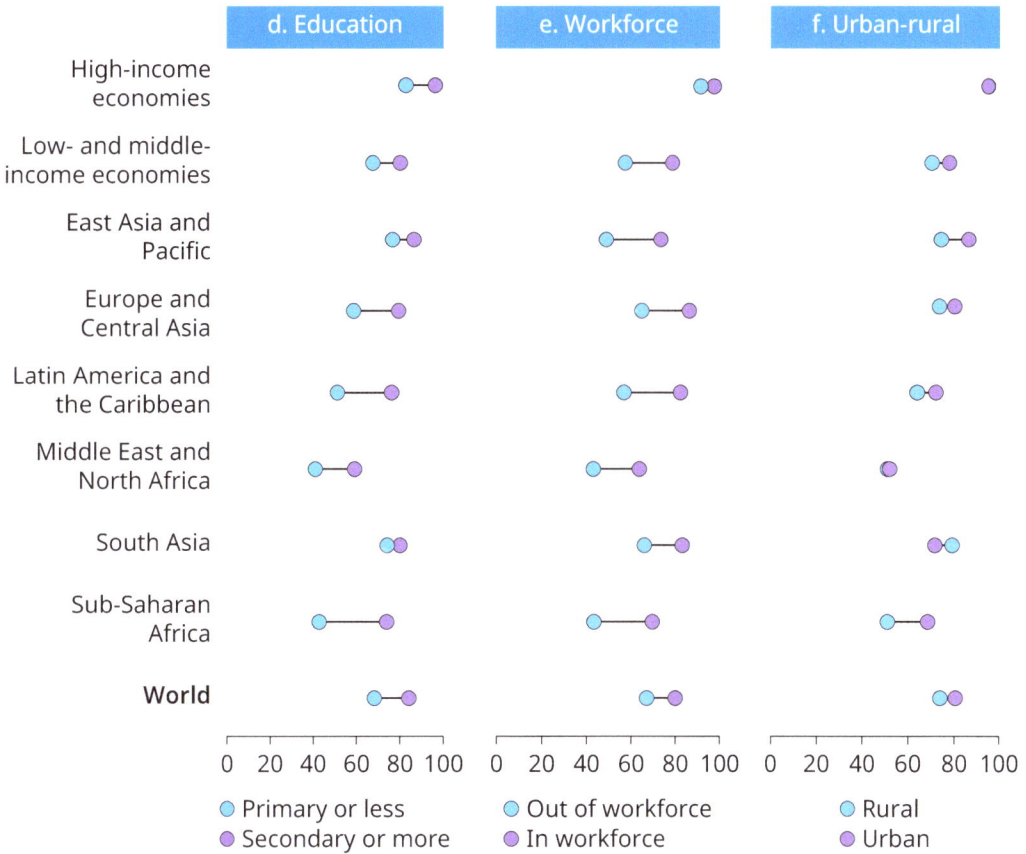

Source: Global Findex Database 2025.

Note: Information on workforce status for adults in China is not available.

Account ownership has increased among both men and women, and the gender gap has narrowed

Globally, 81 percent of men and 77 percent of women have accounts—representing a gender gap of 4 percentage points (refer to figure 2.1.8, panel a). Low- and middle-income economies show a similar gender gap, at 5 percentage points, with 78 percent of men and 73 percent of women having an account. Although account ownership increased among both men and women between 2021 and 2024, the gender gaps remained the same, despite narrowing from 9 percentage points globally and 10 percentage points in low- and middle-income economies between 2011 and 2024 (refer to figure 2.1.9, panel a).[11]

---

11   The 9 percentage point gap is a legacy of how the World Bank Group categorized the world's economies by income group in 2011. Some economies have graduated to high-income status since the first round of data collection. Global Findex 2025 uses the World Bank's fiscal year 2024 income classification for all rounds of data to ensure consistency of group composition for aggregate averages. If the fiscal year 2024 income classification were applied to 2011 data, the 2011 gap would instead be 10 percentage points.

Figure 2.1.9 Gender and income gaps in account ownership narrowed in low- and middle-income economies between 2011 and 2024

Adults with an account (%), 2011–24

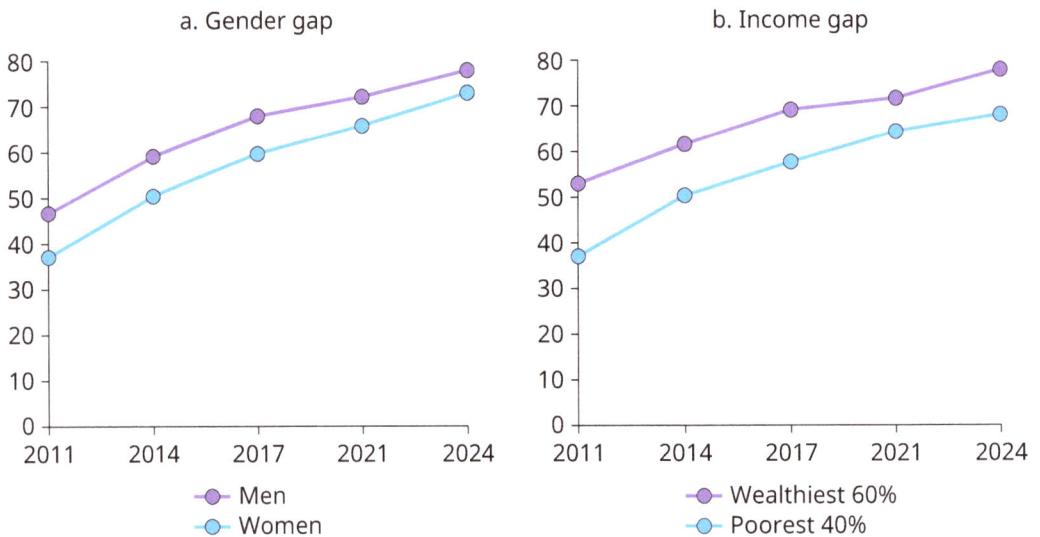

a. Gender gap

b. Income gap

Men
Women

Wealthiest 60%
Poorest 40%

Source: Global Findex Database 2025.

Account ownership particularly benefits women beyond the general positive development outcomes mentioned at the opening of this section. Women with accounts are better able to exert control over their finances and household expenditures and have increased control over their earnings. This helps shift gender norms in their favor.[12]

Sub-Saharan Africa and the Middle East and North Africa continued in 2024 to report gender gaps of 12 and 15 percentage points, respectively—more than twice the average for low- and middle-income economies. In contrast, the gender gap in East Asia and Pacific is not statistically significant. Latin America and the Caribbean and Europe and Central Asia each have gender gaps of 8 percentage points.

The data also reflect appreciable differences within regions. South Asia is a case in point. India, Nepal, and Sri Lanka have gender gaps that are not statistically significant. But gender gaps in Bangladesh (20 percentage points) and Pakistan (30 percentage points) are four or more times greater than the global gender gap.

---

12   Aker et al. (2016); Ashraf, Karlan, and Yin (2010); Field et al. (2021); Heath and Riley (2024); Prina (2015).

On average, high-income economies do not have statistically significant gender gaps in account ownership, because account ownership is nearly universal in these economies.

In Sub-Saharan Africa, mobile money accounts have made access more equal among men and women

The spread of mobile money has been touted as creating new opportunities to better serve financially underserved groups, such as women and poor people.[13] A closer look at Sub-Saharan Africa—the only region with economies in which 20 percent or more of adults have only a mobile money account—shows that ownership of only a mobile money account has increased among both men and women. Whereas on average Sub-Saharan Africa has a gender gap of 11 percentage points in ownership of accounts at a financial institution—that is, among people who have either an account at a bank or similar financial institution or both such an account and a mobile money account—there is no significant gender gap among adults who have only a mobile money account. This finding holds in the three economies outside of Sub-Saharan Africa in which more than 10 percent of adults have only a mobile money account: Colombia, Paraguay, and the Philippines.

The income gap in account ownership remains, despite increases in account ownership among all adults

Poorer adults around the world are less likely than wealthier ones to have an account. Among adults in the wealthiest 60 percent of households within economies, 83 percent worldwide have an account, compared with 72 percent among those in the poorest 40 percent of households within economies (refer to figure 2.1.8, panel b). That represents an income gap of 11 percentage points. This gap was wider in 2024 than it was in 2021, although it was lower than the 15 percentage point gap in 2011. The current level is comparable to that in 2017. In low- and middle-income economies, the income gap is 12 percentage points, similarly up from that in 2021 but again comparable to that in 2017 and down from the same measurement in 2011 (refer to figure 2.1.9, panel b).

Some regions and economies have larger account ownership income gaps. Latin America and the Caribbean and Sub-Saharan Africa have gaps that are larger than average, at 17 percentage points and 18 percentage points, respectively. At 37 percentage points—triple the average for low- and middle-income economies—Viet Nam has the largest income gap in the world. Account ownership grew between 2011 and 2024 for adults both in the wealthiest 60 percent and in

---

13   G20 and GPFI (2020).

the poorest 40 percent of Vietnamese households. The growth rate for adults in the wealthiest 60 percent far outstripped that for adults in the poorest 40 percent, however, resulting in an income gap that widened from 17 percentage points in 2011 to 37 percentage points in 2024.

Meanwhile, the gap in account ownership between adults in richer and poorer households in high-income economies is not statistically significant, on average, because account ownership is nearly universal in these economies. There are some exceptions, however. In 10 high-income economies, the income gap in account ownership is in the double digits. It is as large as 31 percentage points in Panama and 27 percentage points in Romania.

Account ownership differs by age group

Account ownership is higher among older adults—that is, those ages 25 and up—than among younger adults (those between the ages of 15 and 24).[14] Worldwide, 81 percent of older adults have an account, but just 69 percent of younger adults do, for a gap of 12 percentage points (refer to figure 2.1.8, panel c). This gap has narrowed slightly since 2011, when it was 17 percentage points. The gap's size and trend are similar for both high-income and low- and middle-income economies.

The account ownership age gap shows some regional variations. At 15 percentage points, the average age gap in the Middle East and North Africa and Sub-Saharan Africa is about twice the average age gap in other regions. Notably, these two regions have a large share of young adults, with a quarter and a third of their adults, respectively, falling into the younger age bracket.

Gaps in ownership of accounts at banks or similar financial institutions are driving the age gaps in these two regions. In Sub-Saharan Africa, where 20 percent of all adults have only a mobile money account, there is no age gap among those with only a mobile money account. And in economies such as the Republic of Congo, Ghana, and Kenya, the gaps in account ownership at banks or similar financial institutions are the reverse of the age gaps among those who have only mobile money accounts; as a result, overall the gap in account ownership in these economies is not statistically significant. To illustrate, in Kenya, 48 percent of older adults have an account at a bank or similar financial institution, compared with 41 percent of younger adults, for an age gap of 7 percentage points.

---

14   Some countries restrict account ownership to ages 21 and above.

Meanwhile, just 42 percent of older adults have only a mobile money account, compared with 49 percent of younger adults, for a similar age gap of 7 percentage points, but in the other direction.

Account ownership also varies by educational attainment

Among less-educated adults—those who have a primary education or less—account ownership is lower than among adults with at least a secondary education (refer to figure 2.1.8, panel d). In low- and middle-income economies, the gap in account ownership between those two groups is 13 percentage points. This gap was 17 percentage points in 2011, so it has narrowed over the years. Less-educated adults are also more likely to be poor, which may help explain the gap.

At 31 percentage points, Sub-Saharan Africa is the region with the largest gap in account ownership between less- and more-educated adults. There are wide variations, however, in the account ownership education gap across the region's economies. In Ethiopia and Nigeria—the Sub-Saharan-African economies with the largest gaps, both at about 38 percentage points—adults with more education are almost twice as likely to have an account as adults with less education. Kenya's education gap of 13 percentage points is one of the smallest in the region and in line with the average for all low- and middle-income economies.

Workforce participation correlates with account ownership

Adults who are active in the labor force—whether employed for wages or self-employed or looking for work—are more likely to have an account than those who are out of the labor force. Globally, 80 percent of adults who are active in the labor force have an account, whereas just 67 percent of adults out of the labor force have one (refer to figure 2.1.8, panel e). This results in a gap of 13 percentage points. (These data exclude China, for which employment status data are not available.)

The gap is similar in low- and middle-income economies, but smaller by about half in high-income economies. The average gap in labor force participation is similar across regions, although there are appreciable differences across economies within regions. Again, South Asia is a case in point. At 6 percentage points, India's gap is an outlier and similar to those in high-income economies. If data for India are excluded, South Asia's average gap increases from 16 percentage points to 24 percentage points; Pakistan has the largest gap in the region at 29 percentage points.

An urban-rural gap in account ownership exists, but it is hard to quantify precisely

In low- and middle-income economies, in which account ownership is not yet universal or even close to it, account ownership is generally lower in rural areas than in urban areas (refer to figure 2.1.8, panel f). But quantifying the urban-rural gap precisely proves difficult. The distinction could be based on factors such as population density, on the presence and availability of certain services and infrastructure, or on the subjective judgment of interviewers or respondents. Definitional issues of this type become more challenging across economies. What might be considered rural in some economies, for example, might be considered urban in less densely populated economies. The Gallup World Poll—the survey to which the Global Findex survey questionnaire is added—distinguishes between rural and urban areas based on population grids[15] (sometimes, but not usually, informed by local administrative units) that directly capture the spatial concentration of people, instead of relying on respondents' or interviewers' perceptions to classify residences. The Global Findex Database 2025 uses the Gallup World Poll definition to provide account ownership averages for adults living in rural and urban areas.[16]

In low- and middle-income economies, 79 percent of adults living in urban areas have accounts versus 71 percent of those living in rural areas. Sub-Saharan Africa has the largest urban–rural gap: 70 percent of adults in urban areas have an account, compared with 52 percent of adults in rural areas, for a gap of 17 percentage points. However, gaps vary widely by economies within regions. The two economies with the largest urban–rural gaps in the world, incidentally, are outside of Sub-Saharan Africa: Moldova in Europe and Central Asia has a gap of 32 percentage points, and Cambodia in East Asia and Pacific has a gap of 31 percentage points. Consistent with determinants of other gaps, accounts at banks or similar institutions drive the urban-rural gap in Sub-Saharan Africa. The region shows no urban–rural gap among adults who have only mobile money accounts.

Reaching those who remain without accounts

The increases in account ownership since the Global Findex 2021 survey, driven by mobile money and other digital enablers, are a testament to the positive impact of financial inclusion efforts and digital connectivity. Yet the challenge of ensuring everyone who can benefit has access to an account for storing money and making and receiving payments has not yet been fully met. Worldwide, 1.3 billion adults are still unbanked. The next section explores who they are and what barriers they face.

---

15   For additional information, see OECD and EC (2020).

16   For economies in which face-to-face surveys were conducted for the Global Findex 2021 survey, account ownership among adults living in urban and rural areas is available for 2021.

2.2 Expanding access to financial accounts

A reproducibility package is available for this book in the Reproducible Research Repository at https://reproducibility.worldbank.org/catalog/299.

2.2 Expanding access to financial accounts

Around the world, people increasingly have financial accounts. Though nearly half of adults lacked such accounts in 2011, and 26 percent did in 2021, that number had fallen to just 21 percent in 2024. Despite this progress, 1.3 billion adults worldwide still lack financial accounts and are thus unable to benefit directly from the formal financial system.

As account ownership continues to grow, those who remain without accounts are disproportionately more likely to be women or poor or to have no more than a primary school education, making them more vulnerable and difficult to reach than the general population.[1]

To provide a better understanding of adults without accounts *and* how best to reach them, the Global Findex 2024 survey asked questions that explored where they live, who they are, the barriers they face to account ownership, their readiness to use accounts, and opportunities to expand account ownership (refer to box 2.2.1).

Box 2.2.1 Defining adults without accounts and clarifying survey approaches

Global Findex 2025 defines *account ownership* as having an account at a bank or similar financial institution such as a credit union, microfinance institution, or post office or with a mobile money service included in the GSMA's Mobile Money Deployment Tracker.[a] Such an account can be used at a minimum to store money safely and to send and receive payments. *Adults without an account* do not have an individual or jointly owned account at a bank or similar financial institution or a mobile money provider. Refer to chapter 2.1 for a detailed definition of account ownership.

In all regions excluding Sub-Saharan Africa, the Global Findex survey asked adults without an account about the barriers they faced to having an account at a bank or similar financial institution. In Sub-Saharan Africa, adults without an account were instead asked questions on the barriers they faced to having a mobile money account. In Bangladesh, Ethiopia, Nigeria, and the Philippines, adults without an account were asked both sets of questions. Summary statistics for both barriers to bank and similar financial institution accounts and barriers to mobile money accounts are shown as percentages of adults without an account at any financial institution.

(Box continued next page)

---

1   Foundational Building Blocks Working Group (2024).

Most adults without accounts live in just eight economies

Adults in high-income economies enjoy near-universal account ownership. Most adults without accounts live, in contrast, in low- and middle-income economies, and 53 percent of them—more than 650 million adults—reside in just eight: Bangladesh, China, the Arab Republic of Egypt, India, Indonesia, Mexico, Nigeria, and Pakistan (refer to figure 2.2.1).[2]

A large-population economy can have a high rate of account ownership and still be home to many people without accounts. For instance, both China and India have account ownership rates of nearly 90 percent, yet they are also home to the largest number of adults without accounts. Other economies in the list, such as Bangladesh, Egypt, and Pakistan, have large populations but account ownership rates of about 50 percent.

Global Findex 2025 finds that in 29 economies included in the 2024 survey, fewer than half of adults have an account. Ten of these economies are fragile or affected by conflict, and 24 are low or lower middle income.

---

2   These eight countries represent 51 percent of the global population.

The five countries with the largest number of adults without accounts have remained the same since 2011, despite significant increases in account ownership in some of them, such as India.[3]

Figure 2.2.1 More than half of adults without accounts live in just eight economies

Share of global number of adults with no account (%), 2024

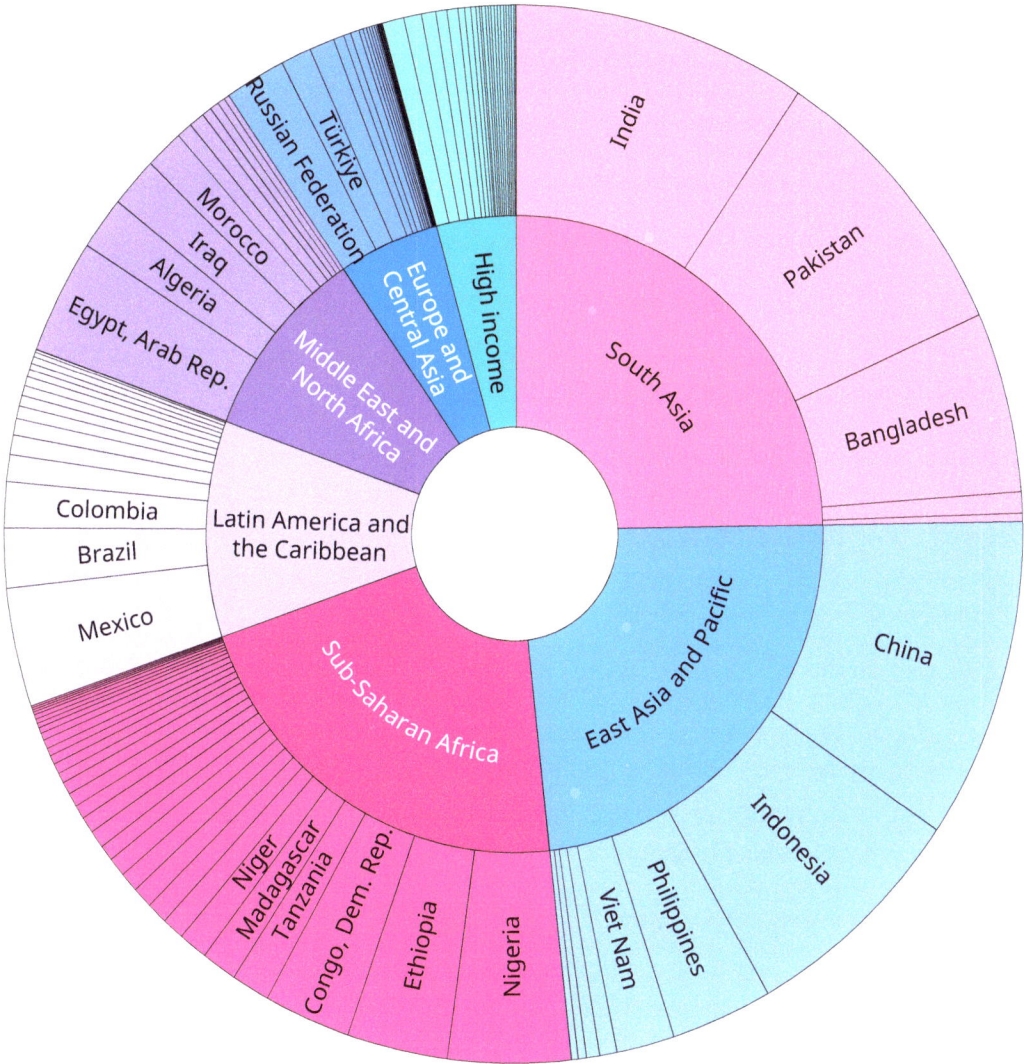

Source: Global Findex Database 2025.

---

3   These five countries are Bangladesh, China, India, Indonesia, and Pakistan. With the exception of Pakistan, they are among the most populous countries in the world.

Adults without accounts are more likely to be women, poor, and young

Understanding who adults without accounts are can help inform targeted policies to expand account access. Adults without accounts are disproportionately likely to come from more vulnerable or disenfranchised populations (refer to figure 2.2.2). Cross-country regression analysis of Global Findex 2025 data confirms that women, lower-income, less educated, younger, and more rural adults are disproportionately less likely to have accounts. Specifically, Global Findex 2025 finds that of the 1.3 billion adults globally without accounts:

- More than 700 million (55 percent) are women.
- 670 million (52 percent) are from the poorest 40 percent of households by income.
- 790 million (62 percent) have a primary education or less.
- 690 million (54 percent) are either out of the workforce or unemployed.
- 380 million (29 percent) are ages 15–24, another 590 million (46 percent) are ages 25–54, and 320 million (25 percent) are ages 55 and older.

Men and women in East Asia and Pacific are equally likely to not have an account, whereas Europe and Central Asia has the largest share of women without accounts at 61 percent (refer to figure 2.2.2, panel a). Türkiye largely drives this high percentage, as it is the second-most-populous economy in the region, and 77 percent of its adults without accounts are women.

By income level, adults without accounts in East Asia and the Pacific, at 58 percent, are disproportionately among the poorest 40 percent in their economies (refer to figure 2.2.2, panel b). In Viet Nam and China, 70 percent and 65 percent of adults without accounts, respectively, live in the poorest 40 percent of households. These are the highest and third-highest rates, respectively, in the world.

Adults without accounts also differ in respect to employment status.[4] Across low- and middle-income economies, 47 percent of adults without accounts are out of the workforce, whereas 20 percent are wage employed, and 27 percent are self-employed. Different interventions may be necessary to encourage adults in each of these groups to open and use an account. For instance, adults who receive formal wages could benefit from efforts to digitalize wages, whereas some adults who are out of the workforce might be better reached by digitalizing pensions or government transfers.

---

4   Data on employment exclude China, for which employment data were not collected.

Figure 2.2.2 Adults without accounts in low- and middle-income economies are disproportionately women and poor adults

Adults without an account (%), 2024

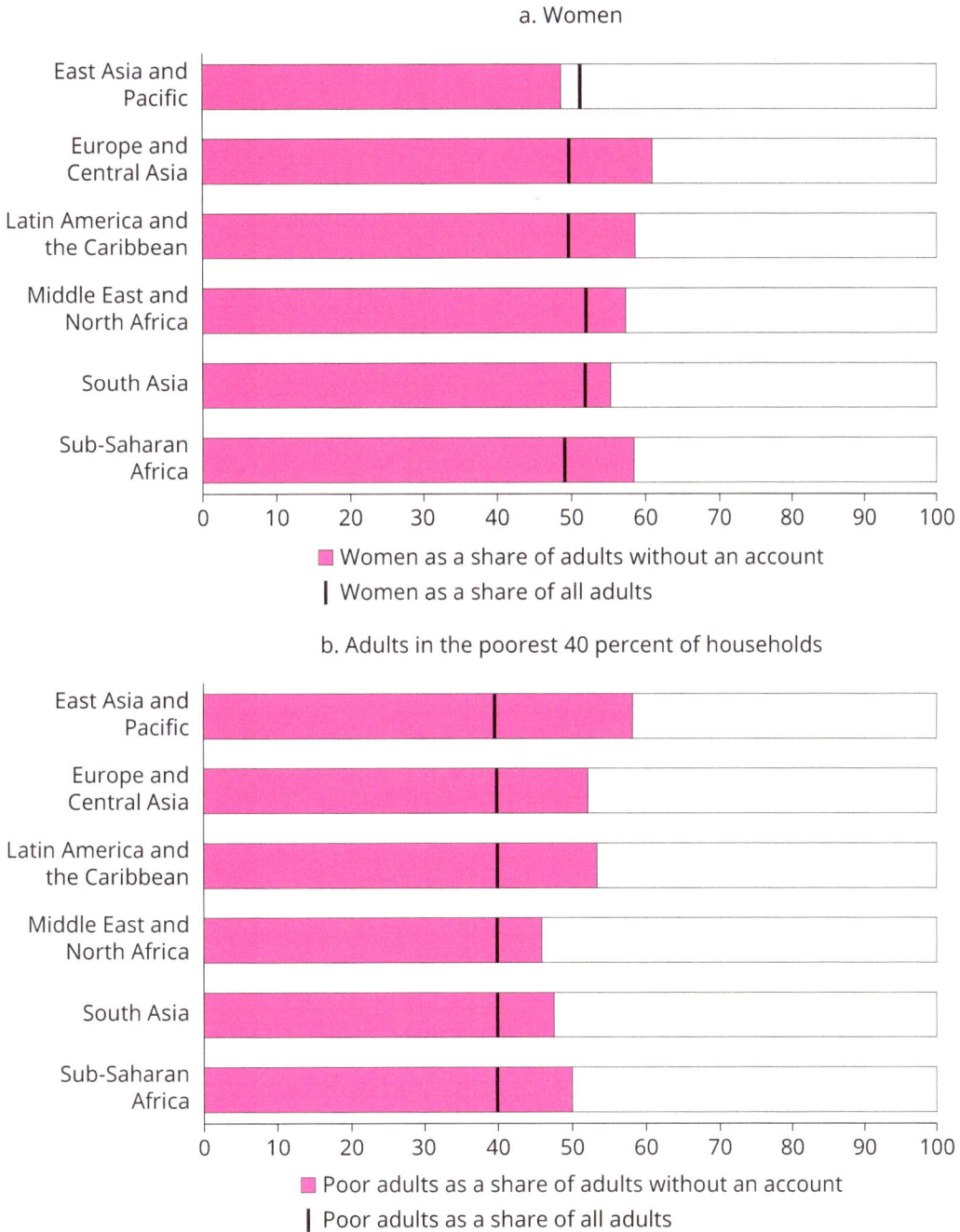

a. Women

- Women as a share of adults without an account
- Women as a share of all adults

b. Adults in the poorest 40 percent of households

- Poor adults as a share of adults without an account
- Poor adults as a share of all adults

Source: Global Findex Database 2025.

Note: This figure indicates whether women (panel a) and poor adults (panel b) are over- or underrepresented among adults without an account. Percentages to the right of the thick black line in each bar indicate that women (panel a) or poor adults (panel b) are overrepresented among adults without an account.

The connection between educational attainment and account access in a region is highly dependent on overall education rates across that region. When the focus is South Asia and Sub-Saharan Africa, the regions with the largest percentage of adults with a primary education or less, 71 percent and 74 percent of adults without an account, respectively, have a primary education or less. Efforts to expand account ownership to adults in this group must consider that they could be disproportionately vulnerable to fraud and might struggle to use an account independently, pointing to the importance of financial education and fraud protection appropriately designed across income- and education-level segments.

Not having enough money is the main barrier to bank account ownership

To provide a better understanding of barriers to account ownership, the Global Findex 2025 asked respondents without accounts at a bank or similar institution why they did not have one. Economies with greater than 89 percent account ownership (China, the Islamic Republic of Iran, Malaysia, Mongolia, and Thailand) were excluded from regional barrier calculations because the samples of adults without accounts were too small to be nationally representative. Data for India are not included in the South Asia average because of the economy's high account ownership rate but are instead reported separately (refer to box 2.2.1). Respondents in most economies in Sub-Saharan Africa (excluding Ethiopia and Nigeria) were not asked questions about bank account ownership but instead answered an alternative set of questions about why they did not have a mobile money account (discussed later in the chapter).

In answering the question, respondents could choose from a set of six barriers:

- They do not have enough money.

- Fees for financial services are too high.

- A family member already has an account.

- Financial institutions are too far away.

- They do not trust institutions.

- They lack necessary documentation.

It was possible to select more than one of these barriers, and most respondents did so (refer to figure 2.2.3).

Not having enough money is the most frequently cited barrier to bank or similar account ownership in East Asia and Pacific, the Middle East and North Africa,

Figure 2.2.3 Lack of money is the main barrier to account ownership for most adults without accounts

Adults without an account citing a given barrier as a reason for having no account at a bank or similar financial institution (%), 2024

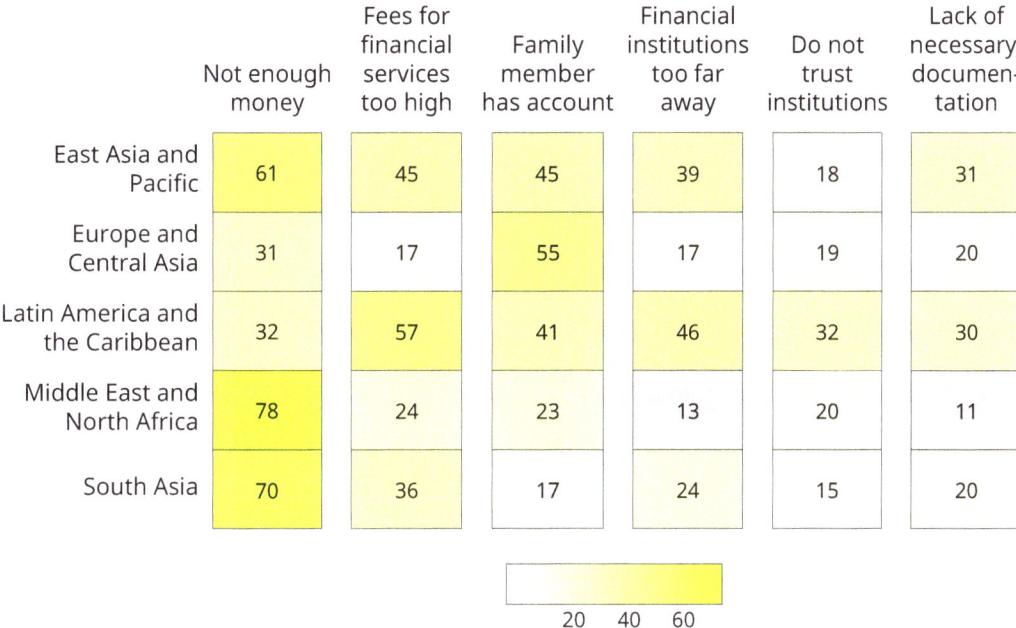

	Not enough money	Fees for financial services too high	Family member has account	Financial institutions too far away	Do not trust institutions	Lack of necessary documen-tation
East Asia and Pacific	61	45	45	39	18	31
Europe and Central Asia	31	17	55	17	19	20
Latin America and the Caribbean	32	57	41	46	32	30
Middle East and North Africa	78	24	23	13	20	11
South Asia	70	36	17	24	15	20

20   40   60

Source: Global Findex Database 2025.

Note: Respondents could choose more than one reason. Respondents in Sub-Saharan Africa without accounts answered an alternative set of questions about the barriers they face to mobile money account ownership. Economies with greater than 89 percent account ownership (China, India, the Islamic Republic of Iran, Malaysia, Mongolia, and Thailand) have been excluded from regional averages calculated.

and South Asia, as well as in both Ethiopia and Nigeria in Sub-Saharan Africa. Across regions, most adults who cited a lack of money as an obstacle listed it in addition to other reasons. Among individual economies, Egypt has the highest share of adults without an account saying a lack of money is the reason why, at 90 percent; for half of them, it was the only barrier they selected. Adults who believe they lack the money for an account may not be able to maintain minimum balances required to avoid service fees or may have so little money that they think an account is not worthwhile. Adults who cited a lack of money as an obstacle might also perceive themselves as too poor to visit a branch and use bank services.

The fees for financial services are the barrier adults without accounts cited next most commonly across almost all regions. These fees might include those for opening and maintaining an account (such as those paid monthly), as well as costs for transactions (such as checking balances, making withdrawals, and sending money). This barrier is most pervasive in Latin America and the Caribbean, where 57 percent of adults without accounts highlighted it. Account fees are also a common barrier in East Asia and Pacific and in South Asia, where more than 40 percent of adults without accounts named them; 24 percent did in the Middle East and North Africa. In Nigeria, 22 percent of adults without accounts reported the cost of financial services as a barrier. These findings highlight the potential demand for more affordable accounts, including mobile money accounts, which may have lower fees.

Using a family member's account comes next among reasons people gave for not owning a personal account. Research underscores the benefits of having a personal account in regard to women's privacy and control over their own money,[5] and adults who share an account are already familiar with financial products, which could facilitate adoption. In Europe and Central Asia, having a family member with an account was the most frequently cited barrier to account ownership; more than half of adults without accounts highlighted it. Women without accounts in the region were 21 percentage points more likely than men to point to a family member's account as a reason for not having their own. Relying on a family member's account could be driven by several factors, including differences in labor force participation and digital receipt of wages, as well as the cost for a family to have multiple accounts.

Distance to the nearest financial institution is the next most commonly cited barrier. More than 40 percent of rural residents without bank accounts highlighted the challenge of distance, unsurprisingly. This issue is also more prevalent in East Asia and Pacific and Latin America and the Caribbean, where about 40 percent of adults without an account cited it, than in other regions. Distance is the second most frequently cited barrier for adults without accounts in Ethiopia and Nigeria, where 30 percent and 47 percent of these adults highlighted it, respectively. Mobile money and fintech products that leverage local agent networks can help reduce the burden of traveling long distances to access financial services, especially in areas with high rates of mobile phone ownership.

Finally, a lack of trust in financial institutions dissuades about 20 percent of adults without accounts across low- and middle-income economies and roughly a third of adults without accounts in Latin America and the Caribbean from having accounts. In Nigeria, 25 percent of adults without accounts mentioned trust as an issue. This concern was often mentioned alongside the high costs of financial services. For instance, about 20 percent of adults without accounts in Latin America and the Caribbean mentioned both concerns. Trust may be related to the perceived safety of keeping money in an account, as well as to understanding and anticipating service fees. This further highlights the importance of targeted and appropriate

---

5   Ashraf, Karlan, and Yin (2010); Field et al. (2021); Heath and Riley (2024); Prina (2015).

Figure 2.2.4 **In India, having a family member with an account is the most common reason adults without accounts give for not having their own**

Adults without an account citing a given barrier as a reason for having no account at a bank or similar financial institution (%), 2024

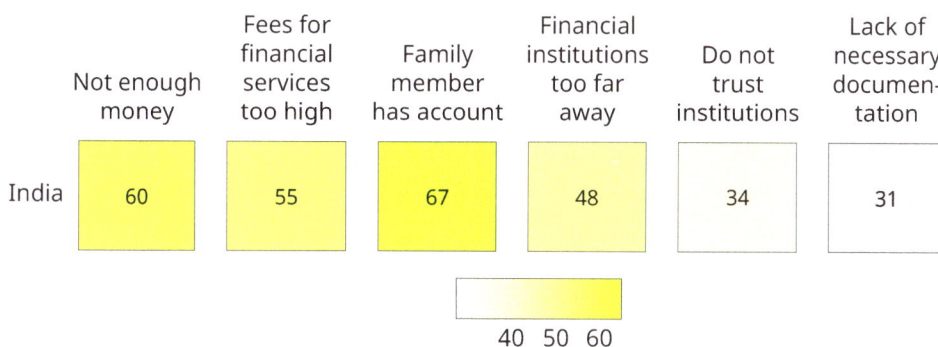

	Not enough money	Fees for financial services too high	Family member has account	Financial institutions too far away	Do not trust institutions	Lack of necessary documen-tation
India	60	55	67	48	34	31

40 50 60

Source: Global Findex Database 2025.

Note: Respondents could choose more than one reason.

financial education, as well as appropriate consumer protection measures, including transparent pricing and terms and conditions, effective handling of complaints and mechanisms for redress, and adequate fraud and cybersecurity protections.

Though India has a 90 percent account ownership rate, its large population means it still has among the largest number of adults without accounts of any economy in the world. The large sample size of Global Findex 2024 survey respondents in India yields results with a high enough degree of statistical significance to allow the barriers to account ownership to be examined. Counter to what is the case in most low- and middle-income economies, the most common reason in India for not having an account is that a family member has one (refer to figure 2.2.4). The share of adults giving this reason is notably higher than the share citing not having enough money for an account, suggesting a potential unmet demand for personal accounts among both men and women. The second-most-common barrier is not having enough money, followed by the cost of financial services and financial institutions being too far away; all three were cited by about half of adults in India without accounts.

Barriers to mobile money account ownership in Sub-Saharan Africa

For economies in Sub-Saharan Africa, the Global Findex 2025 asked why adults without any type of account do not have mobile money. Concentrating on barriers to mobile money in this region, rather than accounts at banks or similar institutions, was both practical and methodological. On the practical side, mobile money accounts are the most common and fastest-growing type of accounts in most economies in the region (discussed in chapter 2.1). The exceptions are

Ethiopia and Nigeria, where banks dominate (and where the survey included both the questions about barriers related to bank account ownership and those about mobile money account ownership). The methodological argument relates to clarity for respondents, who answer dozens of questions and often get confused or impatient if asked to respond to what sound like the same questions twice.

Respondents could choose from the following five options:

• They don't have enough money to use a mobile money account.

• They lack necessary documentation.

• Mobile money agents are too far away.

• Available mobile money products are too expensive.

• They worry about account safety.

The responses they gave for not having mobile money accounts reveal patterns similar to those found with respect to the answers respondents in other regions gave regarding banks (refer to figure 2.2.5).

Figure 2.2.5 A lack of money is the most common reason why adults without accounts in Sub-Saharan Africa do not have mobile money accounts

Adults without an account citing a given barrier as a reason for having no account at a bank or similar financial institution (%), 2024

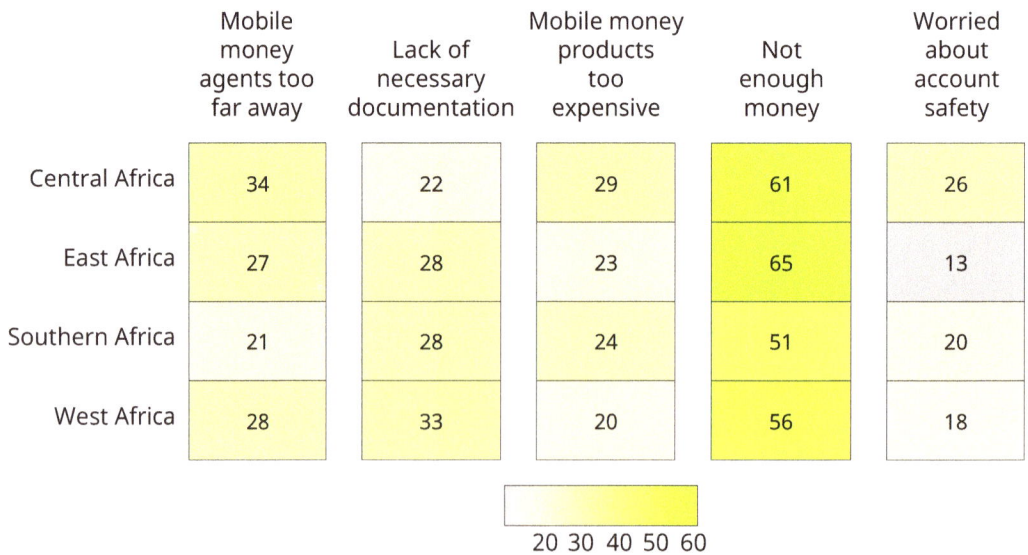

	Mobile money agents too far away	Lack of necessary documentation	Mobile money products too expensive	Not enough money	Worried about account safety
Central Africa	34	22	29	61	26
East Africa	27	28	23	65	13
Southern Africa	21	28	24	51	20
West Africa	28	33	20	56	18

20 30 40 50 60

Source: Global Findex Database 2025.

Note: Respondents could choose more than one reason. Adults without accounts in Kenya are excluded from the East Africa average because account ownership in Kenya is above 89 percent, the cutoff for inclusion.

Across Sub-Saharan Africa, not having enough money was the most frequently cited barrier to mobile money account ownership, with 59 percent of adults without accounts reporting it. This barrier's prevalence varies by subregion, though it is consistently an issue for at least half of adults without accounts in every subregion. As is the case with barriers to bank account ownership, those who said a lack of money is a barrier generally also named at least one other barrier.

Not having necessary documentation is the second-most-common barrier to mobile money account ownership in the region. Depending on the account opening due-diligence requirements for a given economy, the documentation could include the applicant's personal ID as well as some form of address verification, such as a utility bill with their name on it. (Spotlight 1.1 at the end of section 1 provides more information on the challenges people without IDs face in Sub-Saharan Africa.)

Distance to a mobile money agent is an issue for 28 percent of adults without accounts. Although mobile money agents are more pervasive than commercial banks in many of the region's economies,[6] it might still be difficult for some adults to access them, especially in more remote areas. In Central Africa, this is an obstacle for a little more than a third of adults, compared with 21 percent in Southern Africa.

The cost of mobile money products is a barrier for 23 percent of adults without accounts, with limited subregional variation, though wide variation at the level of individual economies: 47 percent of adults without accounts in Chad highlighted costs, whereas just 8 percent did in The Gambia.

Research suggests that competition among mobile money agents could help reduce the costs associated with mobile money accounts. Evidence from Ghana finds that fees decrease after mobile agents enter local markets.[7] Taxes on digital payment services might also be increasing the cost of mobile money transactions, given the existence of such taxes in many economies.[8] In addition to formal costs on transactions and withdrawals, mobile agents might also be overcharging customers; this highlights the importance of agent oversight.[9]

Finally, 18 percent of adults without mobile money accounts worried about account safety. The share of adults without an account who reported this as a barrier ranges from 26 percent in Central Africa to 13 percent in East Africa (see chapter 1.3 for a discussion of safe digital use).

---

6   GSMA (2019).
7   Annan (2024).
8   Hearson et al. (2024).
9   For additional information, refer to Adams et al. (2025).

Continued use of an account is not guaranteed, as some adults without accounts previously owned one

Adults without a bank or similar financial institution account were also asked whether they had previously owned one. In Europe and Central Asia, the Middle East and North Africa, and South Asia, only 10 percent or less of adults without an account at a bank or similar financial institution previously owned one. In East Asia and Pacific, 15 percent of adults without an account at a bank or similar financial institution previously had one; this share was 18 percent in Indonesia. In Latin America and the Caribbean, nearly a quarter of adults without an account at a bank or similar financial institution had an account in the past, a pattern consistent across all economies in the region except Nicaragua.

These patterns might reflect perceived trade-offs between the benefits of having an account and the associated costs, such as fees, bad service, or poorly designed or inappropriate products that do not meet customer needs. The findings suggest that policies to increase account ownership should focus not only on reducing barriers, but also on improving the customer experience and product design to support continued account use and customer retention.

Digital readiness can help increase account ownership in Sub-Saharan Africa

The massive impact that digital financial services have had on financial inclusion over the past decade provides clear opportunities for reaching adults without accounts. In Sub-Saharan Africa specifically, for example, 42 percent of all adults—more than 300 million people—do not have accounts, the highest rate in the world. Of the 50 economies around the world in Global Findex 2025 that have account ownership rates lower than 60 percent, 21 of them are in Sub-Saharan Africa. Given that mobile money accounts are the dominant type of account in the region and are the source of most of the growth in account ownership, it is important to examine what people without accounts might need to open one.

Opening a mobile money account in the region typically has three requirements: personal ID and necessary documentation, a mobile phone, and a SIM card registered in the phone owner's name. (Only a small number of adults report using a SIM card registered to someone else, as discussed in chapter 1.1.) These requirements are sequential: to obtain SIM cards in their names, people must first have personal IDs, and to open mobile money accounts, they must have SIM cards registered in their names.

People without accounts who have identification and own both a mobile phone and a SIM card registered in their name are *digitally ready* to become account owners. Overall, about a quarter of adults without accounts in Sub-Saharan Africa have all three prerequisites, making them digitally ready for mobile money account ownership.

An important caveat is that the ecosystem for mobile money must also be well developed to support mobile money users. This includes investments in infrastructure, such as reliable mobile broadband and electricity, which allow financial services to function consistently and reach rural or underserved areas. A supportive regulatory environment is also important: clear financial regulations, strong consumer protection frameworks, and mechanisms for dispute resolution can build trust in the financial system, encouraging adoption and sustained use. Finally, the private sector plays a central role in designing and offering financial products that are relevant, affordable, and easy to use for people currently outside the financial system. Without appropriate, user-friendly services, the infrastructure alone will not translate into meaningful financial access.

With that caveat, across the region, two-thirds of adults without accounts have IDs, and women are as likely as men to have them, potentially enabling them to easily obtain a SIM card registered in their name. ID possession among adults without accounts varies by subregion (refer to figure 2.2.6). In Central and East Africa, 73 percent and 75 percent of adults without accounts, respectively, have IDs; in West Africa, on the other hand, just 58 percent do. As discussed in spotlight 1.1, in eight Sub-Saharan African economies, less than 70 percent of people have IDs; four of the countries are in West Africa. Government initiatives to expand ID ownership have proven effective on this front.[10]

Regarding mobile phone ownership, just over half of adults without accounts in the region have mobile phones, though there is substantial variation across subregions. For example, whereas almost two-thirds of adults without accounts in West Africa have mobile phones, less than half of adults without accounts in Central and East Africa do. In Ethiopia, only 39 percent of adults without an account have mobile phones. Men and women without accounts are equally likely to have mobile phones, except in East Africa, where 50 percent of men without accounts have phones compared with 37 percent of women.

---

10   Lawson (2023); Tassot and Alberro (2024).

Figure 2.2.6 Digital enablers are necessary for expanding mobile money account ownership in Sub-Saharan Africa

Adults without an account (%), 2024

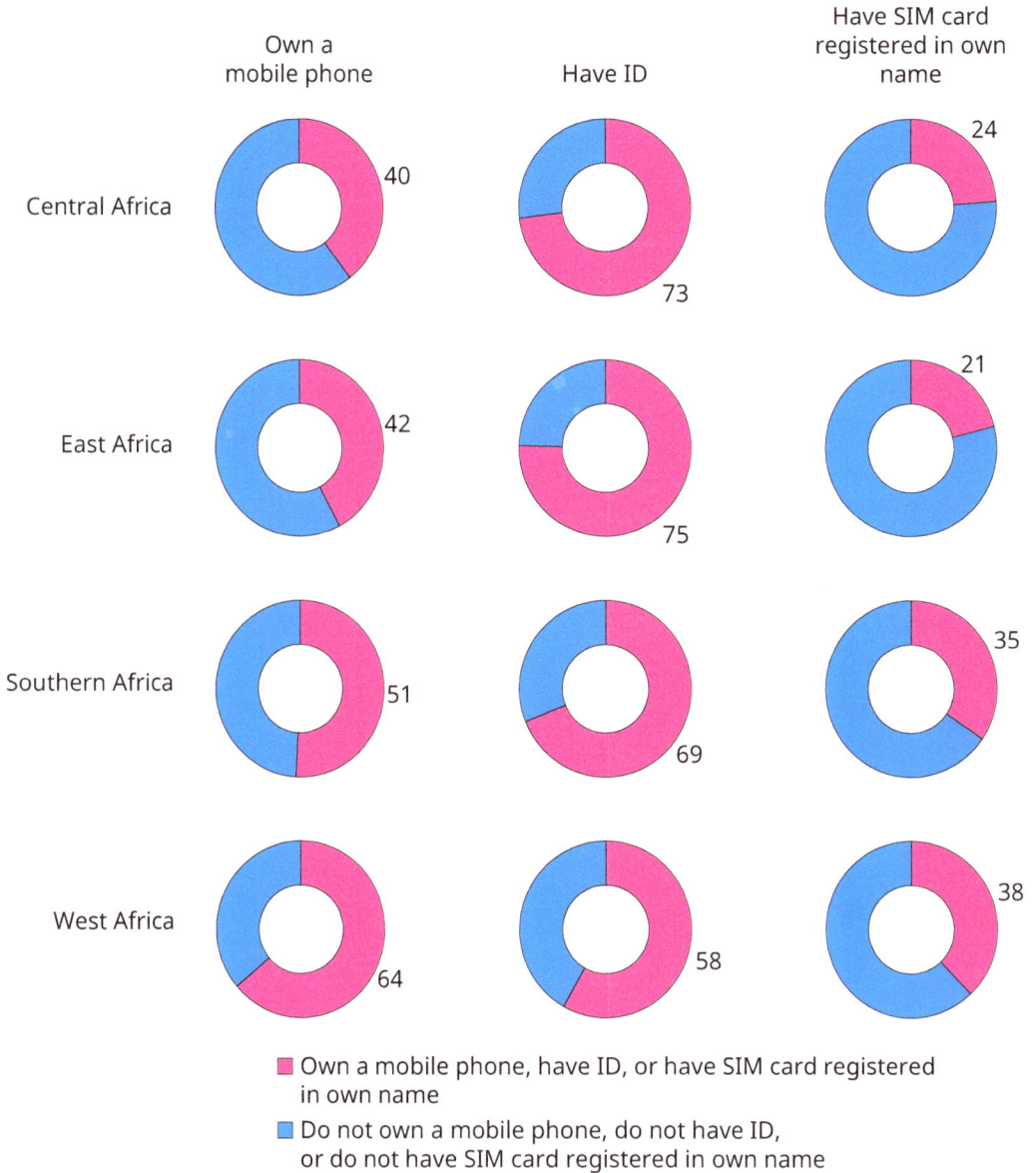

	Own a mobile phone	Have ID	Have SIM card registered in own name
Central Africa	40	73	24
East Africa	42	75	21
Southern Africa	51	69	35
West Africa	64	58	38

■ Own a mobile phone, have ID, or have SIM card registered in own name
■ Do not own a mobile phone, do not have ID, or do not have SIM card registered in own name

Sources: Global Findex Database 2025 and Identification for Development (ID4D)–Global Findex Database 2025.

Finally, about a third of adults without accounts in Sub-Saharan Africa have SIM cards registered in their own names. SIM card ownership ranges from 20 percent or less in the Democratic Republic of Congo, Ethiopia, Madagascar, and Mozambique to more than 70 percent in Botswana and Mauritania. Men and women without accounts are equally likely to have SIM cards across Sub-Saharan Africa, with slight variations in East and Southern Africa, where women are 7 and 5 percentage points less likely, respectively, than men to have SIM cards registered in their own names.

Considering these foundations of digital readiness, there may be existing opportunities to reach some adults without accounts in Sub-Saharan Africa, particularly the 26 percent of them who have IDs, mobile phones, and their own SIM cards. This group totals more than 80 million people, equal shares of them women and men.

The biggest barrier to account ownership among digitally ready adults who lack accounts but have mobile phones, IDs, and SIM cards is that they do not have enough money. About half of them name that as a barrier, whereas about 20 percent cite each of the other barriers offered as responses to the survey question, such as distance to an agent.

The share of digitally ready adults ranges from more than half of adults without accounts in Botswana, Burkina Faso, and Namibia to a quarter or less of adults without accounts in 14 other Sub-Saharan African economies. This variation in readiness points to the importance of having economy-specific strategies to promote financial inclusion. Some economies may be able to reach populations without accounts by digitalizing payments, but others may first need to focus on getting these adults mobile phones or personal IDs, registering their SIM cards, or giving priority in policy making and budgets to supply-side foundations, such as agent networks, cell towers, and other critical regulatory and physical infrastructure.

Smartphone ownership can help increase account ownership and usage of accounts

As discussed in chapter 1.2, smartphones typically enable their owners to access a wider range of digital services than basic phones do. In the context of financial services, banking apps and those associated with mobile money accounts may bring additional benefit by enabling real-time account monitoring and better user experience and by offering features such as bill payments, money transfers, and budgeting tools, enabling users to manage their finances more effectively. Some mobile money providers also offer digital and financial literacy training via their apps. These features and others enhance the benefit of smartphone ownership for all financial account owners, including those with less financial experience. In all regions except South Asia and Sub-Saharan Africa, more than half of adults without accounts have a smartphone (refer to figure 2.2.7).

Figure 2.2.7 In low- and middle-income economies, 42 percent of adults without an account own a smartphone

Adults without an account (%), 2024

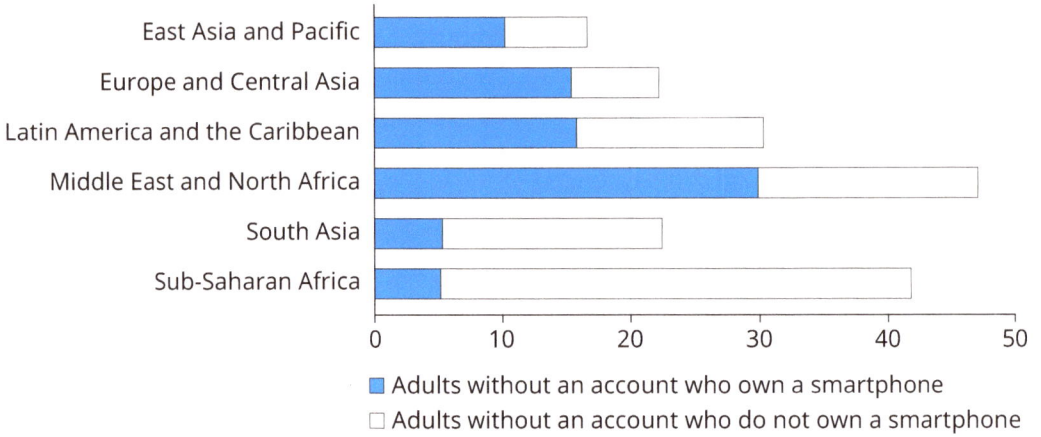

Source: Global Findex Database 2025.

Demonstrating the benefits of use can motivate account adoption

Beyond being digitally ready, people who remain without accounts must also have an incentive to access and use financial services if they are to be persuaded to open and maintain accounts. Without convenient local entry points and compelling, user-friendly financial services, adults without accounts may not find account ownership worthwhile. The next section explores the Global Findex 2025 data on using financial services, specifically saving, borrowing, and payments.

References

Adams, Paul, Francis Annan, William Blackmon, Xavier Giné, Lina Hochhalter, Brian Mwesigwa, and Arianna Zapanta. 2025. *Transaction Cost Index: Year Two Comparative Report*. New York: Innovations for Poverty Action. https://poverty-action.org/sites /default/files/2025-03/Transactional%20cost%20index_8_0.pdf.

Aker, Jenny C., Rachid Boumnijel, Amanda McClelland, and Niall Tierney. 2016. "Payment Mechanisms and Antipoverty Programs: Evidence from a Mobile Money Cash Transfer Experiment in Niger." *Economic Development and Cultural Change* 65 (1): 1–37. https://www.jstor.org/stable/26545224.

Allen, Franklin, Asli Demirgüç-Kunt, Leora Klapper, and Maria Soledad Martinez Peria. 2016. "The Foundations of Financial Inclusion: Understanding Ownership and Use of Formal Accounts." *Journal of Financial Intermediation* 27 (July): 1–30. https://doi.org/10.1016/J .JFI.2015.12.003.

Annan, Francis. 2024. "Randomized Entry." NBER Working Paper 33134, National Bureau of Economic Research, Cambridge, MA. https://doi.org/10.3386/w33134.

Ashraf, Nava, Dean Karlan, and Wesley Yin. 2010. "Female Empowerment: Impact of a Commitment Savings Product in the Philippines." *World Development* 38 (3): 333–44. https://doi.org/10.1016/j.worlddev.2009.05.010.

Beck, Thorsten, Asli Demirgüç-Kunt, and Ross Levine. 2004. "Finance, Inequality, and Poverty: Cross-Country Evidence." NBER Working Paper 10979, National Bureau of Economic Research, Cambridge, MA. https://doi.org/10.3386/W10979.

Bruhn, Miriam, and Inessa Love. 2014. "The Real Impact of Improved Access to Finance: Evidence from Mexico." *Journal of Finance* 69 (3): 1347–76. https://doi.org/10.1111 /JOFI.12091.

Burgess, Robin, and Rohini Pande. 2005. "Do Rural Banks Matter? Evidence from the Indian Social Banking Experiment." *American Economic Review* 95 (3): 780–95. https://doi .org/10.1257/0002828054201242.

Field, Erica, Rohini Pande, Natalia Rigol, Simone Schaner, and Charity Troyer Moore. 2021. "On Her Own Account: How Strengthening Women's Financial Control Impacts Labor Supply and Gender Norms." *American Economic Review* 111 (7): 2342–75. https://doi .org/10.1257/aer.20200705.

Foundational Building Blocks Working Group. 2024. "Foundational Building Blocks for Financial Inclusion: Insights and Call to Action to Reach the Last Mile." Policy Note, United Nations Secretary-General's Special Advocate for Inclusive Finance for Development, New York. https://www.unsgsa.org/publications/foundational-building -blocks-financial-inclusion-insights-and-call-action-reach-last-mile-0.

G20 (Group of Twenty) and GPFI (Global Partnership for Financial Inclusion). 2020. "G20 High-Level Policy Guidelines on Digital Financial Inclusion for Youth,

Women and SMEs." G20 Saudi Arabia 2020, Riyadh. https://www.unsgsa.org/sites
/default/files/resources-files/2021-02/G20%20digi%20fin%20youth.pdf.

Gertler, Paul, Sean Higgins, Aisling Scott, and Enrique Seira. 2023. "Using Lotteries to
Attract Deposits." NBER Working Paper 31529, National Bureau of Economic Research,
Cambridge, MA. https://doi.org/10.3386/W31529.

GSMA. 2019. "Harnessing the Power of Mobile Money to Achieve the Sustainable
Development Goals." London, GSMA. https://www.gsma.com/solutions-and-impact
/connectivity-for-good/mobile-for-development/wp-content/uploads/2019/10/GSMA
-Harnessing-the-power-of-mobile-money-to-achieve-the-SDGs.pdf.

Hearson, Martin, Philip Mader, Mary Abounabhan, Marco Carreras, Awa Diouf, Adrienne
Lees, Hannelore Niesten, Fabrizio Santoro, and Christopher Wales. 2024. "Taxing
Mobile Money in Africa: Risk and Reward." ICTD Policy Brief 10 (version 2),
International Centre for Tax and Development, Institute of Development Studies,
Brighton, UK. https://doi.org/10.19088/ICTD.2024.071.

Heath, Rachel, and Emma Riley. 2024. "Digital Financial Services and Women's
Empowerment: Experimental Evidence from Tanzania." PDF, September 13, 2024.
https://drive.google.com/file/d/1CcpAdDk5-dHvjGZyASnurZi970IjwRMa/view.

Jack, William, and Tavneet Suri. 2014. "Risk Sharing and Transactions Costs: Evidence
from Kenya's Mobile Money Revolution." *American Economic Review* 104 (1): 183–223.
https://doi.org/10.1257/aer.104.1.183.

Karlan, Dean, Aishwarya Lakshmi Ratan, and Jonathan Zinman. 2014. "Savings by and for
the Poor: A Research Review and Agenda." *Review of Income and Wealth* 60 (1): 36–78.
https://doi.org/10.1111/roiw.12101.

Karlan, Dean S., and Jonathan Zinman. 2012. "List Randomization for Sensitive Behavior:
An Application for Measuring Use of Loan Proceeds." *Journal of Development Economics*
98 (1): 71–75. https://doi.org/10.1016/J.JDEVECO.2011.08.006.

Lawson, Cina. 2023. "How Togo Is Charting Its Digital Inclusion Journey through Innovative
Solutions." Forum Institutional, September 19, 2023. https://www.weforum.org
/stories/2023/09/togo-digital-inclusion-journey-to-equitable-access/.

Lee, Jean N., Jonathan Morduch, Saravana Ravindran, Abu Shonchoy, and Hassan Zaman.
2021. "Poverty and Migration in the Digital Age: Experimental Evidence on Mobile
Banking in Bangladesh." *American Economic Journal: Applied Economics* 13 (1): 38–71.
https://doi.org/10.1257/app.20190067.

Munyegera, Ggombe Kasim, and Tomoya Matsumoto. 2016. "Mobile Money, Remittances,
and Household Welfare: Panel Evidence from Rural Uganda." *World Development*
79 (March): 127–37. https://doi.org/10.1016/J.WORLDDEV.2015.11.006.

OECD (Organisation for Economic Co-operation and Development) and EC (European
Commission). 2020. *Cities in the World: A New Perspective on Urbanisation.* OECD Urban
Studies. Paris: OECD Publishing. https://doi.org/10.1787/d0efcbda-en.

Prina, Silvia. 2015. "Banking the Poor via Savings Accounts: Evidence from a Field Experiment." *Journal of Development Economics* 115 (July): 16–31. https://doi.org/10.1016/J.JDEVECO.2015.01.004.

Riley, Emma. 2018. "Mobile Money and Risk Sharing against Village Shocks." *Journal of Development Economics* 135 (November): 43–58. https://doi.org/10.1016/J.JDEVECO.2018.06.015.

Suri, Tavneet, and William Jack. 2016. "The Long-Run Poverty and Gender Impacts of Mobile Money." *Science* 354 (6317): 1288–92. https://doi.org/10.1126/science.aah5309.

Tassot, Caroline, and Luis Iñaki Alberro. 2024. "Identification System in Benin: Increasing Access to Services." *Nasikiliza* (blog), June 26, 2024. https://blogs.worldbank.org/en/nasikiliza/identification-system-in-benin-increasing-access-to-services.

The Global Findex 2025 website has interactive options for using the data.

Account ownership
% adults (age 15+)

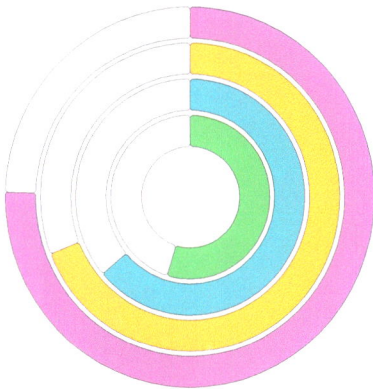

- 2014
- 2017
- 2021
- 2024

Phone ownership and types

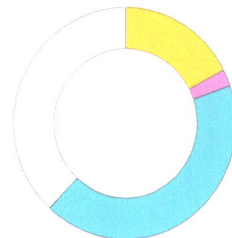

Total

- Basic phone
- Smartphone
- Feature phone
- No phone

Digital payments

GENERATE
variations of any figure in The Global Findex 2025 report including a customized mix of countries.

CLICK THROUGH
to the World Bank's Inclusive Digital Financial Services page to find country-level data visualizations.

EXPLORE
the World Bank's Data360 portal, to gain access to global development data, including Global Findex indicators.

Download the Global Findex database.
HTTP://GLOBALFINDEX.WORLDBANK.ORG/VISUALIZATIONS

Financial use

_____

A reproducibility package is available for this book in the Reproducible Research Repository at https://reproducibility.worldbank.org/catalog/299.

Financial Use

IN LOW- AND MIDDLE-INCOME ECONOMIES

Saving in an account is the most common way to save.

40%

OF ADULTS SAVE THIS WAY, **UP FROM 24% IN 2021.**
AN ADDITIONAL 15% SAVED IN OTHER WAYS,
FOR A TOTAL OF **55% OF ALL ADULTS SAVING.**

NEARLY HALF OF ADULTS WHO SAVED
FORMALLY PUT MONEY AWAY MONTHLY.

36% OF WOMEN SAVED FORMALLY COMPARED
WITH 43% OF MEN.

MORE ADULTS ARE USING
MOBILE MONEY TO SAVE.

In Sub-Saharan Africa,
23% of adults saved
this way.

Only around **39% of people
who save formally** in Latin
America and the Caribbean
receive interest on their savings.

59% OF ADULTS BORROWED MONEY IN 2024.

24%

BORROWED FORMALLY FROM A BANK, OR USING A CREDIT CARD OR MOBILE MONEY ACCOUNT.

THE REST BORROWED FROM FAMILY OR FRIENDS OR THROUGH OTHER INFORMAL METHODS.

CREDIT CARDS DOMINATE FORMAL BORROWING IN FIVE LOW- AND MIDDLE-INCOME ECONOMIES.

7% OF ADULTS IN SUB-SAHARAN AFRICA BORROWED USING MOBILE MONEY, THE SAME SHARE AS IN 2021.

82%

OF ADULTS WITH ACCOUNTS MADE OR RECEIVED A DIGITAL PAYMENT.

73% of government payment recipients and **45% of wage earners** received their money in an account.*

Does not include data for Algeria, China, the Islamic Republic of Iran, Mauritius, and Ukraine.

Only 25% of agricultural sellers in Sub-Saharan Africa were paid in an account.

Digital merchant payments are on the rise.

42% OF ADULTS PAID FOR GOODS WITH A CARD OR PHONE. **THAT'S UP FROM 35% IN 2021, MORE THAN 2 BILLION PEOPLE.**

36% OF ADULTS PURCHASED ITEMS ONLINE, BUT **ONLY TWO-THIRDS OF THEM ALSO PAID ONLINE.**

3.1 Saving

A reproducibility package is available for this book in the Reproducible Research Repository at https://reproducibility.worldbank.org/catalog/299.

3.1 Saving

No matter what their end goals may be, people save money to have more options for the future. They might want to invest in a child's education or a family business, fund their retirement, buy a home or pay for a larger purchase, or set aside resources to address emergencies.

Global Findex 2025 examines saving as a behavior, not as a product. Specifically, the survey asked respondents whether they saved or set aside any money in the past year and whether they used a bank or mobile money account to do so or saved alternatively through a semiformal method such as a savings club (refer to box 3.1.1). The survey did not ask whether people used designated savings accounts or savings products like certificates of deposit or how much they saved. As such, the data do not provide insights on whether respondents held money for long enough or saved a large enough balance to achieve a particular goal or build financial resilience. People's intentions to save and the actions they take are nonetheless foundational for both long-term investments and financial health.

Overall, in low- and middle-income economies, 55 percent of adults saved in the 12 months before taking the survey, an increase of 12 percentage points since 2021. The data show that more adults are saving in any way and more of them are formally saving in an account at a bank or similar financial institution or by using a mobile money account. In fact, the share of adults saving formally grew by 16 percentage points between 2021 and 2024, more than the overall increase in saving.

The remainder of the chapter explores the different forms of saving and then examines trends in formal saving.

> ### Box 3.1.1 What it means to save formally and where the Global Findex survey asked about it
>
> The Global Findex 2025 defines "saving formally" as saving money in an account at a bank or similar financial institution like a credit union, microfinance institution, or post office, or by using a mobile money account included in the GSMA's Mobile Money Deployment Tracker (refer to box 2.1.1 for the full definition of accounts used by Global Findex 2025).[a] The survey collected data regarding these two modes of formal saving separately.[b]
>
> For most high-income economies and the Russian Federation, the survey includes only questions on account ownership, not questions on saving. As a result, this

(Box continued next page)

Most savers used an account

People save money in different ways. In low- and middle-income economies, 40 percent of adults—or 73 percent of those who saved any money in the past year—saved formally in an account at a bank or similar financial institution or by using a mobile money account (refer to map 3.1.1 and figure 3.1.1). Virtually all adults who saved formally have their own account.[1] As in 2021, formal saving is the most common mode of saving in low- and middle-income economies.

Saving in an account lets owners store money privately and securely. Research shows that having an account in which to save reduces reliance on borrowing,[2] increases economic resilience[3] and overall savings volumes,[4] and lets users, particularly women, reallocate household expenditures to better suit their needs.[5]

Alternatively, adults in low- and middle-income economies may save semiformally through savings clubs or by leaving money with a person outside the family; this is a common informal alternative to saving formally in an account. In 2024, 17 percent of adults saved semiformally, including 6 percent of adults who saved only in this way. An equal share of women and men saved semiformally, and a larger share of wealthier adults did than poorer adults—19 percent versus 14 percent.

---

1 In low- and middle-income economies, 1 percent of adults who have saved formally lack an account of any type, suggesting that they might use an account of another person in the household.
2 Pomeranz and Kast (2024).
3 Jones and Gong (2021).
4 Aggarwal, Brailovskaya, and Robinson (2020); Bachas et al. (2021); Bastian et al. (2018); Breza, Kanz, and Klapper (2020); Dupas and Robinson (2013); Habyarimana and Jack (2024).
5 Ashraf, Karlan, and Yin (2010); Prina (2015).

Map 3.1.1 Formal saving was the most common mode of saving across low- and middle-income economies, although formal saving rates varied

Adults saving at a bank or similar financial institution or using a mobile money account in the past year (%), 2024

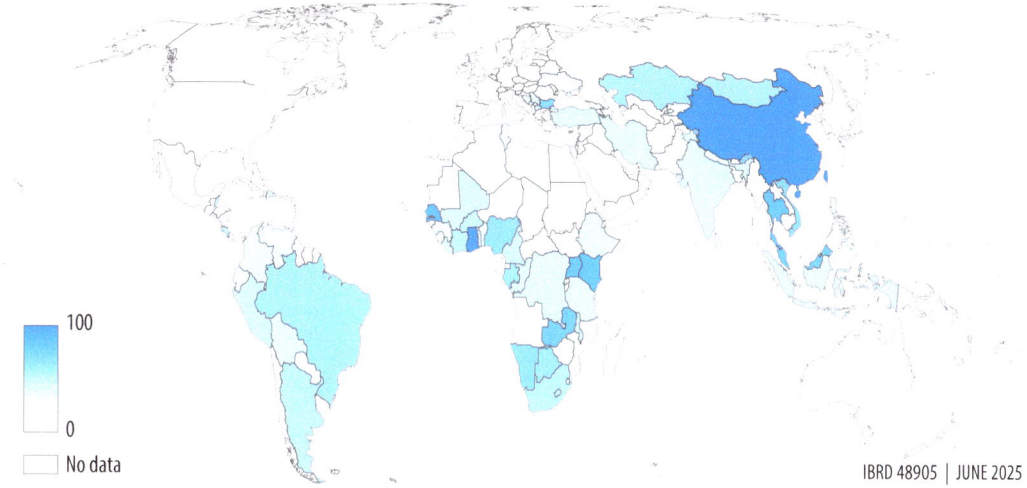

IBRD 48905 | JUNE 2025

Source: Global Findex Database 2025.

Note: Map displays data for low- and middle-income economies only.

Saving semiformally is especially common as a share of saving in South Asia, the only region where the share of adults saving semiformally grew between 2021 and 2024—from 8 percent to 13 percent of adults. It is also popular in Sub-Saharan Africa, where 28 percent of adults saved semiformally in 2024, including 15 percent who saved exclusively this way, about the same as in 2021; 31 percent of women embraced this form of saving in the region compared with 25 percent of men.

Semiformal saving supports social networks and encourages people to build regular saving habits to accumulate lump sums of money, but these savings are also vulnerable to theft, lack flexibility regarding withdrawals, and do not earn interest.[6] For example, rotating savings and credit associations are one common type of savings club, a popular approach to semiformal saving. These associations generally operate by pooling weekly deposits and disbursing the entire amount to a different member each week. Participants get their money, but only when it is their turn to receive cash, making this method potentially unsuitable for dealing with an emergency or unexpected need.

Adults may also save only in some other way "using other methods," as 8 percent of adults in low- and middle-income economies did (about 16 percent of savers). The "other methods" could be saving cash at home or saving in the form of assets

6   Karlan, Ratan, and Zinman (2014).

Figure 3.1.1 The share of adults saving any money, including saving formally, increased across regions between 2021 and 2024

Adults saving any money in the past year (%), 2021–24

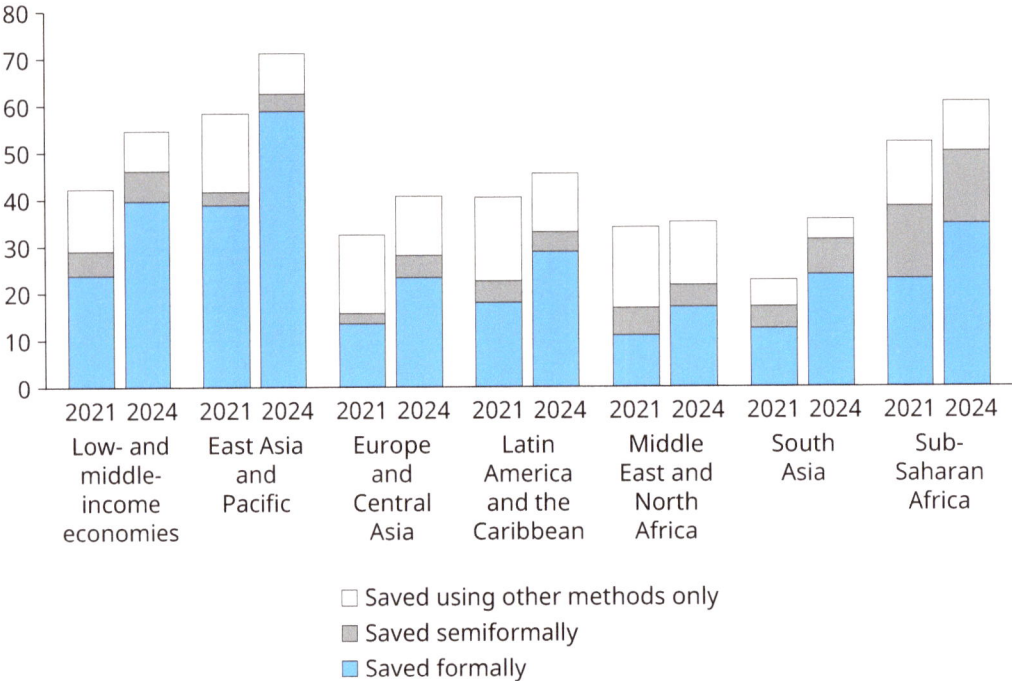

☐ Saved using other methods only
▨ Saved semiformally
▨ Saved formally

Source: Global Findex Database 2025.

Note: People may save in multiple ways, but categories in the figure are constructed to be mutually exclusive. *Saved formally* includes all adults who saved any money in an account. *Saved semiformally* includes all adults who saved any money semiformally but none formally. Because an abridged questionnaire was administered in the Russian Federation in 2024, averages for Europe and Central Asia exclude data for this economy. For comparability across time, averages for earlier years similarly exclude data for Russia and may thus differ from previously published numbers.

such as livestock, gold or jewelry, or real estate, as well as by using market-traded or government-backed securities. Women and poor adults were as likely as men and wealthier adults to save in this way. In 15 low- and middle-income economies, more than half of people who saved used one or more of these alternate vehicles. In Moldova, 33 percent of adults (or 82 percent of savers) saved "using other methods," making it the economy with the highest share of adults, as well as the highest share of savers, exclusively using alternate savings vehicles. It is the exception, however; saving in other ways declined in every region between 2021 and 2024.

The share of adults saving formally grew in every region

The share of adults saving formally in low- and middle-income economies increased across all regions between 2011 and 2024. In low- and middle-income economies it increased by 22 percentage points, from 17 percent in 2011 to 40 percent in 2024 (refer to figure 3.1.2).[7] More than half of that increase occurred between 2021 and 2024, likely driven by changes in macroeconomic conditions, which heavily influence saving behaviors.

This pattern of especially strong growth in formal saving between 2021 and 2024 holds across regions. East Asia and Pacific registered the largest increase, at 20 percentage points, driven by an increase of 22 percentage points in China alone. With China excluded, the share of adults in the East Asia and Pacific region saving formally increased by 9 percentage points between 2021 and 2024.

Figure 3.1.2 **Formal saving rates increased across regions between 2011 and 2024**

Adults saving at a bank or similar financial institution or using a mobile money account in the past year (%), 2011–24

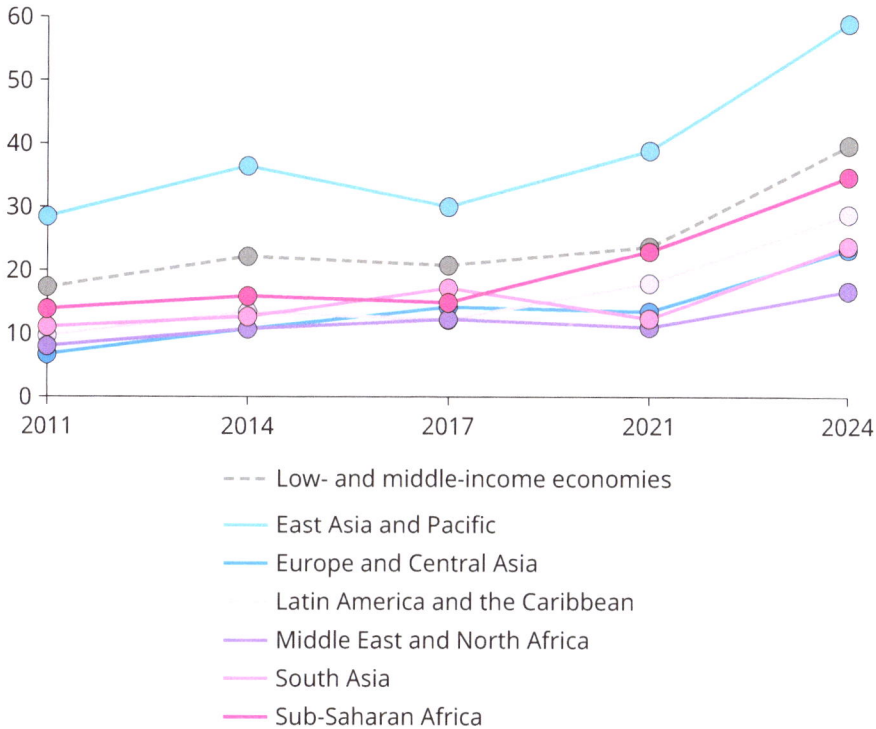

- – – – Low- and middle-income economies
- ——— East Asia and Pacific
- ——— Europe and Central Asia
- ——— Latin America and the Caribbean
- ——— Middle East and North Africa
- ——— South Asia
- ——— Sub-Saharan Africa

Source: Global Findex Database 2025.

Note: Data for 2021 and 2024 include saving using a mobile phone account. Because an abridged questionnaire was administered in the Russian Federation in 2024, averages for Europe and Central Asia exclude data for this economy. For comparability across time, averages for earlier years similarly exclude data for Russia and may thus differ from previously published numbers.

---

7   The Global Findex reports data as whole percentage points, although it calculates that whole based on rounding up or down from the tenths place. As such, any discrepancies between the reported size of a gap and the difference between its end points is due to rounding.

Women, the poor, people who are out of the workforce, and rural adults are less likely than men, the rich, those in the workforce, and urban adults to save in an account

Across low- and middle-income economies, traditionally underserved groups are consistently less likely to save formally than their better-served peers (refer to figure 3.1.3).

For example, 36 percent of women saved formally, whereas 43 percent of men did. Women are less likely than men to have an account, as discussed in chapter 2.1, but account ownership does not explain the difference in formal saving. Even among account owners, women are 6 percentage points less likely than men to save formally: 48 percent of women did so, compared with 54 percent of men.

Gender gaps in the rate of formal saving among account owners vary across regions. East Asia and Pacific has no significant gender gap in formal saving rates among account owners, largely because the same share of both women and men saved in China. When China is excluded, however, the region has a 7 percentage

Figure 3.1.3 Women, poor adults, those out of the workforce, and rural residents were less likely to save formally than men, wealthier adults, the wage and self-employed, and urban residents

Adults with an account (%), 2024

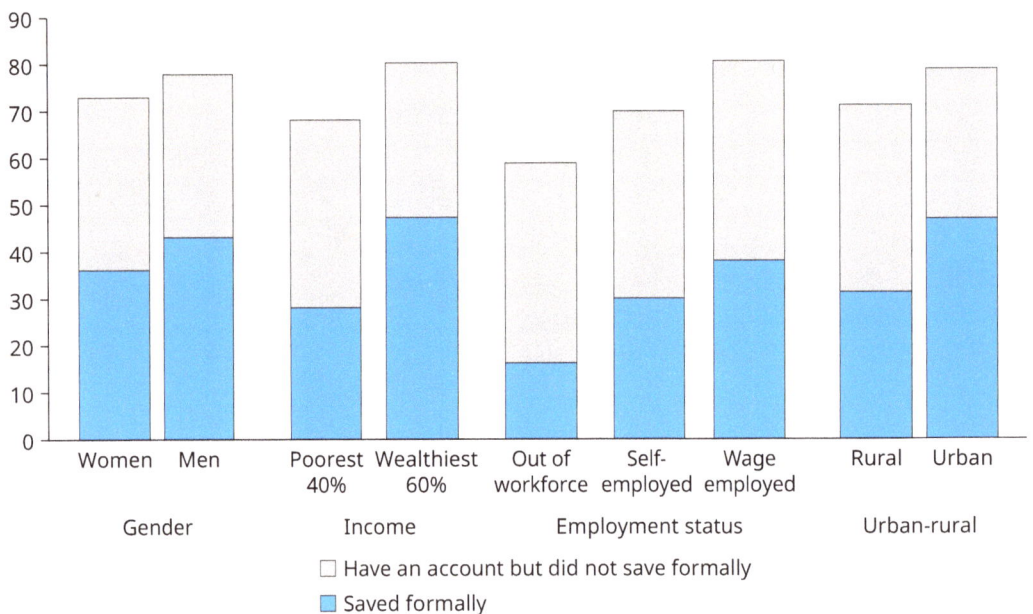

Have an account but did not save formally
Saved formally

Source: Global Findex Database 2025.

point formal-saving gender gap. In contrast, Latin America and the Caribbean and the Middle East and North Africa have the largest gender gaps in formal saving rates among account owners, at 13 percentage points each. In other regions the gap ranges between 7 and 10 percentage points. These gender gaps may partly reflect differences in labor force participation rates across regions.

There are also gaps in formal saving rates based on income and workforce status, which are similarly not related to account ownership. Adults in the poorest 40 percent of households within economies are less likely to have saved formally than adults in the wealthiest 60 percent: 28 percent compared with 47 percent. Among account owners, adults in poorer households are still 18 percentage points less likely than adults in wealthier households to have saved formally: 40 percent compared with 58 percent.

Adults who are out of the labor force are also less likely to have saved formally than those who are active in the labor force, whether wage or self-employed. In low- and middle-income economies excluding China, the shares are 17 percent and 34 percent.[8] Among account owners, adults out of the labor force are 17 percentage points less likely than adults in the labor force to have saved formally: 28 percent of account-owning adults out of the labor force have done so, compared with 44 percent of account owners in the labor force. Within the group of adults in the workforce, account owners who are employed by an employer are most likely to have saved formally, at 47 percent. This suggests that, not surprisingly, even among account owners, those with a steady income are most likely to save formally.

Finally, across low- and middle-income economies, rural residents are less likely to save than urban residents. The share of rural residents who saved formally is 31 percent compared with 47 percent of urban residents. Among account owners, 43 percent of rural residents and 58 percent of urban residents saved.

Mobile money accounts are becoming a popular way of saving formally in Sub-Saharan Africa and elsewhere

As ownership of mobile money accounts has expanded in recent years, so has the use of these accounts to save. In low- and middle-income economies, 9 percent of adults saved formally using a mobile money account in 2024 (refer to figure 3.1.4). This includes 4 percent of adults who saved using only a mobile money account and 5 percent who saved using both a mobile money account and an account at a bank or similar financial institution. (Thirty percent of adults saved formally using only an account at a bank or similar financial institution.) The share of adults saving formally

---

8   Data on employment status for adults in China are not available.

Figure 3.1.4 **More adults used mobile money to save in low- and middle-income economies**

Adults saving any money in the past year (%), 2021–24

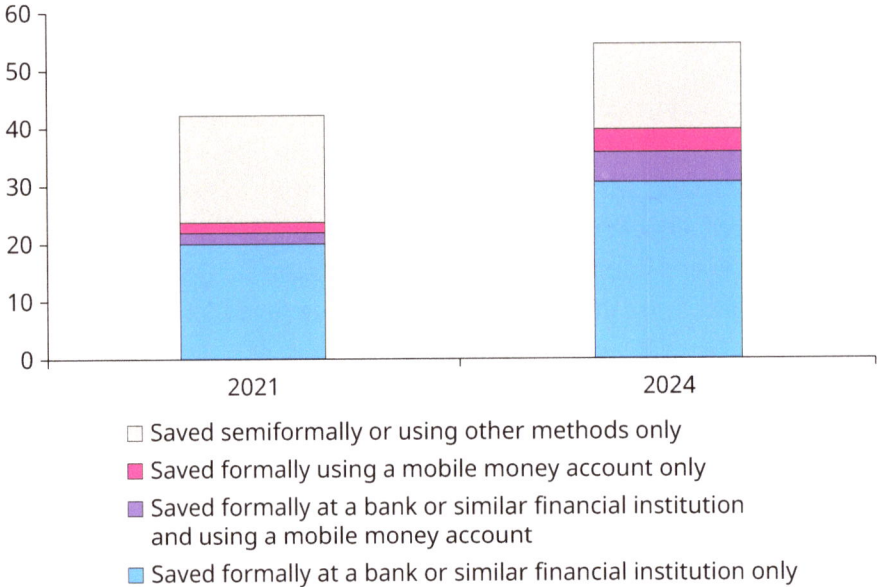

- Saved semiformally or using other methods only
- Saved formally using a mobile money account only
- Saved formally at a bank or similar financial institution and using a mobile money account
- Saved formally at a bank or similar financial institution only

Source: Global Findex Database 2025.

Note: People save in multiple ways, but categories in the figure are constructed to be mutually exclusive. *Saved formally* includes all adults who saved any money in an account. *Saved semiformally* includes all adults who saved any money semiformally but none formally. Because an abridged questionnaire was administered in the Russian Federation in 2024, averages exclude data for this economy. For comparability across time, averages for earlier years similarly exclude data for Russia and may thus differ from previously published numbers.

using a mobile money account is up from the 4 percent of adults who did so in 2021, when the Global Findex survey first asked about saving in these accounts.[9]

Saving using a mobile money account can be more convenient than saving using an account at a bank or similar financial institution. Because mobile money service providers typically have larger retail networks than do banks and similar financial institutions,[10] savers who have mobile money accounts can often make cash deposits locally, more frequently, and in smaller denominations without incurring significant time and transaction costs.[11]

---

9   Because of COVID-19 restrictions, data collection in 11 Sub-Saharan African economies took place in 2022, after the publication of the *Global Findex 2021* report. As a result, some global and regional averages and some for low- and middle-income economies shifted slightly from those that were included in the report. The Global Findex team uses the revised averages in its comparisons. Thus in the case of saving using a mobile money account, the global share of 5 percent reported in *Global Findex 2021* has been revised downward to the 4 percent shown in the chapter here.

10   Economides and Jeziorski (2015).

11   Suri et al. (2023).

The share of adults who saved formally using a mobile money account is much larger in some regions and economies. Sub-Saharan Africa still has the largest share of adults who did so: 23 percent of adults in 2024, twice the share in 2021 (refer to figure 3.1.5). In Latin America and the Caribbean, 19 percent of adults saved formally using a mobile money account, four times the share of adults in these economies who saved this way in 2021. More than 20 percent of adults saved using a mobile money account in Malaysia, the Philippines, and Thailand as well.

At 15 percent, Sub-Saharan Africa also has the highest share of adults who saved using only a mobile money account. In all other regions, that share is less than 6 percent.

Figure 3.1.5 **Mobile money accounts are an important mode of saving in Latin America and the Caribbean and Sub-Saharan Africa**

Adults saving any money in the past year (%), 2021–24

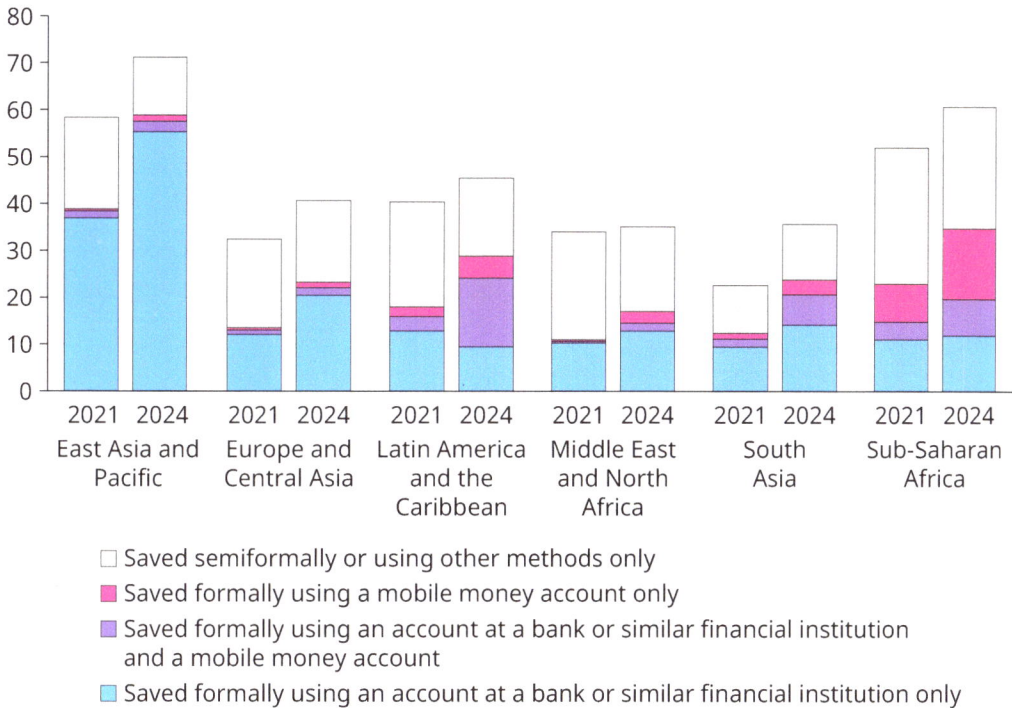

Legend:
- ☐ Saved semiformally or using other methods only
- ■ Saved formally using a mobile money account only
- ■ Saved formally using an account at a bank or similar financial institution and a mobile money account
- ■ Saved formally using an account at a bank or similar financial institution only

Source: Global Findex Database 2025.

Note: People save in multiple ways, but categories in the figure are constructed to be mutually exclusive. *Saved formally* includes all adults who saved any money in an account. *Saved semiformally* includes all adults who saved any money semiformally but none formally. Because an abridged questionnaire was administered in the Russian Federation in 2024, averages for Europe and Central Asia exclude data for this economy. For comparability across time, averages for earlier years similarly exclude data for Russia and may thus differ from previously published numbers.

In the 10 economies with the largest share of adults who saved using a mobile money account, about a third of adults saved this way. The group includes eight economies in Sub-Saharan Africa and two in Latin America and the Caribbean. In five of these economies—Ghana, Kenya, Senegal, Uganda, and Zambia—half of adults or more used mobile money accounts to save (refer to figure 3.1.6). In Sub-Saharan Africa, the increase in the percentage of adults who saved using a mobile money account between 2021 and 2024 boosted the percentage of adults saving any money at all. In contrast, in Argentina and Brazil, although the percentage of adults saving in a mobile money account increased, most adults also saved at a bank or similar financial institution, and the percentage of adults saving only in some other way went down, suggesting that saving formally is replacing saving using only other methods.

Figure 3.1.6 In the 10 economies with the largest share of adults saving using mobile money accounts, these accounts increased the share of adults who save formally

Adults saving any money in the past year (%), 2021–24

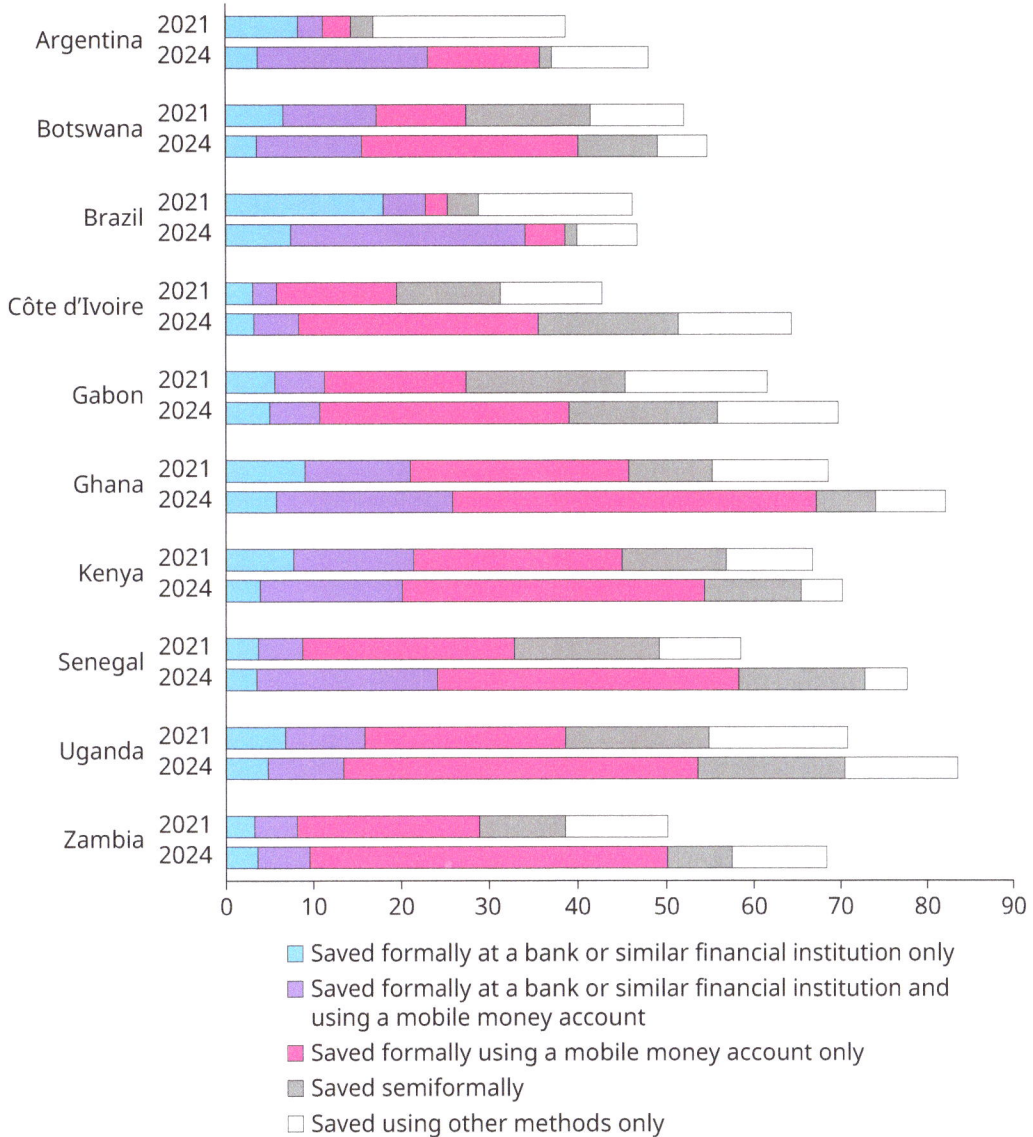

Saved formally at a bank or similar financial institution only

Saved formally at a bank or similar financial institution and using a mobile money account

Saved formally using a mobile money account only

Saved semiformally

Saved using other methods only

Source: Global Findex Database 2025.

Note: People save in multiple ways, but categories in the figure are constructed to be mutually exclusive. *Saved formally* includes all adults who saved any money in an account. *Saved semiformally* includes all adults who saved any money semiformally but none formally.

The share of adults saving formally and receiving interest or additional money for their savings varies across regions

Global Findex 2025 asked adults who saved formally whether they received interest or additional money for the savings in their accounts in the past 12 months. In low- and middle-income economies, 23 percent of adults saved formally and received interest on or additional money for their savings—or just over half of formal savers. However, China drove much of that average: its share of adults saving formally and receiving interest or additional money was more than 50 percent. In East Asia and Pacific excluding China and in all other regions, 15 percent or less of adults saved formally and received interest or additional money for their savings. By region, this represents about a quarter of savers in Sub-Saharan Africa; about a third of savers in Europe and Central Asia, Middle East and North Africa, and South Asia; and about 4 in 10 savers in East Asia and Pacific, excluding China, and in Latin America and the Caribbean (refer to figure 3.1.7). Women formal savers are consistently as likely as men to receive interest, except in Latin America and the Caribbean.

Figure 3.1.7 **In most regions, about 10 percent of adults saved formally and received interest on their savings**

Adults saving at a bank or similar financial institution or using a mobile money account in the past year (%), 2024

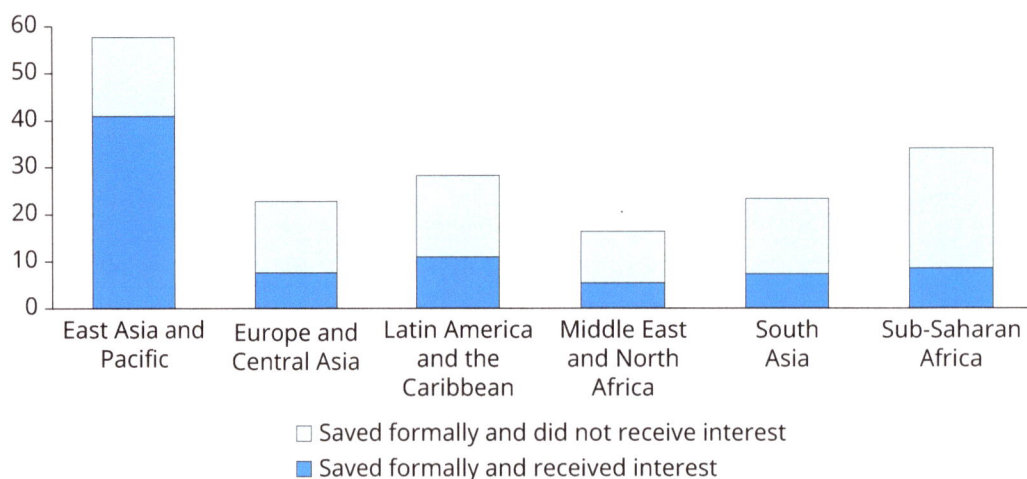

☐ Saved formally and did not receive interest
■ Saved formally and received interest

Source: Global Findex Database 2025.

Most adults who saved formally did so monthly

Global Findex 2025 also asked adults who saved formally how often in a typical month they saved or set aside money in an account: weekly, monthly, or less than monthly.[12] On average, nearly half of adults who saved formally (47 percent) in low- and middle-income economies did so monthly. Another 37 percent saved less than monthly, and just 13 percent saved weekly.

This pattern holds broadly across regions. In Sub-Saharan Africa, a relatively larger share (19 percent) of adults saving formally did so every week. This seems to be driven in part by the prevalence of mobile money accounts in the region. About a quarter of adults in the region who saved formally using a mobile money account did so weekly. That is about double the share of those who saved weekly using only an account at a bank or similar financial institution. Within subregions in Sub-Saharan Africa, adults who saved formally using a mobile money account often made more frequent savings deposits than adults who saved only in a bank or similar financial institution account (refer to figure 3.1.8).

Figure 3.1.8 **In Sub-Saharan Africa, adults who saved using a mobile money account saved more frequently than adults who saved using an account at a bank or similar financial institution**

Adults saving at a bank or similar financial institution or using a mobile money account in the past year, by frequency (%), 2024

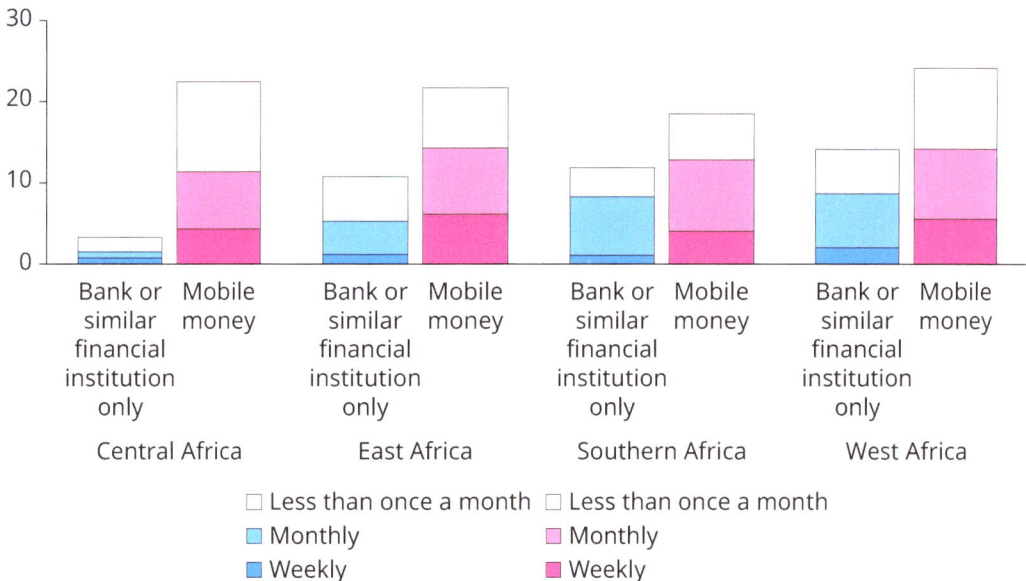

Source: Global Findex Database 2025.

---

12   Data for the question were not collected for all low- and middle-income economies (refer to box 3.1.1).

Saving for old age

Global Findex 2025 asked adults who saved formally whether they specifically saved for their old age.[13] Nearly half of formal savers had done so, resulting in 18 percent of all adults in low- and middle-income economies having both saved formally and saved for their old age. However, the large share of adults who saved formally and for their old age in China drove much of that number. With China excluded, 14 percent of adults in East Asia and Pacific saved formally and for their old age. No more than 10 percent of adults did so in all other regions. Chapter 4.1, "Managing financial worrying," explores saving for old age in more detail.

Opportunities for increasing account use by moving semiformal savings to accounts

The share of adults saving formally has increased in low- and middle-income economies in recent years, but opportunities remain to further increase the use of accounts to save. Moving semiformal or other savings into accounts is one important opportunity. People who save semiformally may be drawn to the social aspects of savings clubs. They also may use semiformal saving methods because they lack affordable and convenient alternatives. Although self-help group interventions tend to show positive impacts, there is limited evidence assessing whether alternative delivery mechanisms could be more effective.[14] In addition, saving only semiformally can be unsafe[15] and limits people's ability to build a relationship and a transaction history with a financial institution that lenders can use to underwrite credit,[16] in turn limiting the saver's access to other financial services. Saving in an account might be more attractive if banks or similar financial institutions or mobile money services providers offered free or low-cost interest-bearing saving products requiring little or no minimum balance.

Encouraging formal savings for those who have saved only semiformally but also have an account is an especially low-barrier opportunity. Among the 6 percent of adults who saved only semiformally in low- and middle-income economies, more than 60 percent—or 190 million adults—already have accounts. In Sub-Saharan Africa, where 15 percent of adults saved only semiformally, more than 40 percent—or 47 million adults, including 28 million women—already have an account.

---

13 In 2021 the Global Findex survey asked all adults, not just those who had saved formally, whether they had saved money for their old age.

14 Gugerty, Biscaya, and Anderson (2018).

15 Collins et al. (2010).

16 Bird et al. (2024); Mukherjee et al. (2024).

Amassing the resources to enable investments

Saving is broadly viewed as bringing unmitigated financial health benefits for individuals and households. Borrowing is another approach people take to access a large enough lump sum of money to address needs or make investments. The following chapter presents the data on borrowing behavior.

3.2 Borrowing

A reproducibility package is available for this book in the Reproducible Research Repository at https://reproducibility.worldbank.org/catalog/299.

3.2 Borrowing

People borrow money when they need cash that they don't have, often for a large expense or investment. The Global Findex 2024 survey asked whether people borrowed any money in the past year and, if so, the source of the funds (refer to box 3.2.1). It therefore captured data on demand for credit and access to and use of it. It did not, however, capture information on the type of loan product, borrowing amounts, or terms, including duration, interest, collateral, and other lending conditions. As such, the data cannot provide insights on whether borrowed amounts were substantial enough to cover expenses or productive investments or whether respondents may have taken on too much credit.

Yet understanding how many people borrowed money in the year leading up to the survey is essential for assessing both individual and national financial health, identifying trends in credit use and debt burdens, and guiding policies that promote economic stability, financial literacy, and overall well-being.

In low- and middle-income economies in 2024, 59 percent of adults borrowed money in the 12 months before taking the survey. This percentage includes all adults who used formal or informal credit. The remainder of the chapter explores the different forms of borrowing and then examines trends in the sources of formal borrowing.

> **Box 3.2.1 What it means to borrow formally and where the Global Findex survey asked about it**
>
> *Global Findex 2025* defines *formal borrowing* as borrowing from a bank or similar financial institution such as a credit union, a microfinance institution, or a post office; through a credit card; or through a mobile money provider included in the GSMA's Mobile Money Deployment Tracker.[a] Each economy identifies the banks and financial institutions that offer credit within that economy and are subject to prudential regulation by a government authority there; the list of institutions may vary from the list included in chapter 2.1, as some economies regulate non-deposit-taking lenders. The Global Findex 2024 survey collected data separately for formal borrowing
>
> • From a bank or similar financial institution
>
> • Using a credit card
>
> • Through a mobile money account (refer to box 2.1.1 for the full definition of accounts used by Global Findex 2025).[b]

(Box continued next page)

An equal share of borrowers relied on formal sources and on family or friends

On average, 24 percent of adults—40 percent of borrowers—borrowed formally in 2024. They got credit through a loan from a bank or similar financial institution or through the use of a credit card or a mobile money account. Formal borrowing's share of total borrowing varied across low- and-middle income economies (refer to map 3.2.1).

Map 3.2.1 The share of adults who borrowed formally varied widely across low- and middle-income economies

Adults borrowing any money from a bank or similar financial institution or through the use of a credit card or mobile money account in the past year (%), 2024

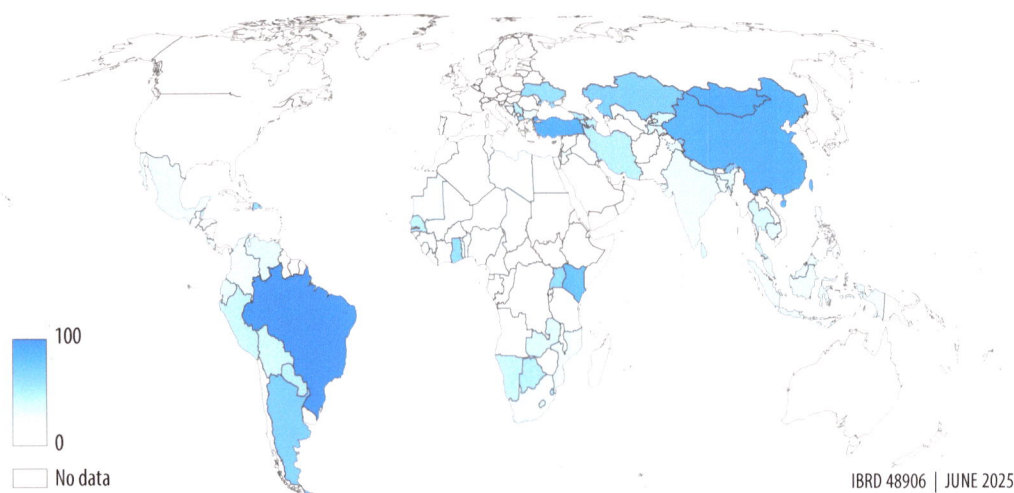

100

0

No data

IBRD 48906 | JUNE 2025

Source: Global Findex Database 2025.

Note: Map displays only data for low- and middle-income economies.

Another 5 percent of adults borrowed semiformally, from a savings club, such as a rotation savings and credit association, including 3 percent of adults who borrowed only semiformally, but not formally.[1] Overall, 31 percent of adults borrowed from family or friends, with 21 percent of adults borrowing only this way and not also formally or semiformally. Other credit sources were tapped by 12 percent of adults (refer to figure 3.2.1); these sources could include buy-now-pay-later options, which have become more popular around the world in recent years.[2] They could also include credit extended for buying groceries, which chapter 4.1 explores in the context of financial health.

Figure 3.2.1 **In low- and middle-income economies, about equal shares of borrowers accessed credit from formal sources as did so only informally from family or friends, though the most common source varied across regions**

Adults borrowing any money in the past year (%), 2024

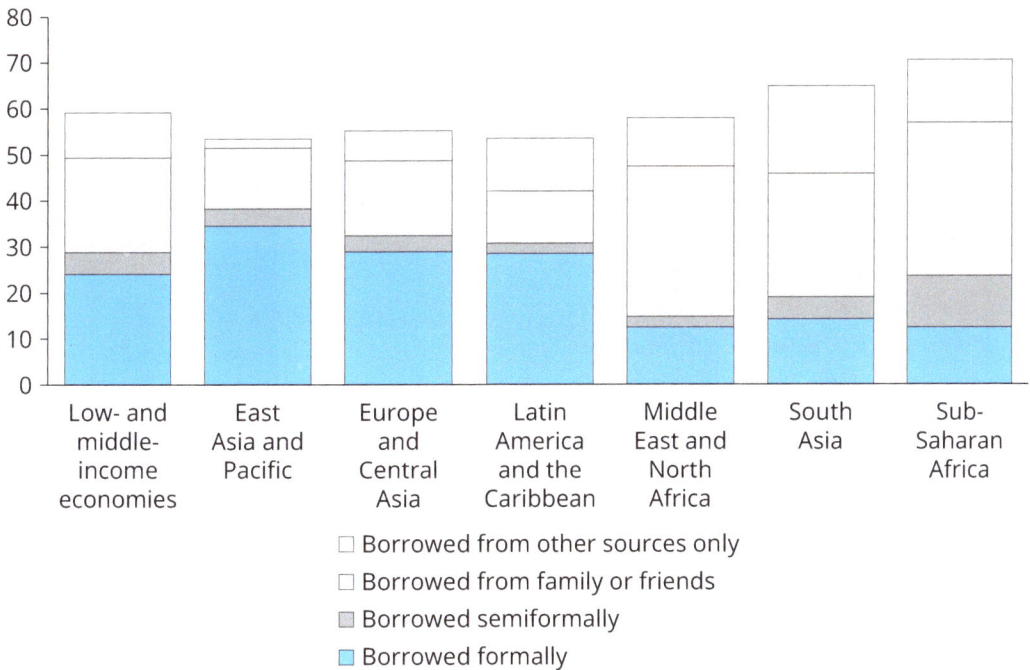

□ Borrowed from other sources only
□ Borrowed from family or friends
▨ Borrowed semiformally
▨ Borrowed formally

Source: Global Findex Database 2025.

Note: People may borrow from multiple sources, but categories in the figure are constructed to be mutually exclusive. *Borrowed formally* includes all adults who borrowed any money from a bank or similar financial institution or through the use of a credit card or a mobile money account. *Borrowed semiformally* includes all adults who borrowed any money semiformally (from a savings club) but none formally. *Borrowed from family or friends* excludes adults who borrowed formally or semiformally.

---

1   The Global Findex 2025 asked only adults who saved semiformally about semiformal borrowing.
2   Cornelli et al. (2023).

The share of adults who borrowed informally only—that is, semiformally, or from family or friends, or from other sources but not formally—varied by region from more than 45 percent of adults in the Middle East and North Africa, South Asia, and Sub-Saharan Africa to just 19 percent of adults in East Asia and Pacific.

In all regions except East Asia and Pacific, women who borrowed were more likely than men who borrowed to do so informally only. Similarly, in low- and middle-income economies, as a share of borrowers, adults living in the poorest 40 percent of households by income were 15 percentage points more likely to borrow informally only than adults from the wealthiest 60 percent of households; this trend held across all regions. Likewise, rural borrowers were 19 percentage points more likely than urban residents to rely on informal credit only across low- and middle-income economies, but in the Middle East and North Africa, South Asia, and Sub-Saharan Africa there were no differences in the use of informal credit only among borrowers. Finally, borrowers who are out of the workforce were 16 percentage points more likely than wage employed and 8 percentage points more likely than self-employed borrowers to borrow only informally.

The share of adults borrowing formally grew in low- and middle-income economies

The average share of adults borrowing formally in low- and middle-income economies increased over time, from 15 percent of adults in 2014 to 24 percent of adults in 2024 (refer to figure 3.2.2).[3]

Figure 3.2.2 **Formal borrowing increased across regions between 2014 and 2024**

Adults borrowing any money from a bank or similar financial institution or through the use of a credit card or mobile money account in the past year (%), 2014–24

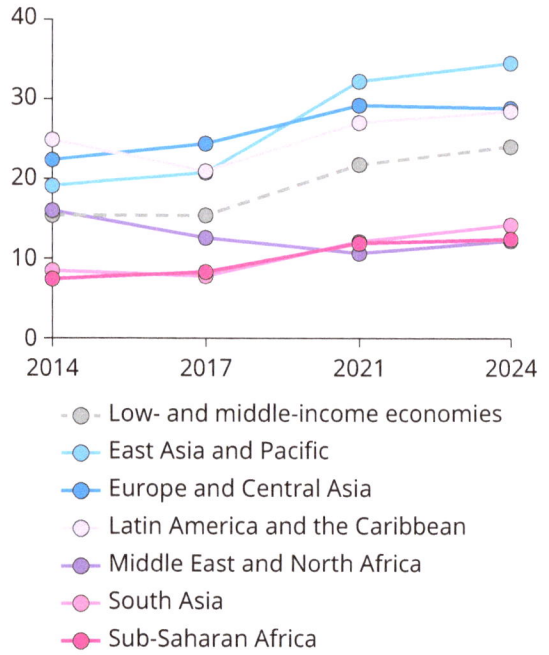

- Low- and middle-income economies
- East Asia and Pacific
- Europe and Central Asia
- Latin America and the Caribbean
- Middle East and North Africa
- South Asia
- Sub-Saharan Africa

Source: Global Findex Database 2025.

Note: Data from 2021 and 2024 include, as part of formal borrowing, borrowing through the use of a mobile money account. Because an abridged questionnaire was administered in the Russian Federation in 2024, averages for Europe and Central Asia exclude data for this economy. For comparability across time, averages for earlier years similarly exclude data for Russia and may thus differ from previously published numbers.

---

3   Past editions of Global Findex reported 16 percent as the share of adults who borrowed in low- and middle-income economies in 2014. Some economies have graduated to high-income status since the first round of data collection, however. Global Findex 2025 uses the World Bank's fiscal year 2024 income classification for all rounds of data to ensure consistency of group composition for aggregate averages.

However, the share of adults borrowing formally varied more widely across regions than over time, from 34 percent in East Asia and Pacific to 12 percent in the Middle East and North Africa and Sub-Saharan Africa.

In East Asia and Pacific, Europe and Central Asia, and Latin America and the Caribbean, formal sources were the most common, used by half or more of borrowers. Meanwhile, in the Middle East and North Africa, South Asia, and Sub-Saharan Africa, only about 20 percent of borrowers accessed formal credit. As mentioned, borrowing only from family or friends was the most common source for borrowing in these regions.

Women were less likely than men to have borrowed formally

Gender patterns around formal borrowing show the opposite trends from those around borrowing informally. Across low- and middle-income countries, 22 percent of women borrowed formally, compared with 26 percent of men (refer to figure 3.2.3). This gender gap persisted among account owners: 29 percent of women with an account borrowed formally, compared with 33 percent of men.

Figure 3.2.3 Women, poor adults, those out of the workforce, and rural residents were less likely to borrow formally than men, wealthier adults, the wage and self-employed, and urban residents

Adults with an account (%), 2024

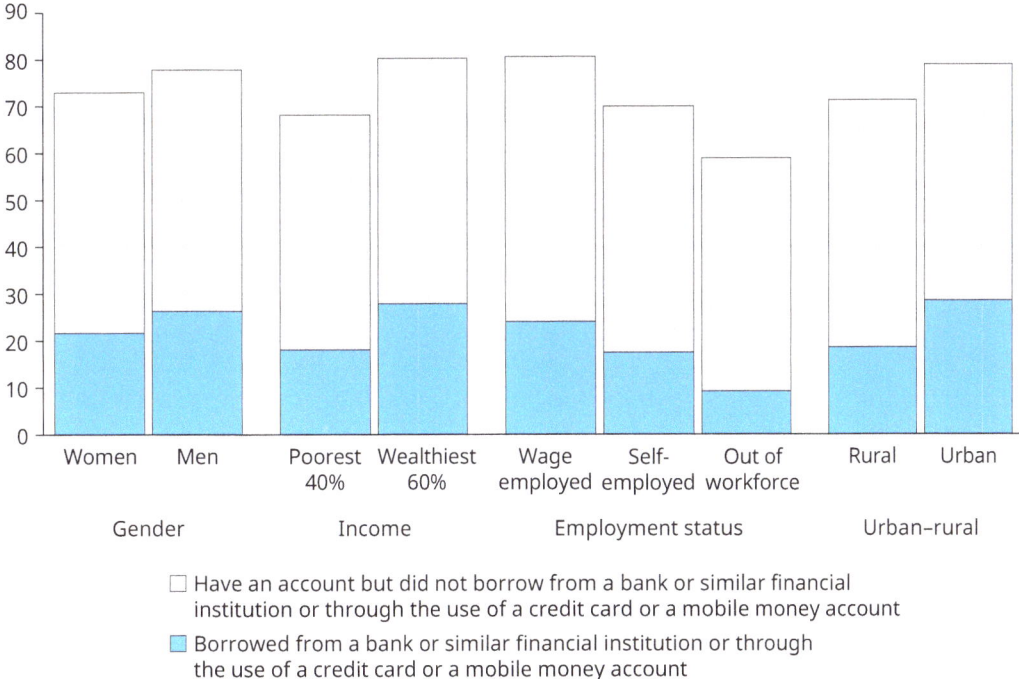

☐ Have an account but did not borrow from a bank or similar financial institution or through the use of a credit card or a mobile money account

☐ Borrowed from a bank or similar financial institution or through the use of a credit card or a mobile money account

Source: Global Findex Database 2025.

Across regions, gender gaps in formal borrowing among account owners ranged from statistically nonsignificant in East Asia and Pacific and the Middle East and North Africa to 8 percentage points in Latin America and the Caribbean. The gender gap was 11 percentage points in Europe and Central Asia, largely because of a gender gap of 21 percentage points in Türkiye. South Asia and Sub-Saharan Africa had gender gaps of 6 and 5 percentage points, respectively. When formal borrowing among adults who borrow is considered, the gender gap remains the same at 4 percentage points.

The data show similar differences for other groups. Adults from the poorest 40 percent of households by income were 10 percentage points less likely to borrow formally than adults from the wealthiest 60 percent, a difference that drops to 8 percentage points when only account owners in each group are considered. One in three wage-employed adults with an account borrowed formally, compared with one in four self-employed account owners and just over one in seven adults who were out of the workforce. Rural residents were 10 percentage points less likely than urban residents to borrow formally, both as a share of adults and as a share of account owners.

The share of adults borrowing formally by using credit cards was generally small, though this type of borrowing dominated in a few low- and middle-income economies

Credit cards are both a payment instrument and a credit source. They provide short-term credit whenever they are used, even when credit card holders pay their balances in full each statement cycle and thus pay no interest on those balances. Credit cards' entry into an economy may therefore affect the demand for and use of other forms of credit.

In low- and middle-income economies in 2024, just 15 percent of adults used a credit card in the past 12 months. As in 2021, the exceptions were Argentina, Brazil, China, Türkiye, and Ukraine, where at least 25 percent of adults did. Credit cards dominated as a source of formal credit in these economies: the share of formal borrowers who used credit cards but did not also borrow from a financial institution or a mobile money account was about 70 percent in Türkiye, about 60 percent in Argentina and Brazil, and about 50 percent in China and Ukraine (refer to figure 3.2.4).[4]

To provide a better understanding of how adults use credit cards, the Global Findex 2024 survey asked whether adults who used a credit card paid off their balances

---

4   This compares with 51 percent of adults who used a credit card in the past 12 months in high-income economies according to the Global Findex 2021 survey. Among formal borrowers in high-income economies in 2021, two-thirds borrowed using a credit card, but not from a bank or similar financial institution or through the use of a mobile money account.

Figure 3.2.4 **Credit card use dominated formal borrowing in some low- and middle-income economies**

Adults borrowing formally in the past year (%), 2024

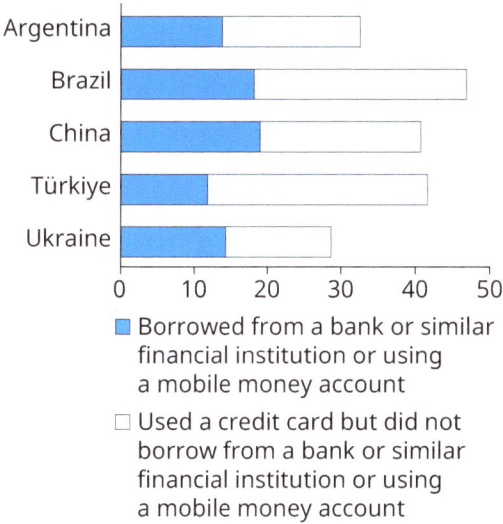

- ■ Borrowed from a bank or similar financial institution or using a mobile money account
- □ Used a credit card but did not borrow from a bank or similar financial institution or using a mobile money account

Source: Global Findex Database 2025.

in full by the due date (note that some adults own a credit card but did not use it in the past 12 months). In the five low- and middle-income economies with high credit card use (defined as having a share of credit card users exceeding 25 percent of all adults), payment patterns among users varied. In China, about 90 percent of credit card users paid off their balances in full, whereas in Argentina and Türkiye, only about 60 percent of credit card users did. In the other two economies in this group, the share of credit card users paying off their balances in full fell between those two percentages (refer to figure 3.2.5).

Figure 3.2.5 **In low- and middle-income economies with high rates of credit card use, most credit card users paid off their balances in full**

Adults with a credit card (%), 2024

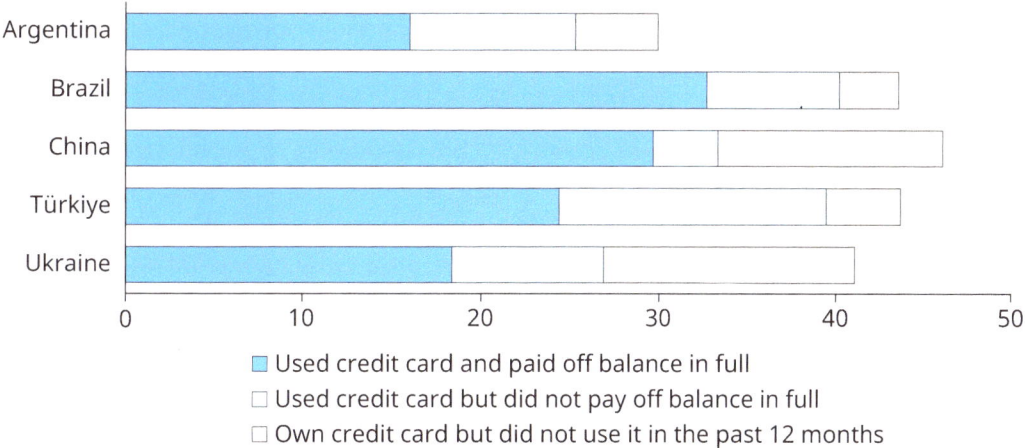

- ▢ Used credit card and paid off balance in full
- □ Used credit card but did not pay off balance in full
- □ Own credit card but did not use it in the past 12 months

Source: Global Findex Database 2025.

Mobile money accounts are the dominant source of formal credit in some economies in Sub-Saharan Africa

As mobile phone ownership and availability of mobile financial services have increased—discussed in chapters 1.1 and 2.1, respectively—so has the range of mobile money account features in some economies that allow those with an account to borrow. If someone is borrowing through a mobile money account, the borrowing could involve money that comes directly from the mobile money provider or from a partnership between the provider and a bank or similar financial institution; it could also take the form of minutes or data. Loans of these types are generally small in value and of short duration (repayment is typically due within a month and often within one to two weeks) and carry high effective interest rates.[5] Evidence suggests such loans can modestly increase consumption, financial health, and subjective well-being without reducing savings or assets, though their effects are not transformative.[6] In 2024, only 4 percent of adults in low- and middle-income economies borrowed through their mobile money accounts.

In Sub-Saharan Africa, where mobile money account ownership is most widespread, just 7 percent of adults borrowed from their mobile money providers. This share is unchanged from the share in 2021, when the Global Findex survey first asked about borrowing from a mobile money provider. Because overall levels of formal borrowing in Sub-Saharan Africa are low, borrowing from a mobile money provider constituted nearly 60 percent of all formal borrowing in the region in 2024.

Economies with some of the highest rates of mobile money account ownership in Sub-Saharan Africa also have the highest rates of people borrowing from their mobile money providers. In Kenya, the region's pioneer in mobile money, 32 percent of adults—or 86 percent of formal borrowers—borrowed from their mobile money providers, including 25 percent of adults who borrowed only in this way (refer to figure 3.2.6). In both Ghana and Uganda, 22 percent of adults—or 74 percent and 76 percent of formal borrowers, respectively—borrowed from mobile money providers, with virtually all of them borrowing *only* from mobile money providers.

In Ghana, the rise in borrowing through a mobile money account between 2021 and 2024 drove an overall increase in formal borrowing over that period. In Kenya and Uganda, the share of formal borrowing remained about the same in 2024 as that in 2021, but a larger share of formal borrowers got a loan through a mobile money account in 2024. In all three of these economies, the share of adults borrowing only from a bank or similar financial institution decreased as a larger share of adults took

---

5   Brailovska, Dupas, and Robinson (2024).

6   For a review of the literature, refer to Cassara, Zapanta, and Garz (2024).

Figure 3.2.6 In Ghana, Kenya, and Uganda, more than 20 percent of adults borrowed from their mobile money providers in 2024

Adults borrowing any money in the past year (%), 2021–24

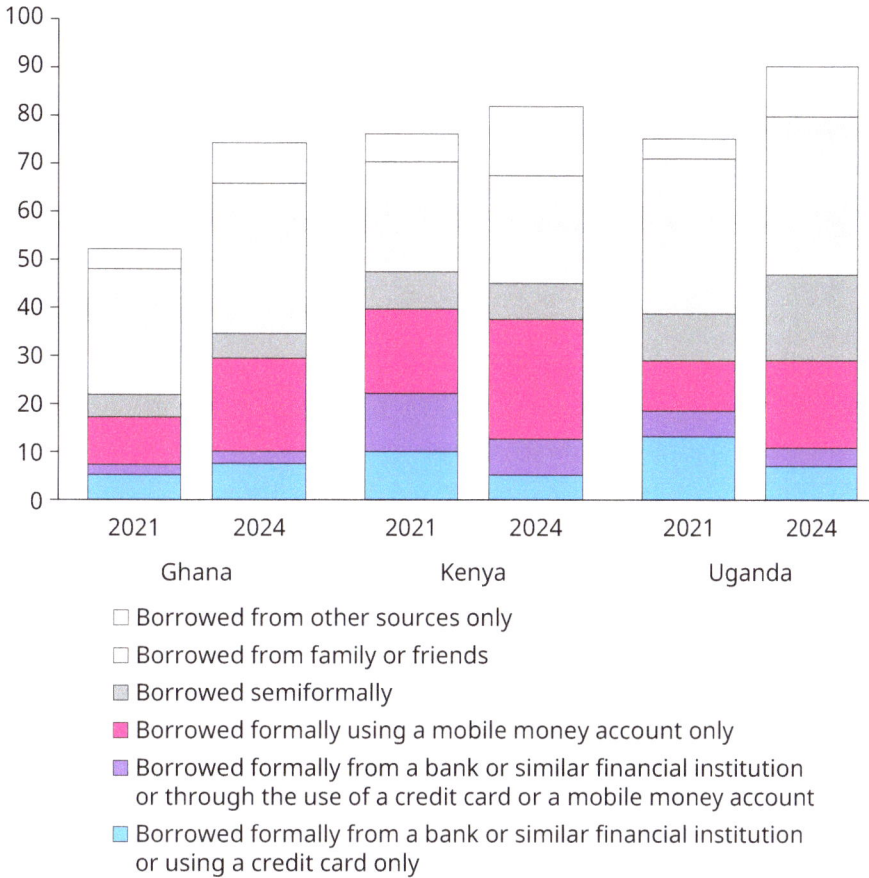

☐ Borrowed from other sources only
☐ Borrowed from family or friends
▨ Borrowed semiformally
■ Borrowed formally using a mobile money account only
■ Borrowed formally from a bank or similar financial institution or through the use of a credit card or a mobile money account
■ Borrowed formally from a bank or similar financial institution or using a credit card only

Source: Global Findex Database 2025.

Note: People may borrow from multiple sources, but categories in the figure are constructed to be mutually exclusive. *Borrowed formally* includes all adults who borrowed any money from a bank or similar financial institution or through the use of a credit card or a mobile money account. *Borrowed semiformally* includes all adults who borrowed any money semiformally (from a savings club) but none formally. *Borrowed from family or friends* excludes adults who borrowed formally or semiformally.

advantage of mobile money borrowing; whether that change was driven by supply (that is, banks pulling back on lending or collaborating with mobile money providers in new business models) or demand (that is, borrowers turning away from banks as an option) is not evident from the Global Findex survey data.

Despite similar levels of overall borrowing by gender in all three economies, borrowing from a mobile money provider differs according to gender in these economies. In Ghana, women are 4 percentage points less likely than men to borrow from this source, whereas in Kenya and Uganda, the gaps are 16 and 13 percentage points, respectively. Similar gaps exist between adults from the poorest 40 percent and wealthiest 60 percent of households by income.

An emerging source of formal borrowing in Sub-Saharan Africa is other digital credit

The Global Findex 2025, in addition to asking questions about borrowing through a mobile money provider, for the first time asked about other sources of digital credit, to capture data on people who do not borrow through a mobile money account, but rather through some other digital method. In particular, the survey asked separately about applying for and receiving a loan through a mobile phone: 1 percent of adults in low- and middle-income economies borrowed only this way (and not through a mobile money account, from a bank or similar financial institution, or through a credit card), including 3 percent of adults in Sub-Saharan Africa. This region is home to all seven of the world's economies in which at least 5 percent of adults report they borrowed through a mobile phone but did not borrow formally otherwise.[7] Although this source of digital credit is one to watch, given the overall small share of adults who used it but did not borrow formally and the uncertainty about who provides the digital credit, *Global Findex 2025* does not include it in its definition of formal borrowing.

Some adults borrowed to pay health or medical bills and some to start or operate a business

The evidence is mixed on the effects of microcredit access among poor adults, especially long-term effects on consumption, health, and women's economic empowerment.[8] Yet some of the literature has found that expanding access to high-interest consumer credit through microfinance loans can improve borrower welfare—boosting consumption, self-sufficiency, and some mental health outcomes—without causing harmful overborrowing, challenging assumptions that such lending is necessarily exploitative.[9] Other studies, however, do not find broader economywide effects but infer that microfinance loans are likely to help households smooth consumption,[10] in the wake of a financial shock as well as at other times.[11]

---

7   The seven economies are Cameroon (5 percent), the Republic of Congo (5 percent), Eswatini (12 percent), Gabon (7 percent), Lesotho (8 percent), Mauritania (8 percent), and Senegal (9 percent).

8   Banerjee et al. (2015).

9   Karlan and Zinman (2010).

10   Banerjee (2013); Banerjee, Karlan, and Zinman (2015). For additional discussion, refer to the CGAP Impact Pathfinder (https://www.impactpathfinder.org/).

11   Suri, Bharadwaj, and Jack (2021).

The Global Findex 2025 also asked adults whether they borrowed money to start or operate a business in the past year. In low- and middle-income economies, 11 percent of adults borrowed money for this reason, with just over half of that group (6 percent of adults) also saying they only borrowed informally (the survey did not ask directly whether adults who borrowed to start or operate a business did so from formal or informal sources).

The Global Findex 2025 additionally asked adults whether they borrowed money to pay health or medical expenses in the past year. In low- and middle-income economies, 19 percent of adults borrowed money for this reason. The proportion was about the same in 2021, but an increase from those in 2014 and 2017, when about 11 percent of adults borrowed to pay health or medical expenses.

Chapter 4.1 explores borrowing for starting or operating a business and borrowing for health or medical expenses in more detail in the context of financial health.

In the context of other financial services, formal borrowing is less common than saving or payments

The data shared in this chapter highlight that borrowing increased between 2021 and 2024. Yet formal borrowing remained much less common in 2024 than saving. It was also less common than using accounts to make or receive payments, the subject of the next chapter.

3.3 Payments

A reproducibility package is available for this book in the Reproducible Research Repository at https://reproducibility.worldbank.org/catalog/299.

3.3 Payments

Payments drive people's financial lives. They are both diverse, in that people make and receive a wide range of different types of payments, and ubiquitous, in that people often pay for things or receive payments daily. Making payments directly from or receiving payments directly in an account—ideally a digitally enabled one that equips the owner to use their money via mobile phone or credit or debit card wherever they are—can have a significant and positive impact on people's finances. Research finds that digital payments are associated with lower risk of theft,[1] greater speed and reliability,[2] and decreased personal costs because they eliminate expenses associated with traveling to make payments in person or collect money.[3]

Making or receiving payments using an account also creates a record of digital transactions that can support credit applications.[4] Finally, research finds that having an account to receive payments increases the frequency and volume of remittances and financial support from family members and friends.[5]

The Global Findex 2025 asked respondents whether they made or received a range of payments in the 12 months before taking the survey and how they did it, in order to understand more about their payment behaviors.

But first, a caveat: although the Global Findex captures trends around end-user behavior, that behavior depends on the context in which it takes place. A supportive enabling environment is essential if digital payments are to replace cash for everyday transactions. Fast and reliable digital infrastructure, widespread connectivity, and interoperable payment systems that make digital transactions seamless and inexpensive all make up the foundations of such an environment. Strong regulation is also critical, including well-designed and well-enforced consumer protection measures that build trust in digital systems. Digital public infrastructure, which includes digital ID and verification systems, data exchange systems, and fast payment systems, also enables secure, real-time, and inclusive financial transactions.[6] When well designed, these systems can lower costs, increase access for underserved communities, and accelerate the shift to digital payments, particularly in low- and middle-income economies.[7]

---

1   Wright et al. (2014).
2   Blumenstock et al. (2023).
3   Aker et al. (2016); Bangura (2016); Glynn-Broderick et al. (2021).
4   Chioda et al. (2025).
5   Lee et al. (2017).
6   Ardic Alper et al. (2023).
7   World Bank, "Project FASTT: Frictionless Affordable Safe Timely Transactions" (https://fastpayments.worldbank.org/).

More than 80 percent of account owners made or received digital payments

Across low- and middle-income economies, 62 percent of all adults—or 82 percent of account owners—either made or received at least one digital payment in the 12 months before taking the survey (refer to map 3.3.1 and figure 3.3.1; refer to box 3.3.1 for how the Global Findex defines making and receiving digital payments).[8]

Whereas the share of adults who made or received a digital payment increased by 6 percentage points in 2024 compared with the share in 2021, the share of account owners using digital payments remained steady at about 80 percent. However, the share of adults using digital payments in low- and middle-income economies almost doubled, from 34 percent of adults in 2014, when the Global Findex first collected data on digital payments, to 62 percent in 2024. In terms of the share of account owners using digital payments, in 2024, 82 percent of account owners did so, up from 63 percent in 2014 and about the same percentage as in 2021, when the COVID-19 pandemic prompted many adults to make their first digital payments.

Map 3.3.1 **The share of adults who made or received at least one digital payment varies widely across low- and middle-income economies**

Adults who made or received a digital payment in the past year (%), 2024

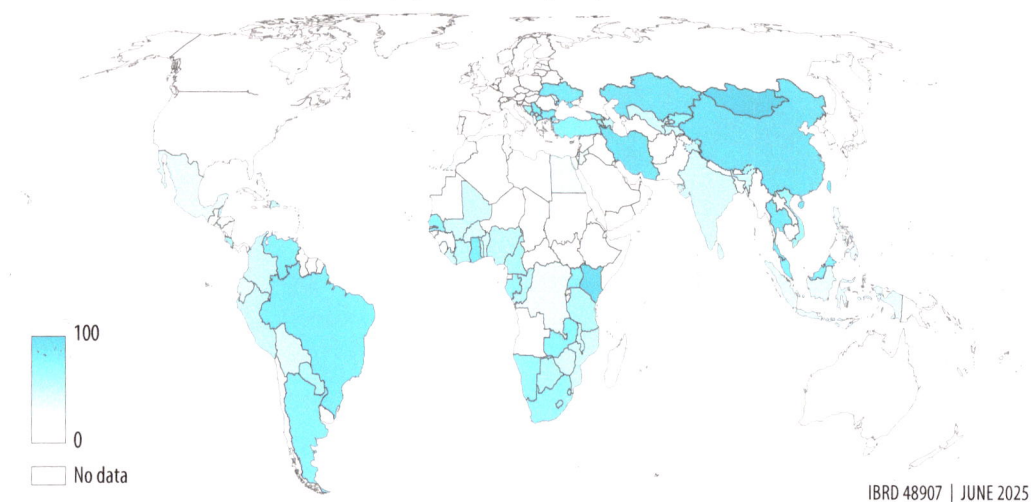

IBRD 48907 | JUNE 2025

Source: Global Findex Database 2025.
Note: In Algeria, China, the Islamic Republic of Iran, Libya, Mauritius, and Ukraine, an abridged questionnaire was administered by phone, and it did not include the questions on receiving payments. For these six economies, adults who made a digital payment or accessed their account using a credit or debit card or phone are identified as having made or received a digital payment.

---

8   The Russian Federation is not included in the averages for low- and middle-income economies or for the Europe and Central Asia region because data on payments were not collected there in 2024. For six economies in which abridged questionnaires were administered by phone—Algeria, China, the Islamic Republic of Iran, Libya, Mauritius, and Ukraine—adults who made digital payments or accessed their accounts using a debit or credit card or phone are identified as having made and received digital payments (refer also to box 3.3.1).

Figure 3.3.1 **In low- and middle-income economies, the share of adults using digital payments grew between 2014 and 2024**

Adults with an account (%), 2014–24

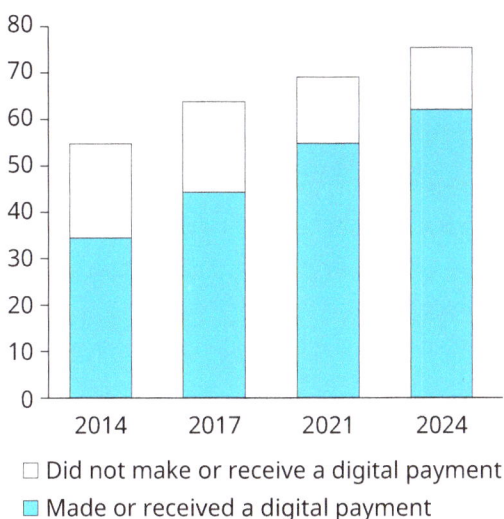

☐ Did not make or receive a digital payment
☐ Made or received a digital payment

Source: Global Findex Database 2025.

Note: In 2024 in Algeria, China, the Islamic Republic of Iran, Libya, Mauritius, and Ukraine, an abridged questionnaire was administered by phone, and it did not include any questions on receiving payments. For these six economies, adults who made a digital payment or accessed their account using a credit or debit card or phone are identified as having made or received a digital payment. Because an abridged questionnaire was administered in the Russian Federation in 2024, averages exclude data for this economy. For comparability across time, averages for earlier years similarly exclude data for Russia and may thus differ from previously published numbers.

These usage levels make digital payments the most popular formal financial service, employed by twice as many adults in low- and middle-income economies as formally saved (40 percent) and more than three times as many as formally borrowed (24 percent).

Digital payment usage among account owners is high across regions, except South Asia

The use of digital payments among account owners is high across all regions except South Asia (refer to figure 3.3.2), where just 57 percent of account owners made or received digital payments. The share ranged from 47 percent in Nepal and 54 percent in India to 78 percent in Bangladesh and as high as 90 percent in Pakistan (albeit based on just 23 percent of adults having an account). In contrast, more than 80 percent of account owners made or received digital payments in all other regions.

Box 3.3.1 **What it means to make or receive a digital payment and where the Global Findex survey asked about it**

The Global Findex 2025 defines a *digital payment* as any payment sent directly from or received directly in an account at a bank or similar financial institution, like a credit union, microfinance institution, or post office, or using a mobile money account

(Box continued next page)

included in the GSMA Mobile Money Deployment Tracker (refer to box 2.1.1 for the full Global Findex 2025 definition of an *account*).

Account owners can make digital payments directly from their accounts using debit or credit cards, mobile phones, or the internet or by transferring funds directly to another account. The survey measures activity around several types of payments people make, including merchant and utility bill payments, as well as making bill payments or domestic person-to-person payments.

The survey also captures whether people received certain types of payments (for example, government payments, including social disbursement and pension payments; wage payments from the government or the private sector; and agriculture payments) and whether they received them directly in an account, in cash, or through another method. Receiving payments also includes receiving domestic person-to-person payments.

For most high-income economies and the Russian Federation, the Global Findex survey includes only questions on account ownership and not questions on payments. As a result, there are no global or high-income averages in this chapter, and Russia is excluded from all averages for Europe and Central Asia.

In Algeria, China, the Islamic Republic of Iran, Libya, Mauritius, and Ukraine, an abridged questionnaire was administered by phone, and it did not include any of the questions on receiving payments. Regarding making payments, the questionnaire in these economies included questions on merchant payments and bill payments, but not on making utility bill payments and making domestic person-to-person payments.

For these six economies, adults who make a digital payment or access their accounts using a credit or debit card or phone are identified as having made or received a digital payment. However, because data for these six economies do not include information on receiving payments, the time series figures for receiving payments have been adjusted to exclude data from these economies in previous years to enable consistent year-over-year comparisons.

The "Methodology" tab of the Global Findex website (http://globalfindex.worldbank .org) provides details on the information collected in each surveyed economy.

Figure 3.3.2 Digital payment use is high among account owners everywhere except South Asia, where rates of adoption vary by economy

Adults with an account (%), 2024

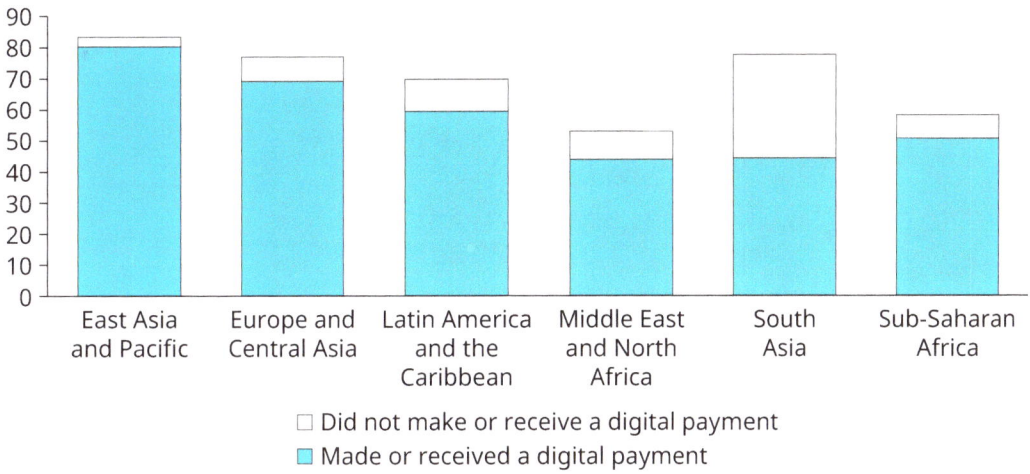

Did not make or receive a digital payment
Made or received a digital payment

Source: Global Findex Database 2025.

Note: In Algeria, China, the Islamic Republic of Iran, Libya, Mauritius, and Ukraine, an abridged questionnaire was administered by phone, and it did not include any questions on receiving payments. For these six economies, adults who made a digital payment or accessed their account using a credit or debit card or phone are identified as having made or received a digital payment.

Digital payment gaps persist among account owners

In low- and middle-income economies, women and poorer adults are less likely than men and wealthier adults to have an account, as documented in chapter 2.1. Use of digital payments is also relatively lower among these groups.

Women are less likely to use digital payments

In addition to the gap among all adults, among account owners, women are also less likely than men to use digital payments. The gender gap is not universal, however. In fact, the gender gap in the use of digital payments among account owners is statistically nonsignificant in most regions. In Europe and Central Asia, however, 84 percent of women with an account use digital payments compared with 93 percent of men. This difference is driven by a 13 percentage point gender gap in Türkiye.

In South Asia, the region with the lowest share of digital payment use among account owners, women are 15 percentage points less likely than men to use digital payments, with just half of women account owners doing so, compared with nearly two-thirds of men account owners (refer to figure 3.3.3). Some economies in the

Figure 3.3.3 In South Asia, the region with the greatest gender gaps in digital payment use among account owners, such gaps are present in every economy except Pakistan

Adults with an account (%), 2024

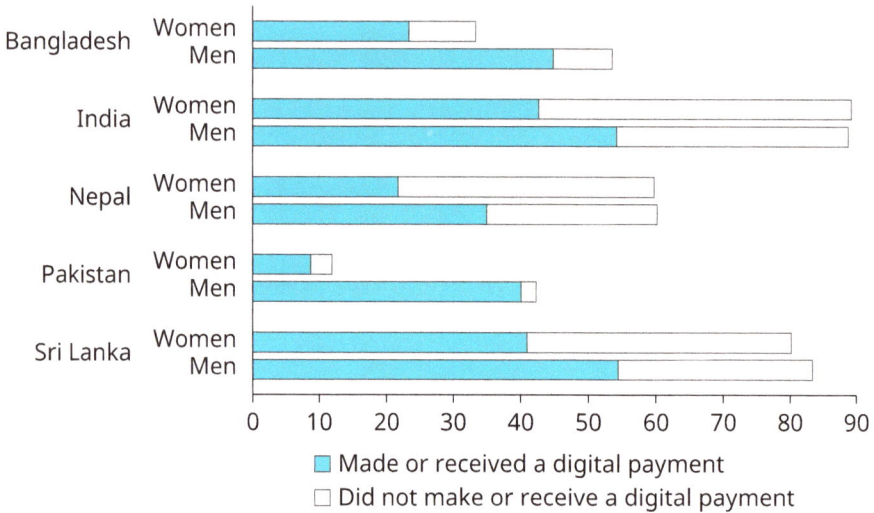

■ Made or received a digital payment
□ Did not make or receive a digital payment

Source: Global Findex Database 2025.

region have even larger gender gaps. Nepal, for example, has a gap of more than 20 percentage points (36 percent of women with accounts versus 58 percent of men), as does Pakistan (74 percent of women with accounts versus 95 percent of men), and the gaps are about 13 percentage points each, also in favor of men, in Bangladesh, India, and Sri Lanka.

Poorer, rural, and young account owners are also less likely to use digital payments

The income gap in the use of digital payments is even wider than the gender gap. Among adults with an account, the income gap is 10 percentage points, with 76 percent of adults in the poorest 40 percent of households within economies using digital payments, compared with 86 percent of adults in the wealthiest 60 percent (refer to figure 3.3.4). This gap has remained unchanged compared with that in 2021 despite a 5 percentage point growth in the use of digital payments among poorer adults.

In most regions, the income gap in digital payment use is about 6 percentage points, but in South Asia it is 20 percentage points. Specifically, 45 percent of poorer adults with accounts use digital payments, compared with 64 percent of wealthier adults in the region. This divide is driven by India, where 42 percent of poorer

Figure 3.3.4 Among adults with accounts, poor people, rural residents, and younger adults are less likely than wealthier people, urban residents, and older adults to use digital payments

Adults with an account (%), 2024

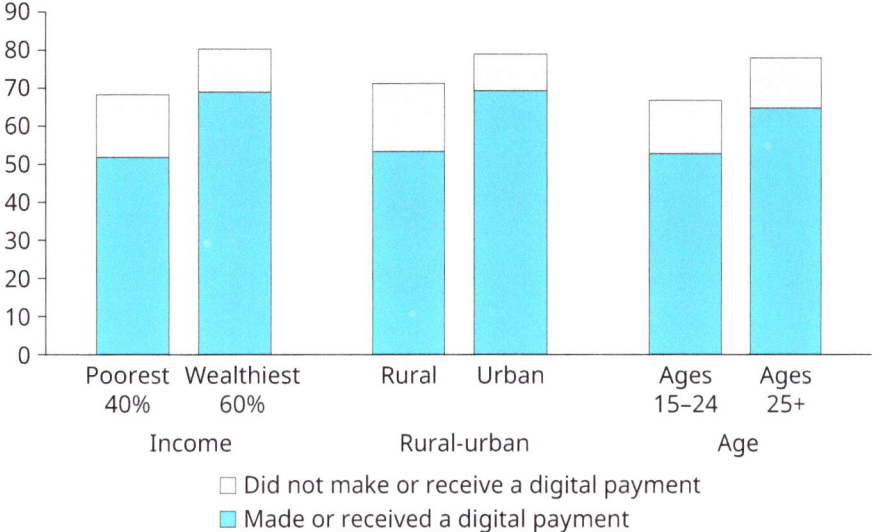

Source: Global Findex Database 2025.

Note: In Algeria, China, the Islamic Republic of Iran, Libya, Mauritius, and Ukraine, an abridged questionnaire was administered by phone, and it did not include any questions on receiving payments. For these six economies, adults who made a digital payment or accessed their account using a credit or debit card or phone are identified as having made or received a digital payment.

adults with accounts and 62 percent of wealthier adults with accounts use digital payments. In other economies in South Asia, the gap among account owners is 10 percentage points or less. In Pakistan, for example, both account ownership and digital payment use are low, yet 90 percent or more of account owners in both poorer and wealthier households use digital payments. This disparity might be driven by the use of accounts for social transfer payments (discussed later in this chapter).

Across low- and middle-income economies, adults living in rural areas are 16 percentage points less likely than adults in urban areas to make a digital payment: 53 percent compared with 69 percent. The gap narrows when measured as a share of account owners: 75 percent of rural account owners use digital payments, compared with 87 percent of urban account owners.

Young adults are more than 10 percentage points less likely than older adults to use digital payments, though among those with accounts, the difference is just 4 percentage points.

The patterns described thus far detailing digital payment use by region and among women and men, poorer and wealthier adults, and rural and urban residents repeat with only slight variations across the different payment types explored in the remainder of this chapter.

Making digital payments

The Global Findex 2025 asks about several common payments people make or send, including merchant payments, payments of utility and other bills, and person-to-person (P2P) payments.[9] The share of adults making any of these types of payments digitally in the economies that answered the full set of questions about payments is 52 percent, or two-thirds (69 percent) of account owners. Compared with that in 2021, the share of account owners making digital payments remained unchanged.

Digital merchant payments show continued growth since COVID-19

Merchant payments are nearly universal: almost everyone pays businesses for something.[10] Whether for food, household supplies, personal items, and clothing or for electronic devices, appliances, and furniture, merchant payments can be of low value and frequent or of high value and occasional. Encouraging payers to make such payments from an account using a debit or credit card or mobile phone (that is, digitally) instead of in cash can benefit payers by making the money transferred safer from theft. Paying digitally also creates a record of payment, which is helpful in cases of disputes and for enabling household financial management. Businesses also benefit from such a digital payment record, because they can use it to document profitability and cash flows, both critical enablers of embedded finance models that can help small businesses grow and create jobs.[11]

The caveat for businesses, however, is that they face multiple constraints to adoption of digital payments, including low payment digitalization in the broader ecosystems in which they operate and potentially high costs of accepting digital payments, including the costs of payment infrastructure (point-of-service devices or smartphones with payment apps) and payment fees. Business informality and distrust of providers of payment services and governments could also dissuade businesses from adopting digital payments.

---

9   The Global Findex 2025 also asked respondents about receiving P2P payments. Making and receiving P2P payments are discussed in the section "Receiving Payments."

10 The survey asked merchants in all low- and middle-income economies except Russia questions about digital payments.

11 CGAP, "Digital Credit Models for Small Businesses," October 2019 (https://www.cgap.org/research/publication /digital-credit-models-for-small-businesses).

For these reasons and others, ecosystems for merchant payments in many low- and middle-income economies continue to be cash driven. That is slowly changing, however. As of 2024, 42 percent of adults made a digital merchant payment either in a store or online (refer to figure 3.3.5).[12] This represents a 7 percentage point increase from 2021, when the Global Findex survey first asked about digital merchant payments. About 40 percent of adults making digital merchant payments in that year started using them for the first time after the beginning of the COVID-19 pandemic.

Most economies have maintained the levels of adoption of digital merchant payments they showed in 2021 and have continued the general trend toward growth. Nonetheless, some economies have much higher levels of adoption of digital merchant payments than average. In China, for example, 80 percent of adults made a digital merchant payment in 2024. When data for China are excluded, the low- and middle-income average for use of digital merchant payments is 24 percent of adults.

Figure 3.3.5 Adoption of digital merchant payments has grown since 2021

Adults who made a digital merchant payment (%), 2021–24

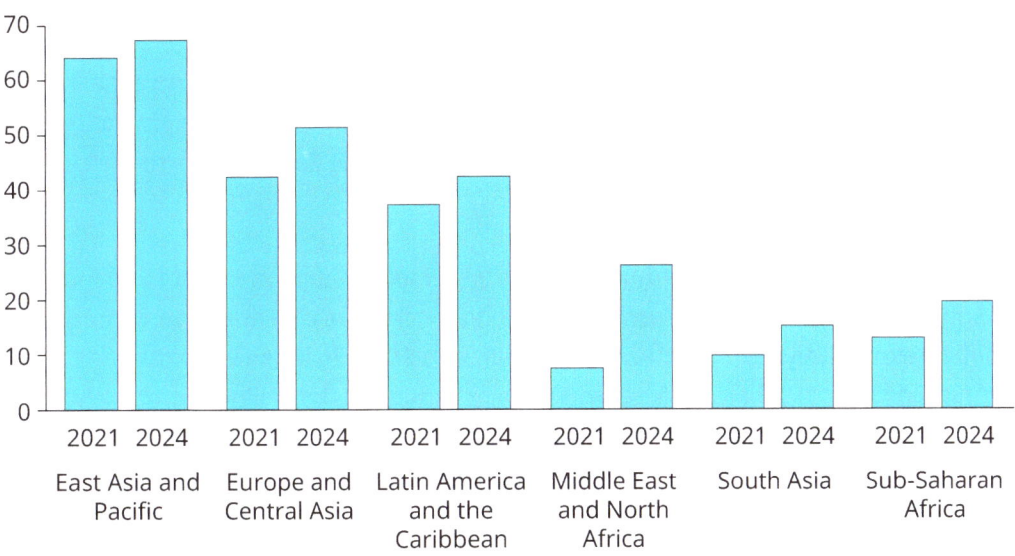

Source: Global Findex Database 2025.

Note: Because an abridged questionnaire was administered in the Russian Federation in 2024, averages exclude data for this economy. For comparability across time, averages for earlier years similarly exclude data for Russia and may thus differ from previously published numbers.

---

12   The Global Findex 2025 includes adults that report paying for an online purchase both in cash and online as making an online digital payment.

Use of digital merchant payments is greatest in East Asia and Pacific, at 67 percent of all adults. This high percentage is driven by that in China, where, as mentioned, 80 percent of adults made a digital merchant payment. This is consistent with the Chinese economy's high levels of smartphone penetration, internet use, and adoption of digital activities, as discussed in chapters 1.1 and 1.2.

When data for China are excluded, 27 percent of adults in East Asia and Pacific made a digital merchant payment, though several economies experienced notable increases between 2021 and 2024. Examples include Cambodia, the Lao People's Democratic Republic, and Viet Nam, where the share of adults making digital merchant payments at least doubled during that period, from 3 percent, 9 percent, and 24 percent of adults, respectively, to 20 percent, 22 percent, and 51 percent, respectively. Among low- and middle-income economies, Mongolia has the highest rate of digital merchant payments at 95 percent (about equivalent to its share of account ownership).

The regions with the next-highest shares of adults making digital merchant payments are Europe and Central Asia at 51 percent (a 9 percentage points increase from 2021) and Latin America and the Caribbean at 43 percent (a slight increase, 5 percentage points). The Middle East and North Africa saw its rate of use of digital merchant payments almost triple since 2021, albeit from a low base, to 26 percent of adults. This increase was driven entirely by a 64 percentage point increase in digital merchant payments in the Islamic Republic of Iran. When data for the Islamic Republic of Iran are excluded, the average for the Middle East and North Africa is 7 percent.

In South Asia, 15 percent of adults made digital merchant payments in 2024, and in Sub-Saharan Africa, 20 percent of adults did, increases of 5 and 7 percentage points, respectively, compared with the shares in 2021. In a few individual economies in Sub-Saharan Africa, the share of adults making digital merchant payments grew twofold or more between 2021 and 2024. They include Cameroon and Zambia, in both of which the share of adults making digital merchant payments is now at about 20 percent; Ghana and Nigeria, where the share reached about 28 percent at the end of that period; and Senegal, where it is 37 percent. In Kenya, adoption of digital merchant payments increased from 37 percent to 56 percent of adults.

Outside of Sub-Saharan Africa, in economies like Armenia, the Dominican Republic, the Kyrgyz Republic, Paraguay, and Tajikistan, adoption of digital merchant payments doubled between 2021 and 2024, albeit from lower shares, reaching 26 percent or more of adults in all five economies.

Women, poorer adults, and rural adults are less likely than men, wealthier adults, and urban adults to make digital merchant payments

Women and men make digital merchant payments at different rates, though the 6 percentage point gap between the two is consistent with the gender gap in account ownership. Among all adults, 38 percent of women made digital merchant payments in low- and middle-income economies and 45 percent of men did. South Asia had the widest gender gap in digital merchant payments at 13 percentage points; East Asia and Pacific, in contrast, had no gap.

Not surprisingly, adoption levels and growth rates of digital merchant payments are lower among adults living in the poorest 40 percent of households within economies compared with the levels and rates in the wealthiest 60 percent of households. Overall, 31 percent of poorer adults made a digital merchant payment, compared with 48 percent of wealthier adults. Both of those shares reflect increases from 2021, when 27 percent of poorer adults made a digital merchant payment and 40 percent of wealthier adults did; the difference for the poorer income group is under the threshold for statistical significance, however.

Variation by rural versus urban context is even greater. Among adults living in rural areas, 28 percent made digital merchant payments, compared with 53 percent of adults living in urban areas. Importantly, this difference is not exclusively driven by differences in account ownership among these groups. When adoption rates for digital merchant payments among account owners are examined, adults living in rural areas are still 27 percentage points less likely to make a digital merchant payment than those living in urban areas. This may be because fewer rural merchants accept digital payments.

Online shopping and digital merchant payments

The subset of digital merchant payments that is specific to online purchases shows distinct patterns among regions of the world. These patterns are mostly consistent with the global trends in smartphone ownership and internet use discussed in chapters 1.1 and 1.2. The regions and economies with higher levels of digital connectivity have higher rates of online shopping behaviors, though rates of digital payment show patterns that are more nuanced.

Overall, in low- and middle-income economies, 36 percent of adults bought something online. Of these online shoppers, nearly 20 percent paid for their online purchases exclusively using cash on delivery.[13]

---

13   In low- and middle-income economies, 5 percent of online shoppers paid both online and on delivery.

East Asia and Pacific had the highest share of online shoppers at 65 percent of all adults, with 87 percent of shoppers also paying for their purchases online (refer to figure 3.3.6). Yet as with the overall trends in digital merchant payments in the region, rates of adoption of online payment are driven mostly by high usage levels in China. When data for China are excluded, online shopping rates for East Asia and Pacific drop to 34 percent of adults, with just over half of them, 18 percent, paying cash on delivery. Rates of this behavior are particularly high in certain of the region's economies. For instance, in Malaysia and Thailand, between 30 percent and 40 percent of adults making online purchases pay cash on delivery; in Indonesia and the Philippines, more than half do (refer to figure 3.3.7).

Latin America and the Caribbean had the highest share of online shoppers who paid digitally: 27 percent of adults shopped online, and 87 percent of them paid online. South Asia had the lowest relative share of online purchasers paying online: 14 percent of adults shopped online, and about half of them paid digitally.

Figure 3.3.6 **In low- and middle-income economies, two-thirds of adults who shop online also pay for their purchases online; the remaining online shoppers pay on delivery**

Adults who made an online purchase (%), 2024

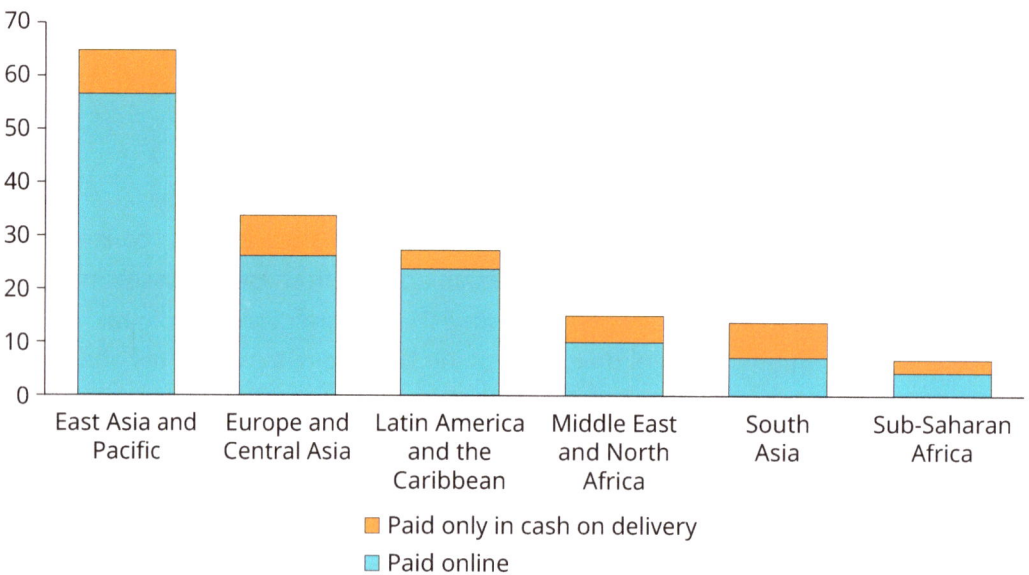

- Paid only in cash on delivery
- Paid online

Source: Global Findex Database 2025.

Figure 3.3.7 In certain East Asian economies, a large share of adults shop online but pay cash on delivery

Adults who made an online purchase (%), 2024

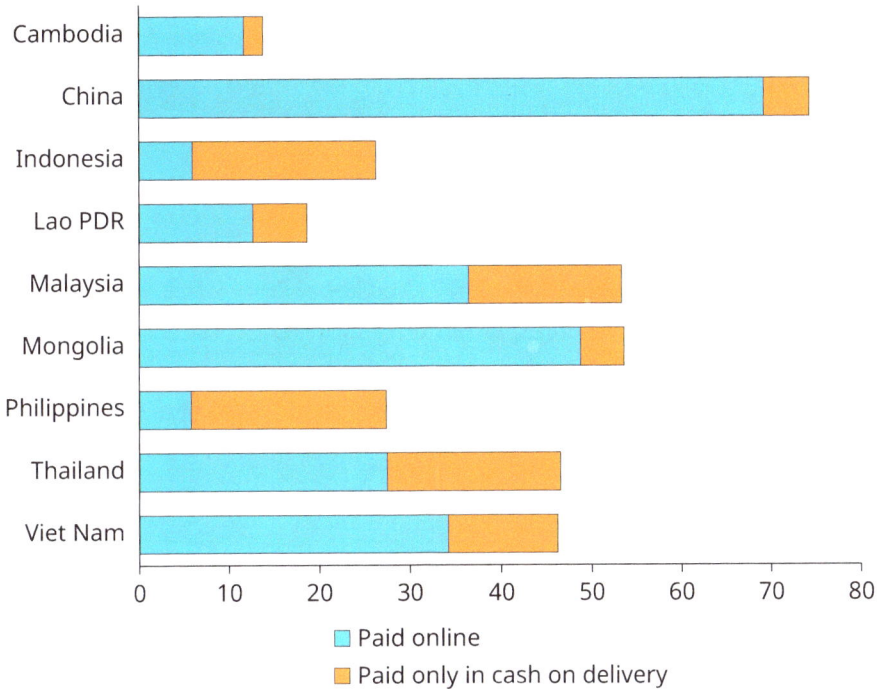

Legend:
- ■ Paid online
- ■ Paid only in cash on delivery

Source: Global Findex Database 2025.

In Sub-Saharan Africa, adults also make digital merchant payments in informal markets

In many parts of the world, people do some or all of their shopping for groceries and household supplies in outdoor markets. To capture digital merchant payments that are not technically in stores or online, the Global Findex 2025 asked people for the first time if they used their debit or credit cards or mobile phones to pay for household food or cleaning supplies. In the low- and middle-income economies in which this question was asked,[14] 18 percent of all adults did so.

Although this specific use case for digital merchant payments is not included in the Global Findex definition for *made a digital payment* or *received a digital payment*, doing so would add 0.5 percent of adults in low- and middle-income economies, including 1 percent of adults in Sub-Saharan Africa. Inclusion of adults who use

---

14   In Algeria, China, the Islamic Republic of Iran, Libya, Mauritius, Russia, and Ukraine, the survey did not ask merchants in informal markets questions about digital payments.

phones or debit or credit cards to pay for groceries, but do not make in-store digital payments, adds 3 percentage points to the low- and middle-income economy averages for digital merchant payments and 4 percentage points to the average for Sub-Saharan Africa. This margin of increase is highest in Kenya (15 percentage points) and in Botswana and Zambia (8 and 9 percentage points, respectively). This suggests possible opportunities for merchants without established physical storefronts to leverage records of their digital payment inflows as proof of income when applying for credit.[15]

Online bill payments

Separate from online shopping, since 2017 the Global Findex has asked, across all low- and middle-income economies, whether respondents paid a bill using a mobile phone or computer. In 2024, 37 percent of adults, or 49 percent of account owners, paid a bill online, up from 28 percent of all adults (41 percent of account owners) in 2021 and 16 percent of all adults (about 25 percent of account owners) in 2017 (refer to figure 3.3.8).

Figure 3.3.8 **In low- and middle-income economies, 37 percent of adults pay bills online**

Adults who made an online bill payment in the past year (%), 2017–24·

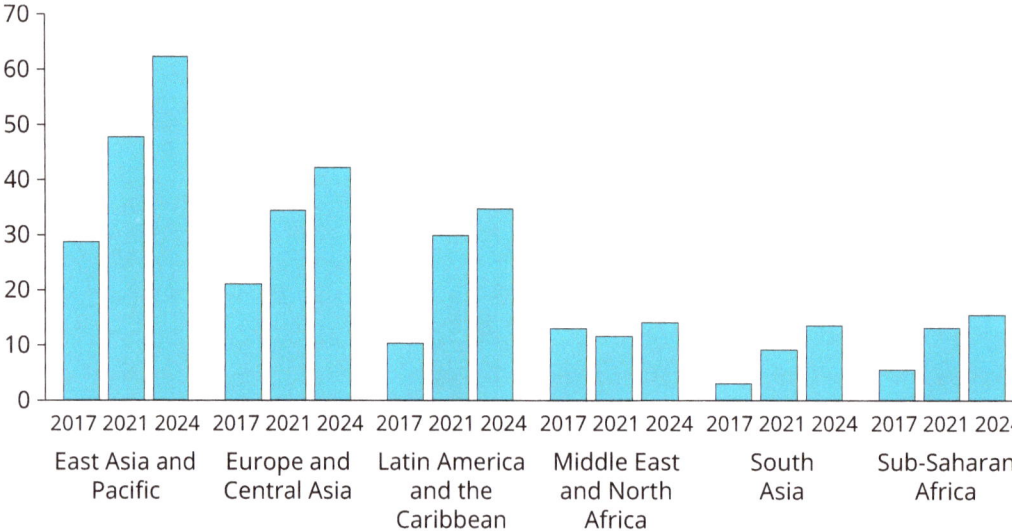

Source: Global Findex Database 2025.

Note: Because an abridged questionnaire was administered in the Russian Federation in 2024, averages exclude data for this economy. For comparability across time, averages for earlier years similarly exclude data for Russia and may thus differ from previously published numbers.

---

15   For a discussion, refer to Krujiff, Sawhney, and Wright (2024).

A few economies have very high rates of online bill payment. In China, 74 percent of adults made an online bill payment, and in Brazil, Kazakhstan, Kenya, Mongolia, Türkiye, and Ukraine, just over half (between 51 percent and 55 percent) of adults did. The regional averages are more modest. For example, in East Asia and Pacific excluding China, 39 percent of adults made an online bill payment. In Europe and Central Asia, 42 percent did, and in Latin America and the Caribbean, 35 percent did. Only about 15 percent of adults paid bills online in the Middle East and North Africa, South Asia, and Sub-Saharan Africa. Across all regions, the share of adults making online bill payments increased between 2021 and 2024.

More adults in low- and middle-income economies are paying their utility bills digitally

Utility bills, as distinct from the more general online bills discussed previously, are interesting from the perspective of adoption of digital payments because they come due at a regular cadence and therefore help promote habitual behavior. They are also associated with access to essential infrastructure like water and electricity. Paying them digitally can increase on-time payment and enable innovations such as pay-as-you-go delivery models,[16] rebates for energy savings, and green energy credits, all of which can inform sustainable infrastructure development.[17]

In low- and middle-income economies,[18] 45 percent of all adults made regular payments for water, electricity, or trash collection, with about 40 percent of these respondents (17 percent of all adults) making those payments digitally.[19] The rest paid only in cash, and a small but declining share paid "some other way." Between 2014 and 2024, the share of adults paying digitally increased from 32 percent to 39 percent of utility bill payers.

Across economies and regions, utility bill payment practices vary. In Europe and Central Asia, Latin America and the Caribbean, and Sub-Saharan Africa, just over half of adults who paid utility bills did so digitally (refer to figure 3.3.9). By contrast, about a third of utility bill payers did so in East Asia and Pacific and South Asia. In the Middle East and North Africa less than 10 percent did so. Notably, in Kenya and Mongolia, close to 100 percent of adults who made utility bill payments did so digitally.

---

16   Gertler et al. (2025); Gertler, Green, and Wolfram (2023).
17   For additional discussion, refer to KPMG (2015).
18   Because an abridged questionnaire was administered in Algeria, China, the Islamic Republic of Iran, Libya, Mauritius, Russia, and Ukraine, averages exclude data for these economies.
19   The Global Findex survey asks whether respondents personally made such payments, not whether households did.

Figure 3.3.9 In low- and middle-income economies, 40 percent of adults who paid utility bills did so digitally

Adults who paid utility bills in the past year (%), 2024

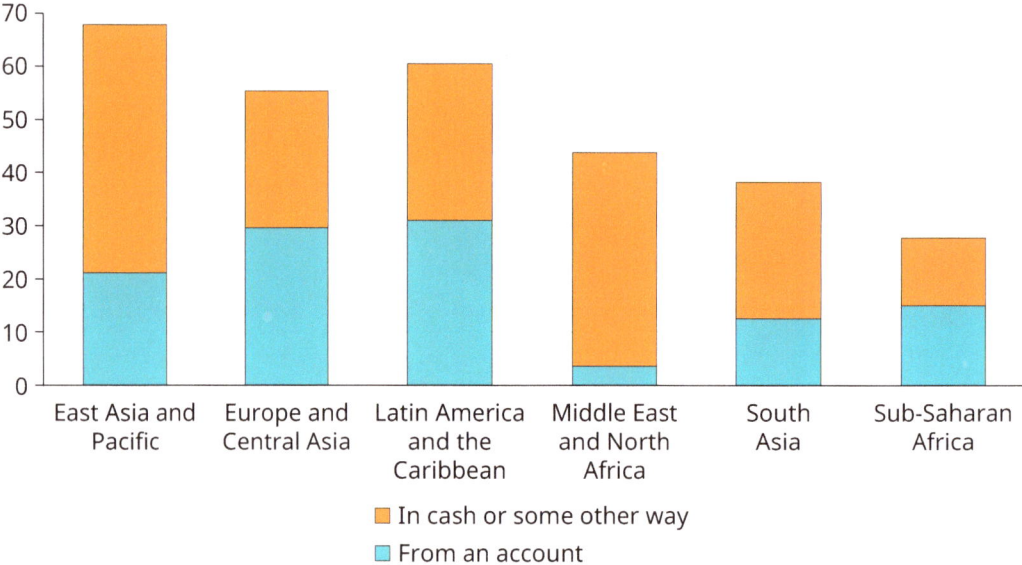

Source: Global Findex Database 2025.

Most people pay in cash out of habit

Efforts to encourage people to make more of their payments digitally cannot assume that people will be compelled to use digital payment options just because they are available. Digital payments need to be perceived as better than cash payments, not simply an alternative to them.

To understand the barriers to adoption of digital payment, the Global Findex 2025 asked respondents with accounts who exclusively make merchant payments in cash why they do not pay digitally. The most common answer is habit: across all regions, people say they are simply used to paying merchants in cash (refer to figure 3.3.10). This may imply that the benefits of making digital merchant payments are not valuable enough to warrant making the switch away from paying in cash.[20] Furthermore, some merchants accept only cash or charge more for digital payments, though those barriers stand out for only a minority of cash users.

---

20   CGAP, "Digitizing Merchant Payments" (https://www.cgap.org/topics/collections/digitizing-merchant-payments
      /value-proposition) and "Cash Is King in Merchant Payments" (https://www.cgap.org/research/publication/cash-is
      -king-in-merchant-payments).

Figure 3.3.10 **In every region, the habit of paying in cash is the most common reason why people do not pay merchants digitally**

Adults who did not make a digital payment for an in-store purchase in the past year citing a given reason as the main reason for using only cash to pay (%), 2024

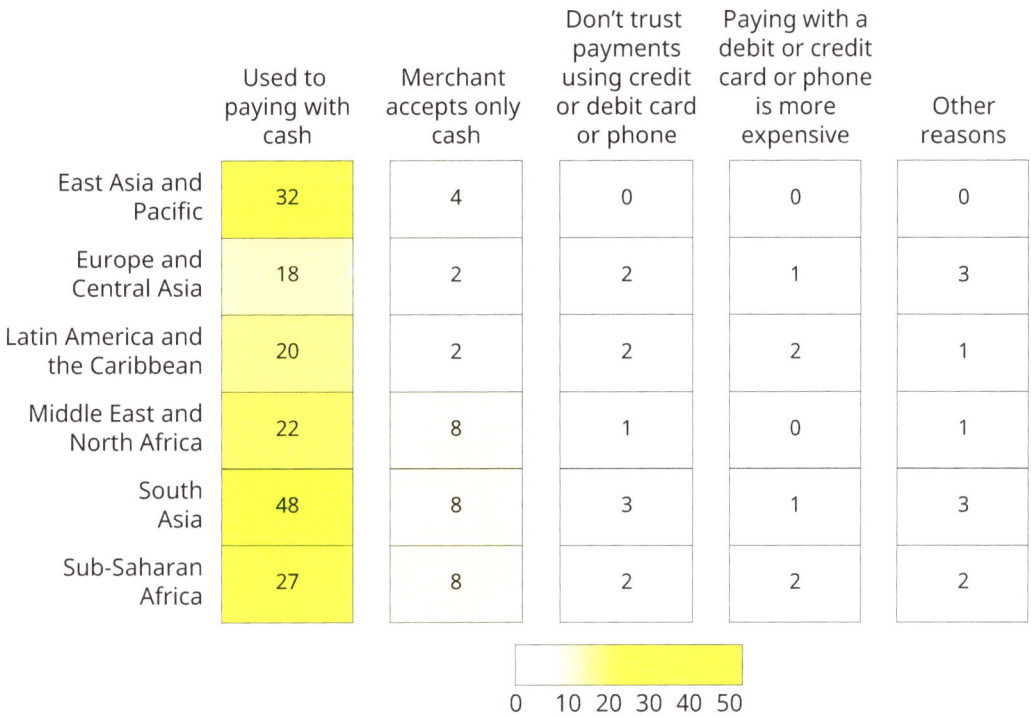

	Used to paying with cash	Merchant accepts only cash	Don't trust payments using credit or debit card or phone	Paying with a debit or credit card or phone is more expensive	Other reasons
East Asia and Pacific	32	4	0	0	0
Europe and Central Asia	18	2	2	1	3
Latin America and the Caribbean	20	2	2	2	1
Middle East and North Africa	22	8	1	0	1
South Asia	48	8	3	1	3
Sub-Saharan Africa	27	8	2	2	2

0 10 20 30 40 50

Source: Global Findex Database 2025.

Digital payments cannot replace cash payments until merchants and other payment recipients operate in a supportive business environment, with affordable and reliable access to a digital ecosystem. For example, most small merchants use much of their revenues to restock inventory. If they are unable to pay their suppliers in cash because their customers pay digitally, then collecting payments digitally adds both time and monetary costs, as it requires them to close their shops, find agents, and pay cash-out fees to access the cash needed to restock. They can avoid all of this by simply accepting only cash payments from the start, which is why many merchants offer no options for digital payment.

Promoting acceptance of digital payment methods among merchants requires delivering clear value propositions, such as, for instance, services built on a digital infrastructure that directly benefit their businesses and expand access to credit. New underwriting models that leverage digital payment data and tools can enable lenders to more accurately assess a merchant borrower's ability to repay a loan. Certain tools can also divert payments directly toward loan repayment, helping lenders better measure and manage risk.

In addition, changing cash-paying habits among buyers requires time and evidence of benefits, the latter of which could become clear as more members of poorer communities acquire accounts and people see others using digital payments.[21] Governments such as the Republic of Korea's have nudged that progress by implementing tax incentives to encourage digital payments,[22] and financial institutions might offer rewards such as cash back or lower fees for using digital methods. These initiatives likely will have to be just one aspect of holistic efforts to transition cash habits to digital ones. Public awareness campaigns could also play a role, for example, by highlighting the often-overlooked costs associated with cash usage, including security risks, withdrawal fees, and the inconvenience of handling physical currency.

Receiving payments

In low- and middle-income economies (not including the six economies in which questions on receiving payments were not asked),[23] 36 percent of adults—or more than half of account owners—had received a digital payment in the last 12 months. These payments included payments from governments, employers, or sale of agricultural products as well as P2P payments from family members or someone in recipients' social networks.

Government payments continue to become digitalized

In the low- and middle-income economies in which questions relating to receiving payments were asked, 23 percent of adults received a government-to-person (G2P) payment in some form, whether a social disbursement, a pension payment, or payment of a public sector wage. About three-quarters of recipients of G2P payments (73 percent) received them directly in an account.[24] This reflects an increase in the share of G2P payments disbursed digitally in these economies from 60 percent in 2017 to 62 percent in 2021. It includes 3 percent of adults who received government wage payments and 14 percent who received government transfers or pension payments. The remaining recipients of G2P payments received them in cash or some other form, such as a voucher.

---

21   Higgins (2024).

22   Sung, Awasthi, and Lee (2017).

23   Because an abridged questionnaire was administered in Algeria, China, the Islamic Republic of Iran, Libya, Mauritius, Russia, and Ukraine, questions on receiving payments were not asked in these economies, and data related to these questions are not included in averages for regions and low- and middle-income economies.

24   This includes less than 1 percent of adults who said they received such payments directly on a payment card issued for the disbursement of wages or government payments and typically linked to an individual account. The Global Findex considers this to be a payment into an account. Refer to the definition of *account* in box 2.1.1.

Although the share of adults receiving G2P payments ranges from 13 percent of adults in Sub-Saharan Africa to about a third of adults in East Asia and Pacific and Europe and Central Asia, in every region more than half of adults receiving such payments were paid digitally (refer to figure 3.3.11). The share is even higher in Latin America and the Caribbean and South Asia, where 77 percent of recipients did so, and in Europe and Central Asia and the Middle East and North Africa, where more than 80 percent of recipients did so. This trend toward G2P payment digitalization is grounded in the myriad benefits it provides both to governments, in terms of accountability, efficiency, and cost saving, and to recipients, in terms of safety and time savings.[25]

South Asia stands out for the growing share of adults in the region receiving digital G2P payments. In India, Nepal, and Sri Lanka, the share of adults receiving G2P payments digitally grew by about 20 percentage points between 2017 and 2024. Other economies, such as the Kyrgyz Republic and Morocco, experienced similarly impressive growth in the share of adults receiving digital G2P payments.

Figure 3.3.11 **More than half of G2P payment recipients in every region were paid digitally**

Adults who received a G2P payment in the past year (%), 2024

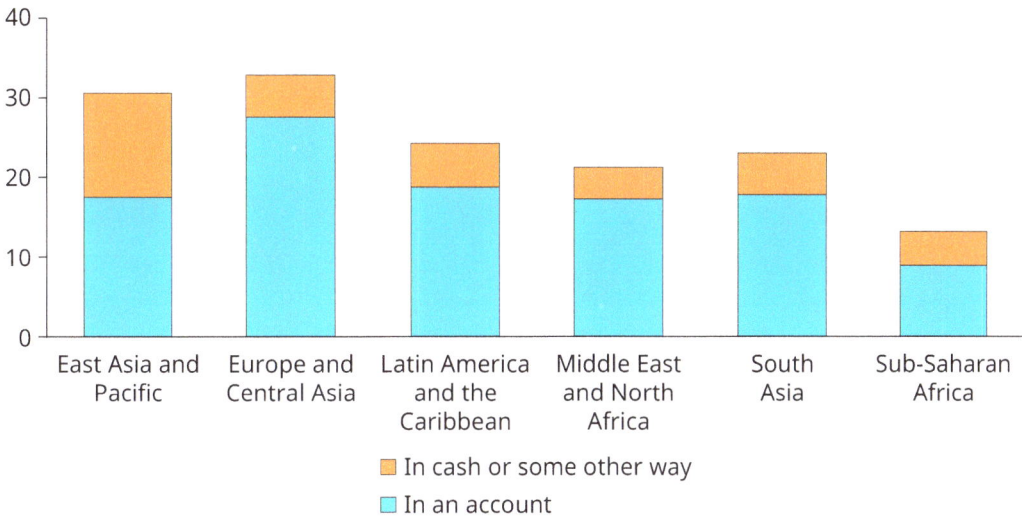

Source: Global Findex Database 2025.
Note: G2P = government-to-person.

---

25   Muralidharan, Niehaus, and Sukhtankar (2016).

On average, women and men who receive a G2P payment are equally likely to receive it digitally. But adults living in the poorest 40 percent of households within economies and receiving G2P payments are 10 percentage points less likely to receive such payments digitally than adults living in the wealthiest 60 percent of households within economies and receiving these payments.

Private sector wages are increasingly paid digitally

In low- and middle-income economies, 28 percent of adults received wage payments from private sector employers. Forty-five percent of those payments were deposited into accounts, an increase from 28 percent in 2014 and about the same share as in 2021.

These averages mask large variations across regions and economies (refer to figure 3.3.12). Europe and Central Asia and Latin America and the Caribbean have the highest shares of private sector wages received digitally at 79 percent and 72 percent, respectively. By contrast, in the Middle East and North Africa, only 20 percent of those receiving a private sector wage payment do so digitally.

Figure 3.3.12 **Half of the recipients of private sector wages in low- and middle-income economies were paid digitally, though the share was much lower in some regions**

Adults who received a private sector wage payment in the past year (%), 2024

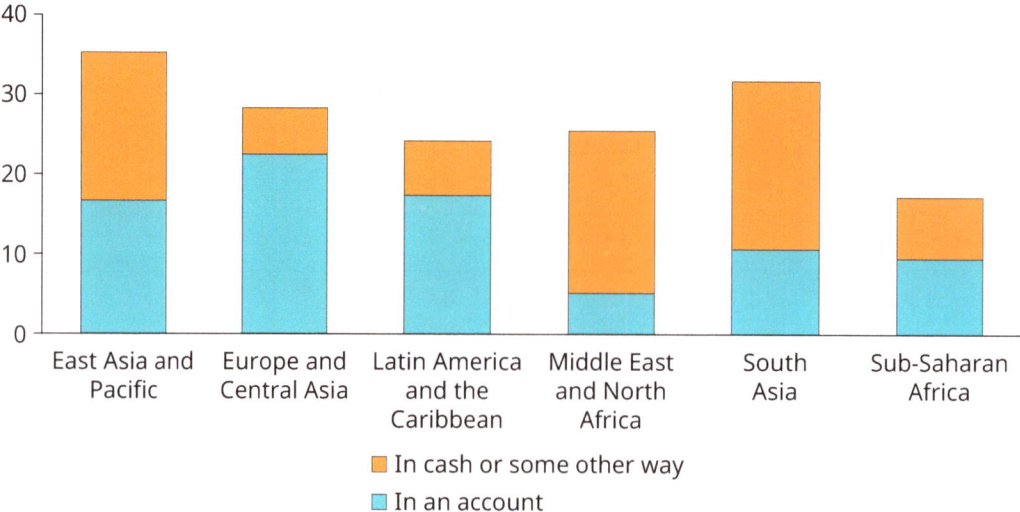

In cash or some other way
In an account

Source: Global Findex Database 2025.

Within regions there can be large variations as well, and an economy's income group does not necessarily predict the share of people within that economy who receive a private sector wage payment in an account. In East Asia and Pacific and Sub-Saharan Africa, for example, roughly half of the adults receiving private sector wage payments do so digitally. That share is about 80 percent in Kenya and Viet Nam, both lower-middle-income economies. Yet in Mongolia, also a lower-middle-income economy, nearly all (94 percent) recipients of private sector wages were paid digitally.

Women and men who receive wages are equally likely to receive them digitally

Women are almost half as likely as men to receive wages in low- and middle-income economies—19 percent versus 36 percent—though the same share of wage-receiving women as wage-receiving men receive them in accounts (refer to figure 3.3.13).

Figure 3.3.13 Though women wage recipients in low- and middle-income economies on average are as likely as men wage recipients to receive wage payments digitally, gender disparities exist in some regions

Adults who received a wage payment in the past year (%), 2024

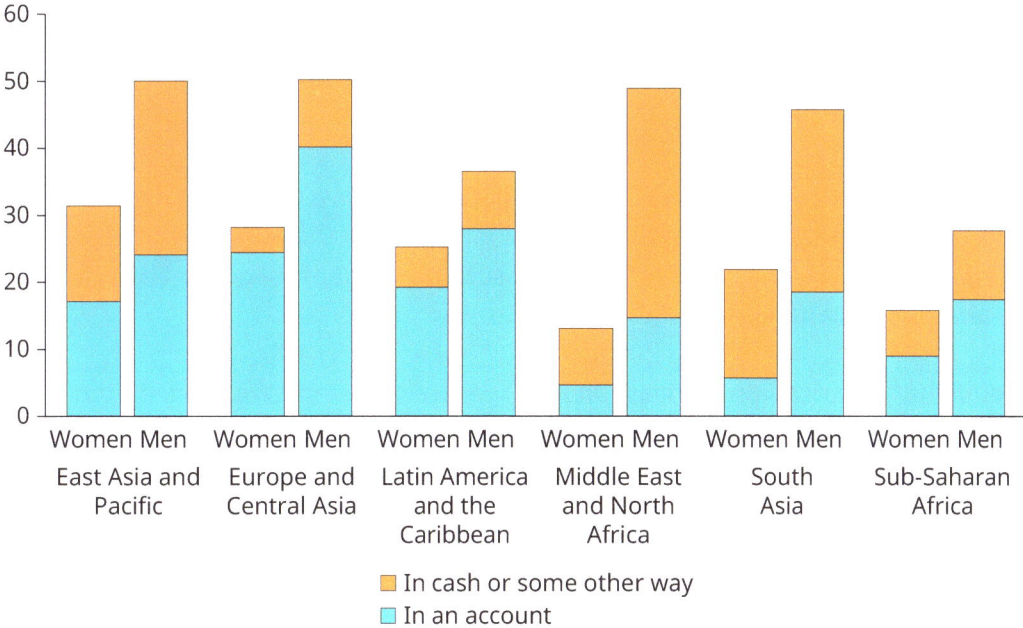

■ In cash or some other way
■ In an account

Source: Global Findex Database 2025.

As with other payment types, there are regional variations. In East Asia and Pacific and Europe and Central Asia, women receiving private sector wage payments are about 6 percentage points more likely than men who receive such payments to receive them in accounts. In Latin America and the Caribbean and the Middle East and North Africa, on the other hand, women and men who receive such payments are equally likely to receive them in accounts. By contrast, in South Asia women receiving private sector wage payments are 14 percentage points less likely to receive such payments in accounts, and in Sub-Saharan Africa, the gap is 6 percentage points, with women again less likely than men.

Adults living in the poorest 40 percent of households within economies are 8 percentage points less likely than those in the wealthiest 60 percent to receive private sector wage payments. They are also consistently less likely to receive payment of those wages in an account: 32 percent versus 52 percent. These disparities hold in every world region, with low-income wage earners consistently less likely to have private sector wages paid into an account than their higher-income peers.

Agricultural payments were received mostly in cash, with some notable exceptions

Farmers, like many others, benefit from formal financial services. Keeping their money in an account can help them save and stretch their income across harvest seasons, finance their purchases of agricultural inputs like seeds and fertilizer, and receive payments for the sale of their products.[26]

Fourteen percent of all adults in low- and middle-income economies received payments for the sale of agricultural goods, and most of these payments were in cash. Only about a quarter of recipients of such payments, or 4 percent of all adults, received them in accounts.

Sub-Saharan African economies, on average, are consistent with this pattern of about 25 percent of agricultural payment recipients being paid into an account, even though 30 percent of adults receive these payments, more than twice the low- and middle-income economy average. In some economies in the region, however, a much larger share of recipients are paid digitally (refer to figure 3.3.14).

---

26   Refer to Nair and Varghese (2020).

Figure 3.3.14 In Sub-Saharan African economies with high rates of digital agricultural payments, most of these payments are made via a mobile phone

Adults who received an agricultural payment in the past year (%), 2024

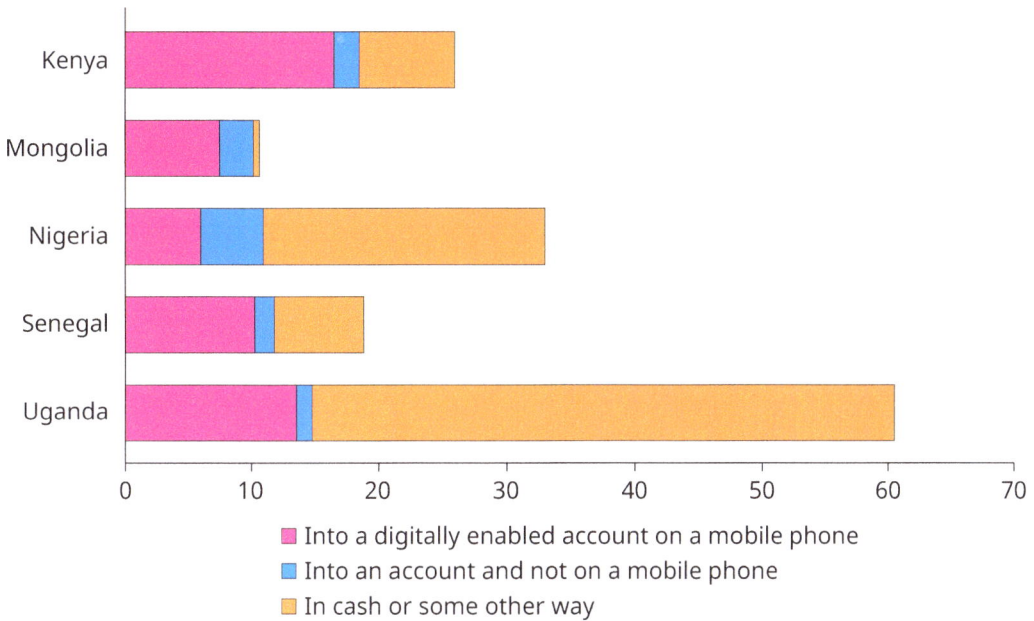

Legend:
- Into a digitally enabled account on a mobile phone
- Into an account and not on a mobile phone
- In cash or some other way

Source: Global Findex Database 2025.

In Kenya, 71 percent of recipients of agricultural payments were paid digitally, as were 63 percent in Senegal and 33 percent in Nigeria. Overall, 10 percent or more of all adults in these three Sub-Saharan African economies receiving agricultural payments did so in accounts, most often mobile money accounts. Compared with that in 2021, the share of adults receiving agricultural payments in accounts more than doubled in 2024 in Nigeria and Senegal.

Outside of Sub-Saharan Africa, Mongolia is the only economy in which 10 percent or more of all adults received agricultural payments in accounts, reflecting nearly 100 percent of all agricultural payments in that economy.

Receiving money from and sending money to family and friends

People within families or social networks exchange money for various reasons. These P2P payments can enable one person to help another through a difficult period, or they may simply be reimbursements for purchases made by one person on another's behalf. The Global Findex survey questions related to such payments do not specify the reasons for payments received from family members or friends. They ask only whether respondents received money from or sent money to family members or friends living in another city within their economies. In previous data collection rounds, these payments were identified as *domestic remittances* rather than by the broader term *P2P payments*.[27]

In low- and middle-income economies in which questions related to P2P payments were asked, 32 percent of adults sent or received such payments from friends or family members living within the same economy but in a different city.[28] Most adults (62 percent) sending or receiving such payments did so digitally. This includes adults who reported sending payments directly from or receiving them directly on their mobile phones, which might involve a mobile money account or app.

Domestic P2P payments are most common in Sub-Saharan Africa, where 52 percent of adults sent or received such payments (refer to figure 3.3.15). The region also has the highest share of such payments being made or received digitally, at 71 percent. In 23 economies in Sub-Saharan Africa, more than half of adults sent or received domestic P2P payments. They include Ghana and Senegal, the economies with the largest shares of adults sending or receiving such payments, at 78 and 76 percent, respectively. In both of these economies, more than 80 percent of those sending or receiving P2P payments did so using accounts or phones. These high rates may be self-perpetuating, as more people sending and receiving these payments leverage digital channels, creating a network effect.[29]

Outside of Sub-Saharan Africa, in every region except for the Middle East and North Africa, more than half of those sending or receiving domestic P2P payments did so using accounts or phones. In the Middle East and North Africa, however, only 34 percent did.

---

27 Chapter 4.2 discusses data on receipt of international remittances, that is, those from friends and family members living in another country. Because less than 10 percent of adults in low- and middle-income economies receive international remittance payments, the Global Findex does not collect data on the mode of transfer.

28 In low- and middle-income economies in which questions related to P2P payments were asked, 20 percent of adults sent such payments and 24 percent of adults received them, including 12 percent of adults who both sent and received such payments.

29 Alvarez et al. (2023).

Figure 3.3.15 Most adults sending or receiving P2P payments did so digitally

Adults who sent or received a domestic person-to-person payment in the past year (%), 2024

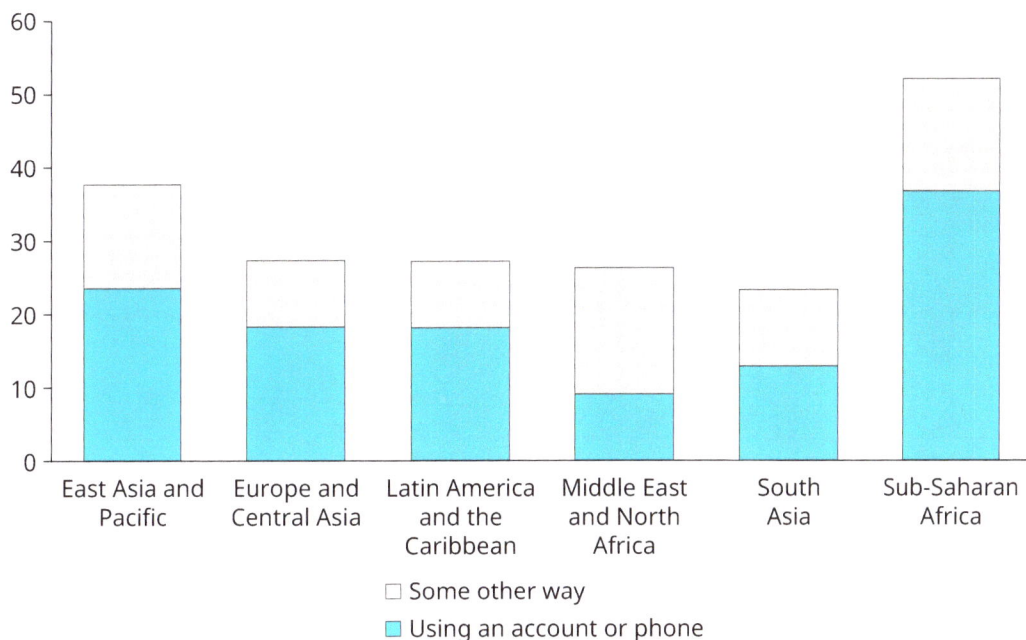

☐ Some other way
☐ Using an account or phone

Source: Global Findex Database 2025.
Note: P2P = person-to-person.

Opportunities remain to leverage payment digitalization to increase all aspects of financial inclusion, including access, use, and financial health

There has been a focused effort across economies over the past 10 years to digitalize government payments, motivated by the potential to reduce costs and loss and increase government accountability.[30]

Across economies, financial inclusion has been boosted by the digitalization of G2P and private sector wage payments. Sending these payments digitally is a proven way to increase account ownership, given that 43 percent of all adults in low- and middle-income economies—or 60 percent of those with an account at a bank or similar financial institution—opened their first account to receive either a G2P payment or a private sector wage payment (refer to figure 3.3.16).[31] Women and men were equally likely to become financially included in this way.

---

30   Aker et al. (2016); Klapper and Singer (2017).
31   This average excludes Russia.

Figure 3.3.16 Between one-third and two-thirds of adults with an account at a bank or similar financial institution opened their first account to receive a G2P or wage payment

Adults with an account at a bank or similar financial institution (%), 2024

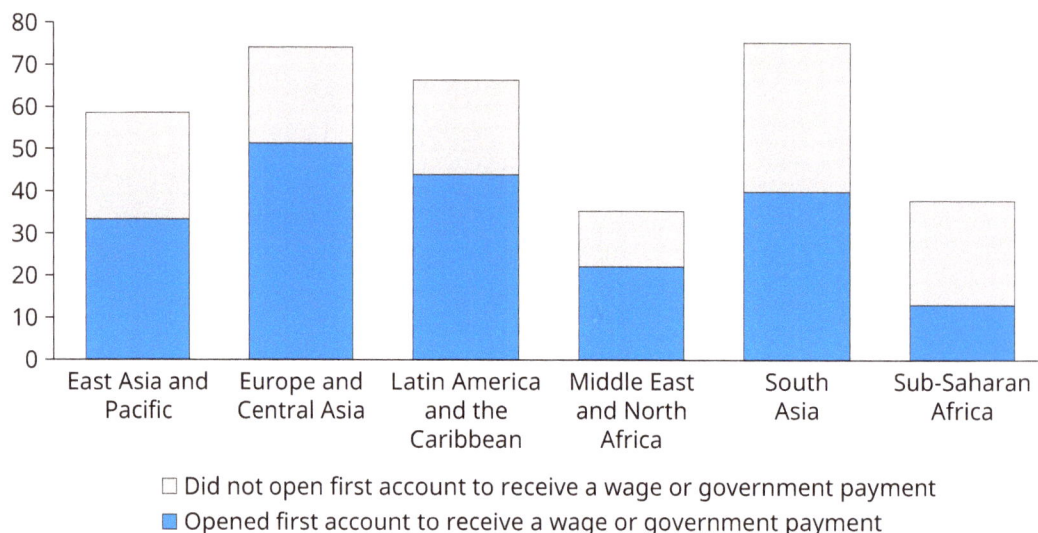

□ Did not open first account to receive a wage or government payment
■ Opened first account to receive a wage or government payment

Source: Global Findex Database 2025.
Note: G2P = government-to-person.

Opportunities remain to take advantage of this association between G2P and wage payments and account ownership, given that 14 percent of all recipients of government payments and slightly less than half of recipients of private sector wage payments still receive these payments in cash or some other way (such as a voucher). Some of the cash recipients already have an account (62 percent) and own a mobile phone (75 percent), including 47 percent who own a smartphone (refer to figure 3.3.17). Those who have accounts could immediately start receiving their payments digitally, if their governments or employers could deliver them and the recipients were willing to receive them that way. People who do not yet have accounts but own mobile phones could be offered digitally enabled accounts for receiving these payments. Thorough onboarding, guidance in how to use such accounts, and a clear explanation of associated rules and fees are essential to ensuring people get the most out of them.

Figure 3.3.17 **Opportunities remain to digitalize government or wage payments to promote financial inclusion**

a. Account ownership among adults who receive G2P or wage payments in cash

Adults who received a G2P or wage payment in cash (%), 2024

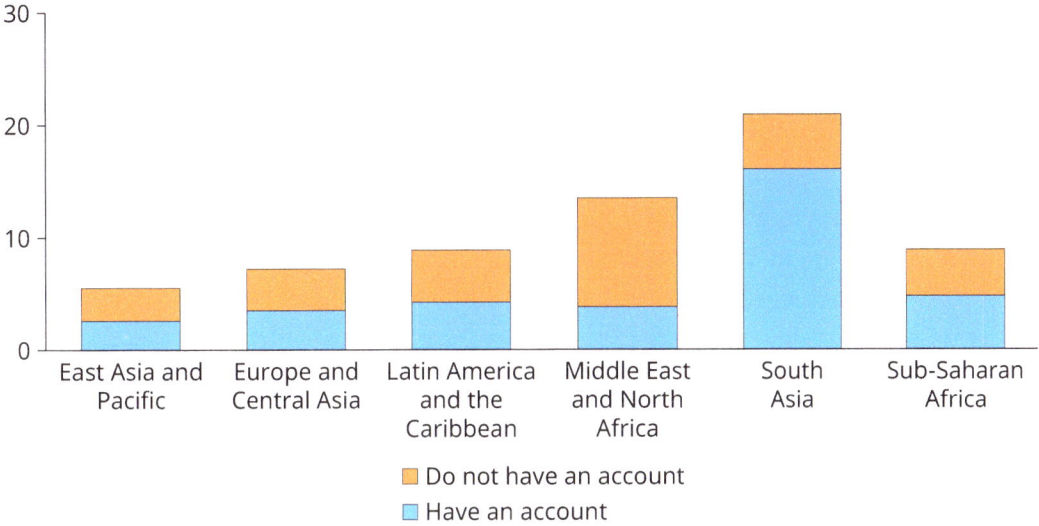

- ■ Do not have an account
- ■ Have an account

b. Phone ownership among adults who receive G2P or wage payments in cash

Adults without an account who received a G2P or wage payment in cash (%), 2024

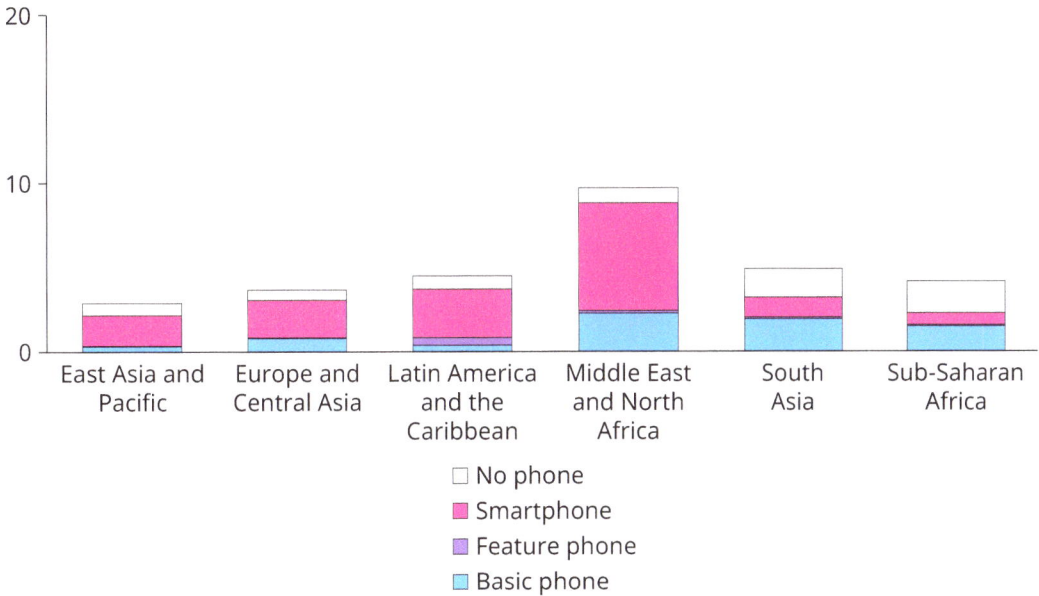

- □ No phone
- ■ Smartphone
- ■ Feature phone
- ■ Basic phone

Source: Global Findex Database 2025.

Note: Basic phone, feature phone, and *smartphone* are defined in chapter 1.1. G2P = government-to-person.

Digital payments help increase people's ability to meet their needs, a key condition for financial health

Digital payments also offer untapped opportunities to help people manage their money more effectively and thereby improve their financial health, a topic explored in the next section. One example of such an opportunity is *payment fractionalization*, or breaking up large one-time payments into smaller, more frequent, and more manageable installments.

For instance, parents who send their children to schools that charge tuition or that require parents to pay for books or other supplies often must pay these fees all at once at the beginning of a semester. That can put significant pressure on tight budgets. Smallholder farmers similarly must also buy supplies at the start of the growing season, when they have limited resources because of the months-long gap since the previous harvest. Digital tools that enable more flexible, incremental payments could thus help households smooth expenses, ease financial stress, and reduce the need for short-term borrowing.

Furthermore, as highlighted throughout this chapter, account owners have frequent and varied opportunities to use digital payments. Doing so helps habituate them to using accounts, not just to make and receive various payment types, but also for accessing a broader range of financial opportunities. This includes saving, which can be thought of as a payment to oneself, and borrowing, with repayments that can be automated.

As individuals expand and deepen their use of financial services, account owners may find they are better able to manage financial stress, build resilience against financial shocks, and strengthen their financial confidence. These are all hallmarks of financial health, explored in the next and final section of this report.

References

Aggarwal, Shilpa, Valentina Brailovskaya, and Jonathan Robinson. 2020. "Cashing In (and Out): Experimental Evidence on the Effects of Mobile Money in Malawi." *AEA Papers and Proceedings* 110 (May): 599–604. https://doi.org/10.1257/pandp.20201087.

Aker, Jenny C., Rachid Boumnijel, Amanda McClelland, and Niall Tierney. 2016. "Payment Mechanisms and Antipoverty Programs: Evidence from a Mobile Money Cash Transfer Experiment in Niger." *Economic Development and Cultural Change* 65 (1): 1–37. https://www.journals.uchicago.edu/doi/abs/10.1086/687578?journalCode=edcc.

Alvarez, Fernando, David Argente, Francesco Lippi, Esteban Méndez, and Diana Van Patten. 2023. "Strategic Complementarities in a Dynamic Model of Technology Adoption: P2P Digital Payments." NBER Working Paper 31280, National Bureau of Economic Research, Cambridge, MA. https:///www.nber.org/papers/w31280.

Ardic Alper, Oya Pinar, Guillermo Alfonso Galicia Rabadan, Ana Georgina Marin Espinosa, Harish Natarajan, Thomas Yann Piveteau, Nilima Chhabilal Ramteke, and Arpita Sarkar. 2023. *G20 Policy Recommendations for Advancing Financial Inclusion and Productivity Gains through Digital Public Infrastructure.* Washington, DC: World Bank Group. http://documents.worldbank.org/curated/en/099092023121016458.

Ashraf, Nava, Dean Karlan, and Wesley Yin. 2010. "Female Empowerment: Impact of a Commitment Savings Product in the Philippines." *World Development* 38 (3): 333–44. https://doi.org/10.1016/J.WORLDDEV.2009.05.010.

Bachas, Pierre, Paul Gertler, Sean Higgins, and Enrique Seira. 2021. "How Debit Cards Enable the Poor to Save More." *Journal of Finance* 76 (4): 1913–57. https://doi.org/10.1111/jofi.13021.

Banerjee, Abhijit Vinayak. 2013. "Microcredit under the Microscope: What Have We Learned in the Past Two Decades, and What Do We Need to Know?" *Annual Review of Economics* 5 (August): 487–519. https://doi.org/10.1146/annurev-economics-082912-110220.

Banerjee, Abhijit, Esther Duflo, Rachel Glennerster, and Cynthia Kinnan. 2015. "The Miracle of Microfinance? Evidence from a Randomized Evaluation." *American Economic Journal: Applied Economics* 7 (1): 22–53. http://www.jstor.org/stable/43189512.

Banerjee, Abhijit, Dean Karlan, and Jonathan Zinman. 2015. "Six Randomized Evaluations of Microcredit: Introduction and Further Steps." *American Economic Journal: Applied Economics* 7 (1): 1–21. https://doi.org/10.1257/app.20140287.

Bangura, Joe Abass. 2016. *Saving Money, Saving Lives: A Case Study on the Benefits of Digitizing Payments to Ebola Response Workers in Sierra Leone.* New York: Better than Cash Alliance. https://btca-production-site.s3.amazonaws.com/document_files/303/document_files/BTCA-Ebola-Case-Study.pdf?1502739794.

Bastian, Gautam, Iacopo Bianchi, Markus Goldstein, and Joao Montalvao. 2018. "Short-Term Impacts of Improved Access to Mobile Savings, with and without Business

Training: Experimental Evidence from Tanzania." Working Paper 478, Center for Global Development, Washington, DC. https://www.cgdev.org/publication/short-term -impacts-improved-access-mobile-savings-business-training.

Bird, Andrew, Michael G. Hertzel, Stephen A. Karolyi, and Thomas Ruchti. 2024. "The Value of Lending Relationships." Research Paper 24-02, Office of Financial Research, US Department of the Treasury, Washington, DC. https://www.financialresearch.gov /working-papers/2024/03/05/the-value-of-lending-relationships/.

Blumenstock, Joshua Evan, Michael Callen, Anastasiia Faikina, Stefano Fiorin, and Tarek Ghani. 2023. "Strengthening Fragile States: Evidence from Mobile Salary Payments in Afghanistan." CESifo Working Paper 10510, CESifo Group, Munich. http://dx.doi .org/10.2139/ssrn.4477998.

Brailovskaya, Valentina, Pascaline Dupas, and Jonathan Robinson. 2024. "Is Digital Credit Filling a Hole or Digging a Hole? Evidence from Malawi." *Economic Journal* 134 (658): 457–84. https://academic.oup.com/ej/article/134/658/457/7296122.

Breza, Emily, Martin Kanz, and Leora F. Klapper. 2020. "Learning to Navigate a New Financial Technology: Evidence from Payroll Accounts." NBER Working Paper 28249, National Bureau of Economic Research, Cambridge, MA. https://doi.org/10.3386/W28249.

Cassara, Dan, Arianna Zapanta, and Seth Garz. 2024. "Mobile Instant Credit: Impacts, Challenges, and Lessons for Consumer Protection." Innovations for Poverty Action, Washington, DC, and Center for Effective Global Action, University of California, Berkeley. https://reports-cega.berkeley.edu/mobile-instant-credit-report/.

Chioda, Laura, Paul Gertler, Sean Higgins, and Paolina C. Medina. 2025. "Fintech Lending to Borrowers with No Credit History." NBER Working Paper 33208, National Bureau of Economic Research, Cambridge, MA. http://www.nber.org/papers/w33208.

Collins, Daryl, Jonathan Morduch, Stuart Rutherford, and Orlanda Ruthven. 2010. *Portfolios of the Poor.* Princeton, NJ: Princeton University Press.

Cornelli, Guilio, Jon Frost, Leonardo Gambacorta, P. Raghavendra Rau, Robert Wardrop, and Tania Ziegler. 2023. "Fintech and Big Tech Credit: Drivers of the Growth of Digital Lending." *Journal of Banking & Finance* 148:106742. https://doi.org/10.1016/j .jbankfin.2022.106742.

Dupas, Pascaline, and Jonathan Robinson. 2013. "Savings Constraints and Microenterprise Development: Evidence from a Field Experiment in Kenya." *American Economic Journal: Applied Economics* 5 (1): 163–92. https://doi.org/10.1257/app.5.1.163.

Economides, Nicholas, and Przemyslaw Jeziorski. 2015. "Mobile Money in Tanzania." Networks, Electronic Commerce, and Telecommunications (NET) Institute Working Paper 14-24, Stern School of Business, New York University, New York. https://doi .org/10.2139/SSRN.2539984.

Gertler, Paul, Brett Green, Renping Li, and David Sraer. 2025. "The Welfare Benefits of Pay-As-You-Go Financing." NBER Working Paper 33484, National Bureau of Economic Research, Cambridge, MA. https://www.nber.org/papers/w33484.

Gertler, Paul, Brett Green, and Catherine Wolfram. 2023. "Digital Collateral." NBER Working Paper 28724, National Bureau of Economic Research, Cambridge, MA. https:///www.nber.org/papers/w28724.

Glynn-Broderick, Kate, Rebecca Rouse, Yoonyoung Cho, Cesi Cruz, and Julien Bernard Labonne. 2021. *Monitoring Digital Financial Payments of Cash Transfers in the Philippines.* Washington, DC: World Bank Group. http://documents.worldbank.org/curated/en/099120003032234458.

Gugerty, Mary Kay, Pierre Biscaya, and C. Leigh Anderson. 2018. "Delivering Development? Evidence on Self-Help Groups as Development Intermediaries in South Asia and Africa." *Development Policy Review* 37 (1): 129–51. https://www.researchgate.net/publication/324538893.

Habyarimana, James, and William Jack. 2024. "High Hopes: Experimental Evidence on Financial Inclusion and the Transition to High School in Kenya." *Economic Development and Cultural Change* 72 (3): 1189–212. https://doi.org/10.1086/723068.

Higgins, Sean. 2024. "Financial Technology Adoption: Network Externalities of Cashless Payments in Mexico." *American Economic Review* 114 (11): 3469–512. https://www.aeaweb.org/articles?id=10.1257/aer.20201952.

Jones, Kelly, and Erick Gong. 2021. "Precautionary Savings and Shock-Coping Behaviors: Effects of Promoting Mobile Bank Savings on Transactional Sex in Kenya." *Journal of Health Economics* 78 (July): 102460. https://doi.org/10.1016/J.JHEALECO.2021.102460.

Karlan, Dean, Aishwarya Lakshmi Ratan, and Jonathan Zinman. 2014. "Savings by and for the Poor: A Research Review and Agenda." *Review of Income and Wealth* 60 (1): 36–78. https://doi.org/10.1111/roiw.12101.

Karlan, Dean, and Jonathan Zinman. 2010. "Expanding Credit Access: Using Randomized Supply Decisions to Estimate the Impacts." *Review of Financial Studies* 23 (1): 433–64. https://doi.org/10.1093/RFS/HHP092.

Klapper, Leora, and Dorothe Singer. 2017. "The Opportunities and Challenges of Digitizing Government-to-Person Payments." *World Bank Research Observer* 32 (2): 211–26. https://doi.org/10.1093/wbro/lkx003.

KPMG. 2015. "PAYGO: Solar Distribution through Pay As You Go Business Models in East Africa." Development in Practice Impact Paper 16, International Development Advisory Services Africa, KPMG, Nairobi. https://assets.kpmg.com/content/dam/kpmg/ke/pdf/idas/thought-leaderships/paygo-development-in-practice-a.pdf.

Krujiff, David, Swati Sawhney, and Richard Leslie Wright. 2024. "Empowering Small Giants: Inclusive Embedded Finance for Micro-retailers." Focus Note, CGAP, Washington, DC. https://www.cgap.org/sites/default/files/publications/FN_Empowering%20Small%20Giants_final.pdf.

Lee, Jean N., Jonathan Morduch, Saravana Ravindran, Abu Shonchoy, and Hassan Zaman. 2021. "Poverty and Migration in the Digital Age: Experimental Evidence on Mobile Banking in Bangladesh." *American Economic Journal: Applied Economics* 13 (1): 38–71.

Mukherjee, Sanghamitra Warrier, Lauren Falcao Bergquist, Marshall Burke, and Edward Miguel. 2024. "Unlocking the Benefits of Credit through Saving." *Journal of Development Economics* 171: 103346. https://doi.org/10.1016/j.jdeveco.2024.103346.

Muralidharan, Karthik, Paul Niehaus, and Sandip Sukhtankar. 2016. "Building State Capacity: Evidence from Biometric Smartcards in India." *American Economic Review* 106 (10): 2895–929. https://aeaweb.org/articles?id=10.1257/aer.20141346.

Nair, Ajai, and Minita Mary Varghese. 2020. *Digitization of Agribusiness Payments in Africa: Building a Ramp for Farmers' Financial Inclusion and Participation in a Digital Economy.* Washington, DC: World Bank Group. http://documents.worldbank.org/curated/en/915271601013162558.

Pomeranz, Dina, and Felipe Kast. 2024. "Savings Accounts to Borrow Less." *Journal of Human Resources* 59 (1): 70–108. https://doi.org/10.3368/jhr.0619-10264R3.

Prina, Silvia. 2015. "Banking the Poor via Savings Accounts: Evidence from a Field Experiment." *Journal of Development Economics* 115 (July): 16–31. https://doi.org/10.1016/J.JDEVECO.2015.01.004.

Sung, Myung Jae, Rajul Awasthi, and Hyung Chul Lee. 2017. "Can Tax Incentives for Electronic Payments Reduce the Shadow Economy? Korea's Attempt to Reduce Underreporting in Retail Businesses." Policy Research Working Paper 7936, World Bank, Washington, DC. https://documents1.worldbank.org/curated/en/105841483990962599/pdf/WPS7936.pdf.

Suri, Tavneet, Jenny Aker, Catia Batista, Michael Callen, Tarek Ghani, William Jack, Leora Klapper, Emma Riley, Simone Schaner, and Sandip Sukhtankar. 2023. "Mobile Money: Issue 2." *VoxDevLit* 2 (2, February). https://voxdev.org/voxdevlit/mobile-money.

Suri, Tavneet, Prashant Bharadwaj, and William Jack. 2021. "Fintech and Household Resilience to Shocks: Evidence from Digital Loans in Kenya." *Journal of Development Economics* 153 (November): 102697. https://doi.org/10.1016/J.JDEVECO.2021.102697.

Wright, Richard, Erdal Tekin, Volkan Topalli, Chandler McClellan, Timothy Dickinson, and Richard Rosenfeld. 2014. "Less Cash, Less Crime: Evidence from the Electronic Benefit Transfer Program." NBER Working Paper 19996, National Bureau of Economic Research, Cambridge, MA. https:///www.nber.org/papers/w19996.

SPOTLIGHT 3.1

Account usage and inactivity

Although owning an account is a critical first step to participating in the greater financial system, to fully benefit from access to finance, account owners should be able to use their accounts to store money and make and receive payments. This spotlight explores how often people use their accounts—and whether they use them at all.

Account activity is high in low- and middle-income economies, with exceptions

The data in section 3 highlight the different ways account owners use their accounts to save, borrow, and make and receive payments. Yet 6 percent of adults in low- and middle-income economies—8 percent of account owners—have only what could be considered inactive accounts. The Global Findex defines *inactive accounts* as those into or out of which no deposits, withdrawals, or incoming or outgoing digital payments have been received or made in the past year.[1] The average 6 percent account inactivity in 2024 is similar to the percentage in 2021.

The share of adults whose accounts are inactive varies across low- and middle-income economies. It is especially high in India, where 14 percent of adults—16 percent of account owners—do not have an active account (refer to figure S3.1.1). If India is excluded from the low- and middle-income average, the share of adults who do not have an active account falls to 3 percent, or 4 percent of account owners.

---

1   In Algeria, China, the Islamic Republic of Iran, Libya, Mauritius, and Ukraine, where an abridged questionnaire was administered, *account inactivity* was defined as cases in which adults with an account had not made a digital payment, had not made a digital merchant payment, and had not accessed their account via a debit or credit card or phone in the past year. Because of a lack of data, the average for low- and middle-income economies excludes the Russian Federation.

Figure S3.1.1 In India, 16 percent of account owners do not have an active account; the average for all other low- and middle-income economies is 4 percent

Adults with an account (%), 2024

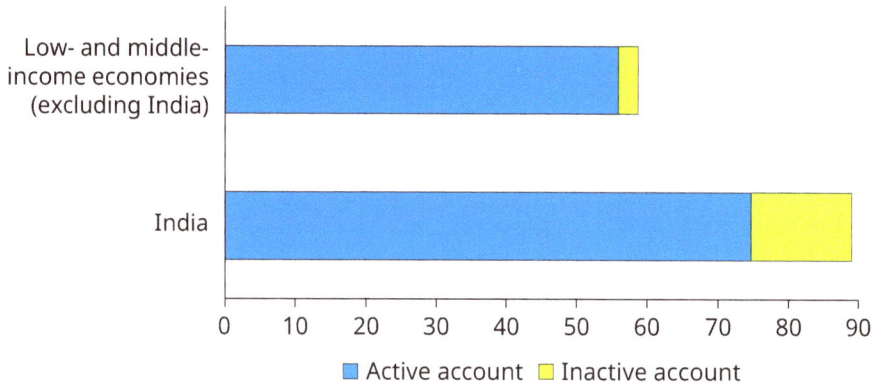

Source: Global Findex Database 2025.

Note: In Algeria, China, the Islamic Republic of Iran, Libya, Mauritius, and Ukraine, where an abridged questionnaire was administered, *account inactivity* was defined as cases in which adults with an account had not made a digital payment, had not made a digital merchant payment, and had not accessed their account via a debit or credit card or phone in the past year. Because of a lack of data, the average for low- and middle-income economies excludes the Russian Federation.

India has made progress in increasing the share of adults with active accounts

Despite its comparatively low rate of active accounts, both the absolute number and the percentage of adults with active accounts in India has increased. In addition, more men than women own active accounts, though the gender gap in ownership of active accounts as a percentage of account owners fell from 12 percentage points in 2021 to 7 percentage points in 2024 (refer to figure S3.1.2). This decrease may be due to the large increase over the same period in women receiving government-to-person (G2P) payments digitally, from 13 percent in 2021 (59 percent of women receiving a G2P payment) to 24 percent in 2024 (81 percent of women receiving a G2P payment).

Figure S3.1.2 In India, the share of both women and men with only inactive accounts decreased between 2021 and 2024

Adults with an account (%), 2021–24

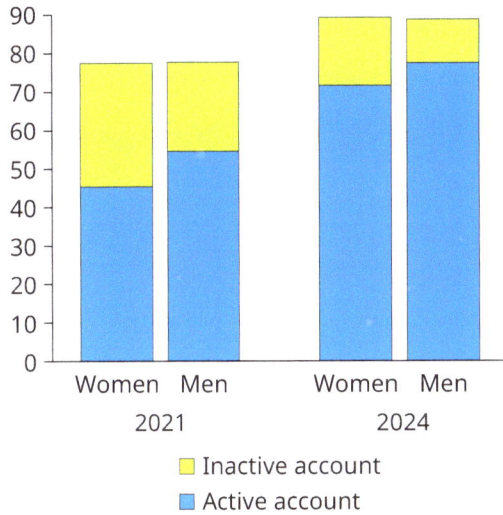

Source: Global Findex Database 2025.

Data on frequency of usage suggest cash is still dominant

The issue of account activity broadly relates to the role of transaction frequency and patterns of account use. To provide data for a better understanding of this, the Global Findex 2025 asks, separately, adults with accounts at banks or similar financial institutions and adults with mobile money accounts in Sub-Saharan Africa about how often in a typical month they deposit money into their accounts and how frequently they withdraw or send money—including as a payment—from their accounts.

Frequency of usage of bank and similar financial institution accounts points to transactions primarily in cash

When inflows are the focus, across low- and middle-income economies, the largest share of owners of accounts at banks or similar financial institutions, 40 percent, deposit money into their accounts at monthly intervals. These monthly deposits might be wages from employers, government transfer payments, or money from family living elsewhere. Only 11 percent of these account holders make deposits weekly.

In comparison, 33 percent of adults with accounts at banks or similar financial institutions send or withdraw money from their accounts monthly, whereas 19 percent do so weekly (refer to figure S3.1.3). In regions such as the Middle East and North Africa, where the majority of adults both deposit and withdraw money at monthly intervals, this pattern suggests that accounts are used primarily for receiving payments. People typically receive wage or transfer payments once a month, withdraw most or all of the money from those payments soon after, and continue to transact primarily in cash.

When monthly inflows of deposits into an account are common but outflows occur weekly or even more frequently, on the other hand, it might suggest the account owner is making greater use of digital payments and other account-to-account transfers.

Another possibility is that account owners use their accounts for safe storage of money and withdraw cash weekly because they do not want too much cash on hand for security reasons. In East Asia and Pacific, Europe and Central Asia, and Latin America and the Caribbean, about 10 percent of adults had monthly inflows into their accounts, but weekly outflows from them.

A more developed digital ecosystem could encourage people to keep money in their accounts, enabling them to store it more safely, reducing impulse spending, and increasing the convenience of making digital payments.

Figure S3.1.3 In many low- and middle-income economies, deposits are monthly and withdrawals are more frequent, indicating increasing use of accounts

Adults with an account at a bank or similar financial institution (standardized to 100%), 2024

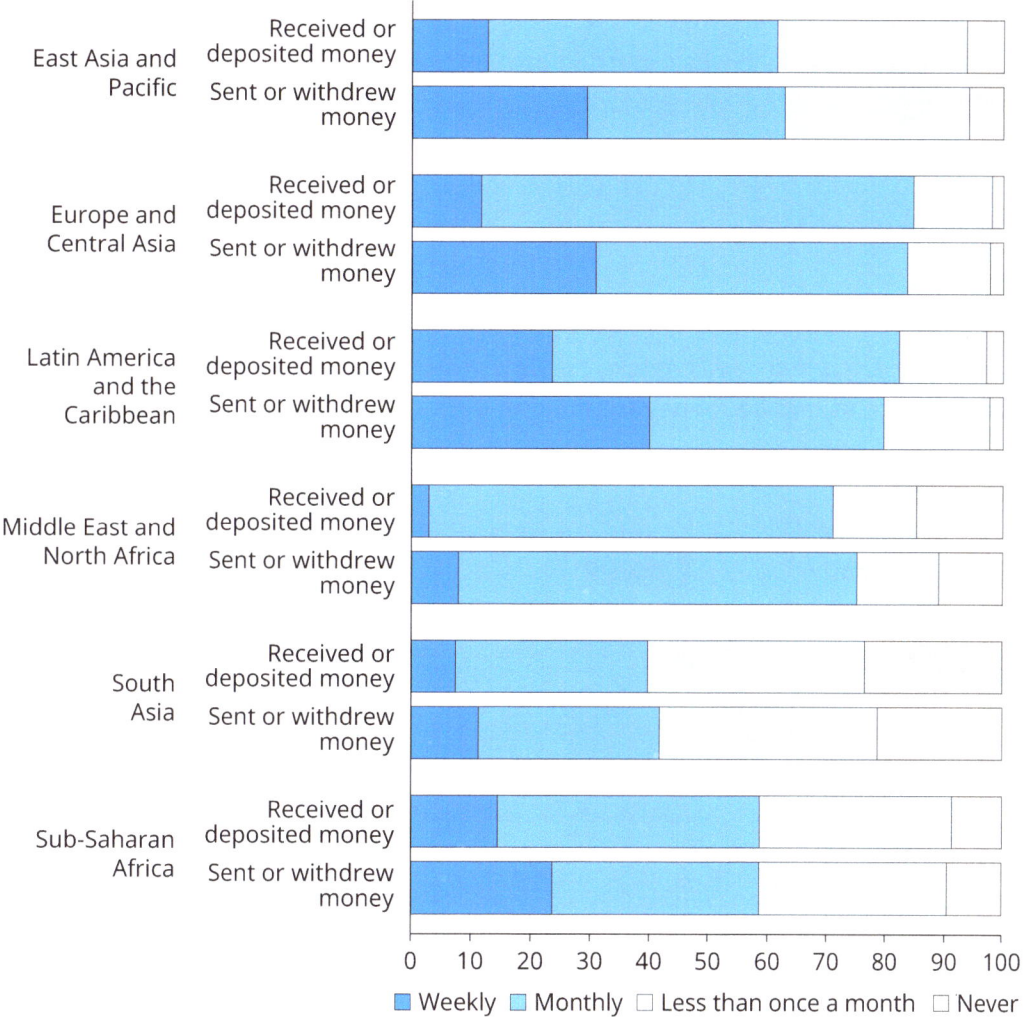

■ Weekly ■ Monthly □ Less than once a month □ Never

Source: Global Findex Database 2025.
Note: Because of a lack of data, averages exclude Algeria, China, the Islamic Republic of Iran, Libya, Mauritius, the Russian Federation, and Ukraine.

Frequency of usage of mobile money accounts in Sub-Saharan Africa points to more use of digital payments

In Sub-Saharan Africa, where many adults own only a mobile money account, the Global Findex 2025 includes similar questions on frequency of use of these accounts. The data show that across the four Sub-Saharan African subregions, adults with mobile money accounts deposit and send or withdraw money at higher frequencies than those with accounts at banks or similar financial institutions (refer to figure S3.1.4). This likely reflects the greater convenience and affordability of depositing money through local mobile money agents, rather than traveling to a bank branch or ATM.

Figure S3.1.4 **Among mobile money account owners in Sub-Saharan Africa, a larger share had more frequent outflows than inflows, pointing to the convenience of mobile money for making digital payments**

Adults with a mobile money account (standardized to 100%), 2024

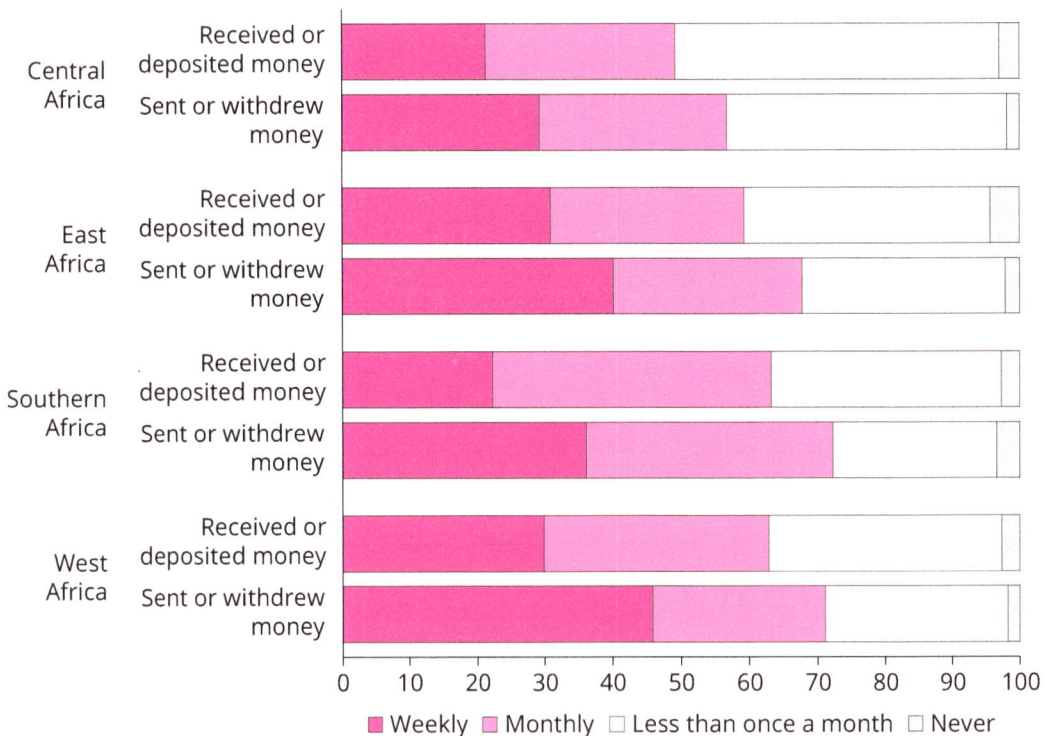

Source: Global Findex Database 2025.

In all subregions with the exception of Central Africa, more than half of adults with mobile money accounts deposit and send or withdraw money at least once a month. Furthermore, about 20 percent make weekly deposits, whereas about 30 percent withdraw or send money at least weekly. The fact that a larger share of owners of mobile money accounts have weekly outflows compared with the share that have weekly inflows suggests that mobile money is especially effective for facilitating frequent transactions, such as sending money or engaging in purchases, making it a convenient platform for everyday digital payments.

These patterns of account use across low- and middle-income economies offer important insights into how people manage their money and use financial services. Although many adults deposit funds on a monthly basis, with the frequency perhaps dictated by wage or government transfer cycles, the frequency of withdrawals and payments varies, shaped by differences in infrastructure, convenience, and digital ecosystems. In Sub-Saharan Africa, mobile money facilitates more frequent transactions, highlighting its role as a convenient channel for day-to-day financial activity. These usage patterns have direct implications for financial health, such as how people manage liquidity, meet financial goals, and cope with shocks, which will be explored in the next section.

Financial health

A reproducibility package is available for this book in the Reproducible Research Repository at https://reproducibility.worldbank.org/catalog/299.

Financial Health

IN LOW- AND MIDDLE-INCOME ECONOMIES

People are **financially healthy** when they can manage their needs, pursue opportunities, deal with financial emergencies, and feel confident about their finances.

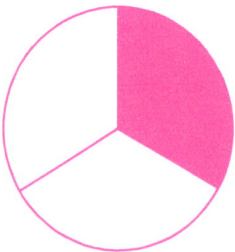

About a third of adults could cover more than two months of expenses if they lost their main income source.

FINANCIAL WORRY

People worry about having enough money for monthly expenses, medical bills, school fees, old age, and business expenses.

MONTHLY EXPENSES ARE THE MOST COMMON SOURCE OF FINANCIAL STRESS, FOLLOWED BY MEDICAL EXPENSES.

IN SOUTH ASIA AND SUB-SAHARAN AFRICA ABOUT 20% OF ADULTS WORRY ABOUT SCHOOL FEES.

26%

OF ADULTS WORRY ABOUT HAVING ENOUGH MONEY FOR OLD AGE, YET ONLY 18% OF ADULTS SAVE FORMALLY AND FOR THEIR RETIREMENT.

About 10% of adults received international remittances in Latin America and the Caribbean.

56%

OF PEOPLE COULD RELIABLY GET HOLD OF EXTRA MONEY TO DEAL WITH **AN EMERGENCY.**

Family or friends are the most popular source of extra money, though savings are more reliable. **Women and poorer adults** are more likely to rely on family or friends for additional funds.

One in four adults **experienced a natural disaster** in the past three years. Two-thirds of them lost income or an asset.

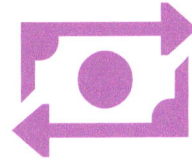

Around 1 in 4 mobile money account owners in Sub-Saharan Africa sent a payment to the wrong person. **Half never got their money back.**

Around **40% of bank account owners have checked their account balances with their phone or a computer,** and the same share have received account information via email or text.

4.1 Managing financial worrying

A reproducibility package is available for this book in the Reproducible Research Repository at https://reproducibility.worldbank.org/catalog/299.

4.1 Managing financial worrying

A major motivation for promoting connectivity, financial access, and use of financial services is to establish the conditions needed to increase people's *financial health*, defined as the ability to meet financial needs without undue stress, pursue goals, deal with financial shocks, and otherwise feel confident managing finances (refer to box 4.1.1). In today's environment, digital and financial inclusion would, in theory, make financial health much easier to attain, though neither type of inclusion offers a guarantee, given other necessary conditions, such as consumer financial protection, financial literacy, and consumer-friendly design of financial products.

In order to understand more about people's financial health and identify the barriers they face to improving it, the Global Findex 2025 asked adults what they worry about in regard to their finances, whether they would be able to manage a financial "shock" such as an accident or a loss of income, and whether they have the financial skills and confidence needed to use financial services to their benefit. This chapter explores the issues around financial *worrying*.

Box 4.1.1 Defining *financial health*

Though many aspects of financial health are subjective, the Group of Twenty's Global Partnership for Financial Inclusion and the UN Secretary-General's Special Advocate for Financial Health, Queen Máxima of the Netherlands, have helped form consensus on four factors that reflect financial health.[a] Financially healthy people can do the following things:

- Manage financial needs and obligations
- Pursue aspirations, fulfill goals, and capture opportunities
- Cope with financial shocks
- Feel satisfied and confident about their financial lives.

The Global Findex 2025 asked a series of questions that align with these indicators of financial health in a way that attempts to capture objective measures of them.

For most high-income economies and the Russian Federation, however, the survey included only questions on account ownership. As a result, this chapter does not report global or high-income economy averages. The "Methodology" tab of the Global Findex website (http://globalfindex.worldbank.org) provides details on the information collected in each surveyed economy.

a. OECD (2024).

Monthly expenses are the main source of financial stress for the largest share of people

Many people worry about having the financial resources to meet their needs, including people who would not seem to have much to worry about. Financial stress is at once universal and highly subjective. People with limited resources in particular worry about financial issues, from paying everyday bills to dealing with medical issues or saving for the future. Yet two people with objectively similar financial situations but in distinct contexts or with different personalities might each experience financial concerns in their own way. Some people hesitate to express money worries; others are simply more anxious than their peers. Two people may also feel financial stress more or less acutely because they assign different priority levels to different parts of their lives.

Acknowledging worry's subjective nature, the Global Findex 2025 asked respondents about which common sources of financial stress concern them most: monthly expenses such as food, housing, or bills; medical costs; school fees; money for old age; and money to support a business. Under the Group of Twenty's definition of financial health, medical bills and monthly household expenses are needs and obligations, whereas money to support a business, school fees, and money for old age relate more closely to the pursuit of goals and opportunities, given the delayed returns on investment provided by money used for these purposes.

The questions asked about financial worries in this round of the Global Findex changed slightly from those in the 2021 survey, which asked first if respondents were very or somewhat worried about any of the first four financial issues (the 2021 survey did not include the option of business expenses as a source of worry), then asked them which was the biggest worry. In 2021, in low- and middle-income economies, about 74 percent of adults said they felt concerned about at least one of the issues, and more than 20 percent said they were very worried about all four.

The Global Findex 2025, however, simply asked respondents to name their biggest financial worry among the issues offered, with no option to say they did not worry about any of them. According to the results, larger shares of people worry about covering their needs and obligations than about their longer-term goals. This could be because their immediate needs are too urgent to allow them to think in the longer term, or because they could feel more secure about their longer-term prospects.

Whichever it might be, across low- and middle-income economies, 30 percent and 26 percent of adults, respectively, are most worried about monthly expenses and medical costs, whereas 14 percent of adults each are most worried about school fees and having money for old age. Among all adults, 9 percent worry most about business expenses; this number increases to 13 percent among self-employed adults.

Monthly expenses are the most frequently cited financial worry in Latin America and the Caribbean, South Asia, and Sub-Saharan Africa. Medical costs tops the list in East Asia and Pacific and is equally prevalent with monthly expenses as a source of worry in Europe and Central Asia and the Middle East and North Africa (refer to figure 4.1.1). The financial pressure posed by medical costs is not new: these costs were the biggest source of financial stress for most adults in the Global Findex 2021 in every world region, with their urgency possibly exacerbated by the recency of the COVID-19 pandemic.[1]

Figure 4.1.1 **The largest share of adults worry most about monthly bills and medical expenses**

Adults identifying their biggest financial worry (%), 2024

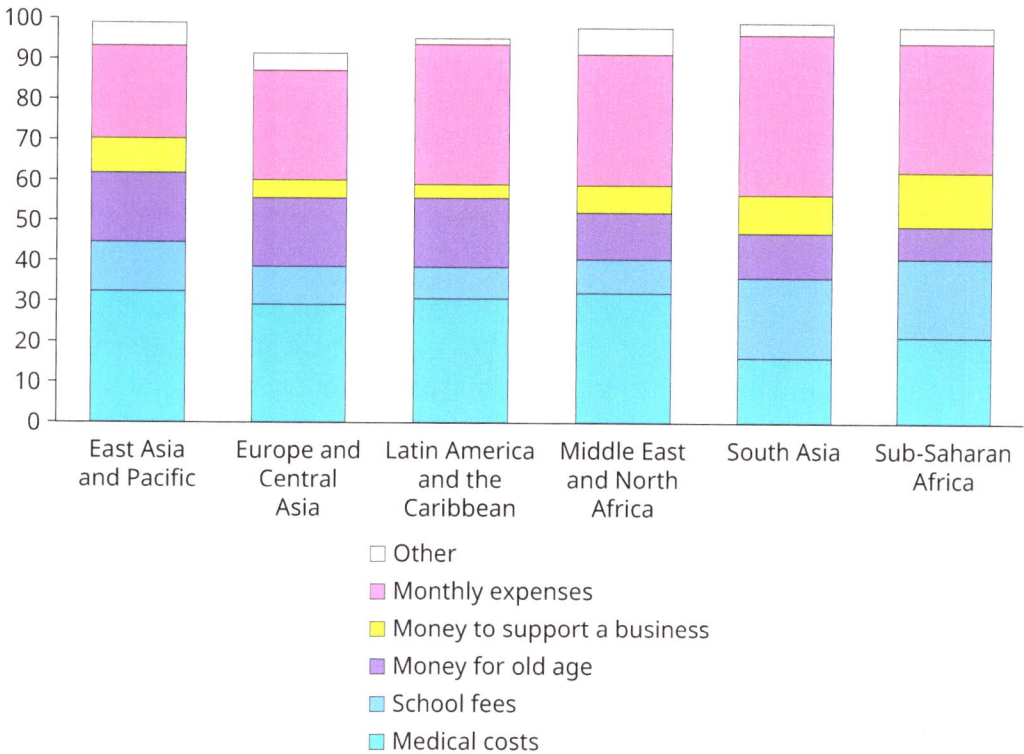

Source: Global Findex Database 2025.

Note: A small share of respondents did not know the answer or declined to answer the question.

---

1   As noted earlier, the Global Findex survey fielded in 2024 structured the questions on financial worrying slightly differently from those in the 2021 survey. As such, the results are not one-to-one comparable and should not be considered a time series, though they can still offer directional insights.

School fees preoccupy about 20 percent of adults in South Asia and Sub-Saharan Africa. Within the latter group, that share is even higher in the subregion of Central Africa at 24 percent (refer to figure 4.1.2). The high share in these two regions may be because private schools are an essential educational option there or because even public schools in certain economies in these regions require that families cover the costs of uniforms, supplies, and meals, among other school-related expenses.[2]

People in a given economy may worry about very different issues than the average adult in the same region. For example, even though a smaller share of people worry primarily about medical expenses in South Asia and Sub-Saharan Africa than in other regions, those expenses are the top concern for the largest share of adults in the Republic of Congo, Ethiopia, Mauritius, and Nepal. Adults in the Comoros, Kenya, Liberia, Sierra Leone, and Uganda are by far more likely to worry about school fees than any other financial issue. Business expenses are a primary worry for approximately 20 percent of adults in a number of economies in Sub-Saharan Africa, including Benin, Malawi, Nigeria, Sierra Leone, and Zambia.

Women and men do not differ widely in their financial worries

In regard to which worries preoccupy the largest share of adults, women and men do not generally worry about different issues at the regional level. The differences between the two tend to be within 3 percentage points—below the significance threshold for the Global Findex 2025.

Concerns about business expenses and school fees, however, show more variation according to gender. Women are 8 percentage points less likely than men to worry about money for businesses and 6 percentage points more likely to worry about school fees.

Figure 4.1.2 **School fees are a major source of financial worry in Sub-Saharan Africa, especially in the Central subregion**

Adults identifying their biggest financial worry (%), 2024

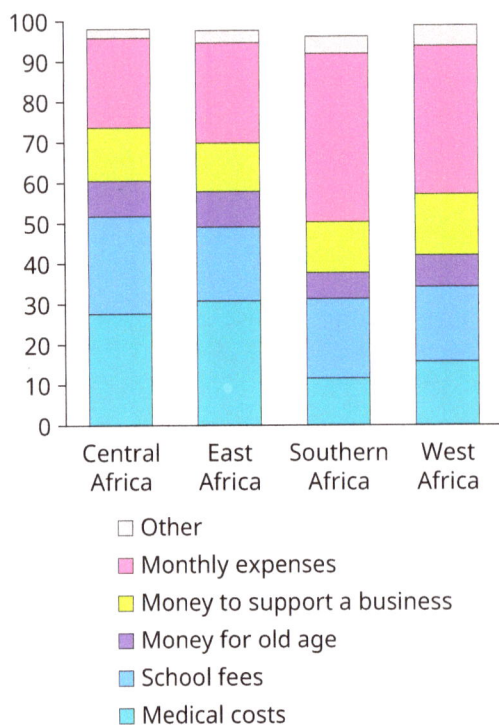

- □ Other
- ■ Monthly expenses
- ■ Money to support a business
- ■ Money for old age
- ■ School fees
- ■ Medical costs

Source: Global Findex Database 2025.

---

2   Maddison and Micah (2022).

Monthly expenses, medical costs, and school fees are still the top concerns in all regions for adults living in the poorest 40 percent and the wealthiest 60 percent of households by income. In a few instances, however, the prevalence of a specific issue shifts for an income group. For example, in South Asia, school fees are the second-most-prevalent worry for wealthier adults, nudging out medical expenses. In Europe and Central Asia, saving for old age occupies third place among wealthier adults, taking precedence by 10 percentage points over the fourth-place worry, school fees.

Borrowing, saving, and insurance could offer people more options for managing needs and pursuing goals

Financial services provide ways for people to manage their financial lives and potentially mitigate their financial worries.

Insurance is the financial product most clearly associated with helping people mitigate stress and manage risk. Insurance coverage is difficult to assess in a survey such as the Global Findex, however, because definitions and availability of insurance products vary widely among economies. For example, *life insurance* refers to term saving products in some places, instead of payments made at death as it does in many others. To avoid confusion around variable definitions, this edition of the Global Findex survey simply asked whether respondents have made any payments to an insurance agent or company.

The responses show that 23 percent of adults across low- and middle-income economies pay an insurer. Payments can be made for a range of insurance products, including life, health, home, and car insurance, as well as saving-oriented products such as policies that help parents save for their children's education. Adults from the poorest 40 percent of households are 10 percentage points less likely than adults from the wealthiest 60 percent to make insurance payments. If China were excluded from the average for low- and middle-income economies, the insurance payment rate would fall by more than half to 11 percent, because more than half of adults in China have a relationship with an insurer. Among low- and middle-income economies, only Mongolia has a similar rate of adults paying an insurer.

If China is excluded from East Asia and Pacific, paying an insurer is most common in Europe and Central Asia, where 18 percent of adults do, and slightly less common than the average in South Asia, where only 9 percent do.

Some borrow to address their everyday needs

Borrowing is another way for people to meet immediate needs and pursue longer-term goals. Borrowing is sometimes a last resort when people do not have enough available cash to cover an expense. This could be an everyday expense, such as household items needed between paydays, or a larger expense, such as a home or car repair. Many people deal with this type of situation using informal credit, such as that from family or friends.[3] Informal loans may or may not incur interest but likely come with the social expectation that the borrower will lend money in turn to the lender when asked. Although this expectation might reflect the typical actions in a tight-knit social network whose members support one another, it can also create a cycle that prevents members from reaching their saving goals.[4]

Borrowing for everyday needs is fairly common. For example, in low- and middle-income economies, 22 percent of adults have purchased groceries on credit. How common this practice is varies widely by region. Almost no one buys groceries on credit in East Asia and Pacific, whereas in South Asia and Sub-Saharan Africa, 40 percent of adults do.

The tendency to make purchases on credit is higher among people in low- and middle-income economies living in the poorest 40 percent of households by income, at 25 percent of adults, compared with 20 percent of adults in the wealthiest 60 percent of households. The difference by income group is about 10 percentage points in Europe and Central Asia, where 22 percent of adults in the poorest 40 percent of households buy groceries on credit compared with 13 percent of those in the wealthiest 60 percent of households, and in South Asia, where 48 percent of the poorest and 37 percent of the wealthiest adults do. The fact that people borrow for basic needs like food serves as a reminder that some people continue to live payday to payday.[5]

Beyond everyday needs, when people do not have sufficient savings for a health emergency, they might also turn to loans, family or friends, or, in a few places, credit cards. About 20 percent of adults in low- and middle-income economies borrowed money for health reasons in the year prior to taking the survey. That is one-third of the 60 percent who borrowed for any purpose, about the same share as in 2021.

---

3   Only 40 percent of borrowers in low- and middle-income economies borrow formally. See chapter 3.2 for more details.

4   Collins et al. (2009).

5   Board of Governors of the Federal Reserve System (2025).

Medical borrowing is higher in South Asia and Sub-Saharan Africa than in other regions, despite a smaller share of adults naming medical expenses as their primary worry in these regions, and the difference is statistically significant. Most people who borrow for health reasons do so informally, given that only a small share of them answered in the affirmative when asked if they borrowed formally in the year before the survey. Only in East Asia and Pacific did more than half of adults who borrowed for medical purposes also borrow formally at 54 percent of borrowers, or 7 percent of all adults in the region (the survey does not enable a determination of whether the formal credit was used for medical purposes).

In every region, a larger share of adults living in the poorest 40 percent of households by income borrowed for medical purposes than the share of adults living in the wealthiest 60 percent (refer to figure 4.1.3). This is in line with existing research suggesting that lower-income people experience greater pressure on household finances from medical bills and often lack income-preserving options for dealing with them, such as affordable and comprehensive health insurance.[6]

Figure 4.1.3 **Poorer adults are more likely than wealthier adults to have borrowed for health purposes**

Adults borrowing for health or medical purposes in the past year (%), 2024

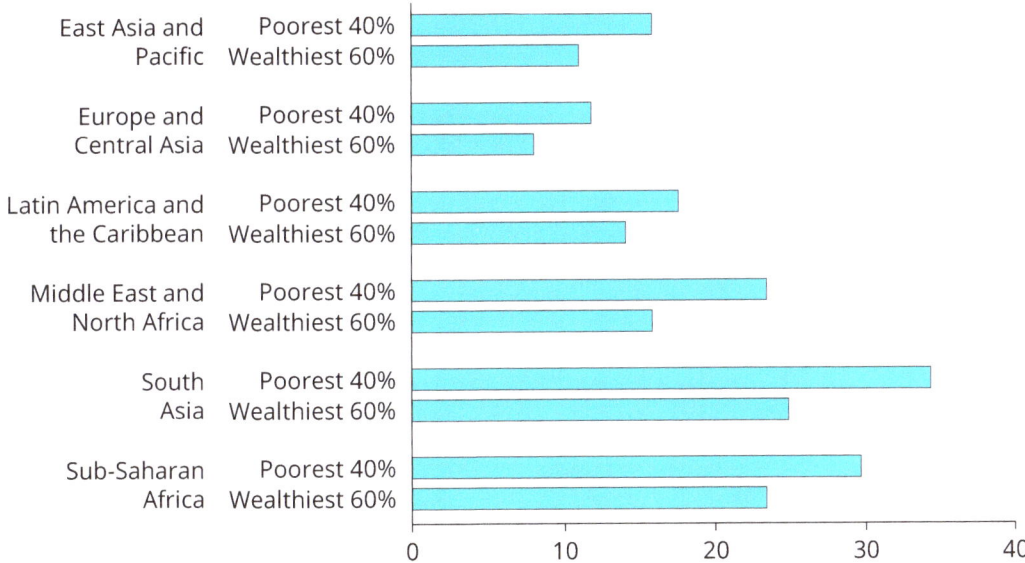

Source: Global Findex Database 2025.

---

6   Alam and Mahal (2014).

In the absence of health insurance, appropriate credit to cover health care costs in the short term could ensure people get the care they need without cutting into household budgets for food or shelter, with the acknowledgment that debt service would add a regular expense that might not be viable for some household budgets. Such an option should also be promoted cautiously, as adults who borrow to cover existing expenses risk becoming overindebted, with negative effects on their financial health.[7]

Borrowing may also help people pursue goals and opportunities, such as building or growing a business. About 11 percent of respondents, or one in six borrowers, in low- and middle-income economies borrowed for a business. Borrowing for business purposes is most prevalent overall in Sub-Saharan Africa, where 16 percent of adults (more than one in five borrowers in the region) borrowed money for such purposes (refer to figure 4.1.4).

As with borrowing for medical purposes, most of the adults who borrowed for a business borrowed only informally (it is not known if those who did have access to formal credit used it for business purposes). In Sub-Saharan Africa, though the share of adults who borrowed for a business was the largest of any region, the smallest share of them had access to formal borrowing compared with those in other regions. It may be that business owners in the region have fewer options for formal credit than business owners in East Asia and Pacific and Latin America and the Caribbean, where about 70 percent of adults who borrowed for business purposes also had access to formal credit through a financial institution, digital credit, or a credit card.

Figure 4.1.4 **Sub-Saharan Africa has the largest share of adults borrowing for a business**

Adults borrowing to start or operate a business in the past year (%), 2024

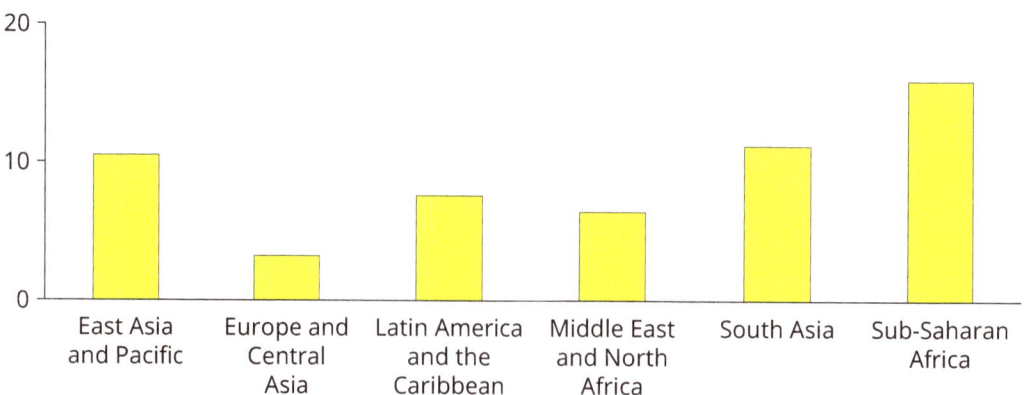

Source: Global Findex Database 2025.

---

7   Karlan, Mullainathan, and Roth (2019); Skiba and Tobacman (2008).

Saving for old age can help mitigate worry about the future

Saving for a specific purpose offers another way for people to manage their financial priorities. For example, across low- and middle-income economies, 18 percent of adults save formally in an account and save for old age. Of adults who report money for old age as their primary financial worry, 29 percent save specifically for this purpose.

The data show sharp regional differences in regard to saving for old age (refer to figure 4.1.5). More than a third of adults in East Asia and Pacific save for old age—a share whose large size is driven by the 43 percent of adults in China saving for this purpose—compared with less than 10 percent in Latin America and the Caribbean, the Middle East and North Africa, South Asia, and Sub-Saharan Africa.

Saving for old age might be difficult, especially because it has a long time horizon and requires long-term commitment to keeping in savings the money intended for use in retirement. Such saving competes with more immediate needs and is particularly hard for people who might need to dip into savings to meet urgent medical or educational expenses or who do not have the ability to store money in a place where it cannot be withdrawn.

Long-term saving is even harder where social insurance is necessary, that is, where a person needs to offer their savings to family or friends so that next time they help you. There might also be expectations of support from children or public pension schemes, which can make saving for old age less of a priority.

Figure 4.1.5 A small share of adults in most regions save for old age

Adults saving formally and saving for old age in the past year (%), 2024

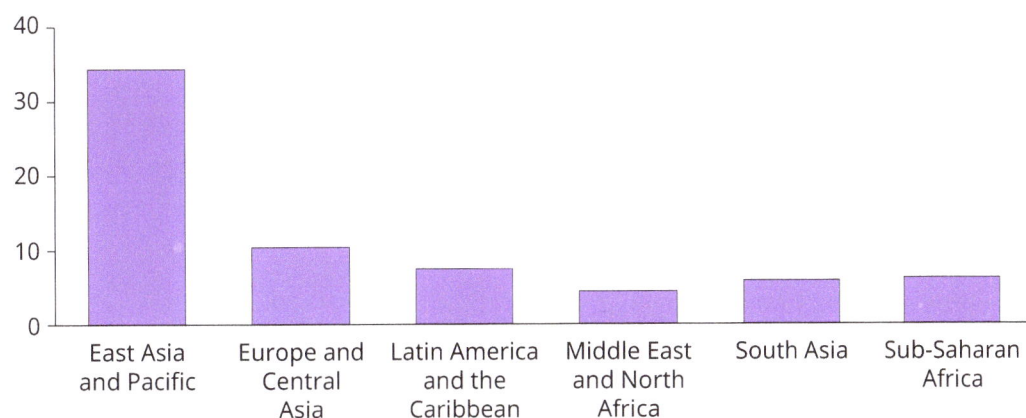

Source: Global Findex Database 2025.

Opportunities exist to leverage financial services to manage financial stress

Although the data show that some people use insurance, borrowing, and saving to address their financial needs and pursue their goals, the fact that most borrowers do so using informal methods suggests opportunities to connect people's needs or goals more effectively with financial services.

Insurance is one area of opportunity, specifically health insurance. Given the high level of stress people feel about medical expenses, there is clearly an unmet demand for ways to get needed health care without sacrificing financial stability. This need is particularly acute among poorer households.

Another clear opportunity is encouraging saving. Some research even finds that emergency savings are a strong predictor of financial health.[8] Generic savings accounts can encourage people to save money to achieve their financial goals[9] and increase their ability to cope with unexpected expenses;[10] commitment savings accounts—those that include "nudging" features to provide account holders with incentives for saving—help increase the amount people save.[11] Informal savings are also shifting to formal accounts, as more affordable and accessible options become available, including ones leveraging mobile technology, as discussed in chapter 3.1.

Though encouraging saving among the poor may be thought of as challenging given their low incomes, research finds that even very poor people are able to save when given the tools to do so, including affordable accounts with no or low transaction fees for small deposits.[12]

Global Findex 2025 data on what private sector earners do with wages paid into their accounts also suggest opportunities. As discussed in chapter 3.3, 32 percent of adults in low- and middle-income economies receive wage payments in financial accounts,[13] and about 36 percent of those receiving wage payments in accounts—or 12 percent of all adults—leave some of that money in their accounts. The share of adults leaving money in accounts is higher than the average in East Asia and Pacific (16 percent), Europe and Central Asia (23 percent), and

---

8   Costa, de la Fuente, and Martino (2025).

9   Karlan and Linden (2025).

10   Jones and Gong (2021); Pomeranz and Kast (2024).

11   Ashraf, Karlan, and Yin (2006, 2010); Brune et al. (2016); Dupas and Robinson (2013); Giné et al. (2018).

12   Banerjee and Duflo (2012).

13   This percentage excludes Algeria, China, the Islamic Republic of Iran, Libya, Mauritius, the Russian Federation, and Ukraine.

Latin America and the Caribbean (17 percent). Behavioral incentives might persuade more people to earmark some of that money for savings, and even for specific purposes, including saving for old age.

Additional incentives, such as awarding interest to people who meet certain thresholds for amounts saved or matching the amounts they save, may likewise help grow savings balances. These balances are key not only for pursuing goals, but also for managing the financial stress that can come from an emergency, loss of income, or financial shock: the area of financial health explored in the next section.

4.2 Financial resilience

A reproducibility package is available for this book in the Reproducible Research Repository at https://reproducibility.worldbank.org/catalog/299.

4.2 Financial resilience

General worrying or financial stress reflects a continuous state of anxiety. Reacting to economic "shocks," on the other hand, is in another category. Often triggered by a sudden loss of income or a major expense, economic shocks often force people to access extra money beyond what they typically need to cover everyday expenses or fill an ongoing income gap.

Aligned with the Group of Twenty's aspect of financial health[1] related to improving people's ability to cope with negative economic shocks, the Global Findex asked whether respondents could access an amount of money equal to 5 percent of their country's per capita gross national income within 30 days. This would be about $4,000 in the United States, 54,000 kwachas in Malawi, 12,000 pesos in Mexico, and so on. The survey first asked respondents about the main source of funding for this amount, and then in a follow-up question, about how difficult it would be to come up with this funding in the next 30 days. The Global Findex 2025 classifies people as *financially resilient* when they can access this amount of money and doing so would not be difficult at all or only somewhat difficult.

Financial resilience in the face of shocks has remained the same since 2021

On average, 56 percent of adults in low- and middle-income economies could access extra money without much difficulty (refer to figure 4.2.1), the same percentage as in 2021. Yet there were modest increases in resilience in Latin America and the Caribbean and the Middle East and North Africa, where it climbed by 6 and 4 percentage points, respectively.

Figure 4.2.1 The share of financially resilient adults in low- and middle-income economies has held steady since 2021

Adults identifying the source of, and assessing how difficult it would be to access, emergency money in 30 days or less (%), 2024

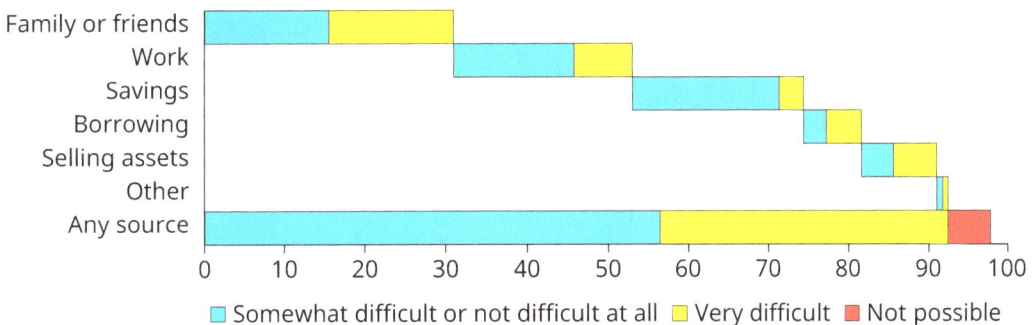

Legend: ☐ Somewhat difficult or not difficult at all ☐ Very difficult ☐ Not possible

Source: Global Findex Database 2025.

Note: A small share of adults did not know or did not disclose their main source of emergency money.

---

1   Refer to box 4.1.1 for the definition of *financial health* used to frame the data described in this chapter.

Family or friends continue to be a dominant source of extra money

People rely on different sources for extra money: family or friends; savings; additional work hours; borrowing from a financial institution, an employer, or a private lender; and selling assets. In most economies, at least 98 percent of people say they would tap one of these resources for emergency funds, although a small share say the money would be impossible to get despite these efforts.

Family or friends are the most common source of extra money, relied on by 31 percent of adults in low- and middle-income economies. This could include people who are local or those who live in other countries (refer to box 4.2.1). In some places, a much higher share of adults turn to family or friends. In the Middle East and North Africa, for example, more than 50 percent of people say they would rely on family or friends (refer to figure 4.2.2, panel d). In 34 economies with diverse geographies and income levels, more than 40 percent of adults name family or friends as their first source of extra money. Examples include Bangladesh, The Gambia, Iraq, Mexico, Kosovo, and Viet Nam.

> **Box 4.2.1** **The role of remittances in increasing resilience**
>
> International remittances provide numerous benefits to both sending and receiving countries. For those who receive them, they offer essential financial support, contributing to poverty reduction, increased consumption, and greater access to education, health care, and housing.[a] In addition, many adults rely on payments from family or friends living inside their country, as discussed in chapter 3.3.
>
> Although the volume of international remittances is often large, the share of adults who receive them is less than 10 percent globally. In 60 low- and middle-income economies included in the Global Findex 2025, 10 percent or more of adults receive them (refer to figure B4.2.1.1). This includes 13 percent of adults in Sub-Saharan Africa and 12 percent of adults in Europe and Central Asia. The five economies with the highest share of adults receiving international remittances are the Dominican Republic, The Gambia, Kosovo, Senegal, and Tajikistan.
>
> Evidence from low- and middle-income economies shows the importance of international remittances for increasing household financial resilience. Remittances act as informal insurance, helping recipient households smooth consumption and cope with adverse shocks such as job loss, health emergencies, natural disasters, and economic downturns.

(Box continued next page)

Box 4.2.1 **The role of remittances in increasing resilience** *(continued)*

Figure B4.2.1.1 **Less than 10 percent of adults in low- and middle-income economies receive remittances from abroad**

Adults receiving money from family or friends living abroad (%), 2024

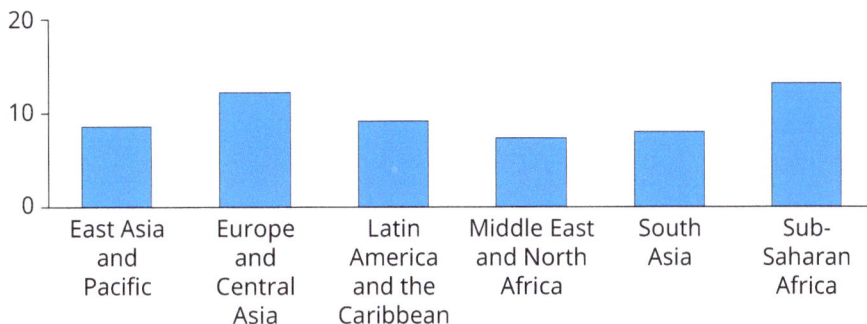

Source: Global Findex Database 2025.
Note: Because an abridged questionnaire was administered in Algeria, China, the Islamic Republic of Iran, Libya, Mauritius, the Russian Federation, and Ukraine, averages exclude data for these economies.

For example, in the Philippines, remittances increase in response to adverse income shocks, such as poor rainfall, acting as a countercyclical insurance mechanism that smooths consumption and buffers against income losses.[b] Furthermore, there is evidence that remittance-receiving households are more likely to invest in health, education, and small businesses, contributing to long-term financial stability and economic mobility.[c] Overall, remittances can serve as a key mechanism for building financial health.[d]

a. Ratha et al. (2024).
b. Yang and Choi (2007).
c. Clemens and Ogden (2020); Rapoport and Docquier (2006).
d. Clemens and Ogden (2020); Rapoport and Docquier (2006); Yang (2011); Yang and Choi (2007).

The Global Findex also asked about the difficulty of accessing extra funds. Among adults who say that it is possible to get extra money, 36 percent also say it would be very difficult to get it from any source: these adults are not resilient.

Even though family or friends are the most common source of extra money in low- and middle-income economies, they are also among the least reliable sources. About half of those who rely on them, or 15 percent of all adults, say the money would be very difficult to get. In Namibia and the Philippines, where about 30 percent of adults rely on family or friends for extra money, three-quarters of those who do rely on them say the money would be very difficult to get.

Figure 4.2.2 In every region except East Asia and Pacific, family or friends are the most common source of extra money

Adults identifying the source of, and assessing how difficult it would be to access, emergency money in 30 days or less (%), 2024

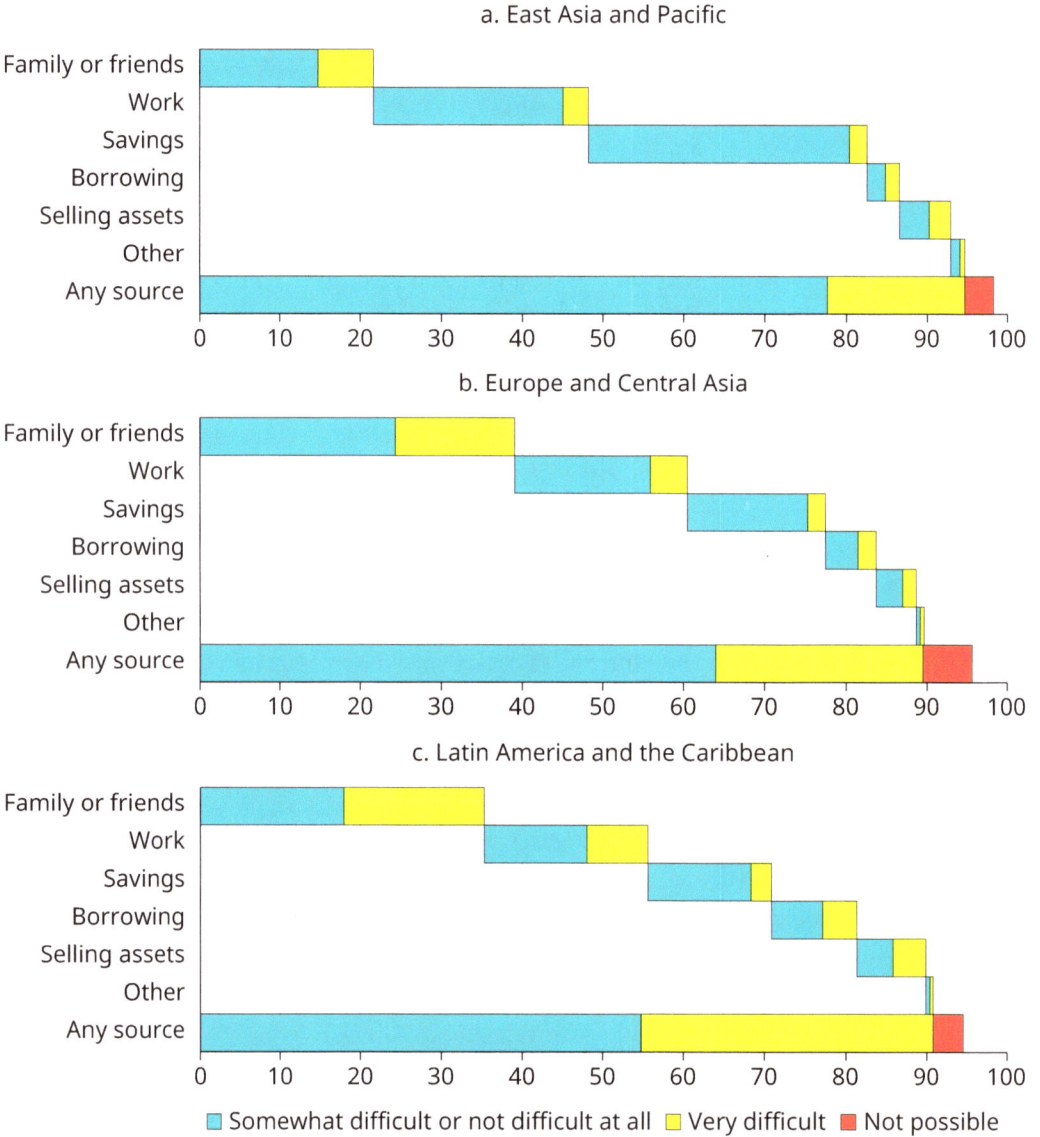

a. East Asia and Pacific

b. Europe and Central Asia

c. Latin America and the Caribbean

■ Somewhat difficult or not difficult at all ☐ Very difficult ■ Not possible

(Figure continued next page)

Figure 4.2.2 In every region except East Asia and Pacific, family or friends are the most common source of extra money *(continued)*

d. Middle East and North Africa

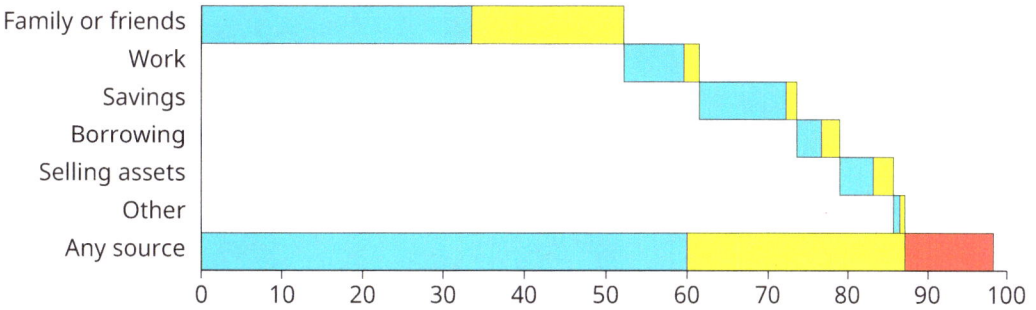

e. South Asia

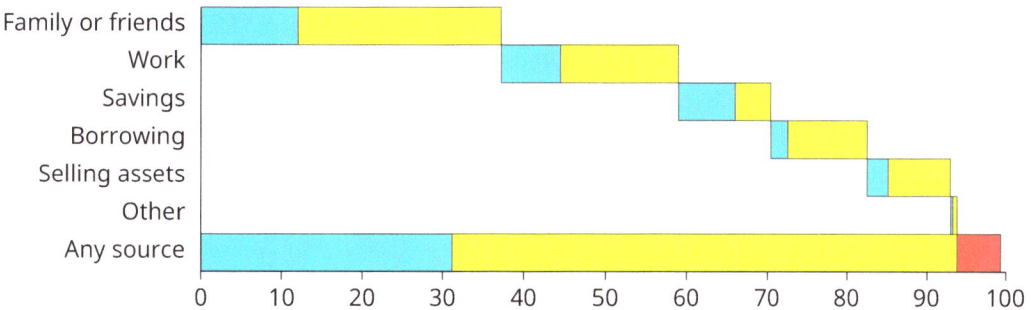

f. Sub-Saharan Africa

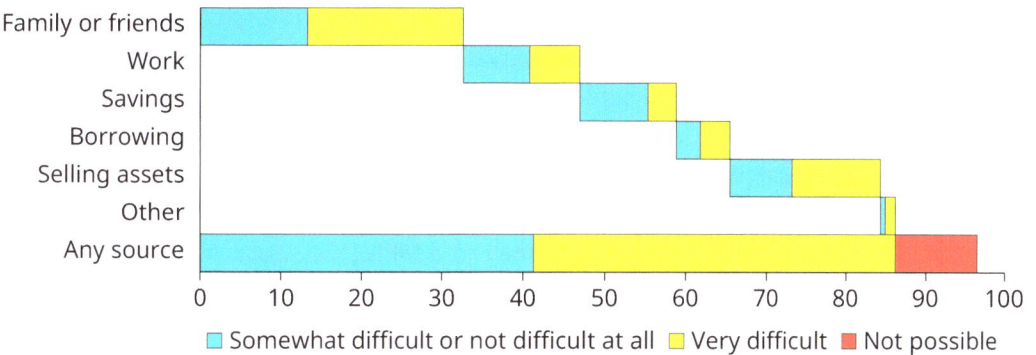

☐ Somewhat difficult or not difficult at all   ☐ Very difficult   ■ Not possible

Source: Global Findex Database 2025.

Note: A small share of adults did not know or did not disclose their main source of emergency money.

There are exceptions to family or friends' low levels of reliability, however. In European and Central Asian economies such as Armenia, Bosnia and Herzegovina, and Montenegro, which also have above-average reliance on family or friends, they are more reliable. In these economies, no more than 20 percent of adults who rely on family or friends for extra money say that it would be very difficult to get.

Overall, the level of reliance on family or friends for extra money was the same in low- and middle-income economies in 2024 as it was in 2021, in terms of both the share of adults who rely on it and how difficult it would be to get the funds. The challenges associated with raising money from family or friends may in part reflect the fact that many events that would motivate people to reach out for help affect an entire community. For example, natural disasters or extreme weather events are becoming more frequent in low- and middle-income economies (refer to spotlight 4.1 at the end of this section for a discussion of natural disasters).

After family or friends, savings and working extra hours are the second-most-popular sources of emergency money, each preferred by about 20 percent of adults across low- and middle-income economies.

The share of adults who can reliably draw money from savings increased by 4 percentage points between 2021 and 2024, which might be related to increases in overall saving rates (formal and informal) of 12 percentage points reported in chapter 3.1.[2] Among adults with any savings in low- and middle-income economies, a third say that they would rely on those savings as a source of emergency money. Of all adults, 21 percent say the same. Among adults who save formally, 38 percent would rely on their savings in an emergency.

Savings are the most reliable source of extra money. Nearly all adults who rely on them say they could access extra money to deal with a shock with little to no difficulty. In East Asia and Pacific and Europe and Central Asia, where overall resilience remained steady, the share of adults who reported having reliable savings to draw from increased by 6 and 5 percentage points, respectively (refer to figure 4.2.3). In East Asia and Pacific, this increase coincided with a decrease in reliance on working for extra money to mitigate a financial shock, and in Europe and Central Asia, with decreased reliance on borrowing.

---

2   Recall that as discussed in chapter 3.1, an increase in the saving rate refers to the share of adults who save, not how much they save.

Figure 4.2.3 **The share of adults relying on savings for extra money increased in low- and middle-income economies**

Adults who could access savings in an emergency in 30 days or less with some or no difficulty (%), 2021–24

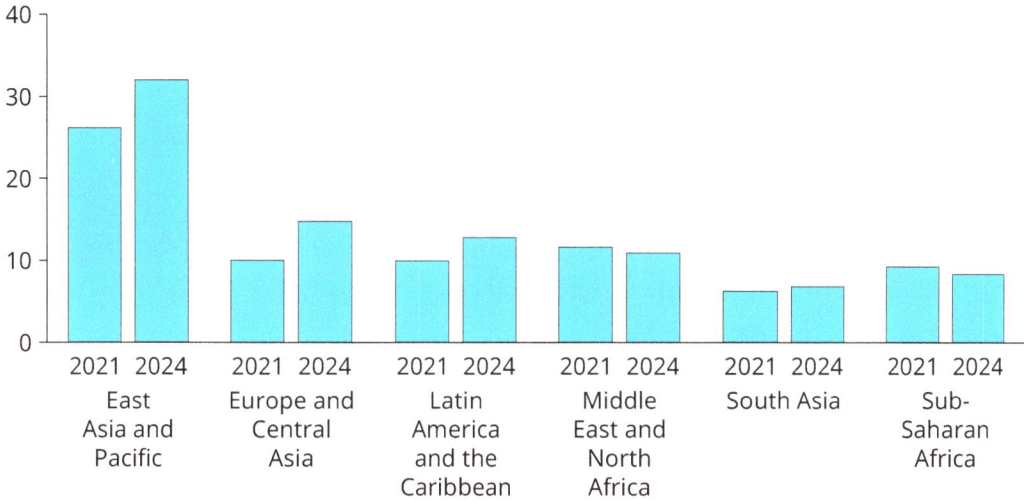

Source: Global Findex Database 2025.

As mentioned, the same share of adults rely on extra work as rely on savings for extra money. Not surprisingly, employment status influences this reliance. Among adults who receive wages, 20 percent say they would rely on work—the same as the overall average. Yet 27 percent of self-employed adults would rely on work. That compares with 15 percent of unemployed adults and 11 percent of adults who are out of the workforce. Wage- and self-employed adults who rely on work for extra money are more likely than the average to say the money would not be hard to get. A quarter of men in low- and middle-income economies would work for extra money, compared with 18 percent of women.

Extra work is nonetheless less reliable than savings, with 7 percent of adults—or one-third of those relying on it—saying the money would be very difficult to get. This may be because in many economies, working more hours might not be possible, especially for people in tight labor markets with low demand for their skills.

For those reasons and others, there is wide variation between the shares of adults relying on savings and those relying on extra work, even in the same geographic region. For example, savings are the option of choice for only 6 percent of adults in Madagascar, compared with 30 percent of adults who choose extra work; in contrast, 20 percent of adults would rely on savings and 13 percent on work in Liberia.

Borrowing money and selling assets are much less popular than any of the other sources of extra money, with 7 percent and 9 percent of adults, respectively, in low- and middle-income economies relying on them in 2024. Both percentages are up slightly since 2021, when 5 percent of adults said they would borrow, and 4 percent said they would sell assets to get emergency cash.

More than 10 percent of adults would borrow to deal with a shock in just 18 economies. These include the Dominican Republic and Malawi, where more than 20 percent of adults report that they would borrow emergency money.

A larger share of adults who borrow and a larger share of those who sell assets say these methods are less reliable than do those who save or rely on family or friends as ways to access extra cash.

Sources of funding for accessing extra money differ according to economies' income group

As was the case in 2021, an economy's income group classification did not necessarily correlate with respondents' financial resilience in the 2024 survey (refer to figure 4.2.4). In Burkina Faso and Togo, both low-income economies, a higher share of adults were resilient than the average across low- and middle-income economies. Their resilience rates were also higher than those in economies such as Eswatini and Nigeria, both lower middle income, and Botswana and Namibia, which are upper middle income.

Adults in upper-middle-income economies are more likely overall to be able to get extra money than adults in low- and lower-middle-income economies (refer to figure 4.2.5). They are also more likely to rely on savings and less likely to sell their assets or ask family or friends for money.

Figure 4.2.4 Income group classification does not reliably correlate with financial resilience

Adults who could come up with emergency money in 30 days or less with some or no difficulty identifying the source of the money (%), 2024

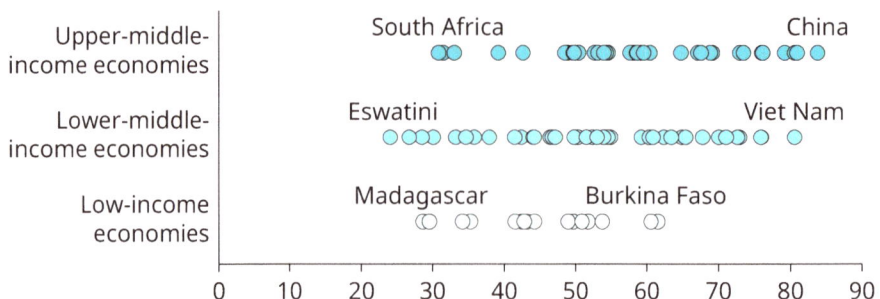

Source: Global Findex Database 2025.

Figure 4.2.5 Choices of emergency money vary by country income classification

Adults who could come up with emergency money in 30 days or less with some or no difficulty (%), 2024

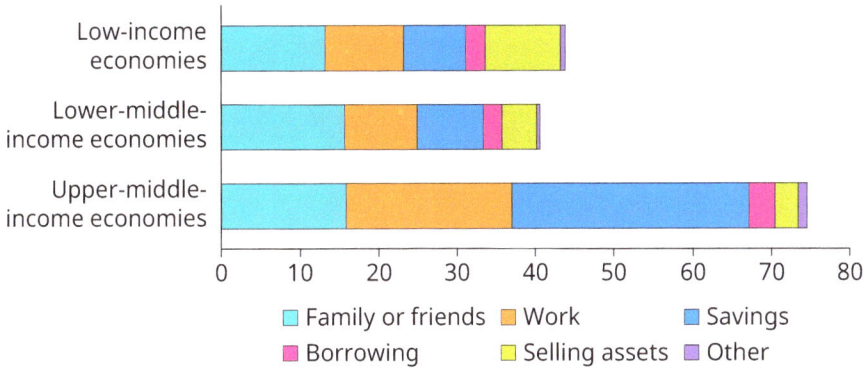

Legend: Family or friends, Work, Savings, Borrowing, Selling assets, Other

Source: Global Findex Database 2025.

A third of adults in upper-middle-income economies rely on savings, more than 20 percentage points more than in low- and lower-middle-income economies, where 12 percent of adults do. Data from China, where 39 percent of adults rely on savings, drive the high level of reliance on savings in upper-middle-income economies. When data from China are excluded, 16 percent of adults in the upper-middle-income group of countries rely on savings.

In contrast, in low-income economies, 22 percent of adults would sell assets to manage a shock. In comparison, 12 percent of adults in lower-middle-income economies and 5 percent in upper-middle-income economies would sell assets. Some economies vary from this norm. In lower-middle-income Tanzania, for instance, 29 percent would sell assets, making it the top choice for funding an emergency in that economy.

Women and low-income adults rely more than men and high-income adults on family or friends for extra money

Financial resilience and sources of emergency money differ according to gender and household income (refer to figure 4.2.6). Across low- and middle-income economies, women and men are equally likely to rely on savings, borrowing, or selling assets for money in an emergency. But women are 6 percentage points more likely to rely on family or friends and 7 percentage points less likely to work for extra money. The gap between women's and men's reliance on work is more than 15 percentage points in nine economies, four of them in Europe and Central Asia: Algeria, Azerbaijan, Bangladesh, Guinea, Niger, Tajikistan, Ukraine, Uzbekistan, and West Bank and Gaza.

Figure 4.2.6 Women and poorer adults are more likely than men and wealthier adults to rely on family or friends for extra money

Adults identifying the source of, and assessing how difficult it would be to access, emergency money in 30 days or less (%), 2024

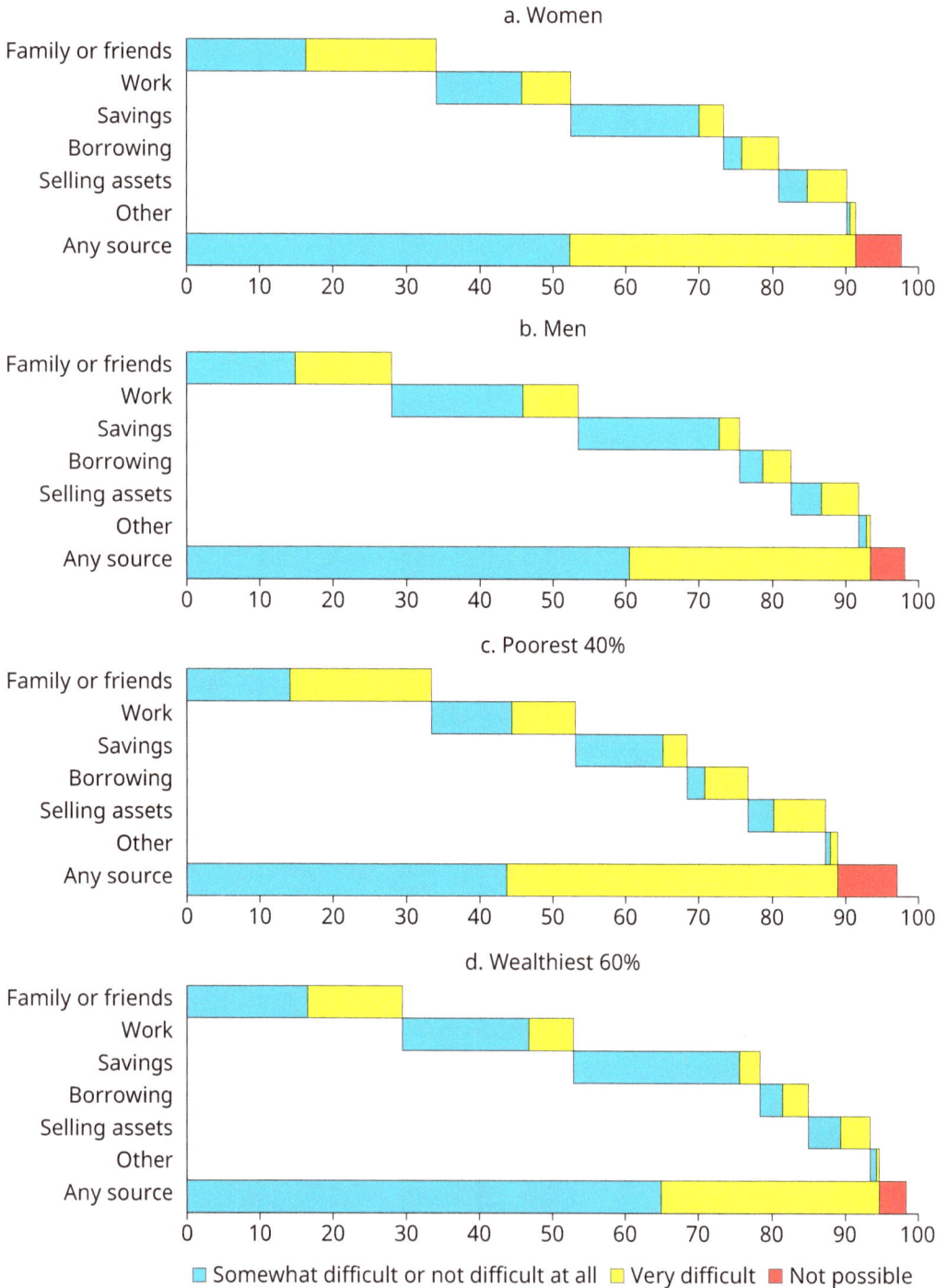

a. Women

b. Men

c. Poorest 40%

d. Wealthiest 60%

☐ Somewhat difficult or not difficult at all ☐ Very difficult ■ Not possible

Source: Global Findex Database 2025.

There are also differences according to income. In low- and middle-income economies, adults living in households in the poorest 40 percent by income are less likely than those in the wealthiest 60 percent to rely on savings for extra money: 15 percent compared with 26 percent. Poorer adults are not significantly more likely to rely on family or friends (33 percent versus 30 percent), nor are they less likely to seek additional work (20 percent versus 23 percent) than their wealthier peers.

One-third of adults could cover more than two months of expenses if they lost their main income source

For the first time in 2024, the Global Findex asked how long people could cover their household expenses if they lost their main income source. About one in three adults in low- and middle-income economies, or 34 percent, said they could cover everyday expenses for more than two months if that happened (refer to figure 4.2.7). About half as many, 17 percent, could cover just about two months. One in four, or 26 percent, could cover one month, and 19 percent could cover less than two weeks.

Figure 4.2.7 **About one-third of adults in low- and middle-income economies could cover more than two months of expenses if they lost their main income source**

Adults identifying how long they could cover expenses if they lost their main source of income (%), 2024

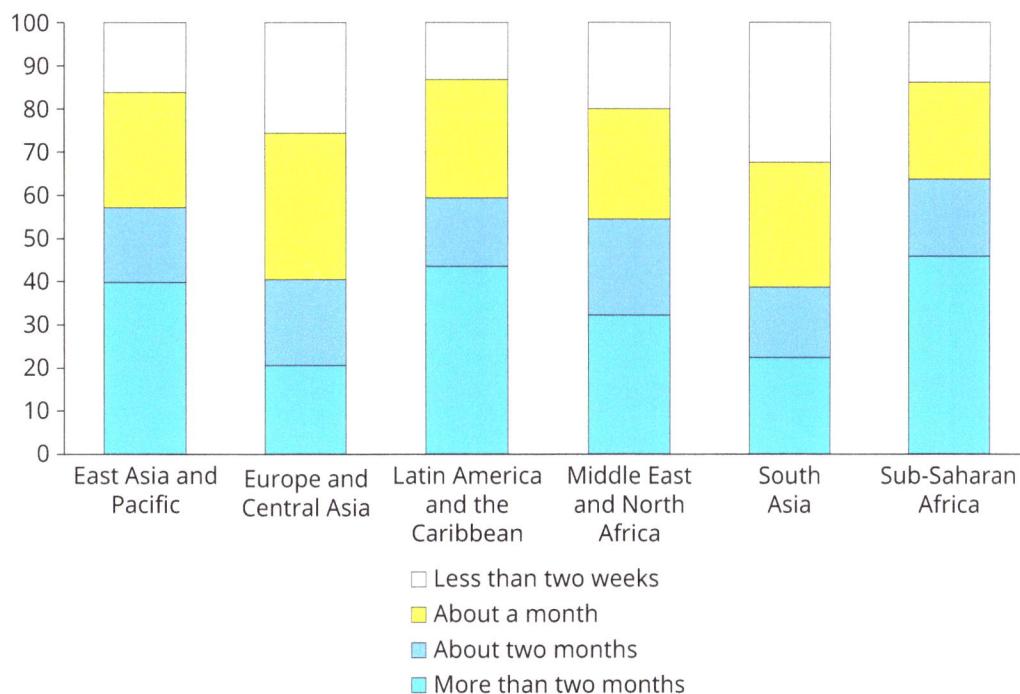

Source: Global Findex Database 2025.

The length of time that respondents could cover their expenses varies by region. The largest share of adults in East Asia and Pacific, Latin America and the Caribbean, the Middle East and North Africa, and Sub-Saharan Africa could cover more than two months of expenses if they lost their main source of income. In Europe and Central Asia and South Asia, in contrast, the largest share of adults could cover only about a month of expenses.

Increasing resilience by building confidence

The trends discussed in chapter 3.1 point toward more adults saving in an account. Over time, as this saving trend continues, it may translate into greater resilience, as more people amass sufficient balances to manage an unexpected expense or loss of income.

Financial confidence, including the ability to manage money and navigate the functions of an account, may also help people make the most of the money they have and maximize their ability to save. That is the subject of the next chapter.

4.3 Gaps in financial capabilities and confidence

A reproducibility package is available for this book in the Reproducible Research Repository at https://reproducibility.worldbank.org/catalog/299.

4.3 Gaps in financial capabilities and confidence

After managing daily needs, pursuing longer-term goals, and preparing for unexpected shocks, feeling confident about one's financial life is recognized as a key aspect of financial health, as defined by the Group of Twenty. Like financial worrying, financial confidence is subjective, shaped by a person's perceptions about their own financial capabilities.

Despite this subjectivity, the Global Findex 2025 attempts to measure financial confidence by asking about behaviors and experiences that suggest people understand how to use their financial accounts and can do so responsibly and confidently. Paying unexpected fees, sending erroneous transactions, relying on others to transact on one's behalf, or expecting to need help to use an account can all result in a lack of confidence in one's ability to use financial services independently. In contrast, people taking proactive steps to manage and safeguard their money tend to show both greater capability and higher levels of confidence.

Yet even when individual experiences are acknowledged, a strong and enforced consumer protection framework is a prerequisite for financial confidence and capability. Financial education and personal financial capability are important and have positive impacts.[1] Yet they are insufficient on their own, and can put too much of an onus on the consumer to navigate financial markets that are often confusing and opaque. Many of the challenges discussed in this chapter, such as unexpected fees or relying on others to navigate financial services, often arise from exploitative pricing practices, poor product design, or a lack of transparency, and not from individual mistakes or ignorance.

For instance, research using mystery shoppers has consistently documented hidden fees, inadequate disclosure of prices and taxes, and unresponsive customer service and complaint mechanisms, particularly in digital financial services such as mobile money.[2] Even when users are aware of official fee structures, they may still overpay as a result of unofficial agent charges or misleading sales tactics.

Financial confidence, therefore, requires a fair financial playing field, one in which users not only understand the rules, but also operate in an environment in which those rules are enforced and abusive practices are curbed. This broader perspective reinforces the view of financial education and consumer protection as complementary, not interchangeable.

---

1   Ansar, Klapper, and Singer (2023); Kaiser et al. (2022).
2   Adams et al. (2025); Annan et al. (2023); Giné and Mazer (2022).

Unexpected fees and erroneous transactions suggest that some adults are financially vulnerable

The Global Findex 2025 asked people who receive a government payment or a private sector wage in an account whether they have paid a higher-than-expected fee to collect their money. The data do not indicate whether such fees, when reported, reflect a recipient's misunderstanding about the fee structure or exploitation by a payment distributor.

Either way, having paid such fees might point to a potential lack of understanding of account rules or a lack of knowledge about recourse options if an account owner encounters difficulties. This highlights the importance of addressing both the inevitability of some fees and the preventability of others through improved regulation and provider practices, as well as increased consumer awareness.

Across low- and middle-income economies,[3] 5 percent of adults paid higher-than-expected fees. In nine economies,10 percent or more of adults paid higher-than-expected fees: Armenia, Bulgaria, Eswatini, Kenya, the Kyrgyz Republic, Malaysia, Morocco, Senegal, and South Africa. Sub-Saharan Africa has the highest share of government payment recipients paying unexpected fees to collect their money, at nearly one in four; Europe and Central Asia has the lowest share, at just one in ten.

In every region, wage payment recipients are more likely than government payment recipients to pay an unexpected fee (refer to figure 4.3.1). Latin America and the Caribbean and Sub-Saharan Africa have the highest shares of wage payment recipients paying extra fees, at about one in four and one in three, respectively.

Those who receive government transfers or wage payments often have limited or no choice about how they get paid. As a result, some unexpected fees may be unavoidable, making them less influenced by an individual's financial knowledge or behavior. Not all unexpected fees are inevitable, however. Regulatory agencies and financial services providers can help minimize exploitative pricing, control agent misconduct, and increase transparency and disclosure around pricing structures. This includes clearer disclosures of taxes, fees, and the consequences of using services such as out-of-network ATMs.

In addition, the cost of financial services can be reduced if consumers are equipped with the tools and information necessary to compare prices and select more affordable options among those available. Increased access to comparable pricing data and greater financial literacy can empower individuals to make more cost-effective financial decisions.

---

3   Because of differences in survey methods and in the survey questionnaire used, this average does not include
     data for Algeria, China, the Islamic Republic of Iran, Libya, Mauritius, the Russian Federation, and Ukraine.

Figure 4.3.1 In every region, the share of adults paying unexpectedly high fees to cash out money is higher among wage payment recipients than among government payment recipients

Adults who receive a wage payment or a government transfer or pension into an account (%), 2024

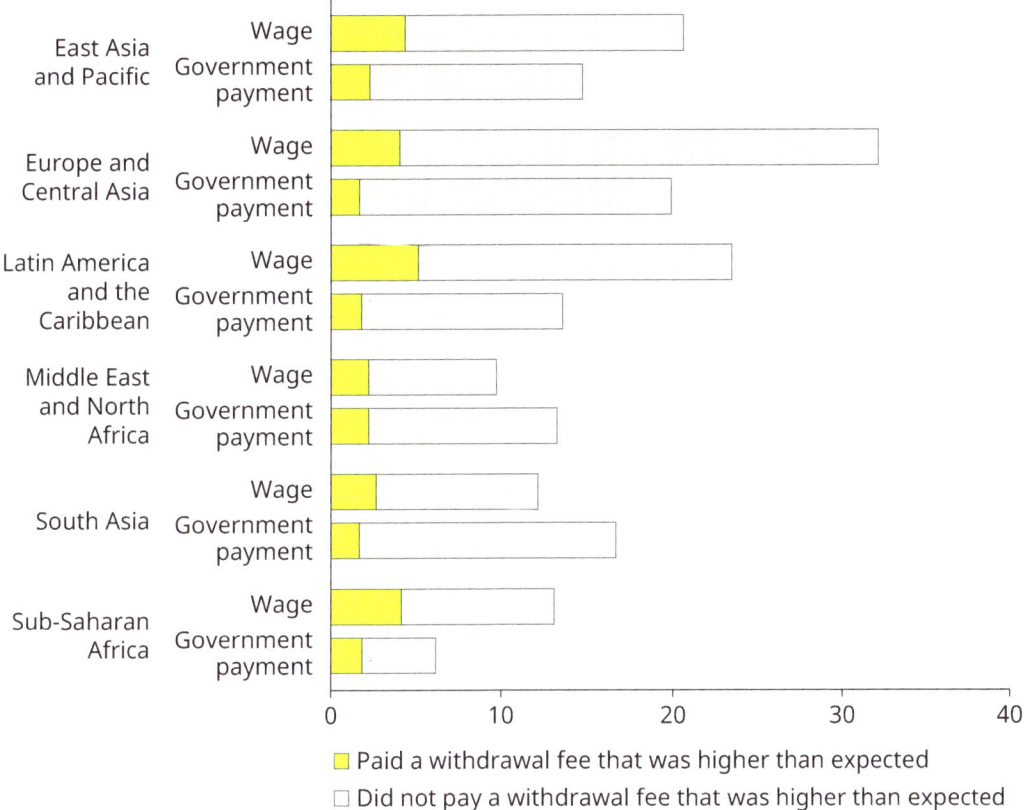

□ Paid a withdrawal fee that was higher than expected
□ Did not pay a withdrawal fee that was higher than expected

Source: Global Findex Database 2025.

Note: Because an abridged questionnaire was administered in Algeria, China, the Islamic Republic of Iran, Libya, Mauritius, the Russian Federation, and Ukraine, averages exclude data for these economies.

Mistakes are common, though potentially avoidable

Though fees are not entirely avoidable, mistakes may be. The Global Findex asked mobile money account owners if they have ever sent money to the wrong recipient. This can happen when an account owner inputs the wrong phone number or a wrong version of another proxy ID before making a payment. Few adults in Latin America and the Caribbean or South Asia have sent money to the wrong recipient, despite these regions' 37 percent and 22 percent mobile money account ownership rates, respectively. In Sub-Saharan Africa, however, 9 percent of people—nearly a quarter of mobile money account owners—have (refer to figure 4.3.2).

Figure 4.3.2 **Only half of mobile money account owners in Sub-Saharan Africa who sent money to the wrong person got it back**

Adults with a mobile money account (%), 2024

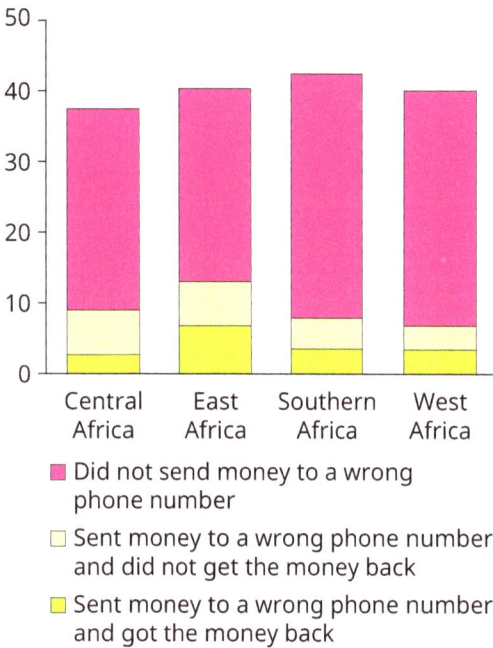

Did not send money to a wrong phone number

Sent money to a wrong phone number and did not get the money back

Sent money to a wrong phone number and got the money back

Source: Global Findex Database 2025.

Fortunately, about half of them got their money back. That average holds across all subregions except for Central Africa, where only about one-third of mobile money users who sent a payment to the wrong person got it back. Overall, 4 percent of adults in Sub-Saharan Africa and 10 percent of mobile money account owners have sent money to the wrong person and not received their money back.

Some providers have created processes for recovering money that has been sent by mistake. Mobile money platforms in Sub-Saharan Africa often have mechanisms to facilitate a transfer reversal or recovery. Customers of Safaricom's M-PESA in Kenya, for example, can dial *456# to request a reversal. Customer support will investigate and potentially freeze the transfer recipient's account until the issue is resolved. In addition, providers have included safeguards to prevent mistaken transfers, including confirmation messages, as well as campaigns and training to educate customers in ways to prevent mistaken transfers, as well as to protect their PINs and avoid fraud.[4]

Relying on others to transact suggests a lack of financial capability

Anyone can accidentally enter the wrong phone number or other ID number for an intended recipient of a mobile payment. Distraction, mistaken information, or poor user experience design can all make that more likely, even for experienced mobile money users. Account owners having family members or friends transact for them, on the other hand, suggests a more distinct lack of financial capability or autonomy.

4   Valenzuela et al. (2022).

Figure 4.3.3 In South Asia, almost one in five adults who received government payments in a bank account relied on a family member or friend to collect the money

Adults who received a government payment in an account in the past year (%), 2024

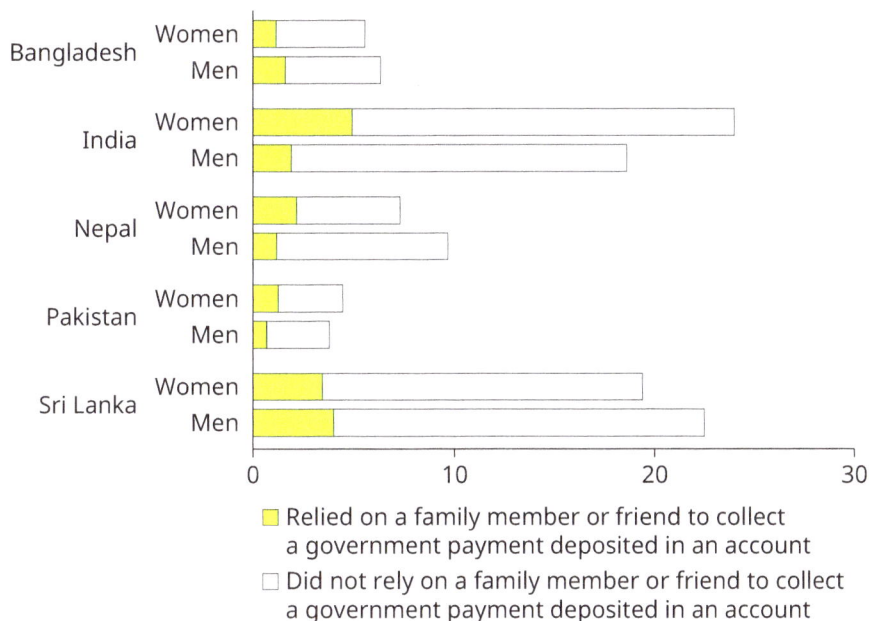

Source: Global Findex Database 2025.

For example, for this edition, the Global Findex survey included a set of questions asked only in South Asia of adults who receive government payments in a bank account. The question asked whether the recipients withdraw the money themselves or rely on a friend or a family member to do it for them. Among adults in the region who receive government payments in a bank account, 17 percent rely on a family member to withdraw the money (refer to figure 4.3.3). Women who receive these payments are equally as likely as men who are recipients to make their own withdrawals.

Responsible use of digital financial services both reflects and enables greater financial confidence

Global Findex 2025 findings highlight the power of mobile connectivity for driving not just increased digital activity, but also increased account ownership, saving, and digital payments. These findings carry through to financial health in the form of leveraging digital channels to engage in responsible financial practices. These practices include keeping track of balances and staying informed about account policies, while taking steps to protect accounts and the money in them.

Approximately 29 percent of all adults in low- and middle-income economies—or 40 percent of bank account owners in those economies—have received information about their account balances through email, text, or some other method on their mobile phones. A similar share of both adults and bank account owners have proactively checked their bank balances using a mobile phone or computer (refer to figure 4.3.4). Research suggests that this kind of real-time balance monitoring can help customers build greater trust in their financial institutions.[5]

Receiving private information electronically makes it more important for users to protect their mobile phones with passwords, a topic discussed in chapter 1.3. This is particularly relevant for mobile money account owners, because even with a mobile money account PIN, anyone with access to an account owner's mobile phone—whether a family member or a phone thief—could potentially access the balance in the associated mobile money account.

Figure 4.3.4 **Forty percent of bank or similar financial institution account owners in low- and middle-income economies received information or checked account balances through digital channels in the past year**

Adults with an account at a bank or similar financial institution (%), 2024

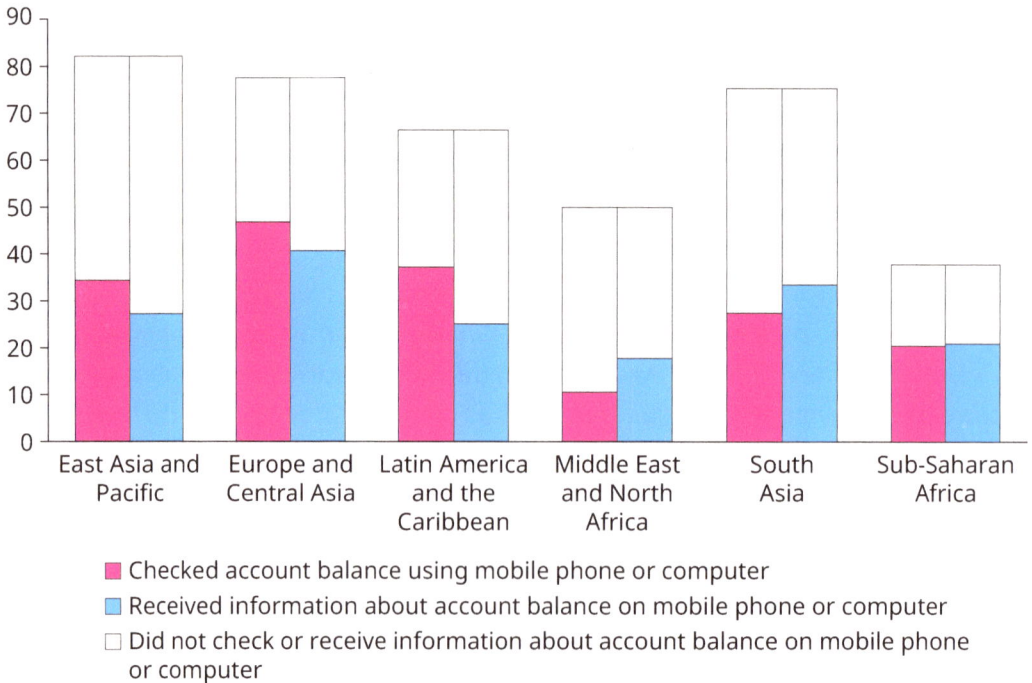

■ Checked account balance using mobile phone or computer
■ Received information about account balance on mobile phone or computer
□ Did not check or receive information about account balance on mobile phone or computer

Source: Global Findex Database 2025.

---

5   Bachas et al. (2021).

Fortunately, password usage is high among mobile money account owners and others with accounts they use through mobile channels. Most have passwords on their mobile phones, even in Latin America and the Caribbean and South Asia, the other regions with significant mobile money adoption. The exception is Sub-Saharan Africa, however, where only about half of mobile money account owners have mobile phone passwords and can change them (refer to figure 4.3.5). This might be because of the higher rates of ownership of basic phones in the region; these phones lack capabilities related to facial recognition and other biometric security measures and require numeric passwords that might be harder to recall or change. Broader awareness and education can help people recognize the importance of having and using passwords.

Figure 4.3.5 **Only about half of mobile money account owners in Sub-Saharan Africa also have passwords on their phones**

Adults with a mobile money account (%), 2024

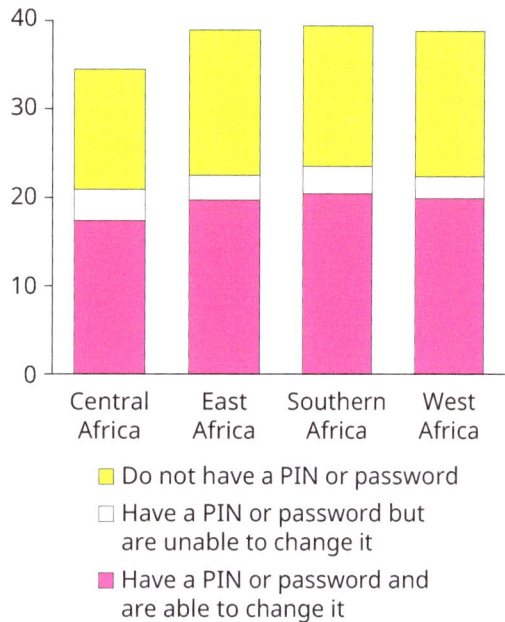

Legend:
- Do not have a PIN or password (yellow)
- Have a PIN or password but are unable to change it (white)
- Have a PIN or password and are able to change it (pink)

Source: Global Findex Database 2025.

A lack of financial confidence may discourage adults who do not have accounts from opening one

The aspects of financial confidence discussed thus far focus on people who already have accounts. Financial confidence may also affect the lives of people who do not have accounts, however, and their willingness to open or use one. To provide greater understanding about that, the Global Findex asked adults without an account at a bank or similar financial institution whether they could use one without help if they were to open one (respondents in Sub-Saharan Africa were not asked this question because of the prevalence of mobile money accounts in the region). Across regions, between 33 percent and 59 percent of these adults say they would need help (refer to figure 4.3.6).

There are statistically significant gender differences across regions in the share of adults without accounts at a bank or similar institution who say they would need help using one. In Europe and Central Asia, the Middle East and North Africa,

Figure 4.3.6 **Two-thirds of adults without an account at a bank or similar financial institution in low- and middle-income economies would need help using one**

Adults without an account at a bank or similar financial institution (%), 2024

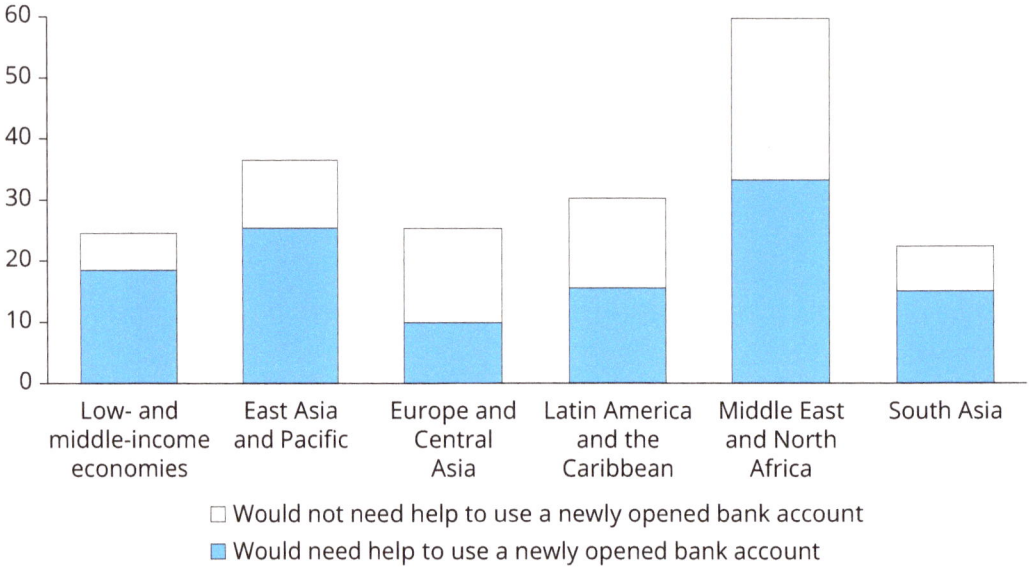

□ Would not need help to use a newly opened bank account
■ Would need help to use a newly opened bank account

Source: Global Findex Database 2025.

Note: Because of the prevalence of mobile money accounts in the region, respondents in Sub-Saharan Africa without an account at a bank or similar financial institution were not asked whether they could use one without help if they were to open one.

and South Asia, women without an account at a bank or similar institution are at least 19 percentage points more likely than men without such an account to say they would need help using one if they opened one. In Latin America and the Caribbean, that gap is 6 percentage points, whereas in East Asia and Pacific, there is a 4 percentage point gender gap.

Regulators and financial institutions play a key role in helping people build financial confidence

Empowering end users and rewarding behaviors that build financial confidence requires collaboration among all parts of the digital and financial ecosystem, including governments and policy makers, financial providers, device manufacturers, and digital platforms.

Behaviors that indicate a lack of confidence, such as paying unexpected fees and relying on others to collect money or otherwise use an account, can be mitigated through experience, awareness building, and targeted financial education programs. These may start among account owners themselves, who can be given safe opportunities to build financial literacy through experience. For example, evidence from an experiment involving women garment workers in Bangladesh finds that first-time account owners who receive their wages in an account learn quickly to use it competently.[6]

Yet the onus should not be put entirely on end users to independently develop the skills they need to use financial services productively. Effective financial account onboarding by providers may also help users, including those with less experience, choose and use products that will give them the most benefit. Clear information in plain language and through accessible media during the sales and onboarding stages of financial product sign-up can ensure people understand the products they sign up for and know how to use them. These types of interventions theoretically benefit both end users and financial providers. Yet regulators and supervisors may nonetheless have to spell out what they expect regulated institutions to offer. In the absence of clear protocols, providers have an incentive to sell the highest-function, highest-fee products, regardless of what a customer needs. Customer service agents may also push higher-priced products, motivated by commissions.

Product design and education also have a role to play. Digital products in particular can help people using them through intuitive user interfaces, alerts, and prompts. In the case of payments, people are less likely to send money to the wrong person if a payment services provider builds identity verification and confirmation steps into the payment process, thereby limiting the potential for mistakes.

Finally, as discussed at the beginning of this chapter, holistic, risk-based consumer protection regimes are essential for setting the expectations and foundations against which all financial services providers must deliver.[7] By making these regimes a priority, government regulators and supervisors can promote a safe and productive financial inclusion environment for everyone.

---

6   Breza, Kanz, and Klapper (2020).
7   Garz et al. (2021).

References

Adams, Paul, Francis Annan, William Blackmon, Xavier Giné, Lina Hochhalter, Brian Mwesigwa, and Arianna Zapanta. 2025. *Transaction Cost Index: Year Two Comparative Report*. Washington, DC: Innovations for Poverty Action. https://poverty-action.org /sites/default/files/2025-03/Transactional%20cost%20index_8_0.pdf.

Alam, Khurshid, and Ajay Mahal. 2014. "Economic Impacts of Health Shocks on Households in Low and Middle Income Countries: A Review of the Literature." *Globalization and Health* 10 (1): 21. https://doi.org/10.1186/1744-8603-10-21.

Annan, Francis, William Blackmon, Xavier Giné, Brian Mwesigwa, and Arianna Zapanta. 2023. *Transaction Cost Index: Year 1 Comparative Report*. Washington, DC: Innovations for Poverty Action. https://poverty-action.org/sites/default/files/2023-09/IPA -Transaction-Cost-Index-Year-1-Comparative-Report.pdf.

Ansar, Saniya, Leora Klapper, and Dorothe Singer. 2023. "The Importance of Financial Education for the Effective Use of Formal Financial Services." *Journal of Financial Literacy and Wellbeing* 1 (1): 28–46. https://doi.org/10.1017/flw.2023.5.

Ashraf, Nava, Dean Karlan, and Wesley Yin. 2006. "Tying Odysseus to the Mast: Evidence from a Commitment Savings Product in the Philippines." *Quarterly Journal of Economics* 121 (2): 635–72. https://doi.org/10.1162/QJEC.2006.121.2.635.

Ashraf, Nava, Dean Karlan, and Wesley Yin. 2010. "Female Empowerment: Impact of a Commitment Savings Product in the Philippines." *World Development* 38 (3): 333–44. https://doi.org/10.1016/J.WORLDDEV.2009.05.010.

Bachas, Pierre, Paul Gertler, Sean Higgins, and Enrique Seira. 2021. "How Debit Cards Enable the Poor to Save More." *Journal of Finance* 76 (4): 1913–57. https://doi.org/10.1111 /jofi.13021.

Banerjee, Anhijit V., and Esther Duflo. 2012. *Poor Economics: A Radical Rethinking of the Way to Fight Global Poverty*. New York: Public Affairs. https://economics.mit.edu/people /faculty/abhijit-banerjee/poor-economics.

Board of Governors of the Federal Reserve System. 2025. "Economic Well-Being of U.S. Households in 2024." Board of Governors, Washngton, DC. https://doi .org/10.17016/8960.1.

Breza, Emily, Martin Kanz, and Leora F. Klapper. 2020. "Learning to Navigate a New Financial Technology: Evidence from Payroll Accounts." NBER Working Paper 28249, National Bureau of Economic Research, Cambridge, MA. https://papers.ssrn.com/sol3/papers .cfm?abstract_id=3753159.

Brune, Lasse, Xavier Giné, Jessica Goldberg, and Dean Yang. 2016. "Facilitating Savings for Agriculture: Field Experimental Evidence from Malawi." *Economic Development and Cultural Change* 64 (2): 187–220. https://doi.org/10.1086/684014.

Clemens, Michael A., and Timothy N. Ogden. 2020. "Migration and Household Finances: How a Different Framing Can Improve Thinking about Migration." *Development Policy Review* 38 (1): 3–27. https://doi.org/10.1111/dpr.12471.

Collins, Daryl, Jonathan Morduch, Stuart Rutherford, and Orlanda Ruthven. 2009. *Portfolios of the Poor: How the World's Poor Live on $2 a Day.* Princeton, NJ: Princeton University Press. https://www.jstor.org/stable/j.ctt7rzr4.

Costa, Paulo, Malena de la Fuente, and Marsella Martino. 2025. "Emergency Savings May Hold Key to Financial Well-Being." Research summary, April 29, 2025. https://corporate .vanguard.com/content/corporatesite/us/en/corp/articles/emergency-savings-may -hold-key-financial-well-being.html.

Dupas, Pascaline, and Jonathan Robinson. 2013. "Savings Constraints and Microenterprise Development: Evidence from a Field Experiment in Kenya." *American Economic Journal: Applied Economics* 5 (1): 163–92. https://doi.org/10.1257/app.5.1.163.

Garz, Seth, Xavier Giné, Dean Karlan, Rafe Mazer, Caitlin Sanford, and Jonathan Zinman. 2021. "Consumer Protection for Financial Inclusion in Low- and Middle-Income Countries: Bridging Regulator and Academic Perspectives." *Annual Review of Economics* 13 (1): 219–46. https://doi.org/10.1146/annurev-financial-071020-012008.

Giné, Xavier, Cristina Martínez Cuellar, and Rafael Keenan Mazer. 2017. "Information Disclosure and Demand Elasticity of Financial Products: Evidence from a Multi-country Study." Policy Research Working Paper 8210, World Bank, Washington, DC. http://documents.worldbank.org/curated/en/513631507130361973.

Giné, Xavier, Jessica Goldberg, Dan Silverman, and Dean Yang. 2018. "Revising Commitments: Field Evidence on the Adjustment of Prior Choices." *Economic Journal* 128 (608): 159–88. https://doi.org/10.1111/ECOJ.12378.

Jones, Kelly, and Erick Gong. 2021. "Precautionary Savings and Shock-Coping Behaviors: Effects of Promoting Mobile Bank Savings on Transactional Sex in Kenya." *Journal of Health Economics* 78: 102460. https://doi.org/10.1016/j.jhealeco.2021.102460.

Kaiser, Tim, Annamaria Lusardi, Lukas Menkhoff, and Carly Urban. 2022. "Financial Education Affects Financial Knowledge and Downstream Behaviors." *Journal of Financial Economics* 145 (2, part A): 255–72. https://doi.org/10.1016/j.jfineco.2021.09.022.

Karlan, Dean, and Leigh L. Linden. 2025. "Loose Knots: Strong versus Weak Commitments to Save for Education in Uganda." *Journal of Development Economics* 174 (May): 103444. https://doi.org/10.1016/J.JDEVECO.2024.103444.

Karlan, Dean, Sendhil Mullainathan, and Benjamin N. Roth. 2019. "Debt Traps? Market Vendors and Moneylender Debt in India and the Philippines." *American Economic Review: Insights* 1 (1): 27–42. https://doi.org/10.1257/aeri.20180030.

Maddison, Emilie, and Angela E. Micah. 2022. "The Steep Price of Education in Africa: Education Is Unaffordable for Many Families in Low- and Middle-Income Countries." Think Global Health: Poverty, August 4, 2022. https://www.thinkglobalhealth.org /article/steep-price-education-africa.

OECD (Organisation for Economic Co-operation and Development). 2024. *G20 Policy Note on Financial Well-Being.* 2024. Paris: OECD Publishing. https://doi .org/10.1787/7332c99d-en.

Pomeranz, Dina, and Felipe Kast. 2024. "Savings Accounts to Borrow Less: Experimental Evidence from Chile." *Journal of Human Resources* 59 (1): 70–108. https://doi .org/10.3368/jhr.0619-10264R3.

Rapoport, Hillel, and Frédéric Docquier. 2006. "The Economics of Migrants' Remittances." In vol. 2 of *Handbook of the Economics of Giving, Altruism and Reciprocity,* edited by Serge-Christophe Kolm and Jean Mercier Ythier, 1135–98. Amsterdam: North-Holland. https://doi.org/10.1016/S1574-0714(06)02017-3.

Ratha, Dilip, Vandana Chandra, Eung Ju Kim, Akhtar Mahmood, and Sonia Plaza. 2024. "Remittances Slowed in 2023, Expected to Grow Faster in 2024." Migration and Development Brief, Global Knowledge Partnership on Migration and Development, World Bank Group, Washington, DC. http://documents.worldbank.org/curated /en/099714008132436612.

Skiba, Paige Marta, and Jeremy Tobacman. 2008. "Payday Loans, Uncertainty and Discounting: Explaining Patterns of Borrowing, Repayment, and Default." Vanderbilt Law and Economics Research Paper 08-33, Law School, Vanderbilt University, Nashville, TN. https://doi.org/10.2139/SSRN.1319751.

Valenzuela, Myra, David Medine, Surbhi Sood, and Arshi Aadil. 2022. "How Are Mobile Money Agents Protecting Customers' Data in Uganda?" Consultative Group to Assist the Poor blog, December 14. https://www.cgap.org/blog/how-are-mobile-money -agents-protecting-customers-data-in-uganda#:~:text=Mobile%20money%20 providers%2C%20including%20Airtel,mitigate%20and%20investigate%20data%20 misuse.

Yang, Dean. 2011. "Migrant Remittances." *Journal of Economic Perspectives* 25 (3): 129–52. https://doi.org/10.1257/jep.25.3.129.

Yang, Dean, and Hwa Jung Choi. 2007. "Are Remittances Insurance? Evidence from Rainfall Shocks in the Philippines." *World Bank Economic Review* 21 (2): 219–48. https://doi .org/10.1093/wber/lhm003.

SPOTLIGHT 4.1

Natural disasters, mobile connectivity, and digital financial services

Worldwide, natural disasters have become more common. The annual number of recorded droughts, floods, earthquakes, wildfires, volcanic events, tornadoes, and similar events increased more than threefold between 1980 and 2023.[1] Since 1980, the United States alone has experienced more than 400 natural disasters that resulted in US$1 billion or more in damage.[2]

Every economy is exposed to natural disasters, though a combination of factors make low- and middle-income economies disproportionately vulnerable to the impacts of such disasters. These factors include vulnerable geography, as with island economies, coastal economies, and nations experiencing desertification; extreme temperatures; or both, as is the case in many low-latitude areas.[3] Exposure to hazards and rising temperatures has been associated historically with decreased economic productivity,[4] lower levels of consumption,[5] and significant business losses.[6]

Within economies, poorer adults also face a threefold challenge: they often live in places that are more exposed to disastrous events; they lose proportionally more when disaster strikes; and they tend to have fewer resources to prepare for, cope with, and recover from such events.[7] Natural disasters are especially damaging to financial access when they harm telecommunications infrastructure,[8] making communications and financial account access difficult, and when they damage physical structures, including homes, government buildings, banks, and local businesses where mobile agents operate.

Given the increased frequency of natural disasters and their potential impact on both connectivity and financial access, the Global Findex 2025 includes questions

---

1   Our World in Data, "Number of Recorded Natural Disaster Events, 1900 to 2023" (https://ourworldindata.org /grapher/number-of-natural-disaster-events). Some of these increases reflect better data reporting rather than an increase in the number of discrete events.

2   National Centers for Environmental Information, National Oceanic and Atmospheric Administration, "Billion Dollar Weather and Climate Disasters" (https://www.ncei.noaa.gov/access/billions/).

3   Mendelsohn, Dinar, and Williams (2006).

4   Burke, Hsiang, and Miguel (2015); Dell, Jones, and Olken (2012); Diffenbaugh and Burke (2019).

5   Bui et al. (2014); Deryugina, Kawano, and Levitt (2018); Gallagher and Hartley (2017).

6   Agarwal, Ghosh, and Zheng (2024); Aladangady et al. (2016); Beatty, Shimshack, and Volpe (2019).

7   Akter and Mallick (2013); Hallegatte et al. (2020).

8   ITU (2022); Rabkin (2005).

on experiences with natural disasters among people in low- and middle-income economies. For the "World Risk Poll 2021: A Resilient World?" the Lloyd's Register Foundation collected data to analyze global perceptions of risk and levels of preparedness, also, like the Global Findex, working with Gallup. Respondents were asked to select from a list of 10 natural disasters (ranging from floods and tsunamis to earthquakes and volcanic eruptions) the most recent type they had experienced. In 2024, the Global Findex survey introduced a new question: "In the past three years, have you personally experienced a natural disaster or severe weather event, such as [insert local examples of natural disasters]?" This question reflects the top three risks identified in the Lloyd's Register Foundation's 2021 report.[9]

One in four adults has experienced a natural disaster

The data show that 24 percent of adults in low- and middle-income economies personally experienced a natural disaster in the three years prior to taking the survey. East Asia and Pacific, South Asia, and Sub-Saharan Africa have higher average exposure rates than other regions (refer to figure S4.1.1, panel a).

Adults in the poorest 40 percent of households by income across low- and middle-income economies were 6 percentage points more likely to experience a disaster than those in the wealthiest 60 percent: 28 percent compared with 21 percent. In the 10 economies with the highest share of adults saying they personally experienced a natural disaster—Armenia, Chad, the Comoros, Madagascar, Malawi, Morocco, Mozambique, the Philippines, Zambia, and Zimbabwe—50 percent or more of all adults were exposed (refer to figure S4.1.1, panel b). These economies are particularly vulnerable, and the people who live there are more likely than average to suffer adverse consequences from a disastrous event.

For example, in Chad, which experienced severe flooding in 2022 and again in 2024,[10] 76 percent of people said they personally experienced a natural disaster. In Morocco, where a 6.8 magnitude earthquake took place in 2023,[11] 64 percent of adults said they were personally exposed to a disaster. Other economies in which more than 60 percent of adults experienced a disaster include Madagascar and Mozambique, an island and a coastal nation vulnerable to floods, respectively, and Malawi and Zambia, neighboring nations that saw severe drought and food shortages in 2024.[12]

---

9   Refer to the web page for the Lloyd's Register Foundation World Risk Poll 2021 report: https://www.lrfoundation .org.uk/sites/default/files/2024-06/LRF_2021_report2-resilienceonline_version.pdf.
10   Lloyd's Register Foundation (2022).
11   Rafferty (n.d.).
12   UN OCHA (2024).

Figure S4.1.1 Poorer and rural adults have higher levels of exposure to natural disasters than wealthier and urban adults, both overall and in high-exposure economies

Adults who experienced a natural disaster or severe weather event in the past three years (%), 2024

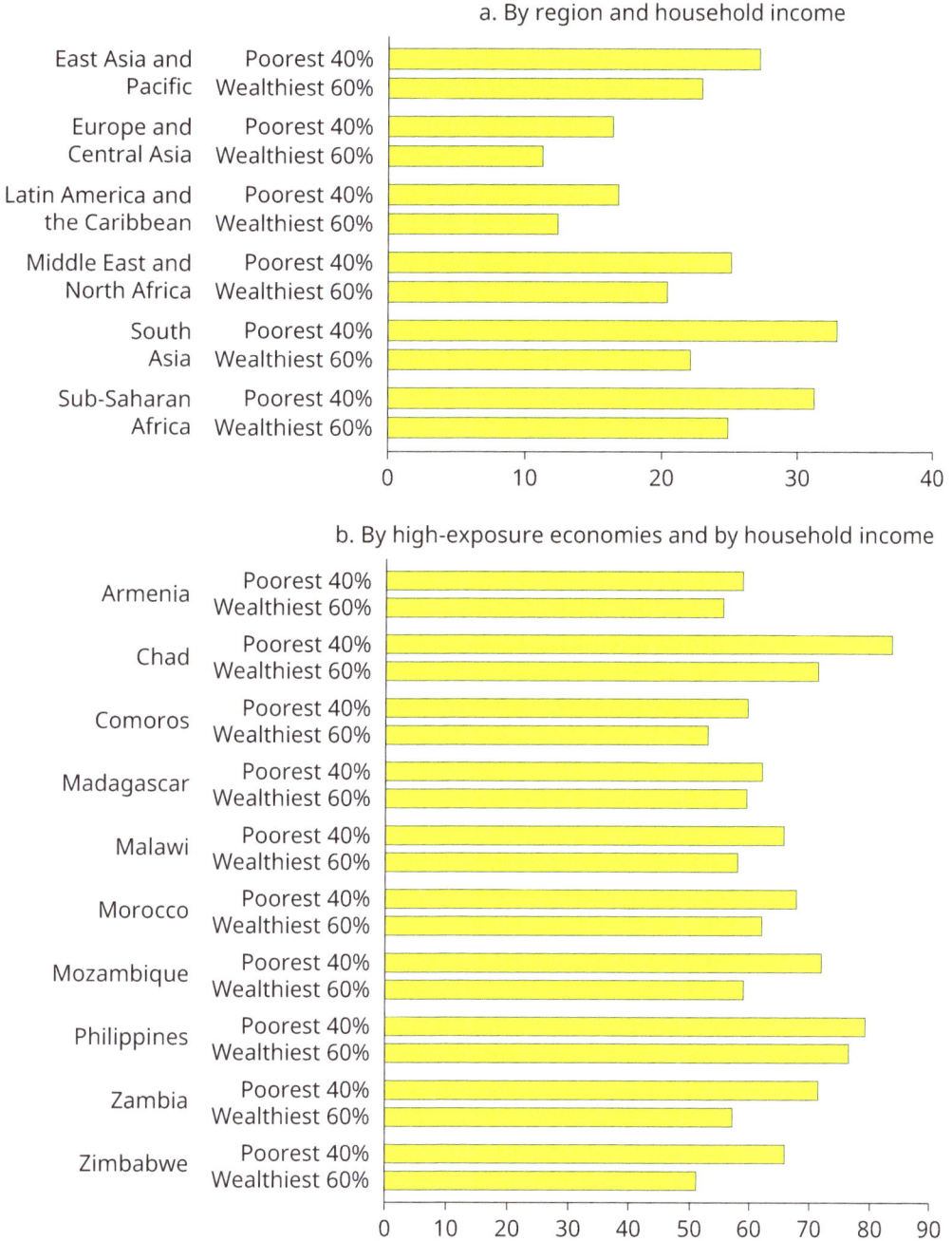

a. By region and household income

b. By high-exposure economies and by household income

(Figure continued next page)

Figure S4.1.1 Poorer and rural adults have higher levels of exposure to natural disasters than wealthier and urban adults, both overall and in high-exposure economies *(continued)*

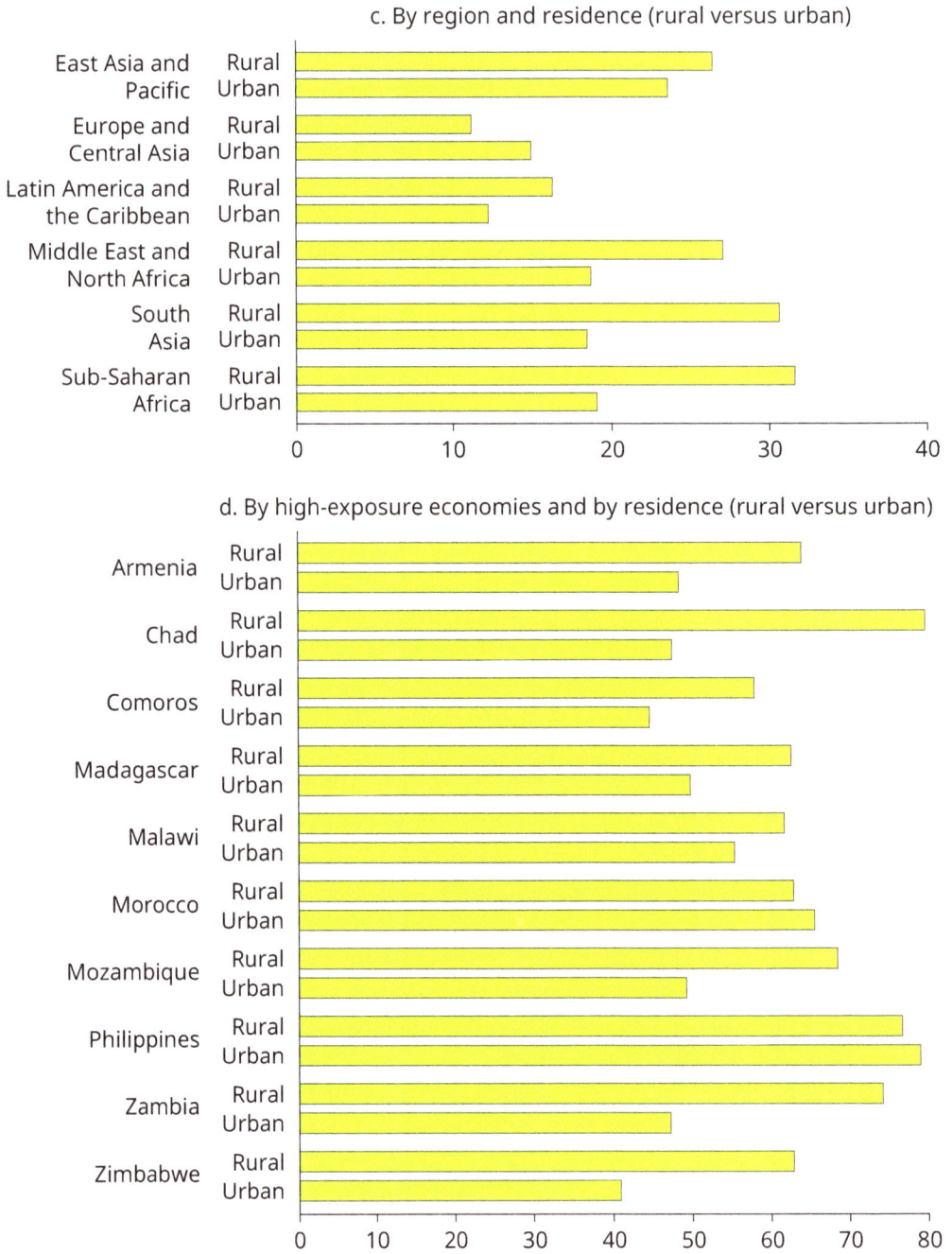

c. By region and residence (rural versus urban)

d. By high-exposure economies and by residence (rural versus urban)

Source: Global Findex Database 2025.

Note: High-exposure economies are defined as those in which 50 percent or more of adults said they had been exposed to a natural disaster or severe weather event in the past three years.

Within high-exposure economies, adults who are poor and those living in rural environments tend to have higher rates of exposure to disasters. For example, in most high-exposure economies, adults living in the poorest 40 percent of households are between 6 percentage points (Morocco) and 15 percentage points (Zimbabwe) more likely to be exposed to a natural disaster than those living in the wealthiest 60 percent. The exceptions are Armenia, Madagascar, and the Philippines, where the differences in exposure by household income are statistically nonsignificant.

People living in rural environments in high-exposure economies are also usually more likely than urban dwellers in those economies to experience disasters (refer to figure S4.1.1, panel d). In Chad, Mozambique, Zambia, and Zimbabwe, rural adults were at least 20 percentage points more likely to experience natural disasters than urban adults. In Armenia, the difference was 16 percentage points, and in the Comoros and Madagascar, the difference was 13 percentage points. Rural adults in Morocco and the Philippines, on the other hand, were no more likely than their urban counterparts to experience disasters.

Two-thirds of people exposed to natural disasters lost either income or assets or both

People who experience a natural disaster often lose income or experience damage to their homes or losses of livestock. Specifically, in low- and middle-income economies in the Global Findex 2025, half of the adults who experienced a disaster lost income, and half saw their homes damaged or lost livestock. About a third of people with disaster exposure experienced both types of loss, so that two-thirds (67 percent) of adults with disaster exposure experienced at least one. That translates to 13 percent and 12 percent of all adults in low- and middle-income economies, respectively, having suffered loss of income, damage to or loss of assets, or both, as a result of a natural disaster.

Income loss and asset damage or loss as a share of exposed adults was higher than the average in South Asia and Sub-Saharan Africa (refer to figure S4.1.2, panel a). That this is the case in the latter region is unsurprising, given the representation of the African continent's economies among high-disaster economies. Differences in the share of adults who experienced income loss or asset damage also reflect the extent of the disaster (widespread or localized) and the quality of the building infrastructure in the affected areas. As such, even high-exposure economies may experience relatively low rates of income loss or asset damage (refer to figure S4.1.2, panel b), particularly if their building codes mandate disaster-resilient construction methods or their disaster-prone areas have relatively low population levels.

Figure S4.1.2 Half of all adults who experienced a natural disaster faced loss of income or property damage

Adults who experienced a natural disaster or severe weather event in the past three years (%), 2024

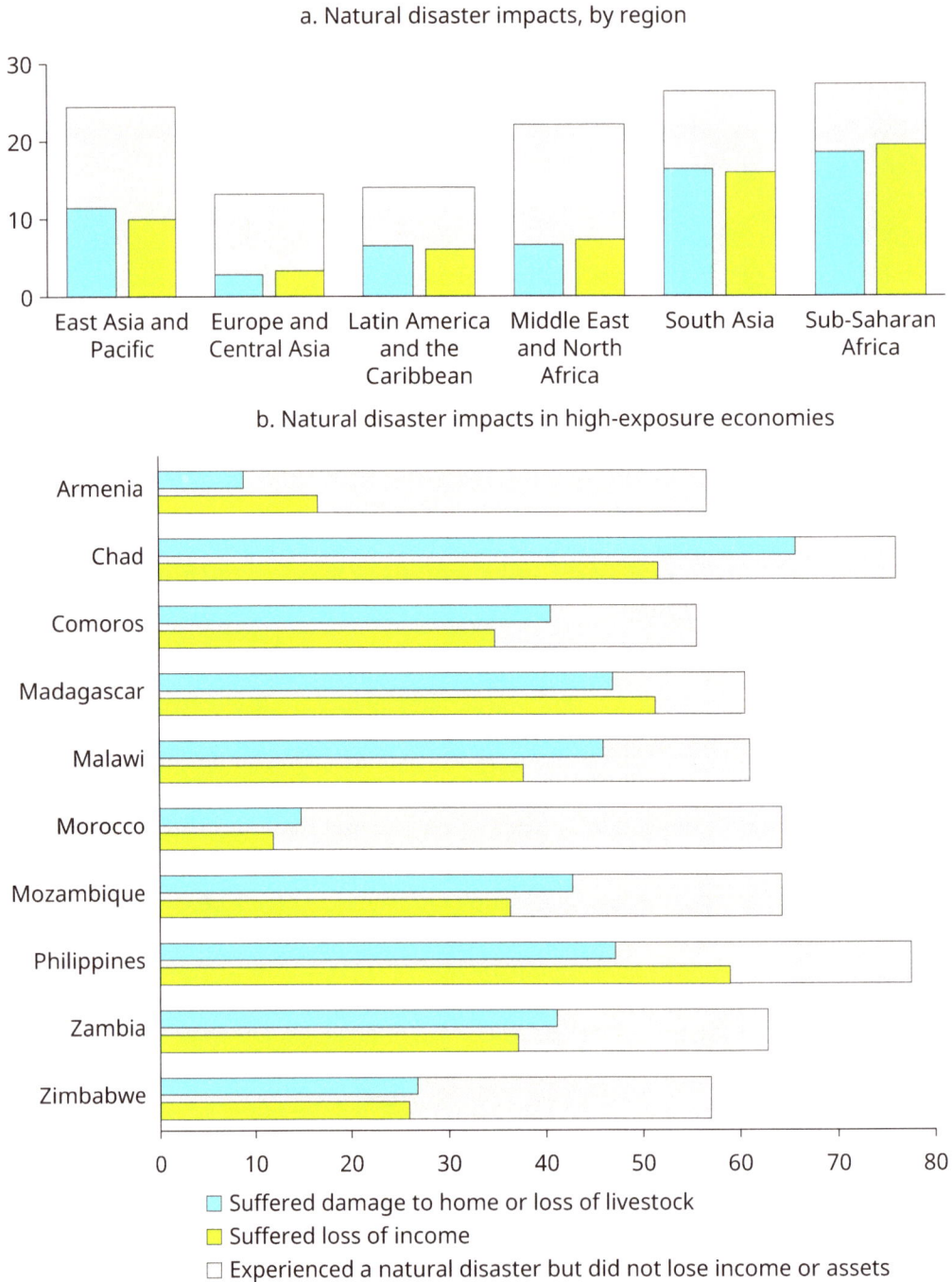

a. Natural disaster impacts, by region

b. Natural disaster impacts in high-exposure economies

☐ Suffered damage to home or loss of livestock
☐ Suffered loss of income
☐ Experienced a natural disaster but did not lose income or assets

Source: Global Findex Database 2025.

Note: High-exposure economies are defined as those in which 50 percent or more of adults said they had been exposed to a natural disaster or severe weather event in the past three years.

Natural disasters are more common and have bigger effects in low-income economies

Low-income economies are more likely than middle-income economies to have high rates of exposure to natural disasters (refer to figure S4.1.3, panel a). Moreover, affected adults in low-income economies are more likely to experience losses of income or damage to assets (refer to figure S4.1.3, panel b). Specifically, 35 percent of adults in low-income economies experienced a disaster, compared with the 24 percent average across all low- and middle-income economies. In addition, 69 percent and 72 percent of disaster-exposed adults in low-income economies lost income or assets or had assets damaged, respectively. Middle-income economies do not show these high rates of negative effects.

Figure S4.1.3 Adults in low-income economies are more likely than adults in middle-income economies to lose income or assets as a result of a natural disaster

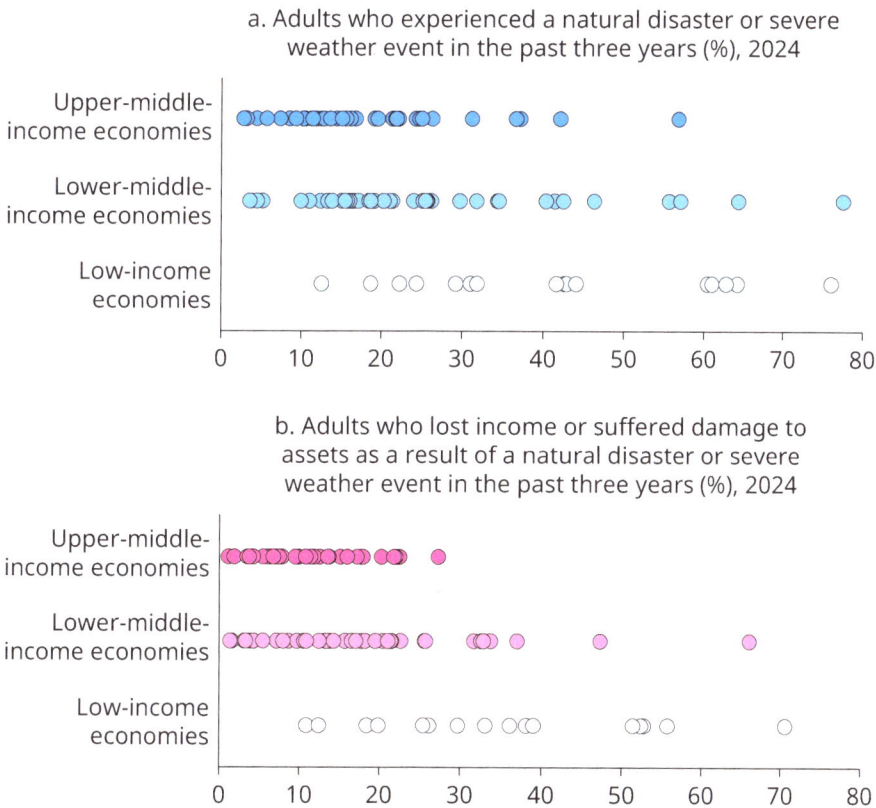

a. Adults who experienced a natural disaster or severe weather event in the past three years (%), 2024

b. Adults who lost income or suffered damage to assets as a result of a natural disaster or severe weather event in the past three years (%), 2024

Source: Global Findex Database 2025.

Connectivity, ID, and digital financial services can mitigate disaster impacts

Phone ownership, personal ID, and financial accounts cannot prevent natural disasters, but these tools can help people mitigate the effects of disasters as part of effective policies relating to disaster preparation and response.

Phone owners may receive more up-to-date information about an impending disaster, including emergency messages from their governments and lockdown or evacuation orders. Forty-two percent of all adults in low- and middle-income economies and half of mobile phone owners say they would prefer their governments to communicate either exclusively by text or through either text or voice message, a preference that grows as the share of connected adults increases. In economies in which mobile phone ownership exceeds 85 percent, for example, 53 percent of all adults and 57 percent of phone owners prefer texts for government communication. Among people who said they experienced a natural disaster, about 30 percent prefer to receive government communication by text and 34 percent by phone call. Governments should leverage texts and phone calls to get out timely communication, as they can help people stay safe and take steps to protect their property.

Similarly, connected individuals who use the internet may have more accurate insights into the trajectory of a wildfire or violent storm and a better understanding of where they can access resources. Among adults in low- and middle-income economies who experienced a natural disaster, 81 percent have any kind of phone, and 58 percent have a smartphone. The share of adults with a phone varies by region, however. South Asia and Sub-Saharan Africa, the two regions with the highest shares of disaster exposure, have the lowest phone ownership rates (refer to figure S4.1.4).

Social media has also become a powerful tool for communicating during a disaster. It can let people tell friends and family they are safe and ask for anything they need. In the United States, during hurricanes, social media platforms have served as a valuable two-way communication channel: governments communicate with citizens, and citizens point out neighbors who need immediate help.[13] Forty percent of adults who experienced a natural disaster used social media in the three months before the survey.

---

13   Pourebrahim et al. (2019).

Figure S4.1.4 Most adults exposed to natural disasters have a mobile phone, though the regions with the highest levels of exposure have some of the lowest levels of digital access

Adults who experienced a natural disaster or severe weather event in the past three years (%), 2024

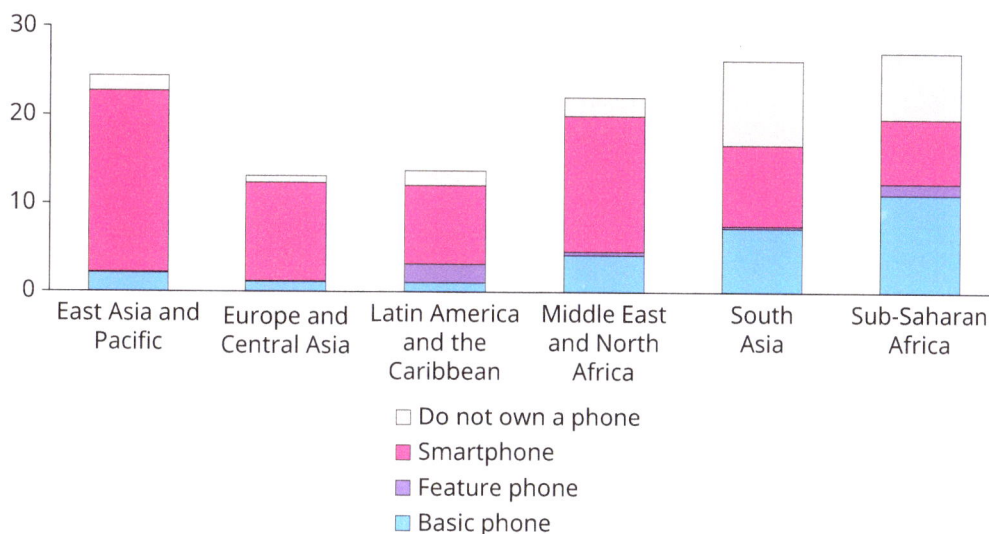

Legend:
- ☐ Do not own a phone
- ■ Smartphone
- ■ Feature phone
- ☐ Basic phone

Source: Global Findex Database 2025.
Note: Basic phone, feature phone, and *smartphone* are defined in chapter 1.1.

Having government-issued ID may also allow people who are displaced by a disaster or whose homes and property are damaged to access government or humanitarian resources. Research on the role of ID in displaced populations highlights that many refugees from natural disasters have to prove who they are and what services they are entitled to—including work privileges—outside their home districts.[14] Governments and humanitarian organizations, for their part, also use ID to coordinate services and track who receives them—all necessary to manage resources and maintain accountability to donor and funder groups.

Among adults in high-exposure economies, 80 percent have ID.[15] Though online digital ID that can be used to access services remotely is less common than foundational ID cards, it is gaining attention as a tool for ID holders to use if displaced after extreme weather events.

Digital financial services might also help make people more resilient to the impacts of natural disasters.[16] Digitally enabled accounts could equip people to receive

---

14   IFRC (2021).

15   ID data for Armenia and Chad have been suppressed because of possible misinterpretation of the question by survey respondents as referring to other acceptable forms of ID that could fulfill a similar purpose. This has been judged to be likely in these economies on account of new ID systems having been rolled out while old systems were still in place and the possibility that administrative data from ID authorities might reflect only the new systems.

16   UNSGSA (2023).

money to cover their essential needs in the wake of a disaster, even if physical bank branches and agent locations are forced to close. This is one of the key lessons from the COVID-19 pandemic, during which several economies used digital channels for government support payments.[17] For example, in Brazil, the Auxílio Emergencial (Emergency Aid) program, launched in response to the COVID-19 pandemic, leveraged digital payments through the creation of free Poupança Social Digital (Digital Social Savings) accounts and the use of Pix instant transfers, benefiting more than 100 million people in nine months. Brazil and other economies embraced digital payments into accounts to disburse support payments in part because they were faster.[18]

Payments from family or friends living elsewhere are also more available to people with financial accounts and mobile phones. Research studies show that people who can receive money into accounts, particularly mobile money accounts, are better able to receive money from their social networks.[19] These payments may come from family or friends living within the same economy, but unaffected by the disaster, or they may be international remittances from friends and family living in different economies, as discussed in chapter 4.2.

Overall, 75 percent of adults affected by a natural disaster have financial accounts. Forty-seven percent of adults have digitally enabled accounts, allowing them to make payments using debit or credit cards or phone, potentially enabling them to make purchases without needing access to a physical branch or agent to withdraw cash. This is crucial, given the small share of adults who have lost access to their accounts during a natural disaster, which is statistically significant only in South Asia and Sub-Saharan Africa (refer to figure S4.1.5).

Savings can also play an important role in helping people to endure a natural disaster. Among adults who lost income or property as a result of a disaster, a third have formal savings. These savings are the most reliable source of money in an emergency, making them extra important for adults at risk of experiencing a natural disaster.

Finally, insurance policies can help protect people from the worst effects of a natural disaster. When affordable, products such as property insurance and flood or fire insurance can give people a lump-sum disbursement they need to rebuild or reimburse them for the loss of an asset.

---

17   Klapper and Miller (2021); Marin, Palacios, and Desai (2022).

18   World Bank (2021).

19   Moore et al. (2019).

Figure S4.1.5 **Most adults who have been exposed to a natural disaster have an account, with some unable to access their account as a result of a natural disaster**

Adults who experienced a natural disaster or severe weather event in the past three years (%), 2024

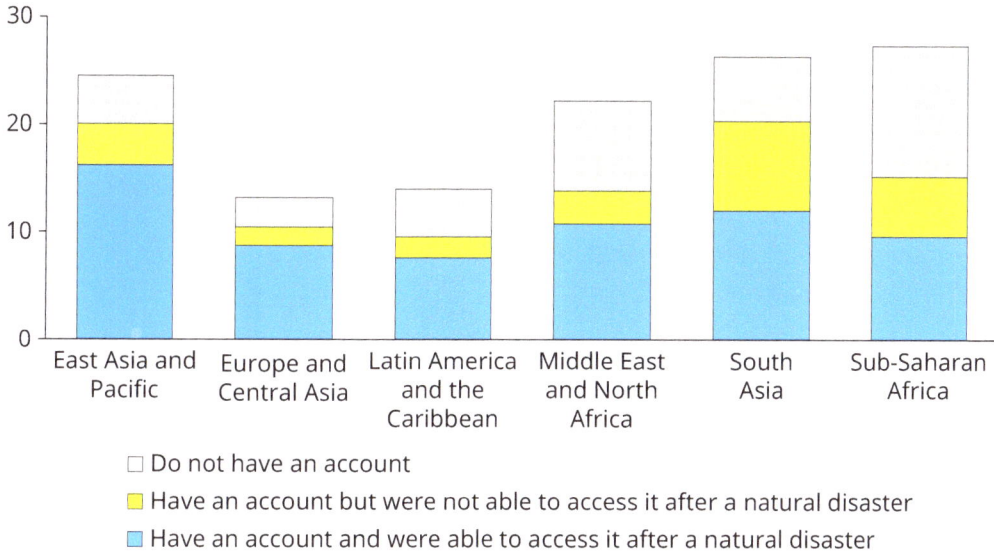

☐ Do not have an account
🟨 Have an account but were not able to access it after a natural disaster
🟦 Have an account and were able to access it after a natural disaster

Source: Global Findex Database 2025.

Building resilience against natural disasters can help

The connection between digital connectivity, identification, and financial inclusion offers ways to help people mitigate the negative financial effects of natural disasters. Making these items available to all adults in communities that are vulnerable to natural disasters could benefit both economies and individuals.

References

Agarwal, Sumit, Pulak Ghosh, and Huanhuan Zheng. 2024. "Consumption Response to a Natural Disaster: Evidence of Price and Income Shocks from Chennai Flood." *Energy Economics* 131 (March): 107323. https://doi.org/10.1016/j.eneco.2024.107323.

Akter, Sonia, and Bishawjit Mallick. 2013. "The Poverty-Vulnerability-Resilience Nexus: Evidence from Bangladesh." *Ecological Economics* 96 (December): 114–24. https://doi.org/10.1016/j.ecolecon.2013.10.008.

Aladangady, Aditya, Shifrah Aron-Dine, Wendy Dunn, Laura Feiveson, Paul Lengermann, and Claudia Sahm. 2016. "The Effect of Hurricane Matthew on Consumer Spending."

FEDS Notes, Board of Governors of the Federal Reserve System, Washington, DC. https://doi.org/10.17016/2380-7172.1888.

Beatty, Timothy K. M., Jay P. Shimshack, and Richard J. Volpe. 2019. "Disaster Preparedness and Disaster Response: Evidence from Sales of Emergency Supplies before and after Hurricanes." *Journal of the Association of Environmental and Resource Economists* 6 (4): 633–68. https://doi.org/10.1086/703379.

Bui, Anh Tuan, Mardi Dungey, Cuong Viet Nguyen, and Thu Phuong Pham. 2014. "The Impact of Natural Disasters on Household Income, Expenditure, Poverty and Inequality: Evidence from Vietnam." *Applied Economics* 46 (15): 1751–66. https://doi.org /10.1080/00036846.2014.884706.

Burke, Marshall, Solomon M. Hsiang, and Edward Miguel. 2015. "Global Non-linear Effect of Temperature on Economic Production." *Nature* 527 (October): 235–39. https://doi .org/10.1038/nature15725.

Dell, Melissa, Benjamin F. Jones, and Benjamin A. Olken. 2012. "Temperature Shocks and Economic Growth: Evidence from the Last Half Century." *American Economic Journal: Macroeconomics* 4 (3): 66–95. https://doi.org/10.1257/mac.4.3.66.

Deryugina, Tatyana, Laura Kawano, and Steven Levitt. 2018. "The Economic Impact of Hurricane Katrina on Its Victims: Evidence from Individual Tax Returns." *American Economic Journal: Applied Economics* 10 (2): 202–33. https://doi.org/10.1257/app .20160307.

Diffenbaugh, Noah S., and Marshall Burke. 2019. "Global Warming Has Increased Global Economic Inequality." *Proceedings of the National Academy of Sciences* 116 (20): 9808–13. https://doi.org/10.1073/PNAS.1816020116.

Gallagher, Justin, and Daniel Hartley. 2017. "Household Finance after a Natural Disaster: The Case of Hurricane Katrina." *American Economic Journal: Economic Policy* 9 (3): 199–228. https://doi.org/10.1257/pol.20140273.

Hallegatte, Stéphane, Adrien Vogt-Schilb, Julie Rozenberg, Mook Bangalore, and Chloé Beaudet. 2020. "From Poverty to Disaster and Back: A Review of the Literature." *Economics of Disasters and Climate Change* 4 (April): 223–47. https://doi.org/10.1007 /S41885-020-00060-5.

IFRC (International Federation of Red Cross and Red Crescent Societies). 2021. "Digital Identity: An Analysis for the Humanitarian Sector." IFRC, Geneva. https://www.ifrc .org/sites/default/files/2021-12/Digital-Identity%E2%80%93An-Analysis-for-the -Humanitarian-Sector-Final.pdf.

ITU (International Telecommunication Union). 2022. *Global Connectivity Report 2022.* Geneva: ITU. https://www.itu.int/hub/publication/d-ind-global-01-2022/.

Klapper, Leora, and Margaret Miller. 2021. "The Impact of COVID-19 on Digital Financial Inclusion." Report for the Italian Presidency of the G20 for the Global Partnership for Financial Inclusion, World Bank, Washington, DC. https://www.gpfi.org/sites/gpfi/files

/sites/default/files/5_WB%20Report_The%20impact%20of%20COVID-19%20on%20
digital%20financial%20inclusion.pdf.

Lloyd's Register Foundation. 2022. "World Risk Poll 2021: A Resilient World? Understanding
Vulnerability in a Changing Climate." Lloyd's Register Foundation, London. https://
www.lrfoundation.org.uk/publications/a-resilient-world-understanding-vulnerability
-in-a-changing-climate.

Marin, Georgina, Robert Palacios, and Vyjayanti Desai. 2022. "The Role of Digital in the
COVID-19 Social Assistance Response." G2Px Initiative, World Bank Group, Washington,
DC. https://documents1.worldbank.org/curated/en/099830009302217091/pdf/P173166
0f8c52f062092ac00d53c648bac7.pdf.

Mendelsohn, Robert, Ariel Dinar, and Larry Williams. 2006. "The Distributional Impact of
Climate Change on Rich and Poor Countries." *Environment and Development Economics*
11 (2): 159–78. https://doi.org/10.1017/S1355770X05002755.

Moore, Danielle, Zahra Niazi, Rebecca Rouse, and Berber Kramer. 2019. "Building Resilience
through Financial Inclusion: A Review of Existing Evidence and Knowledge Gaps." Brief,
Innovations for Poverty Action, Washington, DC. https://www.poverty-action.org
/publication/building-resilience-through-financial-inclusion-review-existing-evidence
-and-knowledge.

Pourebrahim, Nastaran, Selima Sultana, John Edwards, Amanda Gochanour, and Somya
Mohanty. 2019. "Understanding Communication Dynamics on Twitter during Natural
Disasters: A Case Study of Hurricane Sandy." *International Journal of Disaster Risk
Reduction* 37 (July): 101176. https://doi.org/10.1016/J.IJDRR.2019.101176.

Rabkin, Norman. 2005. "Hurricane Katrina: Providing Oversight of the Nation's
Preparedness, Response, and Recovery Activities." US Government Accountability
Office, Washington, DC. https://www.gao.gov/products/gao-05-1053t.

Rafferty, John P. n.d. "Morocco Earthquake of 2023." *Britannica*. Accessed April 22, 2025.
https://www.britannica.com/event/Morocco-earthquake-of-2023.

UN OCHA (United Nations Office for the Coordination of Humanitarian Affairs). 2024.
Southern Africa: El Niño Regional Humanitarian Overview. New York: UN OCHA. https://
www.unocha.org/publications/report/mozambique/southern-africa-el-nino-regional
-humanitarian-overview-september-2024.

UNSGSA (United Nations Secretary-General's Special Advocate for Inclusive Finance for
Development). "Inclusive Green Finance: A Policy and Advocacy Approach." 2023.
Policy Note, UNSGSA, New York. https://www.unsgsa.org/sites/default/files/resources
-files/2023-05/UNSGSA_Inclusive_Green_Finance_Policy_Note.pdf.

World Bank. 2021. *Auxílio Emergencial: Lessons from the Brazilian Experience Responding
to COVID-19.* World Bank Latin American and Caribbean Studies. Washington, DC:
World Bank. https://documents1.worldbank.org/curated/en/099255012142121495/pdf
/P1748361b302ee5718913146b11956610692e4faf5bc.pdf.

Conclusion

The Global Findex 2025 data reflect exciting achievements in digital and financial inclusion. The average worldwide rates of ownership of mobile phones and financial accounts—86 percent and 79 percent, respectively—represent significant development successes, as do the noteworthy increases in rates of formal saving and use of digital payments. Low- and middle-income economies as distinct geographically and economically as Brazil, China, India, Kazakhstan, Kenya, and Mongolia now have rates of account ownership at or close to 90 percent.

In addition to these advances, the Global Findex 2025 data also reveal two important challenges. The first is that too many adults remain either entirely excluded from or with limited access to the digital economy and the formal financial system. Despite high rates of mobile phone ownership, more than 850 million adults worldwide still do not have their own phones, including 325 million women in South Asia alone. Millions more have only basic phones, especially in Sub-Saharan Africa, where these less-expensive devices dominate. This limits these people's ability to participate fully in the digital economy, including to earn income through apps or on digital platforms. And even though device cost dominates as a barrier to phone ownership, free phones may not be the solution. Nor would they address secondary barriers like data costs, illiteracy, and community disapproval of phone ownership that play a role in some economies. Increasing connectivity, in other words, will require holistic attention to device access, network infrastructure, digital literacy, and possibly community norms.

Furthermore, although half of the 1.3 billion adults without financial accounts are concentrated in a relatively small number of economies, these economies all have distinct economic and regulatory environments. As such, the approaches that may work to reach those without accounts in large-population, upper-middle-income economies like China and India—with their high average rates of financial inclusion enabled by strong technical infrastructure and diverse banking sectors—are likely to be very different from what will work in any of the two dozen smaller economies with rates of financial inclusion below 50 percent.

New strategies will also be needed to reach the 6 percent of adults globally— or 30 percent of adults without accounts—who have neither accounts nor mobile phones, given their limited access to the most promising channel for financial inclusion available today. Helping those who have accounts, but engage in only limited activity involving them, transition from informal financial services to formal alternatives will also require distinct approaches. Supportive financial sector infrastructure, such as interoperable fast payment systems, and regulations, such as consumer protection frameworks, could help strengthen future initiatives for financial inclusion.

The second challenge relates to financial health. Even with promising growth in financial access and use, many people still struggle to meet their everyday needs, handle unexpected medical bills, and plan for the future. The data on financial resilience are important to understand, especially the finding that people's perceptions of their ability to manage financial shocks has not improved over the past three years. By extension, the challenges they highlight are crucial to address. For some, these challenges stem from a lack of income or savings. Overall, they point to a need to focus on helping people build both short-term stability and long-term security.

Opportunities to improve financial health may grow over time, as mobile phone penetration continues to advance. This expansion might allow digital financial services to reach more of the world's adults without accounts and enable more account owners to expand their use of digital payments, formal saving, formal borrowing, and, where available, insurance. Such improvements could be faster and more inclusive, however, if governments, advocates, and providers of financial services took coordinated action. Aligning and strengthening regulations, consumer protection, product design, and support for delivery channels with people's needs and challenges could help ensure that financial systems are more effective in bolstering inclusive economic participation and improving long-term financial health.

Survey methodology

The indicators in the Global Findex Database 2025 are drawn from survey data covering more than 140,000 people in 141 economies, representing 96 percent of the world's population (refer to table A.1 for a list of the economies included). The survey was carried out over the 2024 calendar year by Gallup, Inc., as part of its Gallup World Poll, which since 2005 has annually conducted surveys of approximately 1,000 people in each of more than 160 economies and in more than 150 languages, using randomly selected, nationally representative samples. The target population is the entire noninstitutionalized civilian population ages 15 and up.

Interview procedure

In most low- and middle-income economies, Global Findex data were collected through face-to-face interviews. In these economies, an area frame design[1] was used for interviewing. In most high-income economies, telephone surveys were used (refer to table A.1 for detailed information on surveying in each economy). In 2024, face-to-face interviews were again conducted in 22 economies after phone-based surveys had been employed in 2021 as a result of mobility restrictions related to COVID-19. In addition, an abridged form of the questionnaire was administered by phone to survey participants in Algeria, China, the Islamic Republic of Iran, Libya, Mauritius, and Ukraine because of economy-specific restrictions. In just one economy, Singapore, did the interviewing mode change from face to face in 2021 to phone based in 2024 (refer to map A.1 for all changes in survey mode between 2021 and 2024).

---

1   An *area frame design* is a sampling method that divides land into nonoverlapping segments using visible boundaries, such as roads or streams. These segments are then used to select samples for data collection, to ensure comprehensive and unbiased estimates.

A reproducibility package is available for this book in the Reproducible Research Repository at https://reproducibility.worldbank.org/catalog/299.

The survey mode was unchanged in 2024 from that in 2021 in most economies, though it did change in some of them

Survey mode, 2024

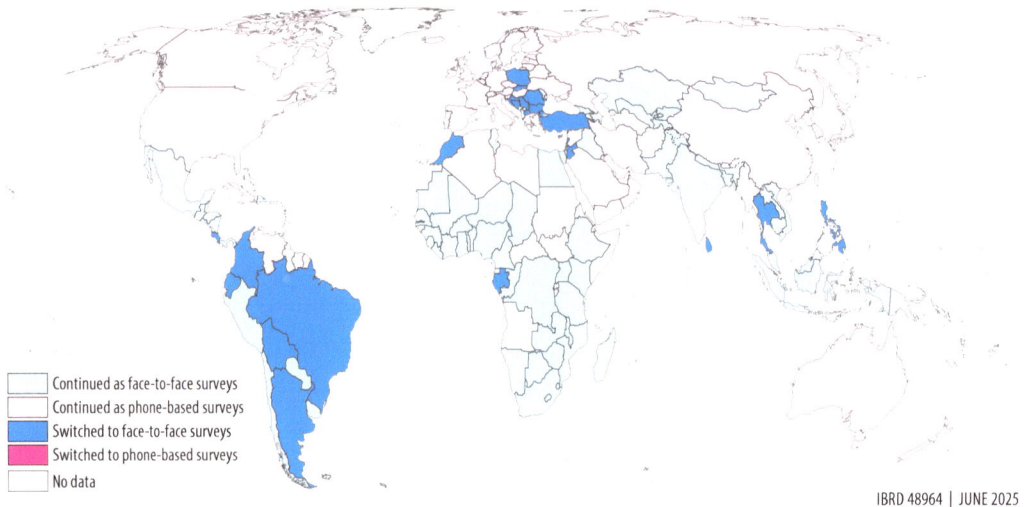

Legend:
- Continued as face-to-face surveys
- Continued as phone-based surveys
- Switched to face-to-face surveys
- Switched to phone-based surveys
- No data

IBRD 48964 | JUNE 2025

Source: Global Findex Database 2025.

Note: A phone-based survey was used in Singapore in 2024, a switch from the face-to-face survey that was used there in 2021. In 2024, China was surveyed using both phone and web-based surveys, and Nicaragua was surveyed using both phone and face-to-face surveys. Bahrain, Kuwait, Libya, and Oman were not surveyed in 2021, but phone-based surveys were continued there in 2024; this was the same mode as was employed the last time they were surveyed. Belize, Montenegro, and Trinidad and Tobago were also not surveyed in 2021, but face-to-face surveys continued there in 2024, the same mode as the last time they were surveyed.

In economies in which face-to-face surveys were conducted, the first stage of sampling was the identification of primary sampling units. These units were then stratified by population size, geography, or both and clustered through one or more stages of sampling. Where population information was available, sample selection was based on probabilities proportional to population size; otherwise, simple random sampling was used. Random route procedures were used to select sampled households. Unless an outright refusal occurred, interviewers made up to three attempts to survey each sampled household. To increase the probability of contact and completion, attempts were made at different times of the day and, where possible, on different days. If an interview could not be completed at a household that was initially part of the sample, a simple substitution method was used to select a replacement household for inclusion.

Respondents were randomly selected within sampled households. Each eligible household member (that is, all those ages 15 or older) was listed, and a handheld survey device randomly selected the household member to be interviewed. For paper surveys, the Kish grid method was used to select the respondent.[2] In economies in which cultural restrictions dictated gender matching, respondents were randomly selected from among all eligible adults of the interviewer's gender.

In economies in which Global Findex surveys have traditionally been phone based, respondent selection followed the same procedure as in previous years, using random digit dialing or a nationally representative list of phone numbers. In most economies in which mobile phone and landline penetration is high, a dual sampling frame was used.

The same procedure for respondent selection was applied to economies in which phone-based interviews were being conducted for the first time. Dual-frame (landline and mobile phone) random digit dialing was used where landline presence and use are 20 percent or higher based on historical Gallup estimates. Mobile phone random digit dialing was used in economies with limited or no landline presence (less than 20 percent).

For landline respondents in economies in which mobile phone or landline penetration is 80 percent or higher, respondents were selected randomly by using either the next-birthday method or the household enumeration method, which involves listing all eligible household members and randomly selecting one to participate. For mobile phone respondents in these economies or in economies in which mobile phone or landline penetration is less than 80 percent, no further selection was performed. At least three attempts were made to reach the randomly selected person in each household, spread over different days and times of day.

Data preparation

Data weighting was used to ensure a nationally representative sample for each economy. Final weights consisted of a base sampling weight, which corrects for unequal probability of selection based on household size, and a poststratification

---

2   A *Kish grid* is a table of numbers used to select an interviewee. In the Global Findex surveys, the interviewer first listed the name, gender, and age of all permanent household members ages 15 and older, whether or not they were present, ordering them from oldest to youngest. Each eligible household member was then assigned a number: 1 for the oldest, 2 for the second-oldest, and so on (to allow for random selection using the Kish grid). Second, the interviewer found the appropriate cell in the Kish grid by identifying the column corresponding to the last digit of the unique serial number assigned to the household's questionnaire and the row corresponding to the number of eligible household members. The number in the intersecting cell was then matched to the assigned household numbers to determine which individual in the household would be interviewed.

weight, which corrects for sampling and nonresponse error. Poststratification weights use economy-level population statistics on gender and age and, where reliable data are available, education or socioeconomic status. Table A.1 shows the data collection period, number of interviews, approximate design effect, and margin of error for each economy, as well as sampling details where relevant.

Additional information about Global Findex data, including the complete database, can be found at http://globalfindex.worldbank.org.

Additional information about the methodology used in the Gallup World Poll can be found at http://www.gallup.com/178667/gallup-world-poll-work.aspx.

Table A.1 Details of survey methodology for economies included in the Global Findex Database 2025

Economy	Region[a]	Income group	Data collection dates[b]	Number of interviews	Design effect[c]	Margin of error[d]	Mode of interviewing	Language(s)	Exclusions and other sampling details[e]
Albania	ECA	Upper middle	May 15–Jun 26	1,000	1.30	3.5	Face to face (HH)	Albanian	People living in remote or difficult-to-access rural areas were excluded from the sample. The excluded areas represent approximately 2% of the population.
Algeria	MENA	Lower middle	Aug 8–Oct 12	1,003	1.73	4.1	Mobile telephone	Arabic	
Argentina	LAC	Upper middle	Jul 6–Aug 12	1,000	1.41	3.7	Face to face (HH)	Spanish	Those living in rural areas with dispersed populations were excluded from the sample. The excluded areas represent about 4% of the population.
Armenia	ECA	Upper middle	Jul 5–Sep 19	1,000	1.40	3.7	Face to face (HH)	Armenian	Settlements near territories disputed with Azerbaijan were excluded from the sample for security reasons. The excluded areas represent approximately 3% of the population.
Australia	HI	High	May 8–Jun 27	1,000	1.37	3.6	Landline and mobile telephone	English	

(Table continued next page)

Economy	Region[a]	Income group	Data collection dates[b]	Number of interviews	Design effect[c]	Margin of error[d]	Mode of interviewing	Language(s)	Exclusions and other sampling details[e]
Austria	HI	High	May 13–Jun 11	1,000	1.73	4.1	Landline and mobile telephone	German	
Azerbaijan	ECA	Upper middle	Aug 5–Sep 6	1,000	1.23	3.4	Face to face (HH)	Azeri, Russian	The East Zangezur and Nakhichevan territories were not included in the sample. The excluded areas represent approximately 8% of the population. (Nagorno-Karabakh was not included in the sampling frame and was not counted in the exclusion percentage.)
Bahrain	HI	High	Aug 20–Sep 13	1,015	1.36	3.6	Mobile telephone	Arabic, English, Hindi	Only Bahrainis, Arab expatriates, and non-Arabs who were able to complete interviews in Arabic, English, or Hindi were included in the sample.
Bangladesh	SAR	Lower middle	Sep 7–Dec 29	1,000	1.27	3.5	Face to face (HH)	Bengali	
Belgium	HI	High	May 16–Jul 12	1,002	1.34	3.6	Landline and mobile telephone	Flemish, French	
Belize	LAC	Upper middle	Aug 26–Nov 1	509	1.54	5.4	Face to face (HH)	English, Spanish	

(Table continued next page)

Table A.1 Details of survey methodology for economies included in the Global Findex Database 2025 *(continued)*

Economy	Region[a]	Income group	Data collection dates[b]	Number of interviews	Design effect[c]	Margin of error[d]	Mode of interviewing	Language(s)	Exclusions and other sampling details[e]
Benin	SSA	Lower middle	Sep 8–Oct 1	1,000	1.84	4.2	Face to face (HH)	Bariba, Fon, French	
Bolivia	LAC	Lower middle	Aug 19–Oct 7	1,000	1.42	3.7	Face to face (HH)	Spanish	Some small, distant locations were excluded from the sample for accessibility or security reasons or both. The areas excluded represent approximately 7% of the population.
Bosnia and Herzegovina	ECA	Upper middle	May 21–Aug 22	1,000	1.46	3.7	Face to face (HH)	Bosnian	
Botswana	SSA	Upper middle	Sep 9–Oct 4	1,000	1.60	3.9	Face to face (HH)	English, Setswana	PSUs of less than 50 people were excluded from the sampling frame. The excluded areas represent approximately 4% of the population.
Brazil	LAC	Upper middle	Jul 27–Sep 8	1,000	1.31	3.5	Face to face (HH)	Portuguese	
Bulgaria	ECA	Upper middle	Jul 4–Oct 29	1,000	1.31	3.5	Face to face (HH)	Bulgarian	
Burkina Faso	SSA	Low	Jul 20–Aug 19	1,000	1.43	3.7	Face to face (HH)	Dioula, French, Fulfulde, Mooré	Some communities across regions were excluded from the sample for security reasons. The excluded areas represent approximately 18% of the population.

(Table continued next page)

Table A.1 Details of survey methodology for economies included in the Global Findex Database 2025 *(continued)*

Economy	Region[a]	Income group	Data collection dates[b]	Number of interviews	Design effect[c]	Margin of error[d]	Mode of interviewing	Language(s)	Exclusions and other sampling details[e]
Cambodia	EAP	Lower middle	Oct 25–Dec 18	1,000	1.65	4.0	Face to face (HH)	Khmer	Kep, Koh Kong, Oddar Meanchey, and Stung Treng provinces were excluded from the sample. The excluded areas represent approximately 3% of the population.
Cameroon	SSA	Lower middle	Jun 4–Jul 10	1,000	1.39	3.7	Face to face (HH)	English, French, Fulfulde	Some arrondissements in the east, north, extreme north, northwest, and southwest regions were excluded from the sample for security reasons. Neighborhoods with less than 50 households were also excluded. The excluded areas represent 21% of the population.
Canada	HI	High	May 15–Jul 6	1,024	1.34	3.5	Landline and mobile telephone	English, French	The Northwest Territories, Nunavut, and Yukon were excluded from the sample. The excluded areas represent approximately 0.3% of the population.

(Table continued next page)

Table A.1 Details of survey methodology for economies included in the Global Findex Database 2025 *(continued)*

Economy	Region[a]	Income group	Data collection dates[b]	Number of interviews	Design effect[c]	Margin of error[d]	Mode of interviewing	Language(s)	Exclusions and other sampling details[e]
Chad	SSA	Low	Oct 17–Nov 11	1,000	1.85	4.2	Face to face (HH)	Chadian Arabic, French, Ngambay	Borkou, Ennedi, Lac, Ouaddaï, Salamat, Tibesti, and Wadi Fira regions were excluded from the sample because of difficult terrain and for security reasons. The North Kanem and Bahr El Gazal North districts were also excluded because of accessibility issues. In addition, quartiers and villages with fewer than 50 inhabitants were excluded as well. The excluded areas represent 23% of the population.
Chile	HI	High	Aug 9–Oct 5	1,000	1.60	3.9	Face to face (HH)	Spanish	
China	EAP	Upper middle	Aug 8–Nov 30	1,009	2.05	4.4	Mobile telephone	Chinese	
Colombia	LAC	Upper middle	Oct 1–Nov 26	1,000	1.28	3.5	Face to face (HH)	Spanish	Ten departments and an additional 19 municipalities were excluded from the sample because they have small populations or for extreme security reasons. The excluded areas represent approximately 5% of the population.

(Table continued next page)

Table A.1 Details of survey methodology for economies included in the Global Findex Database 2025 *(continued)*

Economy	Region[a]	Income group	Data collection dates[b]	Number of interviews	Design effect[c]	Margin of error[d]	Mode of interviewing	Language(s)	Exclusions and other sampling details[e]
Comoros	SSA	Lower middle	Sep 5–Oct 10	1,000	1.95	4.3	Face to face (HH)	Comorian, French	
Congo, Dem. Rep.	SSA	Low	Aug 18–Sep 30	1,000	2.13	4.5	Face to face (HH)	French, Kiswahili, Lingala	Parts of Bandundu, Bas Congo, Équateur, Kasaï Occidental, Katanga Maniema, North Kivu, Orientale, and South Kivu were excluded from the sample for security reasons. The excluded areas represent 19% of the population.
Congo, Rep.	SSA	Lower middle	Jul 3–Aug 14	1,000	1.76	4.1	Face to face (HH)	French, Kituba, Lingala	
Costa Rica	LAC	Upper middle	May 21–Jul 4	1,003	1.24	3.4	Face to face (HH)	Spanish	
Côte d'Ivoire	SSA	Lower middle	Jul 20–Aug 14	1,000	1.43	3.7	Face to face (HH)	Dioula, French	PSUs with fewer than 100 people were excluded from the sample. The excluded areas represent 9% of the population.
Croatia	HI	High	Sep 13–Nov 15	1,000	1.25	3.5	Face to face (HH)	Croatian	
Cyprus	HI	High	May 16–Sep 7	1,010	2.04	4.4	Mobile telephone	English, Greek	

(Table continued next page)

Table A.1 Details of survey methodology for economies included in the Global Findex Database 2025 *(continued)*

Economy	Region[a]	Income group	Data collection dates[b]	Number of interviews	Design effect[c]	Margin of error[d]	Mode of interviewing	Language(s)	Exclusions and other sampling details[e]
Czechia	HI	High	May 3–Jun 25	1,003	1.27	3.5	Landline and mobile telephone	Czech	
Denmark	HI	High	Jun 24–Aug 1	1,005	1.86	4.2	Mobile telephone	Danish	
Dominican Republic	LAC	Upper middle	Jul 9–Aug 6	1,000	1.39	3.7	Face to face (HH)	Spanish	
Ecuador	LAC	Upper middle	Aug 22–Sep 25	1,000	1.43	3.7	Face to face (HH)	Spanish	
Egypt, Arab Rep.	MENA	Lower middle	Aug 23–Sep 16	1,001	1.45	3.7	Face to face (HH)	Arabic	Frontier governorates (Matrouh, New Valley, North Sinai, Red Sea, and South Sinai) were excluded from the sample, as they are remote and represent a small proportion of the population. The excluded areas represent less than 2% of the population.
El Salvador	LAC	Lower middle	Jul 3–Sep 6	1,000	1.64	4.0	Face to face (HH)	Spanish	
Estonia	HI	High	May 13–Jun 27	1,006	1.44	3.7	Mobile telephone	Estonian, Russian	
Eswatini	SSA	Lower middle	Sep 10, 2024–Jan 21, 2025	1,043	1.75	4.0	Face to face (HH)	English, SiSwati	

(Table continued next page)

Table A.1 Details of survey methodology for economies included in the Global Findex Database 2025 *(continued)*

Economy	Region[a]	Income group	Data collection dates[b]	Number of interviews	Design effect[c]	Margin of error[d]	Mode of interviewing	Language(s)	Exclusions and other sampling details[e]
Ethiopia	SSA	Low	Oct 15–Nov 29	1,001	1.69	4.0	Face to face (HH)	Amharic, Oromo, Tigrinya	Amhara was excluded from the sample because of the state of emergency there. Also excluded were the Harari, Somali, and Tigray regions. The excluded areas represent approximately 30% of the population.
Finland	HI	High	May 15–Jul 1	1,000	1.77	4.1	Mobile telephone	Finnish	
France	HI	High	May 13–Jun 14	1,000	1.42	3.7	Landline and mobile telephone	French	
Gabon	SSA	Lower middle	Sep 17–Oct 19	1,000	1.77	4.1	Face to face (HH)	Fang, French	
Gambia, The	SSA	Low	Sep 16–Dec 12	1,016	1.36	3.6	Face to face (HH)	English, Malinke, Pulaar, Wolof	

(Table continued next page)

Table A.1 Details of survey methodology for economies included in the Global Findex Database 2025 *(continued)*

Economy	Region[a]	Income group	Data collection dates[b]	Number of interviews	Design effect[c]	Margin of error[d]	Mode of interviewing	Language(s)	Exclusions and other sampling details[e]
Georgia	ECA	Upper middle	Jun 29–Aug 27	1,000	1.46	3.7	Face to face (HH)	Georgian, Russian	Abkhazia and South Ossetia were excluded from the sample for security reasons. In addition, very remote mountainous villages and those with fewer than 100 inhabitants were also excluded. The excluded areas represent approximately 8% of the population.
Germany	HI	High	May 13–Jun 13	1,000	2.44	4.8	Landline and mobile telephone	German	
Ghana	SSA	Lower middle	Oct 7–Nov 6	1,000	1.34	3.6	Face to face (HH)	Dagbani, English, Ewe, Hausa, Twi	Localities with fewer than 100 inhabitants were excluded from the sample. The excluded areas represent approximately 4% of the population.
Greece	HI	High	Jun 12–Jul 19	1,004	2.09	4.5	Landline and mobile telephone	Greek	
Guatemala	LAC	Upper middle	Jun 6–Sep 7	1,000	1.59	3.9	Face to face (HH)	Spanish	
Guinea	SSA	Low	Oct 5–23	1,000	1.74	4.1	Face to face (HH)	French, Malinke, Pular, Susu	

(Table continued next page)

Table A.1 Details of survey methodology for economies included in the Global Findex Database 2025 *(continued)*

Economy	Region[a]	Income group	Data collection dates[b]	Number of interviews	Design effect[c]	Margin of error[d]	Mode of interviewing	Language(s)	Exclusions and other sampling details[e]
Honduras	LAC	Lower middle	Jun 3–Aug 29	1,004	1.88	4.2	Face to face (HH)	Spanish	PSUs with fewer than 50 people, along with the Gracias a Dios and Islas de la Bahía departments, were excluded from the sample. The excluded areas represent approximately 4% of the population.
Hong Kong SAR, China	HI	High	Aug 24–Oct 30	1,006	1.28	3.5	Landline and mobile telephone	Chinese	
Hungary	HI	High	May 27–Jun 21	1,006	1.65	4.0	Landline and mobile telephone	Hungarian	
Iceland	HI	High	Jun 11–Jul 13	500	1.25	4.9	Landline and mobile telephone	Icelandic	
India	SAR	Lower middle	Aug 1–Dec 29	3,086	1.42	2.1	Face to face (HH)	Assamese, Bengali, Gujarati, Hindi, Kannada, Malayalam, Marathi, Odia, Punjabi, Tamil, Telugu	The northeast states and remote islands, as well as Jammu and Kashmir, were excluded from the sample. The excluded areas represent less than 10% of the population.

(Table continued next page)

Table A.1 Details of survey methodology for economies included in the Global Findex Database 2025 *(continued)*

Economy	Region[a]	Income group	Data collection dates[b]	Number of interviews	Design effect[c]	Margin of error[d]	Mode of interviewing	Language(s)	Exclusions and other sampling details[e]
Indonesia	EAP	Lower middle	Aug 21–Sep 30	1,073	1.28	3.4	Face to face (HH)	Bahasa Indonesia	
Iran, Islamic Rep.	MENA	Lower middle	Oct 14–21	1,008	1.40	3.6	Landline and mobile telephone	Farsi	
Iraq	MENA	Upper middle	Aug 20–Nov 24	1,000	1.50	3.8	Face to face (HH)	Arabic, Kurdish	
Ireland	HI	High	May 13–Jun 13	1,000	2.08	4.5	Landline and mobile telephone	English	
Israel	HI	High	Jul 7–Aug 16	1,001	1.21	3.4	Face to face (HH)	Arabic, Hebrew	East Jerusalem, as well as unsafe and evacuated areas near the border, were excluded from the sample.
Italy	HI	High	May 9–Jul 24	1,001	1.99	4.4	Landline and mobile telephone	Italian	
Japan	HI	High	Jul 3–Oct 5	1,008	1.33	3.6	Landline and mobile telephone	Japanese	
Jordan	MENA	Upper middle	Sep 30–Nov 4	1,006	1.37	3.6	Face to face (HH)	Arabic	

(Table continued next page)

Table A.1 Details of survey methodology for economies included in the Global Findex Database 2025 (continued)

Economy	Region[a]	Income group	Data collection dates[b]	Number of interviews	Design effect[c]	Margin of error[d]	Mode of interviewing	Language(s)	Exclusions and other sampling details[e]
Kazakhstan	ECA	Upper middle	Jul 29–Sep 3	1,000	1.24	3.4	Face to face (HH)	Kazakh, Russian	
Kenya	SSA	Lower middle	Oct 7–30	1,003	1.37	3.6	Face to face (HH)	English, Kiswahili	
Korea, Rep.	HI	High	Aug 16–Oct 8	1,003	1.60	3.9	Landline and mobile telephone	Korean	
Kosovo	ECA	Lower middle	Jun 5–Sep 28	1,000	1.73	4.1	Face to face (HH)	Albanian, Serbian	
Kuwait	HI	High	Sep 18–Dec 19	1,003	1.66	4.0	Mobile telephone	Arabic, Bengali, English, Hindi	Only Kuwaitis, Arab expatriates, and non-Arabs who were able to complete interviews in Arabic, Bengali, English, or Hindi were included in the sample.
Kyrgyz Republic	ECA	Lower middle	Aug 4–Sep 11	1,000	1.24	3.5	Face to face (HH)	Kyrgyz, Russian	
Lao PDR	EAP	Lower middle	Sep 21–Nov 1	1,000	1.65	4.0	Face to face (HH)	Lao	Xaisomboun and Xayaboury provinces were excluded from the sample, as were some communes that are unreachable; other communes were excluded for security reasons. The excluded areas represent approximately 7% of the population.

(Table continued next page)

Table A.1 Details of survey methodology for economies included in the Global Findex Database 2025 *(continued)*

Economy	Region[a]	Income group	Data collection dates[b]	Number of interviews	Design effect[c]	Margin of error[d]	Mode of interviewing	Language(s)	Exclusions and other sampling details[e]
Latvia	HI	High	May 20–Jul 2	1,001	1.64	4.0	Mobile telephone	Latvian, Russian	
Lebanon	MENA	Lower middle	May 28–Jul 2	1,004	1.17	3.4	Face to face (HH)	Arabic	Baalbak, Bint Jbeil, Hermel, and neighborhoods in Beirut's south suburbs that are under the strict control of Hezbollah were excluded from the sample. The excluded areas represent approximately 10% of the population.
Lesotho	SSA	Lower middle	Sep 5, 2024– Jan 13, 2025	1,020	1.98	4.3	Face to face (HH)	English, Sesotho	
Liberia	SSA	Low	Sep 17–Nov 2	1,000	1.43	3.7	Face to face (HH)	English, Pidgin English	
Libya	MENA	Upper middle	Jul 21–Aug 31	1,000	1.15	3.3	Mobile telephone	Arabic	
Lithuania	HI	High	Jun 11–Aug 26	1,012	2.16	4.5	Mobile telephone	Lithuanian	
Madagascar	SSA	Low	Jun 6–Jul 22	1,000	1.38	3.6	Face to face (HH)	French, Malagasy	Unreachable regions were excluded from the sample, as were other regions for security reasons. The excluded areas represent approximately 17% of the population.

(Table continued next page)

Table A.1 Details of survey methodology for economies included in the Global Findex Database 2025 *(continued)*

Economy	Region[a]	Income group	Data collection dates[b]	Number of interviews	Design effect[c]	Margin of error[d]	Mode of interviewing	Language(s)	Exclusions and other sampling details[e]
Malawi	SSA	Low	Sep 25–Oct 11	1,002	1.32	3.6	Face to face (HH)	Chichewa, Chitumbuka, English	
Malaysia	EAP	Upper middle	Aug 2–Sep 23	1,000	1.76	4.1	Face to face (HH)	Bahasa Melayu, English	
Mali	SSA	Low	Jul 18–Aug 10	1,000	1.41	3.7	Face to face (HH)	Bambara, French	Gao, Kidal, Mopti, and Tombouctou regions were excluded from the sample for security reasons. Quartiers and villages with fewer than 50 inhabitants were also excluded. The excluded areas represent 23% of the population.
Malta	HI	High	April 10–Jun 3	1,006	1.22	3.4	Landline and mobile telephone	English, Maltese	
Mauritania	SSA	Lower middle	Aug 15–Sep 5	1,000	1.68	4.0	Face to face (HH)	French, Hassaniya Arabic, Pulaar	Some communes in Hodh Ech Chargui and Hodh El Gharbi regions were excluded from the sample for security reasons. The excluded areas represent approximately 4% of the population.

(Table continued next page)

Table A.1 Details of survey methodology for economies included in the Global Findex Database 2025 *(continued)*

Economy	Region[a]	Income group	Data collection dates[b]	Number of interviews	Design effect[c]	Margin of error[d]	Mode of interviewing	Language(s)	Exclusions and other sampling details[e]
Mauritius	SSA	Upper middle	Apr 22–Jun 15	1,000	1.83	4.2	Landline and mobile telephone	Creole, English, French	
Mexico	LAC	Upper middle	Jul 30–Sep 18	1,038	1.34	3.5	Face to face (HH)	Spanish	
Moldova	ECA	Upper middle	Jul 3–Sep 10	1,000	1.22	3.4	Face to face (HH)	Moldovan Romanian, Russian	Transnistria (Prednestrovie) was excluded from the sample for security reasons. The excluded area represents approximately 13% of the population.
Mongolia	EAP	Lower middle	Aug 15–Sep 16	1,000	1.21	3.4	Face to face (HH)	Mongolian	
Montenegro	ECA	Upper middle	Aug 30–Oct 25	1,000	1.60	3.9	Face to face (HH)	Montenegrin	
Morocco	MENA	Lower middle	Sep 9–Oct 2	1,019	1.26	3.4	Face to face (HH)	Moroccan Arabic	The southern provinces were excluded from the sample. The excluded area represents approximately 3% of the population.
Mozambique	SSA	Low	Oct 15–Dec 21	1,000	2.28	4.7	Face to face (HH)	Emakhuwa, Portuguese, Xichangana	Cabo Delgado Province, as well as a small number of districts in other provinces, were excluded from the sample for security reasons. The excluded areas represent 11% of the population.

(Table continued next page)

Table A.1 Details of survey methodology for economies included in the Global Findex Database 2025 *(continued)*

Economy	Region[a]	Income group	Data collection dates[b]	Number of interviews	Design effect[c]	Margin of error[d]	Mode of interviewing	Language(s)	Exclusions and other sampling details[e]
Namibia	SSA	Upper middle	Sep 21–Oct 21	1,000	1.53	3.8	Face to face (HH)	Afrikaans, English, Oshiwambo	
Nepal	SAR	Lower middle	Jul 26–Sep 5	1,000	1.35	3.6	Face to face (HH)	Maithili, Nepali	
Netherlands	HI	High	May 13–Jun 20	1,004	1.47	3.8	Landline and mobile telephone	Dutch	
New Zealand	HI	High	Apr 24–May 30	1,000	1.46	3.7	Landline and mobile telephone	English	
Nicaragua	LAC	Lower middle	F2F: Jul 20–Aug 9 CATI: Nov 1–Dec 28	1,129	2.03	4.2	Face to face (HH) and mobile telephone	Spanish	
Niger	SSA	Low	Aug 14–Sep 12	1,000	1.63	4.0	Face to face (HH)	French, Hausa, Zarma	Some communes in the Agadez and Diffa regions were excluded from the sample for security reasons. In addition, PSUs with fewer than 25 households were also excluded. The excluded areas represent approximately 8% of the population.

(Table continued next page)

Table A.1 Details of survey methodology for economies included in the Global Findex Database 2025 (continued)

Economy	Region[a]	Income group	Data collection dates[b]	Number of interviews	Design effect[c]	Margin of error[d]	Mode of interviewing	Language(s)	Exclusions and other sampling details[e]
Nigeria	SSA	Lower middle	Oct 21–Nov 13	1,000	2.01	4.4	Face to face (HH)	English, Hausa, Igbo, Pidgin English, Yoruba	Adamawa, Borno, and Yobe states were excluded from the sample for security reasons and because of the Boko Haram insurgency. In addition, disputed areas of Taraba state were also excluded. The excluded areas represent roughly 7% of the population.
North Macedonia	ECA	Upper middle	Jun 20–Sep 13	1,005	1.38	3.6	Face to face (HH)	Albanian, Macedonian	
Norway	HI	High	May 3–Jun 24	1,007	1.90	4.3	Mobile telephone	Norwegian	
Oman	HI	High	Aug 18–Sep 16	1,003	1.62	3.9	Mobile telephone	Arabic, Bengali, English, Malayalam	Only Omanis, Arab expatriates, and non-Arabs who were able to complete interviews in Arabic, Bengali, English, or Malayalam were included in the sample.
Pakistan	SAR	Lower middle	Jul 27–Oct 2	1,000	1.78	4.1	Face to face (HH)	Urdu	Azad Jammu and Kashmir and Gilgit-Baltistan regions, as well as parts of the Federally Administered Tribal Areas, were excluded from the sample. The excluded areas represent approximately 5% of the population. Gender-matched sampling was used during the final stage of sample selection.

(Table continued next page)

Table A.1 Details of survey methodology for economies included in the Global Findex Database 2025 *(continued)*

Economy	Region[a]	Income group	Data collection dates[b]	Number of interviews	Design effect[c]	Margin of error[d]	Mode of interviewing	Language(s)	Exclusions and other sampling details[e]
Panama	HI	High	Jul 8–Aug 22	1,010	1.35	3.6	Face to face (HH)	Spanish	
Paraguay	LAC	Upper middle	Aug 19–Oct 9	1,000	1.43	3.7	Face to face (HH)	Jopara, Spanish	
Peru	LAC	Upper middle	Aug 23–Oct 27	1,000	1.38	3.6	Face to face (HH)	Spanish	
Philippines	EAP	Lower middle	Aug 29–Nov 6	1,000	1.31	3.5	Face to face (HH)	Bikol, Cebuano, Filipino, Hiligaynon, Iloco, Waray	
Poland	HI	High	Aug 3–Sep 25	1,000	1.24	3.5	Face to face (HH)	Polish	Low-population areas were excluded from the sample. The excluded areas represent approximately 5% of the population.
Portugal	HI	High	May 2–Jun 28	1,001	1.61	3.9	Landline and mobile telephone	Portuguese	
Romania	HI	High	Jun 12–Aug 2	1,000	1.33	3.6	Face to face (HH)	Romanian	
Russian Federation	ECA	Upper middle	Jul 15–Oct 4	1,000	1.62	3.9	Mobile telephone	Russian	

(Table continued next page)

Table A.1 Details of survey methodology for economies included in the Global Findex Database 2025 *(continued)*

Economy	Region[a]	Income group	Data collection dates[b]	Number of interviews	Design effect[c]	Margin of error[d]	Mode of interviewing	Language(s)	Exclusions and other sampling details[e]
Saudi Arabia	HI	High	Jun 23–Jul 22	1,018	1.24	3.4	Landline and mobile telephone	Arabic, English, Hindi, Urdu	Only Saudis, Arab expatriates, and non-Arabs who were able to complete interviews in Arabic, English, Hindi, or Urdu were included in the sample.
Senegal	SSA	Lower middle	Oct 7–27	1,000	1.52	3.8	Face to face (HH)	French, Wolof	Sindian commune in Zinguichor region was excluded from the sample for security reasons. Quartiers and villages with fewer than 50 households were also excluded on account of their small populations. The excluded areas represent 18% of the population.
Serbia	ECA	Upper middle	May 20–Aug 16	1,000	1.31	3.5	Face to face (HH)	Serbian	
Sierra Leone	SSA	Low	Oct 3–Nov 9	1,000	1.39	3.7	Face to face (HH)	English, Krio, Mende	
Singapore	EAP	High	Jun 14, 2024–Jan 1, 2025	1,000	1.68	4.0	Mobile telephone	Bahasa Malay, Chinese, English	
Slovak Republic	HI	High	Jun 21–Aug 6	1,001	1.26	3.5	Face to face (HH)	Hungarian, Slovak	
Slovenia	HI	High	Apr 18–Jul 8	1,001	1.59	3.9	Landline and mobile telephone	Slovene	

(Table continued next page)

Table A.1 Details of survey methodology for economies included in the Global Findex Database 2025 *(continued)*

Economy	Region[a]	Income group	Data collection dates[b]	Number of interviews	Design effect[c]	Margin of error[d]	Mode of interviewing	Language(s)	Exclusions and other sampling details[e]
South Africa	SSA	Upper middle	Aug 27–Oct 4	1,000	1.44	3.7	Face to face (HH)	Afrikaans, English, Sesotho, Xhosa, Zulu	
Spain	HI	High	May 13–Jun 11	1,000	1.75	4.1	Landline and mobile telephone	Spanish	
Sri Lanka	SAR	Lower middle	Aug 24–Nov 17	1,000	1.59	3.9	Face to face (HH)	Sinhala, Tamil	
Sweden	HI	High	Jul 2–Aug 24	1,004	1.89	4.2	Mobile telephone	Swedish	
Switzerland	HI	High	May 13–Jun 14	1,000	1.52	3.8	Landline and mobile telephone	French, German, Italian	
Taiwan, China	HI	High	Jun 28–Jul 22	1,000	1.46	3.7	Landline and mobile telephone	Chinese	
Tajikistan	ECA	Lower middle	Jul 4–Aug 13	1,000	1.47	3.8	Face to face (HH)	Tajik	
Tanzania	SSA	Lower middle	Jun 3–Jul 5	1,001	1.47	3.8	Face to face (HH)	Kiswahili	

(Table continued next page)

Table A.1 Details of survey methodology for economies included in the Global Findex Database 2025 *(continued)*

Economy	Region[a]	Income group	Data collection dates[b]	Number of interviews	Design effect[c]	Margin of error[d]	Mode of interviewing	Language(s)	Exclusions and other sampling details[e]
Thailand	EAP	Upper middle	Sep 7–Dec 13	1,003	1.81	4.2	Face to face (HH)	Thai	Narathiwat, Pattani, and Yala provinces in the southern region were excluded from the sample for security reasons. In addition, a few districts in other provinces were excluded as well. The excluded areas represent less than 4% of the population.
Togo	SSA	Low	Sep 21–Oct 15	1,000	2.10	4.5	Face to face (HH)	Ewe, French	PSUs with less than 100 people were excluded from the sample. The excluded areas represent approximately 7% of the population.
Trinidad and Tobago	HI	High	Sep 30–Dec 5	502	1.55	5.4	Face to face (HH)	English	
Tunisia	MENA	Lower middle	Jul 26–Nov 29	1,000	1.29	3.5	Face to face (HH)	Arabic	
Türkiye	ECA	Upper middle	Sep 9–Nov 2	1,000	1.23	3.4	Face to face (HH)	Turkish	Gaziantep and Şanlıurfa provinces, as well as portions of Adana, Hatay, and Malatya provinces, were excluded from the sample as a result of an earthquake in February 2023. The excluded areas represent approximately 4% of the population.

(Table continued next page)

Table A.1 Details of survey methodology for economies included in the Global Findex Database 2025 *(continued)*

Economy	Region[a]	Income group	Data collection dates[b]	Number of interviews	Design effect[c]	Margin of error[d]	Mode of interviewing	Language(s)	Exclusions and other sampling details[e]
Uganda	SSA	Low	Nov 19–Dec 10	1,009	1.58	3.9	Face to face (HH)	Ateso, English, Luganda, Runyankole	The Kotido, Moroto, and Nakapiripirit districts in the northern region were excluded from the sample for security reasons. The excluded areas represent 2% or less of the population.
Ukraine	ECA	Lower middle	Aug 13–29	1,000	1.78	4.1	Mobile telephone	Russian, Ukrainian	Some occupied territories under entrenched Russian Federation control were excluded from the sample because of lack of coverage by Ukrainian mobile operators. The excluded areas represent approximately 12% of the population.
United Arab Emirates	HI	High	Sep 19–Oct 7	1,000	1.40	3.7	Mobile telephone	Arabic, English, Hindi, Urdu	Only nationals of the United Arab Emirates, Arab expatriates, and non-Arabs who were able to complete interviews in Arabic, English, Hindi, or Urdu were included in the sample.
United Kingdom	HI	High	May 13–Jun 14	1,000	1.56	3.9	Landline and mobile telephone	English	

(Table continued next page)

Table A.1 Details of survey methodology for economies included in the Global Findex Database 2025 *(continued)*

Economy	Region[a]	Income group	Data collection dates[b]	Number of interviews	Design effect[c]	Margin of error[d]	Mode of interviewing	Language(s)	Exclusions and other sampling details[e]
United States	HI	High	Jun 28–Aug 1	1,000	1.99	4.4	Landline and mobile telephone	English	
Uruguay	HI	High	Aug 13–Oct 26	1,000	1.30	3.5	Face to face (HH)	Spanish	
Uzbekistan	ECA	Lower middle	Jun 13–Aug 12	1,000	1.42	3.7	Face to face (HH)	Russian, Uzbek	Karakalpakstan was excluded from the sample. The excluded area represents 6% of the population.
Venezuela, RB	LAC	Upper middle	Nov 4–Dec 19	1,002	1.33	3.6	Landline and mobile telephone	Spanish	
Viet Nam	EAP	Lower middle	Jun 23–Aug 31	1,000	1.33	3.6	Face to face (HH)	Vietnamese	
West Bank and Gaza	MENA	Lower middle	Jul 7–Aug 10	1,000	1.25	3.5	Face to face (HH)	Arabic	Includes the West Bank and East Jerusalem. The Gaza Strip was excluded. Areas with less than 1,000 people were excluded from the sample, as were Jewish Israeli-majority areas within the West Bank and East Jerusalem. The excluded areas represent approximately 2% of the population of West Bank and East Jerusalem.

(Table continued next page)

Table A.1 Details of survey methodology for economies included in the Global Findex Database 2025 (*continued*)

Economy	Region[a]	Income group	Data collection dates[b]	Number of interviews	Design effect[c]	Margin of error[d]	Mode of interviewing	Language(s)	Exclusions and other sampling details[e]
Zambia	SSA	Low	Dec 1–21	1,002	1.89	4.3	Face to face (HH)	Bemba, English, Lozi, Nyanja, Tonga	
Zimbabwe	SSA	Lower middle	Jul 27–Aug 25	1,001	1.31	3.6	Face to face (HH)	English, Ndebele, Shona	

Source: Global Findex Database 2025.

Note: CATI = computer-assisted telephone interviewing; EAP = East Asia and Pacific; ECA = Europe and Central Asia; F2F = face to face; HH = handheld (data collection); LAC = Latin America and the Caribbean; MENA = Middle East and North Africa; PSU = primary sampling unit; SAR = South Asia; SSA = Sub-Saharan Africa.

a. Regions exclude high-income (HI) economies, and the composition of economies included in each region, as well as the region in which any particular economy is classified, may differ from common geographic usage.

b. All data collection dates are 2024, except where noted otherwise.

c. The design effect calculation reflects weights used and does not incorporate intraclass correlation coefficients. Design effect calculation: $n*(sum\ of\ squared\ weights)/[(sum\ of\ weights)*(sum\ of\ weights)]$.

d. The margin of error was calculated around a proportion at the 95 percent confidence level. The maximum margin of error was calculated assuming a reported percentage of 50 percent and takes into account the design effect (DE). Margin of error calculation: $\sqrt{(0.25/n)}*1.96*\sqrt{(DE)}$. Other errors that can affect survey validity include measurement error associated with the survey questionnaire, such as translation issues, and coverage error, which results from the fact that a part of a target population has a zero probability of being selected for the survey.

e. Samples are nationally representative unless noted otherwise.

Summary economy-level statistics on financial account and mobile phone ownership and use, 2024

Table B.1 Financial account and mobile phone ownership and use

Adults (%), 2024

Economy	Has an account	Made or received a digital payment	Saved formally	Borrowed formally	Owns a mobile phone	Used the internet in the past 3 months
Albania	46	35	15	11	93	83
Algeria	35	13	17	7	98	83
Argentina	82	72	36	33	90	88
Armenia	71	61	11	23	95	88
Australia[a]	98				95	92
Austria[a]	100				93	94
Azerbaijan	56	52	17	22	90	86
Bahrain[a]	82				98	97
Bangladesh	43	34	11	13	82	44
Belgium[a]	98				94	95
Belize	68	51	34	19	86	86
Benin	52	48	23	13	77	34
Bolivia	57	44	26	19	87	79
Bosnia and Herzegovina	77	62	24	12	90	85
Botswana	61	57	40	23	88	47
Brazil	86	77	39	47	92	88

(Table continued next page)

A reproducibility package is available for this book in the Reproducible Research Repository at https://reproducibility.worldbank.org/catalog/299.

Table B.1 Financial account and mobile phone ownership and use *(continued)*

Economy	Has an account	Made or received a digital payment	Saved formally	Borrowed formally	Owns a mobile phone	Used the internet in the past 3 months
Bulgaria	85	78	48	14	92	79
Burkina Faso	51	48	33	8	88	31
Cambodia	39	32	11	17	81	81
Cameroon	61	60	31	10	78	46
Canada[a]	98				89	95
Chad	21	18	14	11	53	11
Chile[a]	85				96	87
China	89	89	67	41	97	86
Colombia	57	49	25	14	88	81
Comoros	45	28	20	11	72	43
Congo, Dem. Rep.	39	37	27	9	54	32
Congo, Rep.	56	54	29	6	73	34
Costa Rica	71	60	35	14	92	87
Côte d'Ivoire	58	56	36	6	89	47
Croatia	93	88	46	38	97	87
Cyprus[a]	96				98	90
Czechia[a]	92				97	93
Denmark[a]	99				99	98
Dominican Republic	65	53	29	29	89	89
Ecuador	65	43	22	16	88	83
Egypt, Arab Rep.	43	36	14	10	85	55
El Salvador	43	28	14	11	87	81
Estonia[a]	99				99	97
Eswatini	65	61	30	24	86	52
Ethiopia	49	21	26	4	58	14
Finland[a]	100				99	94
France[a]	99				91	96
Gabon	68	67	39	6	87	69
Gambia, The	38	28	25	6	80	65
Georgia	79	69	19	24	95	82
Germany[a]	98				92	95

(Table continued next page)

Table B.1 Financial account and mobile phone ownership and use *(continued)*

Economy	Has an account	Made or received a digital payment	Saved formally	Borrowed formally	Owns a mobile phone	Used the internet in the past 3 months
Ghana	81	80	67	29	88	55
Greece[a]	89				95	91
Guatemala	38	23	11	9	81	71
Guinea	36	32	23	11	82	31
Honduras	42	30	18	11	81	75
Hong Kong SAR, China[a]	97				98	89
Hungary[a]	87				97	91
Iceland[a]	100				99	99
India	89	48	27	15	66	46
Indonesia	56	43	27	15	80	70
Iran, Islamic Rep.	91	86	29	24	87	77
Iraq	30	25	10	12	91	76
Ireland[a]	98				93	95
Israel[a]	89				96	86
Italy[a]	86				99	89
Japan[a]	99				94	83
Jordan	46	38	11	13	88	89
Kazakhstan	87	85	38	33	92	88
Kenya	90	89	54	38	93	60
Korea, Rep.[a]	97				96	87
Kosovo	64	47	16	10	91	96
Kuwait[a]	74				95	96
Kyrgyz Republic	72	67	20	18	96	92
Lao PDR	38	27	16	7	84	70
Latvia[a]	95				98	94
Lebanon	23	20	3	6	94	94
Lesotho	62	58	35	17	79	46
Liberia	52	50	30	13	70	33
Libya	33	23	16	12	100	81
Lithuania[a]	99				99	89
Madagascar	24	22	11	7	46	11

(Table continued next page)

Table B.1 Financial account and mobile phone ownership and use *(continued)*

Economy	Has an account	Made or received a digital payment	Saved formally	Borrowed formally	Owns a mobile phone	Used the internet in the past 3 months
Malawi	50	49	31	11	59	21
Malaysia	89	77	52	15	95	87
Mali	55	52	30	12	84	46
Malta[a]	97				97	93
Mauritania	27	24	16	13	85	60
Mauritius	90	64	32	19	94	77
Mexico	53	41	17	15	83	78
Moldova	56	50	7	10	92	79
Mongolia	98	95	36	42	98	87
Montenegro	75	64	23	16	94	84
Morocco	44	32	6	1	90	65
Mozambique	54	51	20	15	62	27
Namibia	73	68	44	22	80	56
Nepal	60	28	21	16	78	50
Netherlands[a]	99				95	96
New Zealand[a]	98				94	95
Nicaragua	23	16	9	8	85	75
Niger	15	12	5	3	54	16
Nigeria	63	54	43	9	84	38
North Macedonia	84	75	32	26	90	83
Norway[a]	99				100	98
Oman	70	60	24	9	98	92
Pakistan	27	25	13	8	63	36
Panama	64	52	33	16	84	75
Paraguay	61	55	20	22	94	84
Peru	59	52	31	21	86	78
Philippines	50	40	24	12	78	71
Poland	86	82	46	19	95	81
Portugal[a]	91				95	86

(Table continued next page)

Table B.1 Financial account and mobile phone ownership and use *(continued)*

Economy	Has an account	Made or received a digital payment	Saved formally	Borrowed formally	Owns a mobile phone	Used the internet in the past 3 months
Romania	71	64	26	20	95	77
Russian Federation[a]	79				94	93
Saudi Arabia	79	76	42	31	98	99
Senegal	76	73	58	23	87	70
Serbia	83	77	26	23	93	79
Sierra Leone	39	37	22	9	59	33
Singapore[a]	98				97	93
Slovak Republic[a]	92				97	88
Slovenia[a]	99				95	88
South Africa	81	67	36	13	87	68
Spain[a]	98				97	97
Sri Lanka	82	47	23	18	77	43
Sweden[a]	99				99	98
Switzerland[a]	98				91	94
Taiwan, China[a]	96				96	90
Tajikistan	55	49	10	17	78	63
Tanzania	60	57	26	9	78	20
Thailand	92	83	54	18	92	86
Togo	57	53	32	13	83	44
Trinidad and Tobago[a]	75				92	86
Tunisia	38	24	22	5	96	68
Türkiye	82	71	28	42	97	87
Uganda	73	71	54	29	79	38
Ukraine	88	83	21	29	97	95
United Arab Emirates[a]	71				100	86
United Kingdom[a]	99				92	96
United States[a]	97				98	98
Uruguay[a]	74				95	91
Uzbekistan	60	50	9	12	82	74

(Table continued next page)

Table B.1 Financial account and mobile phone ownership and use *(continued)*

Economy	Has an account	Made or received a digital payment	Saved formally	Borrowed formally	Owns a mobile phone	Used the internet in the past 3 months
Venezuela, RB	87	76	23	15	95	89
Viet Nam	71	62	45	8	98	88
West Bank and Gaza	40	21	10	7	95	94
Zambia	73	71	50	18	79	39
Zimbabwe	50	47	14	6	82	32

Source: Global Findex Database 2025.

Note: SAR = special administrative region.

a. Blank cells indicate that the relevant data for this economy were not collected for 2024.

www.ingramcontent.com/pod-product-compliance
Lightning Source LLC
Chambersburg PA
CBHW050900210326
41597CB00002B/30